D1599336

THE GREAT CIVILIZED CONVERSATION

THE
Great Civilized Conversation

EDUCATION FOR A
WORLD COMMUNITY

Wm. Theodore de Bary

COLUMBIA UNIVERSITY PRESS

NEW YORK

Columbia University Press
Publishers Since 1893
New York   Chichester, West Sussex
cup.columbia.edu
Copyright © 2013 Columbia University Press
All rights reserved

Library of Congress Cataloging-in-Publication Data
De Bary, William Theodore, 1919–
    The great civilized conversation : education for a world community / Wm.
Theodore de Bary.
        p. cm.
    Includes bibliographical references and index.
    ISBN 978-0-231-16276-0 (cloth : alk. paper) —
ISBN 978-0-231-53510-6 (e-book)
    1. East and West—Study and teaching. 2. Civilization, Oriental—
Study and teaching. 3. Asia—Civilization—Study and teaching. 4. China—
Civilization—Study and teaching. 5. Comparative civoilization. 6. Educa-
tion, Humanistic.   I. Title.

    CB251.D39   2013
    909—dc23   2012042156

Columbia University Press books are printed on permanent and durable
acid-free paper.
This book is printed on paper with recycled content.
Printed in the United States of America

c 10 9 8 7 6 5 4 3 2 1

Jacket design by Jason Alejandro

References to websites (URLs) were accurate at the time of writing. Neither
the author nor Columbia University Press is responsible for URLs that may
have expired or changed since the manuscript was prepared.

Contents

Preface

The essays selected here are representative, I hope, of my academic work as a whole, but what they have most in common is that they all stem from a happy accident of my early life as a college student. As a freshman at Columbia in 1937, attending my first class in the core course Contemporary Civilization taught by Harry J. Carman (later dean of the college), almost the first thing he said was, "Of course you realize that when we talk about contemporary civilization, it is just Western civilization. Some of you should start to think about how we can expand this to Asia." I took him up on that suggestion, and almost everything in this book flows from it—scholarship in the interests of an educational core curriculum including Asia. And just as this book stems from my encounter with Carman, most of the essays included here are the outcome of my response to someone else's initiative.

Just after Congress enacted the National Defense Education Act in 1958, the very thoughtful head of the Office of Education, Donald Bigelow, sponsored a conference to discuss what should be the larger education parameters within which this new federally sponsored program for language learning, intended initially to serve military purposes, should fit. The keynote address that he asked me to give (later published in the *Journal of Liberal Education* in 1964) summed up all I had learned in following up on Dean Carman's suggestion. Much progress has been made since then, but even fifty years later this keynote still expresses for me the purposes that have guided most of the academic work I have done since—including research in East Asian sources that would enable me to carry out that broader aim.

The essays in part 2 all partake of that same intention, but for me they represent the discovery of aspects of major Asian traditions that shared many of the same educational needs and purposes in their own historical and cultural contexts.

Part 3 reflects in a different way accidents of my own personal history—invitations received to give lectures in honor of distinguished teachers I have known. The cases reproduced here are only a sampling of the larger number of scholar-teachers who have influenced my work. At the risk of seeming arbitrary and invidious, I mention here only a few, historians like Carlton, J. H. Hayes, and Jacques Barzun; Ernest Nagel and James Gutman in philosophy; and Mark Van Doren (through his writings), as representative of a larger number of devoted teachers in the Columbia core curriculum not dealt with here. Mostly, I dwell on testimonials to East Asian scholars who fulfilled the same ideal.

For his help in the final proofreading of this manuscript, I am greatly indebted to Alexander Sullivan, and for its final processing, William Gaythwaite.

Over the years, Jennifer Crewe has presided over the publication of my books at Columbia University Press, and I take this occasion to thank her again for her ready understanding of my work and her wise counsel.

Finally, I close, as in all other prefaces I have ever written, with a tribute to my wife of sixty-seven years, Fanny Brett de Bary, and my mother, Mildred Marquette de Bary, both of whose heroic examples have inspired my whole life's work. Both were notable exemplars of keen intelligence, generosity of spirit, leadership ability, and Christian self-giving in service to family and community.

Introduction

For centuries, a conversation has been going on in both Asia and the West about the values that could sustain a human community, but there has been only limited exchange *between* the two conversations. Today, the challenges of the contemporary world are such that the civilizing process can only be sustained through an education that includes (at least in part) sharing in the traditional curricula developed on both sides, based on classics now recognized as not only enduring but world class.

The essays in this book speak first of all to the nature of a core curriculum as it has developed recently in the West, then how a kind of core curriculum also developed in East Asia as part of a liberal education "modern" for its own time. Finally, examples are given of recent Chinese and Japanese scholars who have helped us share in Asian classics by articulating their more traditional values in a modern context.

Paradoxically, among the things that threaten this sharing of the wisdom traditions in a new world community is the idea much touted recently of the globalization of education as an accompaniment to the spread of a global economy. This "globalization" calls for college curricula to include a large component of multicultural studies and to promote study abroad at new centers around the world that are in touch with current trends. Ironically, this movement only extends a process of globalization that has already enveloped much of Asia, as education there has become more and more geared to the world market. It dictates how young people can qualify for and compete in this market, most often at the expense of any continuing discourse with either their own or others' humanistic traditions.

So far, the proponents of globalization have seen its open-endedness and unlimited variety as goods in themselves, depending only on how well they fit prevailing economic trends and develop a mentality keyed to the opportunities of the free market. The idea is to open educational free markets anywhere in the world, counting on the already considerable appeal of "study abroad" programs and further enhancing them.

To some degree, this study-abroad idea can indeed be compatible with a core curriculum already incorporating a balanced program of humanistic learning at the center (required of all students) along with one or another elective specialization. In such cases, the study-abroad program can well fit in with the specialized elective, especially where language learning is a key to the study of another culture. Whether it would do anything for the core humanities program is another matter.

The problem becomes particularly acute at colleges where an attempt has been made to incorporate Asian civilizations within the scope of the core. In most cases, this necessitates extending the core into the third and fourth years, which tends to conflict with study abroad at a center that likely does not itself offer such core courses. In such an event, any kind of priority given to study abroad tends to be at the expense of a truly global core—it will privilege one particular culture at the expense of an approach that should emphasize human commonality as well as cultural diversity.

In effect, this means that it is truly difficult to define a "globalization" program that also has a genuine core. It depends, of course, on what one means by core and whether or not that core is based on classics or great books representative of more than one cultural tradition.

A main purpose of the essays that follow is to argue that either a true core or true multiculturalism must draw on classics from more than one such tradition because the process of reading and discussing the classics should itself involve the bridging of cultures in order to establish the terms of equivalence or difference that are not themselves culture bound.

At this point, however, I want to step aside to East Asia in order to establish a kind of universality we can hope to talk about, one contrary to the impression created by one "great books" program highly promoted in the twentieth-century West, i.e., the Hundred Great Books or Hundred Great Ideas, which were seen by Mortimer Adler and Robert Hutchins as exclusively to be found in the West. Those finite numbers quickly yield to the recognition that the classics of the Asian tradition merit like, if not equal, attention, as already many of the most influential minds in the modern West have recognized by the interest they have shown in Indian, Chinese, and Japanese classics.

Moreover, the idea of providing a defined program for the reading and discussion of the classics—a curricular core—is not peculiar to the West. Without going into its long history in the West before the twentieth century, let me just point out that it has as long a history in East Asia as it does in the West.

It goes without saying that almost any school of learning in early times had to decide what its own classic canon consisted in—what would be the heart of its curriculum. In early China, this became a matter of public (not just private, scholastic, or sectarian concern) in reaction to the unification of the imperial state. Although early Chinese schools had their own way of referring to a classic canon on which they founded their teachings, the most notable efforts to certify classics for public or official purposes came in response to the repressive measures of the newly unified empire of the Qin dynasty (221–207 b.c.e.) when it acted to suppress the Confucian classics through the infamous "Burning of the Books." This led to efforts under its successor, the Han dynasty, to restore the classics by certifying certain surviving texts as authentic for public purposes. When I say "for public purposes," it means primarily for the preparation of those aspiring to serve in positions of public office. This leadership class was limited to those who had access to education and a literacy that would enable them to communicate with a bureaucratic ruling class. Among Confucians, this meant a concern for individual self-cultivation balanced with service to others.

After a subsequent long period of disunity, the question arose again with the reunification of China by the Sui (589–618) and Tang (618–906) dynasties. Reunification brought a massive attempt to re-create a bureaucratic structure staffed through civil-service exams. One of the examination fields dealt with the Confucian classics, but it was only one of several paths to accreditation, others of which included belles lettres, Daoist texts, hydrology, military arts, law, and astronomy. In this case, however, we could not consider the Confucian classics as a true "core" and the others as technical specialties because the most sought after and prized degree was the one in literary styles (not surprising in a Tang culture with a strong aesthetic orientation), and the "classics" exam, which stressed rote learning of the classic texts, was regarded by most candidates as too routine and mechanical and was criticized by serious scholars as altogether too lacking in either moral seriousness or intellectual challenge.

Such was the prestige of the Tang dynasty, however, that its neighbors Korea and Japan readily adopted the Tang examination system and curriculum as features of a new advanced world culture "modern" for its time. Attending this was a new educational system that even leading Buddhist thinkers such as Saichō (767–872) and Kūkai (774–835) tried to incorporate in the training of monks. In these cases, their aim was to combine Confucian learning with Buddhist spiritual training, so that monks would be able to provide social service along with religious instruction. In this connection, both Saichō and Kūkai incorporated the study of Confucian classics along with Buddhist scriptures into a basic core training, which Saichō said should consist of two-thirds study of Buddhist texts and one-third Chinese classics.[1]

Kūkai, citing the Chinese example of universal schooling for commoners as well as the elite, recommended the establishment of a School of Arts and Sciences that would include the study of Confucian and Daoist classics, as well as Chinese histories, along with Buddhist texts, in a program of universal schooling both religious and secular, citing sayings of both Buddha and Confucius: "The beings in the three worlds are all my children, roars the Buddha [in the *Lotus Sutra*]." And there is the beautiful saying of Confucius (*Analects* 7): "All within the Four Seas are my brothers. Do honor to them" (SJT 1:171).

The third example of the defining of a new core curriculum comes with the rise of Neo-Confucianism in Song-period (960–1279) China. In this case, the Neo-Confucians sought to reassert the primacy of the Confucian classics, arguing that Buddhism and Daoism had failed to deal with the civil disorders of the late Sui and Tang dynasties (eighth–tenth c.) and that only Confucian teaching based on substantive moral values could do so. At the same time, they reinterpreted the classics (especially the *Classic of Changes*) to provide an alternative to the metaphysics of Buddhism and Daoism.

The culmination of this process came with the synthesizing of a new curriculum based on the so-called Four Books and Five Classics but including new "classics" based on the writings of Zhu Xi's recent predecessors in the Song. The Four Books included, besides the *Analects* and *Mencius*, texts drawn from the *Record of Rites* entitled the *Great Learning* and the *Mean*. This represented an intense focusing on a few texts that could provide a core for the structuring of a new curriculum, aimed at defining a systematic learning process (in the *Great Learning*) and mind cultivation (in the *Mean*) that would serve as a foundation for the political process and social improvement that neither Buddhism nor Daoism could provide. Starting with the Eight Stages of the *Great Learning* ("the investigation or recognition of things," "extending of knowledge," "rectification of the mind," etc.), it applied this process to the methodical study of the classics in the light of interpretations and speculations found in the writings of Zhu's Song predecessors, who had developed a Confucian metaphysics as an alternative to Buddhism and Daoism. Primary features of this new core, in contrast to earlier, more compendious collections of classics, were its intense focusing on a few primary texts and from this base working out to a larger body of texts, listed by Zhu in the more extended curriculum he set forth for advanced study in higher schools and in preparation for civil examinations. In this larger curriculum he included Daoist classics, Legalist writings, and a wide range of histories as well as recent thinkers in the Song.

Later, Zhu's anthology of recent thought, the *Jinsilu* (*Reflections on Things at Hand*) became a fixture of the Neo-Confucian core curriculum. It was organized under the headings found in the first chapter of the *Great Learning*, so that even the outer ranges of learning were to be directed in accordance with the same initial principles Zhu had foregrounded in his study sequence—a focused core to start with, leading out to open horizons, the exploration of which would still be guided by core principles.

One might notice here a striking omission—no Buddhist texts. The fact is that even in the Tang period, which was so powerfully infiltrated by Buddhism, the examinations had no provision for Buddhist texts, nor was there in the Song. Later, when a Yuan-dynasty prime minister, catering to the Mongols' nominal identification with Buddhism, proposed that there be such exams on Buddhist scriptures, a leading Chan (Zen) master came to court to protest it, arguing that Buddhism does not rely on texts, public discourse, or public service. This fact did not keep Zhu Xi from taking Chan seriously and engaging with it philosophically, but its depreciation of textual study and public discourse disqualified it from inclusion in the core curriculum.

This limitation on Chan, however, did not at all apply to Neo-Confucianism or disqualify Zhu's core curriculum from widespread adoption all over East Asia—in Korea, Tokugawa Japan, and Annam (Vietnam). What might have been thought primarily a Chinese revival of Confucianism was quietly recognized by the Mongol conquerors of China in the thirteenth and fourteenth centuries as a universal teaching, a basic humanistic ethic, which could serve to pacify and consolidate their own rule. Then it was from the Mongols' own official adoption and sponsorship of it that the Koreans and Japanese came to know about and accept the Neo-Confucian core as the latest and best answer to the key problem of their time—the need for national and international stability based on a shared public trust.

Indeed, when Fujiwara Seika (1567–1709), the leading Japanese proponent of Zhu's teaching as adviser to the founder of the Tokugawa Shogunate, had to deal with a problem in the expanding Tokugawa commerce with Annam (in the "free market" of the time), he appealed to the Neo-Confucian ethic as a means of resolving a trade dispute, citing the virtue of mutual trust as the underlying principle of the Neo-Confucian humanist ethic—trust as true to the core.

Perhaps this much of the Neo-Confucian experience will suffice to provide an Asian perspective on the importance of the core in Asia as well as in the West, and more particularly on the importance of Neo-Confucian contributions to a great civilized conversation, the main subject of this book.

THE GREAT CIVILIZED CONVERSATION

Part 1

EDUCATION AND THE CORE CURRICULUM

I

Education for a World Community

It is a good sign that today, as we meet to consider how the new world situation may affect our college education, our theme should suggest an awareness not only of the revolutionary changes going on around us but of the undiminished importance of liberal education. "Liberal Learning in a Changing World" are the terms in which one recent book has formulated the matter for us in 1964.[1] To me, it is a favorable indication of the progress made in over a decade of continuing discussion. In 1950, one had to argue the point with proponents of so-called non-Western studies that a broadening of the curriculum should be considered in the context of liberal education as a whole and not simply offered as a response to the shift in the world power balance. Now that the political factor has been brought into proper relation to the broader human aspects of the problem, we may be prepared to pursue its liberal implications further.

One of these is certainly to recognize that liberal learning has *always* taken place in a changing world. This is not the first era to experience revolutionary change, nor are we the first teachers to deal with it. It is false to think of the West as living in a world all its own, unchallenged until now by expanding horizons. Before Plato's time, Greece had experienced invasion from Asia, and by Alexander's it was more deeply involved in that continent than we are today. Aristotle, the father of scholastic philosophy and also Alexander's mentor, contemplated no static world: his bust in stone, discovered in the ruins of northern India, bears silent witness to the cultural revolution that swept East and West in those days, from Gibraltar to the Japan Sea. Nor was medieval Europe immune to change and unresponsive to the East. Its confrontation with Islam helped stimulate the revival and creative development of scholastic philosophy. And if we look beyond the Western tradition to other countries in which some kind of "liberal learning" developed, there is China, perhaps the most stable of the great civilizations, yet it was no changeless world, either. Confucius and Mencius too, as educators, faced a revolutionary situation.

The point, of course, is that "liberal learning" has always been conscious of change yet at its best has responded to it without being swept away by it. In the midst of the historical flux, it has tried to preserve what was least mutable and most universal in learning as a core around which new experience and new insights could be ordered and passed on. Mark Van Doren says, concerning the education of the young man: "His job is not to understand whatever world may flash by at the moment; it is to get himself ready for any human world at all."[2] This may seem to belittle change, but still the humane learning Van Doren reaffirms is grounded in a fundamental truth: that there is an inescapable tension between permanence and change in our lives that cannot be overcome by simply cutting ourselves adrift from the past.

Often, it seems to me, the advocates of greater world awareness often fail to reckon with this problem in its real depth. They make little allowance for the need to have deep roots in the past if one is to cope with the sudden, bewildering complexity of the present. Slowness to reform they see as motivated simply by a desire to preserve the status quo in education or to defend traditional departmental interests. Western learning, they think, has been too content with itself. Our scholars and teachers have been parochial, smug, and resistant to change.[3]

There is truth in this, but it is difficult to judge how much. We have no universal scale by which to measure our deficiencies against those of others, and we may be myopic in viewing our own myopia. If our knowledge of Asia, for instance, has been found wanting, so too has the Asian peoples' knowledge of one another. If one argues that their ignorance reflects only the limitations of a Western-oriented education forced upon them in the contest for survival, one must nevertheless allow that the Asians' seeming self-satisfaction or preoccupation with their own cultures reflected inherent limits in their environment that gave domestic needs priority over foreign ventures. Japan, and then only fitfully in its past, serves as perhaps the one exception to Jacques Barzun's claim for Western civilization that "it is the only civilization which has had an unlimited curiosity about other civilizations."[4]

Properly viewed, the great postwar upsurge of interest in other languages and cultures is a further extension of this unlimited curiosity, now that we have more means and opportunities to satisfy it. It represents especially the incorporation into the educational sphere of a type of learning that has ripened enough in the minds of scholars and thinkers so that the seeds may be more widely sown. We may be aware of the great lengths to which that dissemination must go to be truly effective, and we may look forward to advances in learning that will make our past gains seem insignificant, but progress will be surer if based more on respect for what has been accomplished than on contempt for what has not.

Consequently, in approaching our problem today, we will accept it as a challenge not to our past but to us in the present. We will recognize it as a unique opportunity for our educational system today, without justifying this new departure on the dubious ground that Western learning has been too narrow and self-centered until now. And we will regret that a book so laudable in its aims, so reasonable in its recommendations as *The College and World Affairs* should yield to the current compulsion to deprecate the past in order to enhance the present opportunity. It regrets that before 1945 so little had been done to "escape from the historical confines of Western culture":

> There was little change . . . in the general concept of the liberal arts. As late as 1943 Mark Van Doren could write a book on liberal education that neither took into consideration its application to cultures other than those of the West, nor sought new

meanings in those cultures. Alfred North Whitehead also confined himself to the traditional West when he wrote on education in 1929 (although he did mention Chinese as a preferred language for study), even as he discussed in the same volume the educational implications of "Space, Time, and Relativity."[5]

Admittedly, this problem has not been dealt with directly by Van Doren or Whitehead, but their writings as a whole do show an acquaintance with what lies outside the Western tradition and an appreciation of its significance to their own studies.[6] If they have not chosen to discuss the so-called non-West as a separate problem in liberal education, it is perhaps from a disinclination to dichotomize their subjects in this way. But who yet has said anything more fundamental about the problem than Van Doren when discussing the role of imagination in liberal education? Since this passage may have escaped his critics, permit me to cite it:

Imagination always has work to do, whether in single minds or in the general will. It is the guardian angel of desire and decision, accounting for more right action, and for more wrong action, than anybody computes. Without it, for instance, the West can come to no conclusions about the East, which war and fate are rapidly making a necessary object of its knowledge. Statistics and surveys of the East will not produce what an image can produce: an image of difference, so that no gross offenses are committed against the human fact of strangeness, and an image of similarity, even of identity, so that nothing homely is forgotten. The capacity for such images comes finally with intellectual and moral virtue; it is not the matter of luck that some suppose it, though single imaginations of great power are pieces of luck that civilization is sometimes favored with. It is a matter of training, of the tempered and prepared character which all educated persons can share. This character is a condition for the solution of any huge problem, either in the relations of peoples—and such relations, beginning at home, call first for knowledge of self, so that in the centuries to come it will be as important for the West to know itself as to know the East, which means to know itself better than education now encourages it to do—or in the ranges of pure speculation.[7]

Along with Van Doren and Whitehead, there are many other poets and philosophers whose work was affected by acquaintance with the Oriental world well before the postwar boom of Oriental studies. Besides Pound, whose passion for Confucius is well known, there is Paul Claudel, who encountered Zen years ahead of the Beats, and T. S. Eliot, who plunged early into the study of India and Buddhism (though it only produced, he says, "enlightened mystification"). And besides Whitehead, there are among philosophers of this century Bertrand Russell, who wrote *The Problem of China* after visiting there; John Dewey, whose personal encounter with young China reflected his consciousness of it as a world-regional rather than an East/West problem; and William Ernest Hocking, philosophically as much at home in China as in New England—to say nothing of others reaching back to William James, Thoreau, Emerson, Nietzsche, Schopenhauer, and Leibniz, or, among writers, to Yeats, Tolstoy, Wordsworth, and many more. A dialogue with the East has been going on for centuries, since the Jesuits first introduced the learning of India and China to Europe while at the same time bringing Western learning to Asia. And today it serves poorly to advance this dialogue if we imply that little has been gained by it so far.

This is why I cannot join in scolding the West, though it has become almost a ritual introit to all praise of "non-Western studies," as in this opening to *Non-Western Studies in the Liberal Arts College*:

> Until quite lately higher education in the United States of America has been almost completely under the sway of an illusion shared by nearly everybody of European descent since the Middle Ages—the illusion that the history of the world is the history of Europe and its cultural offshoots; that Western experience is the sum total of human experience; that Western interpretations of that experience are sufficient, if not exhaustive; and that the resulting value systems embrace everything that matters.[8]

In my estimation, such sweeping accusations only obscure the real issues. In the first place, the educational picture, if it ever was that black, is certainly more mixed today. Among the social sciences, some, like anthropology and political science, have been quick to reexamine basic premises and methodologies in the light of foreign-area studies; others, like economics, have been notoriously resistant. In large areas of the South and Midwest, there are now more voices raised in behalf of Asian studies; in other sections, the interest in language and area studies is lively and intense. The curiosity of educators, teachers, and students and their desire to do more is limited only by the available means. Financial help and professional guidance are what they need; encouragement and support, not prodding and preaching.

In the second place, to indict the Western academic tradition will get us nowhere. We must rather show how a world outlook is rooted in and deeply relevant to the traditional concerns of liberal learning. Superficially, one might expect the humanities to be the stronghold of Western classicism and traditionalism, whose defense mechanisms would have to be broken down before a broader, more progressive position could be established. Yet at Columbia, a pioneering movement for Oriental studies in the core curriculum was spearheaded by professors of French, English, philosophy, and American history (without an "Orientalist" on the committee). The first Oriental humanities course was launched jointly by a professor of Greek and Latin (Moses Hadas) and a political scientist (Herbert Deane). Their standpoint was not progressive or iconoclastic but liberal and humane.

And this attitude of mind seems to me crucial. If we have failed at all in our efforts to broaden the scope of education, I suspect that the fault lies less with teachers and scholars in the past—the "dreamy" poet whose thoughts were perhaps off with Du Fu in China, the philosopher whose "ivory tower" may actually have afforded a glimpse of Al Ghazali and Sankara, the philologist whose absent mind was probably fixed on a difficult Sanskrit text—and more with the "practical" men of our own society—on foundation boards, in congressional committees, and even in our highest political offices—who have often disbursed vast sums in the field of international studies and cultural exchange without educating themselves to the task. It is not that they have lacked experience in international affairs or sometimes even training in specific areas like Asia and Africa. They are handicapped just as much by ignorance of the West, of their own liberal traditions, and of a liberal learning about the East that is already ours. Hence, our problem in respect to broadening the scope of liberal education is complicated by the continuing failure of many college graduates to receive any kind of liberal education at all, Western or "non-Western."

I shall not cite here cases of foundation preoccupation with contemporary problems, of fellowship applicants who have had to contrive justifications for classical research in terms of "contemporary relevance," of governmental support for language study in the interests of "national defense." "Everyone knows," says Arthur Wright in his contribution to the *Report of the Commission on the Humanities*, "it is easy to persuade the board to give $950,000 to young economists working over the meager data on China's present economy, difficult to get $120,000 for a seven-year project in the humanities (here pre-modern history) involving all the senior Chinese scholars in the country."[9]

We need not deprecate what has been accomplished in current research on Communist China—the scholarly world is less ignorant of conditions there than some would have us believe—in order to demonstrate the futility of a policy that is completely preoccupied with the contemporary scene and the supposedly quantifiable factors in it.[10] Wolf Ladejinsky, one of our most experienced economic advisers in the Far East, years ago indicated that the economic problem in Vietnam could be solved yet everything lost through ineptitude in dealing with the human factors. Today, South Vietnam's economy thrives, and the country is near collapse. Americans, having poured millions into economic and military aid, are stupefied at what is happening and totally unprepared to cope with it. Why? Because no one bothered to find out what was going on in the minds of the Vietnamese people; no one was trained to analyze the religious factors in the situation. You cannot acquire an understanding of Buddhism in a few days, as the ineptitude of our journalistic efforts shows. But do we have to wait until Buddhists are rioting in the streets to realize that the traditional religions of Asia are important fields of study? And without such study, how is one to judge what kind of "Buddhists" they are, when so many of their violent acts are inconsistent with Buddhism? Thus we fail even in the handling of current problems if we lack insight into the minds and hearts of these people, into the political uses that are made of traditional beliefs, into long-term trends that alone give current data meaning and predictive value.

What a tragedy, then, that our newest multi-million-dollar foundation efforts should continue the same sterile policy, only on a grander scale, of promoting more contemporary research that will speculate over the same "meager data" and probably be out of date or irrelevant next week!

It is some consolation that the superficiality of thought around the concentrations of educational power and money is, to some degree, offset by the growing number of able men who serve as skillful mediators between scholarship and the bureaucracy, public and private. In not a few cases they have stretched the letter of an unreasonable law to provide for legitimate needs or interpreted short-sighted policies to allow for far-sighted projects. But we have to look beyond our immediate frustrations and minor successes to a long-range goal that will direct our hitherto confused efforts.

That goal I have identified as "education for a world community." I put it this way because "education for world affairs" suggests the same preoccupation with the current world scene, of which we have grown wary. Research and reporting on the international situation is indeed essential in government, business, and our democracy for all educated people participating in it. But the first essential is to have educated people. They must be educated to live, to be truly themselves, in a world community. They must undergo the kind of intellectual chastening that is prerequisite to the exercise of any power or influence in the world. They must know themselves better than they know world affairs so that the responsibilities they assume are commensurate with their capabilities and not swollen with self-conceit—personal, national, racial, religious, social, political, and so on. Confucius and his teaching were strongly oriented to public service, to world affairs, yet he had to reconcile himself to serving *out* of office. Finding it impossible to engage in the politics of his time and remain true to himself, he chose the latter. We must know how to be like that.

I say "education for a world community" because, next to self-understanding, the emphasis in education should be on the bonds uniting men in a true community—not the passing world scene, but what men have most deeply in common as a basis for coming together. This is where imagination, as Van Doren says, has work to do, in helping us do justice to one another, in respecting similarities and differences among men. Increasingly, our education must be formed by such an image and such a vision. And this is why I prefer "vision" to "strategy."[11] "Strategy" seems to imply that the objective is clear enough if only the forces can be mobilized and marshaled to take it. It takes the end for granted and concentrates on the means, whereas much thinking remains to be done about both: our end—the world community—and the means of attainment that must be proportionate to it. What we have now is not in fact a clear goal but only a sense of direction or, better, a sense of being attracted by a vision that we cannot fully make out and measure because it is growing with us.

For similar reasons, I would avoid the expression "non-Western studies." The disadvantages of this term have been discussed most recently in the report of the Commission on International Understanding, but the authors, like many others, resort to it for want of any other term that will cover the same ground—all of the neglected areas in our studies. Some of these areas, however, are as Western as we (Latin America), and for those that are not, "non-Western" sets us off in the wrong direction to find and place them in our educational system. It tends to perpetuate whatever isolationism or parochialism we have suffered from by suggesting that the significance of other civilizations lies primarily in their difference from European and North American civilization. It confirms the arbitrary separation of the world into Western and non-Western categories and therefore is divisive rather than constructive of the new sense of community that must be the basis and aim of our education. And finally, it does violence to the individual members of that community. As I have said elsewhere,

> the seeming impartiality with which so many civilizations are thus equated (actually negated) tends to obscure the true proportions of their respective contributions. The positive significance of Asia in particular tends to be obscured when it is simply lumped together with other areas equally different from the modern West, which by implication becomes the norm for all.[12]

As used and popularized by Vera Micheles Dean, "non-Western" signified those societies that were underdeveloped and alike in their need to modernize quickly. Since, from this standpoint, their common problem was to catch up with the advanced industrial states of Western Europe and North America, the latter obviously provided the norm or yardstick to which the underdeveloped societies would be expected to measure up, hopefully by telescoping centuries of "Western" growth into decades of non-Western forced development. No doubt this distinction served to emphasize a major problem on the contemporary scene and recommend itself to students of current world affairs. But for purposes of liberal education, a longer view and wider perspective are needed. If we are not to conceive of the new world community as homogeneous with our own megalopolis, then we must arrive at a better understanding of what these other civilizations represent in themselves and what potentially they could bring into the new community that, at this early stage, it is not yet conscious of.

I realize that no one who has grown accustomed to using "non-Western" for a host of nations and a variety of sins will consider anything like "the new world community" a convenient substitute. For practical purposes, it will be satisfactory to use "language and area studies," "regional studies," or "international studies" as a general category, representing this new community in its diversity. Such divisions or subdivisions as "Asian studies," "African studies," "Russian studies," or "East European studies" will adequately represent it in its particularity, standing for basic geographical or cultural units of more than current topical interest, which should retain their distinctive identity and significance even in the community of the future. For some, the name "Oriental studies" may be ruled out as too old-fashioned, musty with the odor of classical archeology and philology in the Near East, or considered guilty by association with such bigotry as found expression in the Oriental Exclusion Act. From a genuine scholarly viewpoint, however, this term has traditionally given recognition to the major civilizations of Asia as worthy fields of study and as generous contributors to Western culture. Such an intrinsically positive concept should not, in any case, be sacrificed to the negative and dubiously new-fashioned "non-Western" label.

Liberal education consists of any study that liberates man for a better life. Thus it is broad and inclusive but also involves a process of growth and maturation, implying distinctions of order and priority. It liberates man by giving him, first of all, power over himself, and only then perhaps power over things and over others. By disciplining his faculties, it frees them for constructive use. The arts of language, for instance, are among the most fundamental of such disciplines, so recognized in both classical and modern education. There is almost no level on which they cannot make their contribution. And the learning of foreign languages is, among these arts, one that will contribute most to the building of a new world community because it is the most genuine compliment that a man can pay to another people and their culture. That he should put himself to the trouble of learning another's language, that he should subject himself to the discipline of study, and often of monotonous drill, is immediate evidence of a man's readiness to humble himself, to put himself, so to speak, at another's disposal, in order that he may enter into genuine communication with him. Understanding others makes that much difference to him.

Still, foreign language study is only one of the language arts so indispensable to civilization. To learn well one's own language and literature—in the broadest sense—is hard enough and must retain some priority. Most of us recognize the folly of "collecting languages" when none of them is learned well, and learning well (that is, to the point of reading and enjoying a foreign literature) is all the more unlikely if one's powers of appreciation and discrimination have not been nourished at home before they are called upon for service abroad. No doubt the language-learning capabilities of most young Americans are far from overtaxed, and more yet can be demanded of them in both secondary and higher education. Nevertheless, the polyglot cannot be our educational ideal. Overemphasis on foreign languages can stunt intellectual growth in other directions. It is futile if we learn to speak in several languages but end up with nothing to say. The gift of tongues will do little to grace a shallow mind.

Thus, most of the work of college education will remain to be done in English, and this applies to the study of foreign areas as well as to any other. I have been dismayed at the number of cases in which small liberal arts colleges have held off doing anything about Asian studies until they could offer one or more of the languages involved. No such program would be respectable, they thought, unless it were based on language study. Yet for the number of students who might take Chinese, Japanese, Hindi, or Arabic with the expectation of pursuing them to real fluency, this would be an uneconomical arrangement, an exotic frill. As a consequence, they have done nothing. Procrastination has been justified on grounds of academic respectability, abetted by a simple misconception as to educational priorities.

Language study is ultimately important for any student ready to commit himself seriously to area training. It is not essential, however, for a liberal education, and even for the college major its unavailability does not preclude substantial accomplishment. We need not choose between all or nothing. Enough scholarly research and translation has been done already so that enormous advances can be made in dispelling the ordinary student's ignorance of Asia without exhausting the material in Western languages. Yet where resources permit, our educational system should have a place and a proper sequence for both general study in the medium of Western languages and specialized studies in other foreign languages. Experience has shown, moreover, that the greater the diffusion of this general knowledge and the more energetic the college in providing introductory courses, the more spontaneous and irrepressible is the demand generated for the addition of language instruction. It is at this stage that an effort should be made to launch language study in at least one area that would provide an opportunity for specialization.

This natural sequence in the development of the college curriculum also corresponds to the natural order in which students should get their exposure to other areas and cultures, moving from general education to special training. Language study need not necessarily be preceded by a general introduction to the area, but such an introduction should be available to all students—including the great majority who will never take up language study—during the early years of college. Its primary purpose should be to form an integral part of their liberal education, and as a secondary purpose it should expose an increasing number of students to the possibilities for specialization in time to make a decent start on the language.

The manner in which foreign areas are represented in undergraduate education will vary according to the college. In principle, we should encourage a plurality of methods, recognizing the diversity of needs, purposes, and capabilities. There is just one condition I would set. We must be prepared to justify any innovation in terms of the established curriculum and stated educational aims of our colleges. This might seem no more than obvious, but I am convinced that it is widely ignored or evaded. With the increasing mobility of both teachers and students, facilitated by liberality in granting leaves, canceling courses, and adjusting requirements in favor of study abroad, there seems to be less and less conception of the college program as an integrated learning experience. Not that there is lack of respect for the "integrity" of the curriculum—the traditional piety is still there—but fewer people have any idea of what it is.

In such circumstances, those who advocate an increasing role for language and area studies all too often rely on convenient but essentially irrelevant arguments on behalf of their proposals. An eloquent appeal is backed up by no more substantial argument than the popularity of our new courses among students or some vague assertion about the educational wave of the future. While statistical surveys of rising enrollment in language and area programs around the country may suggest to a curriculum committee that it give serious thought to what should be done in this direction, they do not render "any argument about whether such studies fit into the curriculum . . . purely academic."[13] Or if they do, we must understand "purely academic" in the legitimate rather than the pejorative sense of the term.

The nature of courses offered to students should properly be determined by the subject matter and the requirements of the disciplines pertaining thereto. Whether courses so defined fit into a planned curriculum must then be decided in relation to the college's conception of itself. If it has no such idea of what it is about, the real need of that college is to become more conscious of itself before it talks about greater "awareness" of the other half of the world. Most particularly, this applies to core courses that will have to transcend departmental boundaries in order to serve their purpose. They must have some higher justification than the mere assertion of one department's interests or popularity over against another.

Opportunism, I concede, may gain momentary redress from an imbalance that has long worked to the detriment of education for a world community. We must seize our chances where we find them. But these occasions also should find us ready to explain and justify our goals in relation to the aims of undergraduate education—in terms meaningful to those outside our own area and discipline. In the long run, unless our purposes can be constantly exposed and upheld before the college community as a whole, our gains will be insecure.

Is it unrealistic or visionary to suggest that such discussion can be conducted within a college faculty or curriculum committee in terms meaningful to all? Admittedly, many of our colleagues are still strangers to the world of which we speak. For this very reason, however, we should welcome any opportunity for discussion or debate as a means of educating and informing them. And welcome it at the same time as a means of educating ourselves. For without an appreciation of their curricular aims and choices, we cannot adjust and refine our own. Without this we, too, run the risk of becoming parochial and self-serving.

For instance, if at Columbia I know that there is no room in the basic (Western) humanities course for such philosophers as Plotinus and Pascal, it will affect my judgment as to how many and which Oriental philosophers I shall try to make room for in the Asian Humanities course. How can I claim that any college graduate ought to have read Sankara and Ramanuja if he has not read these others? If there is time enough only for the *Iliad* but not the *Odyssey*, for Milton but not Chaucer, for *Lear* and *The Tempest* but not *Hamlet* and *Macbeth*—can I ask students to read works of Oriental literature, however important in their own traditions, that do not measure up to some more universal standard? When the *Psalms*, the *City of God*, Dante's *Paradiso*, St. John of the Cross, and Kierkegaard find no place on the Western list, how many Vedic hymns, Sufi poets, or Buddhist mystics can I include in the Asian "must" list? And, coming out of the classical world into the modern, if, in the light of all that crowds in upon the lower college program, my colleagues in charge of the core curriculum have decided not to insist upon each student's receiving a basic introduction to, say, the economic problems of American society, what right have I to insist that the same student should acquaint himself with the economic problems of so-called underdeveloped countries?

On questions such as these, we are constantly forced to make practical judgments, even though we possess no final answers to many of them. In one sense, the works and writers I have cited are not truly comparable. They have a claim on our attention precisely because of their standing in their own traditions rather than because their universality can be immediately recognized or their stature fully gauged. In other words, the traditions of which they are an expression can be better understood as complementary to our own than as comparable. From this standpoint, we can only teach as much of all of them as is possible, knowing that it will never be enough.

Nevertheless, our practical choices ought to reflect some overall view of the curriculum, and from this standpoint our judgments of what should be taught about other civilizations must take into account what is taught of our own. If we ask for reexamination and readjustment of the traditional curriculum, we should be prepared to reciprocate. From a continuing faculty discussion on this basis, great mutual benefits would flow. There is no better way to promote the gradual integration that should overcome the opposition between "West" and "non-West" and generate from within the college community the new educational consciousness appropriate to a world community. More to the point here, it will help us define the relationship between education for world citizenship and specialized language and area study for the advancement of learning.

We face at least two basic problems: How much of the world can we hope to embrace in a core curriculum? And how far can we press for specialized language study in college without sacrificing other essential ingredients of a liberal education?

One approach to the first problem is to provide introductory courses to different areas or civilizations and give the student his choice. The minimum requirement then would be only that his program should include at least some exposure to another culture or another society. This will give him a different perspective on his own way of life and open his eyes to new possibilities. But a more concentrated exposure to one civilization will usually be gained at the expense of exposure to any others. In a college without the resources to offer a wider range of choice, nothing will have been lost. In better circumstances, however, some familiarity with still another civilization should provide a triangulation point for the comparisons a student tends to make between the "other" civilization and his own.

Thus arises a second approach: a survey covering several areas or civilizations in a single course.[14] Whether these civilizations are introduced singly or in combination, a judgment must still be made as to which areas or civilizations have the first claim on our attention. Teaching and library resources are rarely sufficient to deal with all continents and countries, nor is the time available to the student. For this reason, again, a distinction is useful between a core curriculum and specialized training. Some civilizations merit consideration because we realize, if only imperfectly, that their achievements and experiences are no less significant than those of Western civilization. These should be represented in the core. Others simply have not attained that distinction. As problem areas in the modern world they cannot be ignored, but it will suffice if they are offered only for some students to investigate and not for all.

I have already identified four major Asian civilizations—Islamic, Indian, Chinese, and Japanese—as meriting inclusion in the first group and have explained that

> to assign a higher priority . . . to the major Asian civilizations is justified by the greater richness and depth of their traditions, by the historical contributions to and influence upon other peoples beyond their own borders, and by the impressive continuity and stability of their traditional institutions down through the ages. It is little wonder that the natural interest of Westerners today should spontaneously incline them to learn about Asia, for here are the peoples whose technological "underdevelopment" can never be mistaken for immaturity of culture or society. Their social experience—their population problems, their political institutions, their economic dilemmas—in many ways anticipate those of the modern West. Their arts, literature, philosophy and religion in some respects achieved a refinement surpassing our own.

To focus, then, on Asian civilizations in a core curriculum is only to signify that there is more than enough matter here worthy of the student's attention and reflection, on a level with and as challenging for him as that which he encounters in Western civilization. Global scope—with Russia, Africa, South America, and what not thrown in—need not be the criterion, when to discover any one of the major Asian civilizations is virtually to discover a whole new world, and two or three of them a new universe.[15]

On this basis, we are entitled to ask that an introduction to at least some of these civilizations be offered in the early years of college. The second year seems a good one in which to begin, assuming that the first is taken up with a basic introduction to Western history, thought, and literature (that is, so far as the humanities are concerned). It is not that Western civilization should always have priority, but it must *for us*. We are Americans and start from there—or we make a false start. For Indians and Japanese, the priorities will be different. Nothing I have said about citizenship in the world community can change that. This latter goal may give us some common direction in the future, but it does not erase our past.

Considering this basic fact of our lives and the distinctive character of the major civilizations, I question whether an omnibus course in world civilization or world literature could do justice to its individual parts. A well-thought-out sequence over at least two years might perhaps do it, but tacking Mao Zedong and Nehru on to the modern end of a contemporary civilization course or just adding the *Analects* and the *Tale of Genji* to the Hundred Great Books will not.

Another conclusion I draw from this basic fact is that study of the more remote and difficult languages should not take priority over the Western languages traditionally emphasized in our colleges and universities. If a knowledge of French or German, and sometimes Latin or Greek, has been thought essential to liberal education in the West, our new situation should not tempt us to substitute, for example, Chinese or Japanese. We can only aim at their addition beyond the normal requirements for those students whose aptitude and industry enable them to undertake more. Both types of language study qualify as liberal disciplines, but the former serve a double purpose. They are more intimately related to our own language and involved in our own culture, which means that they can help us understand our own past. The latter do this, if at all, only reflexively.

Here some may feel that I am showing altogether too much respect for tradition. At this rate, we will never move out of our own backyard. The curriculum will be so weighted down with Western baggage that few students will get the chance to specialize in a foreign language and area with hopes of achieving real competence. After two years devoted entirely to a core curriculum and fulfilling other basic requirements, how can the student squeeze in the minimum three years of language study needed for his or her field of specialization? Moreover, since this "field" means not just an area but also a standard discipline that he or she can bring to bear on that area, how can he or she further squeeze in the basic methodology of that discipline?

We are indeed in a tight spot, but rescue may not be impossible if help comes from enough different directions. One of these is the improvement of language teaching so that acceleration relieves the threatened congestion. We must hope that the satisfaction of Western-language requirements can be accomplished largely on the basis of secondary-school study. We may look forward even to some high school students coming into college with at least an introductory knowledge of Russian or Chinese, so that rapid advancement in specialization need not be at the expense of the core curriculum. We have the means also, through intensive summer study supported by NDEA, almost to double the amount of language learning possible in the last two years of college.

Thus the language problem is far from hopeless, but what about area specialization? I can be optimistic about this only if we reconsider the conventional components of an area-studies major. It is unrealistic to think that, in his junior and senior years, the student can both ground himself in a given discipline such as history, anthropology, government, or economics and also follow an interdisciplinary program that covers his area from every angle. Compelled to opt for one or the other, we can only choose the former. We must be satisfied if on graduation from college the student has received a general introduction to the area, a basic discipline that he can work in, and a command of the language appropriate to his discipline. A more comprehensive knowledge of the area will have to wait, either upon practical experience in the field or upon an interdisciplinary regional studies program at the M.A. level.

Exceptions must be allowed for, and one of them is the college that cannot afford the appropriate language instruction but happens to have a group of area specialists in established departments who can staff a respectable interdisciplinary program. Assuming, however, that aid will be forthcoming for more liberal arts colleges to launch programs in uncommon languages, the desirability of starting difficult languages early would give them priority over area study.

What we end up with is a sequence that looks something like this:

1. A core curriculum in the lower college, with an introduction to the major Asian civilizations and humanities for *all* students—following the basic Western courses in the second year (or where necessary the third).
2. A major in the upper college emphasizing:
    a. language study begun as early as the student's preparation for college allows, without sacrificing some Western language competence, and using summers for intensive study;
    b. initiation into the basic methodology of a discipline or profession;
    c. application of language and discipline to seminar research in the senior year.
3. An interdisciplinary area study program at the M.A. level *or* travel, study, and practical experience in the area. Both will be necessary for most students who look forward to careers as area specialists.
4. Ph.D. work in a given discipline, with all the skills and experience gained thus far brought to focus on a specific topic of research.

In this scheme, travel and study abroad would, for most students, be substituted for intensive language work in summer school or come naturally just after graduation from college. Only those who have fulfilled all other requirements and accomplished at least two years of fairly intensive language study as freshmen and sophomores should be allowed to spend their junior year abroad because only students this serious and determined will benefit from it. Otherwise, it seems unjustifiable to break up a four-year program carefully designed, balanced, and pruned to provide a true liberal education. The values of such a program derive only from planning and persistent application. Travel, though a valuable experience, is not educational in the same way. It should be considered a reward for disciplined study, not a substitute. Or it should be considered a supplement to the language program, providing a summer's intensive conversational practice.

Unless the "global centers" so much promoted today can satisfy these same needs and requirements, they should be considered more in the category of summer excursion than as serving the purposes of a more integrated curriculum.

My discussion so far has been within the context of the established curriculum in American colleges. If there were time, I should have liked to consider the possibility that our conception of liberal education itself may be enlarged and enriched by knowledge of other teaching traditions. For instance, in China, Japan, and Korea it was always considered a mark of the educated man, the humane man, that he was capable of composing poetry on the significant occasions of life and of rendering it in calligraphy that was a true expression of his character and personality. The reading of poetry is still a part of our college education, but how many of us have expressed ourselves in it since leaving fifth or sixth grade? To some G.I.'s in the Pacific, for a defeated Japanese general to spend his last moments writing a final poem seemed a somewhat silly ritual. But in this respect, did not the general show his superiority over his conquerors? We shall mourn the passing of poet-generals like Lord Wavell and General Yamagata as war becomes more and more of a specialized business of destruction and as we lose the creative touch that ennobled even this most inhumane of human occupations. In the rush and din of modernization, such humane traditions are fast disappearing even in the East. As we move into the world community, to save and preserve them becomes our responsibility. This will require not merely a sense of appreciation but an effort at creation.

I have given an illustration of only one among many forms of training—physical, artistic, and spiritual, as well as intellectual—that in the East have been thought both to liberate and civilize the individual. A few of them are peculiarly "Oriental," but some of them, like poetry, are not. A continuing encounter with Eastern forms of learning may help us to rediscover and possibly revive some of our own classical arts and spiritual traditions. Whether anything can be done to restore them in the liberal education of the future is a question. The advancing pressures and demands of modern life have long since put them to flight, and the resulting wasteland may not attract their return. On the other hand, we are aware of a profound unrest among our students, a resistance to these pressures for uniformity and conformity, and a spirit of revolt against the "establishment" that can undermine the finest curriculum and the most expert teaching. We face the paradox that the "deeper spirit" of our times is a deeply troubled spirit rather than one serenely flowing beneath the agitated surface. Compulsory chapel and assembly are gone, only to be replaced by the compulsion to seek a meaning for life somewhere off campus. An unnamed restlessness impels students to march or ride instead of sit, read, and think. The situation may be better in some places, worse in others, but no one can deny the strong, worldwide undercurrent. And in these circumstances, our established curriculum cannot achieve fully even its own purposes.

Salvador de Madariaga says of Europe that its destiny

> was never more clearly defined than in our day. The twofold message which she incarnates is fast being forgotten. Both the freedom of the mind for which Socrates died and the divine spark within the humblest man for which Christ died are in danger today. The Factory State is fast developing, reducing man to the level of a computer. Quantity is driving quality to the wall. And if Europe does not unite to save quality and the individual, both will perish.[16]

When we come to realize it, however, the same concern is expressed in only slightly different terms by spokesmen for every major tradition today. Madariaga's problem is not just Europe's but the world's. That is why a solution can be found only in the context of a world community that respects the dignity and destiny of each civilization.

That is why, too, our study of our neighbors in this community must approach them on a human level rather than on a mechanical level. The reason our foreign policy has lacked dynamism and our foreign aid has been abortive is that they have dealt with people largely in a mechanical way, with no regard for the human spirit living and working in them. Though we think of ourselves as always wishing to help others and always ready to make sacrifices for them, our goodwill and generosity do not touch the hearts of others as long as it is expressed only in dollars and cents, howitzers and helicopters. Some deeper bond, some more vital basis, must be found for the community we hope to form with them. And this can be done only if we are reeducated for the task. But it will not be done until the officials responsible in government, the foundations, and the schools are ready to support work in the humanities—Eastern and Western—on something like the scale of the physical and social sciences.

There is urgency to this now. We have squandered our opportunities and now find the times unreceptive to our noblest aims. Though technologically the world is coming together, in other respects the barriers to genuine communication are rising. In Europe as well as in Asia and Africa, the trend toward nationalism, sectarianism, and communalism militates against the international community. We can anticipate that our vision of a world community may appear anachronistic in the days immediately ahead—a mere echo of the time when we fought "to make the world safe for democracy." We must expect to be haunted by our failures in the past. And still, we must see beyond all this.

The West need not repudiate itself in order to redeem its position in the world. It needs to know itself better, as well as others. It needs to emulate the pioneering work of its scholars and thinkers, who helped prepare us for this day, while it also heeds the voices of other peoples unheard till now. The great force of Western expansionism has spent itself, but we should not forget that with the Wellesleys into India went Sir William Jones, who led the revival of Sanskrit studies; that from the East India Company's trade in India and China came not only unprecedented profits but the first social sciences spanning East and West; that missionaries dedicated to the propagation of their own faith, like James Legge, Timothy Richard, Seraphim Couvreur, and Karl Reichelt, were devoted enough to truth and the peoples among whom they worked to labor for a better understanding of Confucian and Buddhist teachings.

We suffer justly and inevitably for the sins of imperialism and colonialism, even though the specific charges against us are often distorted because their aim is retaliation or revenge, not justice. But we are false to ourselves if we forswear our inheritance not because it is untainted but because we cannot wash our hands of it without forsaking the obligations it imposes. That obligation is to go out into the world, bringing forward all that is good from the past, as the basis for a new understanding, a new world community in which all peoples will contribute to the building. Earlier generations may have misconceived the task or misjudged the degree of self-denial that leadership of such a world order would entail. Great ideals often invite great self-deception. But the challenge of building such a world order is not one that we can decline any more than they could. The world will be ordered now, for better or worse. It will be for better if the education we now plan is education for a world community, education that has learned lessons from the past—that is, everyone's past, which we share by virtue of our common present and future. That will be the kind of liberal learning Confucius talked about: "Even when walking in a party of no more than three, I can always be learning from those I am with. There will be good qualities that I can select for imitation and bad ones that will teach me what requires correction in myself."[17]

2

"Starting on the Road" with John Erskine & Co.

The beginning of what would become Columbia's Core Curriculum lies in the World War I era, when two courses were started that soon became the heart of the Columbia College program later known as the "Core." One of these was the prewar General Honors course of John Erskine (1879–1951), which sought to conserve the values of classical liberal education in the face of the growing trend toward specialization in the research university. Along with this latter trend came the threat to classical learning that arose from the abandonment by the college of the requirement for Latin and Greek, the languages in which most of the classics had been read.

Erskine argued that the most essential values of the ancient classics could be conveyed in translation. If modern laymen could feel comfortable reading the Bible in English, the same could be done for other classic works. Indeed, translations into the vernacular had the advantage of bringing the classics within reach of laymen in general rather than preserving them as the special province of classical scholars.

Such an understanding was implicit in the title of Erskine's pioneering course: General Honors. As an experimental venture it was offered first as a challenge to a select group of promising students—who were attracted to it as a special honors course. At the same time, it had a new and democratic appeal for them in its aim to reach the generally educated person or layman. In these features of the original course lay the germs of what would later become spoken of as "general education."

The central focus and subject matter of this course, however, was the classics. These were texts that had proven themselves capable of speaking to generations of humankind in terms that could still be meaningful to their own life and times, reaching into their own hearts and touching them personally.

This was how the texts were to be read—in the raw, directly, and not mediated too much by scholarly introduction or commentary. No doubt, such a reading could result in somewhat different personal understandings, and to deal with these differences—as a no less essential part of Erskine's next step on the road—was the method of engaging in small group discussions, led by a pair of teachers who could help students to articulate, share, and compare with others their own reading of the texts.

Among academics, Erskine was unusual in being a creative artist himself: a notable poet, musician, novelist, and playwright. To him, a classic text was a great work of art not only in its literary perfection but in its appeal to the heart, the senses, and the aesthetic imagination. It was not just an object for the exercise of critical reason and analysis. In this respect, he resisted the increasing enshrinement of "critical thinking" as the be all and end all of learning, which could only result in a narrowing and impoverishment of the self, unless it included sympathetic appreciation and synthesis as well as critical analysis.

In the printed syllabus for the course (which would serve as the syllabus for its direct successor, the "Colloquium"), Erskine entitled his preface "The Enjoyment of Reading the Classics," which expressed the essential features of this learning experience in these terms:

Just before the United States entered the World War, a course of reading for Juniors and Seniors in world masterpieces of literature was proposed in the faculty of Columbia College. The plan lapsed during the next two years, but when the College re-organized itself in 1919, the so-called Honors Course was inaugurated—a system of weekly meetings in small groups of students, each group presided over by two or more members of the faculty, for the purpose of discussing some great book in the field of history, philosophy, economics, science, or literature. The ideas underlying the course were simple. It was thought that any fairly intelligent person could read with profit any book (except, of course, highly specialized science) which had once made its way to fame among general readers. Even without the introductory study which usually precedes our acquaintance with classics in these various fields, any reader, it was thought, can discover and enjoy the substance which has made such books remembered. It was thought, also, that in a weekly discussion of the reading, such an exchange of ideas as might occur in any group which had read an interesting book, would be more illuminating than a lecture. It was thought, also, that the result of such reading and discussion over a period of two years would be a rich mass of literary information, ideas and principles, even emotions.

In practice this course has been so successful that the list of readings has been somewhat expanded, and is here published in the thought that others outside of the College group might care to follow it, Any such list, however expanded, must remain somewhat arbitrary. The reader will think of many titles which to him seem to deserve a place here, or which seem more important than some of the titles here given. Undoubtedly we get a better historical approach to anything that is old if we have the time to study its environment and its associations. But in art it is not the history of a masterpiece which makes it famous so much as qualities of permanent interest. It is precisely those qualities which we recognize first when we take up an old book without prejudice, and read it as intelligently as we can, looking for what seems to concern our times. I personally would go rather far in protest against the exclusively historical approach to literature or any other art.[1]

From this we can see that Erskine's early list was not thought of as complete but as open-ended. He was not defining a fixed canon (such as later was promoted with great fanfare as the Hundred Great Books by Mortimer Adler at the University of Chicago). But it did involve a process of induction, of constructive reasoning, from the legacy of enduring classics, as to what might be considered central concerns of human life, judging from the experience of one's forbears. It was not a fixed quantity but a process of focusing on perennial issues. In other words, though open to new experience, it was not open-ended in the sense of being open to the indefinite, indeterminate, and potentially infinite exploration of any and all possible forms of new knowledge. If such exploration should occur, quantitatively speaking, it should be accompanied by a parallel process of qualitative reflection and judgment.

The point is illustrated by what occurred when the followers of Erskine succeeded in converting his Honors course into a course required of all undergraduates, a decision of the College faculty in 1936 and first enacted in 1937. This was a signal achievement for the movement, underscoring for its proponents (as for Erskine) that the "general" part of General Honors aimed at a general audience and its active assimilation of the classics, not just a generality or diffusiveness of knowledge.

The point is underscored when one recognizes that the same followers of Erskine persisted in offering the General Honors course as a junior-senior level "Colloquium on Important Books" (known in the 1930s, 1940s, and on into the 1970s and 1980s as the "Colloquium"). Why, since they had succeeded in establishing the Humanities course as a requirement for all freshmen, was there any need for a an almost identical junior-senior colloquium—especially considering the heavy duplication in the readings?

At least one view of this seeming anomaly was that the upper-college course enabled students in the humanities to pursue this as a form of specialized study, just as other students would follow the other required course with an upper college major in one or another discipline that would serve their professional needs. Indeed, one observer of this process described it as yielding to the insistent trend toward professionalization that still exerted strong pressure on the college program. "The Colloquium represents a rather narrow scholarly enterprise: the desire to prepare would-be scholars for further study. . . . [It was] designed to provide specialized academic training of future liberal arts graduate students rather than for all students."[2]

To whatever extent this may have been so, the Colloquium continued to draw students destined for professions outside the humanities
(e.g., natural sciences, medicine, and engineering), and the advocates
of the Colloquium saw it otherwise than as specialized training: they
thought of it as a continuing parallel to specialized study, alongside
and complementary to it.

Erskine himself had emphasized that the classics were to be read
and reread many times, sometimes in the company of other classics one
had not had a chance to consider the first time around or even in the
new contexts of expanding research. Later, the continuing reflection
on classic works should be a constant accompaniment to specialized
study, a core understood as central to all new learning, as an integrative
function bringing old and new together.

Strong evidence for this view comes from the fact that the Colloquium was based on the same syllabus as the original General Honors
course, which included Erskine's own succinct rationale for the process. Here, he especially disputed the idea that classics should only be
read in historical context or with the benefit of expert commentary.

The titles here suggested are arranged chronologically without
regard to different fields of knowledge. The reading of these
books will not be training in history, nor in economics, nor in
literature—we should not like to imply that any subject or special field is here completely represented. But of course it is the
critic, not the artist, who invents distinct fields of knowledge. In
life these fields all overlap. The reading of this list consecutively
would give, we believe, something better than an introduction
to special fields—it would exhibit the mind of western Europe,
moving for two thousand years or more through the various
interests, imaginative, intellectual, scientific, and emotional,
which have occupied it from century to century. Great books
read simply and sensibly are an introduction to the whole life;
it is the completeness of their outlook which makes them great.[3]

In the circumstances that attended publication of this syllabus in
1927, two notable features stand out. First, Erskine's preface is followed
by a statement by Everett Dean Martin of the People's Institute of New

York, where teachers in the Columbia program also taught an audience
made up of labor union members and other adults. Martin testified
that the same course conducted for Columbia College students had

> been used by the People's Institute in various reading and dis-
> cussion centers in New York City: In the present instance we
> were able to secure the services of a number of the faculty of
> Columbia University, who had given the course in that univer-
> sity. The experiment in taking the course off-campus and giving
> it to groups of average readers, led to the belief that there may be
> persons everywhere who would be interested in such a course in
> the humanities.[4]

To all of this we can easily imagine Erskine saying Amen, when he
agreed to have it included in his published syllabus along with a statement by a supporting cast of scholars who readily lent their names to
the enterprise, i.e. the Columbia College Colloquium, as heir to the
original syllabus of General Honors, published first in 1927. The fact
that it was published by the American Library Association for the use
of a national audience speaks for the wide appeal just noted by Everett Dean Martin and testifies to the eagerness of many distinguished
scholars to lend it their endorsement. Here is the list of signatories:

M. J. Adler, J. B. Brebner, J. M. Barzun, R. L Carey, I. Edman,
J. Erskine, J. Gutmann, M. Hadas, J. Hutton, C. W. Keyes, S. McKee
Jr., R. P. McKeon, E. E. Neff, P. H. Odegard, H. Peterson, H. W.
Schneider, J. Storck, L. Trilling, R. G. Tugwell, M. Van Doren,
R. M. Weaver, H. T. Westbrook, A. Whitridge, P. N. Youtz.[5]

Each of these signers was a distinguished scholar in his own right,
and some achieved national importance, e.g., Rexford Guy Tugwell,
an economist who became a leading member of FDR's "Brain Trust";
Herbert Schneider of UNESCO; and Peter Odegaard, later president
of the University of Washington. (I need not emphasize the obvious
importance of Mortimer Adler and Richard P. McKeon in taking the
movement to Chicago in the form of general education and the Great
Books program). The continuity at Columbia was extended from

Erskine to both the Humanities course and the Colloquium on Important Books by J. B. Brebner (among those just listed), Jacques Barzun, Irwin Edman, James Gutmann, Moses Hadas, Herbert Schneider, Mark Van Doren, Raymond Weaver, and Harold Westbrook. Several of them doubled in importance as contributors to the development of the Contemporary Civilization course, as did Robert Carey. Although both CC and Humanities experienced many vicissitudes over the years, the fact that so much of what Erskine advanced when he "started on the road" endured into the twenty-first century is attributable to their persistent efforts in a long-term collegial effort.

Of the two original Core initiatives mentioned at the beginning of this essay, I have yet to say something about the origins of the second major initiative, which first appeared in the form of the Peace Issues course. Although it would eventually emerge as one of the two main components of the Columbia program, to be known as the Core, its origins are quite different from those of its counterpart, General Honors, later the Colloquium. The latter, as we have seen, was born of the growing contest between the earlier liberal education of the American college gentleman and the increasing emphasis on professional specialization in the emerging research university of the twentieth century. Peace Issues, by contrast, exploded on the Columbia campus as a direct hit from World War I, from the insistence of university leaders like President Nicholas Murray Butler and Dean Herbert Hawkes that Columbia gentlemen face their civic responsibility for supporting the Allied cause, which was variously advertised as the "War to Save [Western] Civilization" and the "War to End All Wars." The political heat and patriotic fervor at the moment was such that the College plunged into action to pursue these big questions without much resistance but with many educational issues left unaddressed.

A further accounting of these issues will be attempted in later chapters. Important to note here is that there were no preexisting answers or historic models to draw upon. A wide range of possibilities presented themselves. It was not immediately apparent that any of the classics would offer readymade solutions to the problems of war and peace. This became all the more apparent when the war ended and the issues of peace took center stage. Many of these issues were immediate and pressing, but since the war had ostensibly been fought to save

"Civilization," it did not take long for current problems to take civilizational values as a framework for discussion. It was the contemporary situation that had forced itself on the college's attention, and the terms of the discussion were therefore sought in the modern period. John Herman Randall's *Making of the Modern Mind* became a standard text for years. A further compilation of major historical documents (postmedieval) and scholarly articles, published as the syllabus of the Contemporary Civilization course, became widely used as a model for similar courses elsewhere.

Problems of staffing and pedagogy beset Contemporary Civilization from the start, and these remained, even after the adding of a second year entitled Contemporary Civilization B, which addressed immediate social, economic, and political issues in a kind of hands-on way (including local field trips). CCB did not last; ironically, it eventually fell victim to the demands for political relevance of the antiwar movement in the sixties, insisting on radical action instead of considered reflection on longer-term values.

Much more can be said about the checkered and tortuous history of Contemporary Civilization. For the present purpose, however, it may suffice to point out two salient developments over the ninety-odd years of local history as to what became of its ideas and methods as adopted and adapted elsewhere: First, Contemporary Civilization (like the Peace Issues course) was the first to become required of all College students, and insofar as its required status marked it as the essential feature of what became known as "general education," Contemporary Civilization stood as an historical landmark, whereas Humanities A, the successor to Erskine's General Honors course, only became a general requirement for all students in 1936–1937. Nevertheless, the earlier (Honors) Colloquium, with which Erskine "started on the road" in the pre–World War I era, emerged in the longer run as contributing the two most durable formulations of the essential Core Curriculum: a direct personal reading of enduring classics by each student and the discussion method ("colloquium") as superior to lectures for their shared serious engagement with perennial issues that were also "contemporary." These twin formulations may not capture all that was meant to be made available in general education, but I think they come close to pointing at the heart and practice of the Core.

3

The Great "Civilized" Conversation

A CASE IN POINT

Those familiar with the early history of the movement at Columbia identified with John Erskine's Honors Course and the "Classics of the Western World," known later in Chicago and St. John's as the "Great Books Program," will recall how its early advocates, including, among others, Mark Van Doren and Stringfellow Barr, referred to the dialogue among the great writers and thinkers as the "Great Conversation." They thought of it as the great minds speaking to one another over the centuries about the perennial issues of human life and society. Contrary to those who misperceived the process as one of handing down fixed, eternal truths, for them it was a vital process of reengaging with questions that had continued human relevance, age after age. One could not afford to ignore what had been said about those issues earlier because civilization depended on building upon the lessons of the past. Thus tradition, like civilization, continued to grow. It was cumulating and cumulative, not fixed.

Not all of the issues engaged in this conversation had to do with civilization and society—some religious issues might go beyond that—

but sustaining the conversation itself required a civilized life, a willingness to show a decent respect for what others have learned or thought for themselves, what others have valued or held dear—indeed, it was an appreciation for human life as it has been lived.

In the earlier phases of this movement, the conversation was largely within the Western tradition and was closely tied to the question of how classics, originally expressed in the classical languages of the West, especially Latin and Greek—could still survive in the modern vernacular as part of a classical education. But it was easily assumed that translation into the vernacular was possible because of a continuity of both language and culture into the later period. Such continuity in cultural values overrode historical change. As we shall see, this was largely (but not entirely) true of the major Asian traditions as well. They too had longstanding traditions of a Great Conversation, as later writers spoke to and reappropriated their own classics and thus engaged with the great minds of the past.

It was not, however, a matter simply of conserving received tradition. It was, as the word "conversation" suggests, the present speaking to the past in its own voice, actively repossessing and renewing the classics in modern terms that spoke to contemporary concerns as well. In other words, these traditions had within themselves the capacity for reexamination and self-renewal.

In modern times, this meant reflecting on the classics in a way that responded to the new cultural situation in which modern writers found themselves. As homegrown classics but also recognizably human, they became world classics. By the eighteenth century, at least, Western writers recognized that Asian traditions had classic thinkers who spoke to the same issues and concerns, though perhaps in somewhat different terms. Thus Enlightenment thinkers began to speak to the thinkers of classical China as well as to Western classics, and the New England Transcendentalists spoke also to philosophers of ancient India. Benjamin Franklin, at the founding of the American Philosophical Society, dedicated it to the study of Chinese philosophy as well as Western. All this had an effect on early twentieth-century writers such as W. B. Yeats, Ezra Pound, T. S. Eliot, and others too numerous to mention. But as of the twentieth century, though the most creative minds were already extending the Great Conversation to Asia, it had as yet little effect on Western education at the base level. Asian classics did not become part of the Great Books program. They were not among Mortimer Adler's "Hundred Great Books," nor did his "Hundred Great Ideas" include any Asian concepts.

Another limitation on the inclusion of Asian classics in the Great Conversation as conducted in the modern West was the tendency to focus the conversation on the classic writers of the Asian traditions, but not as part of a continuing conversation over time that matured well beyond ancient times. Thus Ezra Pound thought he could directly engage with the Confucian classics and even translate them himself with minimal sinological expertise. Sometimes he succeeded brilliantly in intuiting and appropriating them for his own poetic purposes, but this fell short of explaining what the *Analects* or *Great Learning* had meant to later Chinese, Japanese, and Korean civilizations. In other words, it was more of an extension of Pound's own culture, his own exploratory venture into a past idealizing Confucianism, than it was a substantial engagement with Chinese culture or civilization in its mature forms.

The time has come, however, for us to extend the conversation to twenty-first-century education in ways that do justice to Asian classics not just as museum pieces but also as part of the historical process to be factored into an emerging world civilization. Given the domination of education today by economic and technological forces—the same forces that drive world business—the preservation of any humanities education at all is problematic now anywhere in the world. Chapter 4 speaks to the crisis in East Asian education: as in the West, modern Asian universities have found it difficult to sustain the reading of even their own classics in the undergraduate curriculum. But the reasons for it are the same as those that militate against any classical education at all, even in the West. For the most part, Chinese or Japanese classics are read only by a few East Asian students majoring in classics departments. Meanwhile, most students want to concentrate on economics, science, and technology, and for these English is the relevant language. Thus the problem for Asian education is little different from that in the West: how to sustain any place at all for the humanities in the curriculum. It is a global problem and raises the question everywhere whether traditional humanistic learning can be sustained as part of a new global culture that would otherwise be dominated simply by the market and technology.

Let me now cite a case close to "home." It comes from a publication entitled *Inside Academe*, which speaks for an organization dedicated to upholding academic standards and traditional values in American education. In its summer 2007 issue, *Inside Academe* had an article entitled "Where's the Bard?" reporting on a new survey, headlined "The Vanishing Bard," of more than seventy universities, which reported that only fifteen among them require their English majors to take a course on Shakespeare. Instead, it says, "English majors are being offered an astonishing array of courses on popular culture, children's literature, sociology, and politics."

The article goes on to cite a long list of American publications, from *USA Today* to *The New Republic*, which regarded these survey results as significant. I doubt that many of us familiar with college education in the United States will consider this news. But for those concerned with how traditional humanistic learning stands in today's curriculum, the real significance of the report lies in its narrow focus on what is happening in English departments, to English majors—an academic vested interest—and how that is similar to what is happening to their counterpart departments in East Asia, i.e., the erosion in the study of their own classics, as upwardly mobile students choose to study the going language of English as the lingua franca of the twenty-first century. What adds to the irony in this case is that, before this, educated East Asians in the nineteenth and twentieth centuries had already come to admire Shakespeare as a world classic.

For traditionalists of almost any stripe, it would be a matter of concern that Shakespeare was being put on the shelf, unstudied, in any English department, but the reason for it is something antecedent to the state of the English major. If there is no place for the humanities in a globalized market for education, then even English majors will turn away from so great a figure as Shakespeare to whatever finds favor in the current media or marketplace.

My point is that mere conservatism—holding to an old line that has long since been overrun—will not avail today unless we can establish a place for local tradition in a global humanism that has something to say about what values might direct and control a runaway market economy and technology. Put in such global terms, the magnitude of the problem may seem overwhelming—how can one deal with the problem locally except in the larger context of global education? On the other hand, how can one get a handle on something so massive and complex as global education? If we have to think globally (as the saying goes), how can we act locally to work our way toward that goal? The answer, it seems to me, is that even if we have to deal within the limits of what is practicable in our local situation, we can begin the process of sharing our goals and experiences on a wider scale, so that the resources of the larger scholarly and educational community can be brought to bear upon beneficial, incremental change.

One way to get at this is to share our views on what has been considered "classic" in the major mature traditions of the civilized world and on how these can best be incorporated into our pooled educational resources—to put it simply, to make these resources available in a form that can be adapted to local systems. Thereby, one might hope to establish some kind of working consensus in the same way that the United Nations established a consensus on human rights in its Universal Declaration of 1948. The Universal Declaration did not effectively become "law," but it did set an international standard few could disagree with and that almost all states formally "ratified," however much or little they actually complied with it. Activists, always a minority, at least had a standard they could invoke in working toward its implementation. Fortunately, the English text of the declaration had the benefit of multicultural consultation and was less culture bound than would otherwise have been the case. Something like that should be done to establish "Classics for an Emerging World."

Let us compare our situation to that in American education a century ago. No sooner had President Eliot of Harvard set up his Five-Foot Shelf of Classics than he went over to a system of free electives, which meant that students could wholly ignore the Five-Foot Shelf. Columbia responded by making its "Classics of the Western World" a required Humanities course (a core course for all undergraduates). The Chicago version of this was dubbed "general education," with the idea of its being intended for students in general, young or old, elite or popular (as the Columbia program itself had been). But "generality" was its undoing when general education at Harvard succumbed to diverse academic interests and disciplines—to "ways of knowing" (among other methodologies) that could lead anywhere. The "core" of the classics earlier had been "ways of living," i.e., what the "Good Life" could mean in human terms, but this was premised on what it meant to be human. "Ways of knowing" was one aspect of this, but only one. Without a core of central human concerns, Ways of Knowing could lead to a diffuse unboundedness out on the so-called cutting edge of knowledge.

The "elective" character of even general education at Harvard was congenial to the free market that has dominated almost all aspects of cultural life in the past century, and it has benefited from the affluence—the great range of choices—that free enterprise has afforded the better classes, based on the pervasive assumption of unlimited growth and expansion. Education in the twenty-first century, however, without the luxuries of a bubble prosperity, will find itself constrained to make choices within much stricter limits. Choices are still there to be made, but just as the economy will have to live with much less exploitation of natural and human resources, society will have to make harder choices—giving up some of the freedom our affluence has afforded in order to preserve other values judged more essential. Education will have to do the same—make judgments as to what is most essential. Without closing the door on intellectual growth, we will have to prepare people to make qualitative judgments as to what is most conducive in the longer run to "the good life" and as to what human goods are sustainable.

4

A Shared Responsibility to Past and Future

When Chinese Confucian scholars escaped from Mao's armies and his anti-Confucian campaign, taking refuge in Hong Kong, Taiwan, and elsewhere, Qian Mu and Tang Junyi set up New Asia College in Hong Kong in the hope of conserving Confucian studies there (somewhat like the New School in New York as a "university in exile"). Much later, when Mao's successors shelved the Marxist-Leninist class struggle and turned back to Confucian "harmony" as a better basis for a stable political and economic order, Confucian studies began slowly to resume on the mainland. Still, it was a sign of the times—of the displacement of Confucian studies abroad—that when honorary lectureships were established at the New Asia College in the names of Qian and Tang, an American scholar like myself would have been asked to inaugurate them.

It was, however, only when I went to honor Tang Junyi at the Chinese University of Hong Kong that I learned from my hosts what a parlous state Confucian studies were actually in and why—now it was neglect, not repression.[1] This was disappointing news to me but not entirely a surprise. The problem, it turned out, was cultural rather than political. The long-term trend toward technological modernization and economic globalization had caught up with the Chinese here as every-where else—not just in high-tech Singapore. As the educational center-piece of a port city open to the world, the Chinese University of Hong Kong wished to establish itself as being in the very forefront of what was then called "internationalization." Even the People's Republic's eventual concession to the idea that Confucianism would provide the essential Chineseness of "Chinese socialism" did not count for much compared to the growing importance of a global culture now expressed in English. Hong Kong increasingly attracted Chinese students from the mainland itself because they could gain quicker access to English as the lingua franca of the new economic, scientific, and technological culture. It is no more than what had already been occurring in places like Singapore and Taiwan—and to some degree, all over Asia.

But if this could have a detrimental effect on the humanistic tradi-tions of Asia, the process had already begun well before this in Europe and America—the process of abandoning classical languages in favor of modern languages, the dropping of language requirements in Latin and Greek for entrance to the most prestigious colleges in the United States, and the replacement of Latin as the language of science up to the eighteenth century—all these changes presaged the global trend that would overtake the classical cultures of Asia as well.

In this respect, the worry of my colleagues at the New Asia Col-lege—that even there it would be difficult to sustain the reading of Chinese classics in the original—was anticipated by developments at Columbia in the early twentieth century, when John Erskine and his colleagues insisted that, if the great classics of the Western tradition were no longer to be read in Latin and Greek, they should still be read in English as part of a required core curriculum.

In view of the problems that have arisen at the Chinese University of Hong Kong as well as at the general education programs in Taiwan National University and Chiao Tung University (the MIT of Taiwan), and earlier at the Singapore National University, it seems to me the time has come to move to a third stage, that is, to identify the classics of the major world traditions that could constitute a master list for a global counterpart in English to the scientific and technological lingua franca that now dominates the educational scene. Nothing guarantees the enduring dominance of English, and nothing says that it is the most beautiful of languages, but the *New York Times* (May 15, 2007) confirms the simple fact of the matter today: it reports that hundreds of thousands of South Koreans are competing to take the TOEFL English test and that thousands more scramble to gain access to it in other countries, so as to qualify for admission to universities abroad and even for employment in South Korean businesses.

If this seems unduly to privilege English as a global second language, it is in accord with the long-term historical trend and should not be thought wholly prejudicial or unmanageable (i.e., a dead loss to other languages and cultures). The Bible is rarely read in its "original languages" but is still the most widely read book in the world. Leaders of India including Gandhi and Nehru first read Sanskrit classics in English, and Martin Luther King read Gandhi in English. If world-class classics can survive in a global curriculum, their inherent appeal will lead some to go back to classic texts that they might not otherwise have even known of.

WHAT TO DO

The process can be manageable, as I have said, if it is done in stages. First, it must be recognized that in using the word "classics" we do so in a way that confirms this concept as understood in its original discursive contexts. Every major tradition has its own canon or canons, and in considering what texts might be worthy of global attention we start first with the idea that their classic status has been confirmed over time by the respect they have continued to receive in their own tradition. These are works that have commanded attention, been appreciated or contested, and have survived scrutiny over the ages. In this sense, they are the surviving artifacts of a civilization and warrant the respect we show to what has endured. We do not read them because they conform to our own ideas or norms but to show respect to what other human beings have valued. It is, on our part, an act of civility, without which we cannot expect to live in the company of others whose traditions differ from ours (though we hope these are not wholly different or "other"). We are looking for common ground, but respect for differences is part of the process.

For this reason, our initial listings in what follows are given in terms of the traditions from which they emerge. Sometimes, these represent the convergence of several traditions, in which cases cross-referencing is in order. In conformity with this basic postulate, we assume that no such "classic" will first be read outside its own cultural company. How much company—how many other works of the same tradition are necessary in order to establish the context—is not a fixed quantity and depends partly on the genre or nature of the works in question. But it would be prejudicial to the whole enterprise if one simply removed a work (for its first reading) from its own context and inserted it, by itself, in strange discursive company, which only encourages one-sided comparisons. From our experience at Columbia, a minimum of four or five related works are needed to establish the classic context of each tradition.[2]

When it comes to "modern" classics, however, different criteria apply. Most of these cannot be judged primarily as products of largely self-contained traditions with their own norms and canons. Many respond to challenges from abroad and in turn enter into a larger realm of discourse. Their "classic" importance is enhanced by the way they take up themes of major importance in the larger world and contribute to new cross-cultural dialogues. This applies especially to representations of late developing cultures that become articulate as literate discourse only in modern times.

A prime example of a "modern classic" is Mahatma Gandhi, who, in his autobiography, speaks of the deep impression made on him not only by the New Testament but also by the modern writer John Ruskin, reminding us that Ruskin was a major nineteenth-century influence on other "modern classic" writers, such as William Morris, Friedrich Engels, Karl Marx, and Clement Atlee, as well as Gandhi.

Another example is Okakura Kakuzō, a prominent twentieth-century Japanese contributor to the East-West values debate who, in his "classic" *Book of Tea*, acknowledged a deep indebtedness to the American John La Farge, less well known in the West today than he was as a leading voice in American arts and crafts in the early twentieth century.

These cases obviously do not conform to the model of traditional classics. They have not endured the test of time, they have not met the test of "canonization," nor have they even survived "canonization" itself; indeed, they are not even by "dead white boys," as some black critics of the "canon" would have it.

If this distinction between traditional and modern classics is acceptable, I believe we could proceed to update the original syllabus of Erskine, Barzun, Van Doren, et al. in four stages, by workshops or seminars dealing with:

1. A review of the master lists of classics used in the core curriculum at Columbia and elsewhere (including Asia as well as the United States, but in this first stage focusing on Western classics as the original syllabus did), to produce a master list of recommended works, which might be drawn upon at local option to fit specific educational programs.

2. A review of classics of the major Asian traditions that might qualify for treatment in courses parallel to those in the Western classics, updating the *Columbia Guide* of 1989, on the basis of input from Asian programs of general education (Chinese University of Hong Kong, National Taiwan University, etc.).

3. A review of "modern classics" of the nineteenth and twentieth centuries that might produce another master list from which selections could be made for courses or programs that focus on nineteenth-century–twentieth-century interactions among major world traditions on core issues, i.e., perennial human issues that are reexamined in a comparative light and in a modern context.

4. Preparation of guides or manuals corresponding to each of these stages, listing available translations, scholarly studies useful for general education purposes, and core issues or genres exemplified by each work.

5

Asia in the Core Curriculum

The term "general education," as it gained currency in mid-twentieth-century America, was originally applied to efforts at the reform of university education, which had become dominated by departmental specialization and by an elective system in undergraduate colleges that lent itself, by the choice of a major, to the same trend toward specialization. The earlier history of these reform movements, as well as their subsequent history in America, tells us something about why "general education," whether as a term or as a practice representing a diffuse generality, is somewhat anachronistic today and would better be replaced by the concept of a central and centered "core curriculum." Yet the recent rise of the movement for what is called "multicultural education" underscores the need for equipping that central core with multicultural dimensions.

The genesis of these educational reform movements took place, as we have seen, at Columbia College in the post–World War I era. As background factors, one can cite at least two main trends toward the modernization of education at that time. One was the abandonment earlier of the classical "liberal" education that had prevailed in British and American colleges, wherein the required languages had been Greek, Latin, and sometimes Hebrew. When those language requirements were abandoned in the early twentieth century, a serious question arose as to how the humanistic values of a classical education would survive if students could no longer read these classics in the original.

Another educational challenge arose from the sense that, following the end of World War I, there was occurring both a civilizational crisis and a new intellectual opportunity. The great aim (or at least the great ideological slogan) of that war had been "to make the world safe for democracy." With its hope and concern for the establishment of a new world order based on the peaceful solution of human problems, it is not stretching things to say that the central concern of this new course and its syllabus was "civility" in its broadest sense.

The topical treatment, the concern for values and ideas, the contemporary interest combined with historical background, and above all the use of challenging source readings as the basis for class discussion became defining characteristics of the Contemporary Civilization course. Another defining characteristic was that it was required of all students, a break from the dominant elective system of which Harvard's had stood as the preeminent model.

The justification for CC's being required was a civic one: along with the inescapable trend toward academic specialization, Columbia should educate its students to deal in an informed way with the shared problems of contemporary society. Preparation for leadership and citizenship was undoubtedly among the course's aims, but the method of personal engagement with urgent contemporary problems, through active class discussion (rather than just listening to lectures), was almost an end in itself. In other words, the discussion method promoted active civil discourse on the nature of civility—learning by doing.

These, then, were the shared moral and social concerns, along with a sense of the college's corporate responsibility to address them in a collegial fashion, that justified limiting the students' full freedom of election—while also, it is important to add, limiting the faculty's freedom to teach whatever its individual members chose in the way of their own specialties. In the interests of education, the faculty had to subordinate their personal research interests to the needs of a common curriculum taught in a collegial fashion.

Subsequently, the idea of having a "required core" spread widely, but one hardly need mention today that the original sense of corporate responsibility and esprit de corps, on the part of the faculty, has since proved difficult to sustain. Thus the true esprit de *core* has often been dissipated, and today "core" at many places only means "what is required," and few remember why. Usually, it amounts only to a distribution requirement—at best a methodological smorgasbord—and not a genuinely collegial effort to bring a range of disciplines to focus on questions of common contemporary concern.

This is what has happened at the University of Chicago and at Harvard, which adopted the idea of general education in the 1930s and 1940s with much fanfare. At Chicago, the program was initially identified closely with the Great Books program promoted by Robert Hutchins and Mortimer Adler, but subsequently the Great Books program was spun off as a separate adult education foundation, and the university adapted it to a divisional structure tailored more to disciplinary groupings (humanities, social sciences, etc.). Thus a common core was no longer required of all undergraduates. At Harvard, the so-called general education program quickly became departmentalized, and the subsequent reform inaugurated by Dean Henry Rosovsky did little to arrest this gradual fragmenting of the core. In effect, the forces of academic specialization reasserted themselves, "general education" became converted into a distribution program based on a sampling of different methodologies, and the idea of core concerns, key human issues, and major classic texts to be addressed by all students in common became less central to the program.

In the light of this experience, one can say that the very generality and flexibility of so-called general education lent itself, adapted itself, too readily to centrifugal tendencies in academia. And it is likewise from this experience that one may draw an important lesson concerning the need to refocus attention on the concept of a common educational core—difficult though it is to sustain that struggle against the persistent departmentalization and specialization of academic research. It goes to the heart of the educational enterprise—whether it is to be centered on a common humanity. Though "a common humanity" may itself be a difficult philosophical question, if it ceases even to be a question, a key issue for shared discussion, we are in deep trouble and become exposed to all the divisiveness of ethnic and political conflicts.

Core then, in the true sense, has referred not just to content or canon but to process and method—to a well-tested body of challenging material, cultivated habits of reflective critical discourse, and procedures for reexamination and redefinition. A viable core, it was thought, could neither be slave to the past nor captive to the preoccupations, pressures, or fashions of the moment. It should serve rather to advance the students' intellectual growth and self-awareness, cultivate their powers of thought and expression, and prepare them to take a responsible part in society. The focus has differed in the two basic courses: on society and civility in the CC course and more on the individual and on a shared but at the same time diverse humanity in the Humanities course. In either case, the method has emphasized practice in civil discourse in a collegial setting.

Almost from the beginning, however, the proponents of this core were conscious of its initial Western focus and anxious to extend its horizons. This consciousness is reflected in the course title, "Contemporary Civilization in the West," and in the original syllabus of the honors course, "Classics of the Western World"; "West" in both cases signified an acknowledgment of cultural limitations, not an affirmation of Eurocentrism. And no sooner had the Humanities course been added to the Core in 1937–1938 than leaders of the movement (though none of them Asianists themselves) began to agitate and plan staff development for counterpart courses in Asian civilizations and humanities, which were added as soon as was practicable after World War II.

The way in which this was done is highly significant for the present debate on multiculturalism: that its focus was on core concerns, humanity, and civility and that the method of instruction continued to put a premium on collegial discussion, that is, practice in civil discourse. No assumption was made of the superiority of Western ways or values or the primacy of a European canon but only of the presence in other major civilizations, and in other major traditions of great depth, complexity, and longevity, of comparable discourses on perennial human concerns and issues, which we should try to make our own to the extent that translation allowed.

This assumption of a parallel discourse had no difficulty gaining confirmation from the Asian works themselves, but, there being no such thing as an "Asian tradition" (in the sense of "pan-Asian"), some judgment had to be exercised in identifying the major traditions or civilizations to be focused on in a one-year course; in our case, Islamic, Indian (including both Buddhist and Hindu traditions), Chinese, and Japanese (with the late addition of Korea). That judgment, however, was almost made for us, given our prior and most fundamental assumption concerning the nature of any tradition or canon: that it be self-defining and self-confirming. Thus it was not for us to find counterparts to Western classic models but only to recognize what Asians themselves had long since ratified as works commanding special respect, either through enduring appeal or irrepressible challenge.

Within each major tradition, this dialogue has taken place through a process of constant, repeated cross- and back-referencing internal to the tradition and largely independent of external involvement except to the extent that, from at least the seventeenth century onward, writers in the West, great and not so great, have confirmed for themselves what important writers in the Islamic, Indian, Chinese, and Japanese traditions have long held in esteem. Thus in the Islamic tradition Al Ghazali and Ibn Khaldun have based themselves on the Quran and commented on the great Sufis, while European writers, no less than middle Eastern, from medieval times onward have also recognized the greatness of Al Ghazali and more recently Ibn Khaldun. Something similar is true of India, with the Upanishads and the *Ramayana* taking up the discourse from the earlier Vedas, the Gita from the Upanishads and Shankara from both. And it is true too of China, with Mencius drawing on Confucius, Xunzi commenting on both Confucius and Mencius, the *Laozi* and Zhuangzi taking issue with the Confucians, and so on. Almost all of the great classics of the Asian traditions have established one another as major players in their own league, members (even if competitors) in their own discursive company.

It is of crucial importance, however, that enough of the original discourse be reproduced so that this internal dialogue can be recognized and meaningfully evaluated by the reader. For the reader (discussant) to recognize and judge the adequacy of one writer's representation of another requires some familiarity with the original work. Further, though the particular examples given here are drawn more from the religious and philosophical domain, the same is no less true of the literary. Indeed, in any domain the matter of genre, voice, and medium of expression enters strongly into the judgment of what is considered either classic form or canonical wisdom.

(At this point, I should add parenthetically that our program included parallel courses in Asian humanities and Asian civilizations, with a more historical, developmental, and social emphasis in the latter, as well as other courses in Asian music and art humanities. Thus the overall program is less bibliocentric than the discussion thus far might lead one to believe. But it is in the discussion of the classic works that one can most easily observe the kind of internal give and take that should be incorporated in the larger discourse aimed at here.)

So fundamental are the foregoing considerations to any kind of multicultural education that just to include one or two such works in a world civilization, world history, or world literature course is almost worse than including nothing at all. It is tokenism, and even if such a course is equally and uniformly sparing in its representation of all cultural artifacts, then it is only tokenism on a grander and more dangerous scale. If one's initial framework is a civilization or humanities course already established to deal with Western models, the addition of just one or two Islamic, Indian, or Chinese works will almost always be prejudicial, no matter how innocently intended, for in such a case the individual Asian work, bereft of its own context, will inevitably be read in a Western frame of reference by Western readers. Even if the instructor tries to compensate for this by lecturing about the breadth and variety of the culture in question, the information still comes to the student secondhand, so the latter must depend on the instructor's word instead of the original word of an Asian author.

No one can prescribe a fixed number or minimum of classic works to be included in any such multicultural program. Nevertheless, one could offer, as a rule of thumb, that five or six such works are the minimum necessary to establish the context of any particular discourse to which one might hope to gain access, assuming that the works are well chosen to complement one another and suggest not only the range of possibilities within a given tradition but also how it has grown and developed from within. For unless the cumulative nature of the discourse—its continuities, discontinuities, and mature syntheses are adequately represented, the tendency of the reader is to see individual works as in themselves embodying some static essence of the culture rather than as landmarks along the way.

Today, in a multicultural education that serves human commonality as well as cultural diversity, both content and method may vary in different educational situations, but a core program should make the repossession (both sympathetic and critical) of a given society's main cultural traditions the first priority and then move on, in a second stage, to a similar treatment of other major world cultures. Further, to the extent that time and resources allow, it would provide for the consideration of still other cultures that, for a variety of historical and geographical reasons, have not so far played such a dominant role in world history. (In the East Asian context, I would certainly point to Korea and Vietnam in this respect.)

At least two other general principles seem applicable to this educational pattern or approach. One is that it is best, if at all possible, for the process to extend to more than one culture other than one's own, so that there is always some point of triangulation and so that a multicultural perspective predominates over a simplistic we/they, self/other, East/West comparison. Thus, the Columbia "Asian Humanities" course includes reading from several of the major Asian traditions, which allows for significant cross-cultural comparisons quite apart from those the student naturally makes between his own and any one other culture.

If the effect of this is to underscore diversity, the second principle would be that any such treatment, whether of one's own or other cultures, should give priority to identifying central concerns. Above, I have suggested "civility" and "humanity" (to which "the common good" or "commonality" could well be added) as basic categories or core concepts, but a main reason for starting the process with source readings or original texts has been to proceed inductively—to ask, in the reading of these works: what are the primary questions being addressed in each, what are the defining concepts and values of the discourse, and in what key terms have they expressed both their proximate and ultimate concerns? Such questions may well be left open-ended, but for the time being, at this stage of the learning process and for purposes of cross-cultural discussion, we should be looking for centers of gravity, points of convergence, common denominators.[1] Why? Because as a matter of educational coherence it is best to work out from some center, however tentatively constructed, to the outer reaches of human possibility. And for purposes of establishing the grounds for carrying on civil discourse, some working consensus, initially tradition-based but increasingly multicultural, is needed.

The priorities and sequence just proposed would, it seems to me, be applicable to almost any cultural situation. If one recognizes that other peoples will set their own priorities, one would naturally expect each educational program to repossess its own classics first and then move on to ingest those of others. Indeed, one would concede this possibility to others as of right—that in China's schools for instance, a course entitled "Chinese Civilization" would have priority over "European Civilization"; in India, "Indian Civilization," and so forth. Starting from the premise that every person and people needs its own self-respect, as well as a minimum of respect from others, it is essential for each to have a proper self-understanding—to come to terms with its own past. This is essential not only to its own cultural health but to healthy relations all around.

The key to success in such an endeavor is how well one identifies core human issues and how one selects the texts that can illuminate these issues from among the larger body of works recognized as perennial classics in the respective traditions. This requires constant reflection, reexamination, and dialogue among world traditions. But as each civilizational tradition participates in this multicultural discourse, we can hope gradually to expand the horizons of civil discourse and the scope of shared civilizational values, which will be a key to the solution of our common global concerns about the environment, human rights, and world peace.

6

What Is "Classic"?

What is classic? To answer this question, I do not believe we need agreement at the start on how to define a "classic." In fact, it is important not to theorize about this until we have taken into account what representatives of the major world traditions have considered classic, whatever the terms or genres of expression they propose. From this base of reference arrived at inductively, not deductively from our own premises, we might also ask to what extent have certain classics, sprung from one tradition, come to be recognized by others, as many Chinese classics came to be accepted by other East Asian traditions, insofar as, for example, the classic literature of Korea and Japan incorporated Chinese classics into their own canon. Since, in the nineteenth and twentieth centuries, Western classics in philosophy, religion, and literature (as well as in music and the arts) often became widely recognized in East Asia as "classic" (e.g., Shakespeare, Dostoevsky, Mozart, and Beethoven), this convergence of classics in modern curricula should also be taken into account.

In recognizing works of other traditions as "classic," however, those who did so accepted them in two ways: they responded to something important in them that spoke to their own sensibilities, something "human" in their moral and rational makeup and cultural susceptibilities, but they also saw something in the original that expressed these sentiments in a special way and to a preeminent degree. It was not a case of simply seeing them as either the same as or other than oneself or one's own but as both common (universal) and diverse (particular) at once.

In this process, we shall be taking as "classic" what has survived into modern times, and this survival itself has an important claim on our consideration. These are works that have lasted, and their enduring character is what compels our attention: they are artifacts of human civilization, "hard facts" of historical survival that cannot be ignored. What else cannot be ignored, however, is that they are the products of that history. They take the form history has given them, and as "received" later, many can no longer be taken simply as representing the original text that generated the classic tradition.

The most obvious example of this is the so-called Four Books of the Confucian tradition, consisting of the *Analects, Mencius, Great Learning*, and the *Mean*. When educated East Asians referred to the Confucian "classics" in the seventeenth through twentieth centuries, they almost always spoke of the Four Books, which were the texts as processed by the great Neo-Confucian scholar Zhu Xi (1130–1200), texts that became standard in the curriculum promoted by Neo-Confucians in a broad educational movement that extended into the immediate "premodern" period. Thus they were "traditional classics" as received in later times.

It did not take long, however, for textual critics even in the Neo-Confucian schools to point out differences between these supposedly "traditional classics" and the versions that had prevailed before the Neo-Confucians put their own stamp on them. This led inevitably to efforts by modern textual critics to "discover" or reconstruct what might be considered the *Original Analects*, etc. If we want to incorporate any of these texts into our own core curricula, however, which version are we to include? It is unrealistic to think that any curriculum today that tries to provide a humanistic component for an undergraduate

program can get into all the difficulties that this historical complexi-
fication entails. If we read what some modern scholar reconstructs as
the "original *Analects*," it may not be what later tradition would have
recognized; it is not what would have entered into the intellectual and
moral formation of generations of East Asians. It would simply be an
academic discovery.

There is no perfect solution to this educational dilemma, but if we
are willing to think not of final or definitive solutions but rather of
working ones, then we can try to provide a repertoire of approaches
that at least may be drawn upon by those trying to adapt these resources
to their own educational situation and system.

For this purpose, I propose making a distinction among (1)
"generic" classics, (2) traditional classics, and (3) modern "classics."
A selective combination of these might enable the student to gain a
perspective on those classics inspiring enough to become the seedbed
of tradition; others that are given such brilliant articulation later as to
become dominant in the subsequent received tradition; and "modern
classics," which reaffirm traditional concerns in a modern setting but,
because of their relatively short life, cannot yet be considered to have
endured the test of time. If one chooses among these possibilities, one
can put together a combination selected so as to represent both the
age-old "generic" classics; the "traditional" classics, which confirm the
centrality of the generic ones but articulate these in much broader historical and cultural terms; and finally "modern" classics, which again
confirm the relevance of the generic and traditional classics in a way
that students today can recognize as pertinent to their own lives and
present situations.

For the time being, however, we approach the matter not as one of
definition but as one of actual practice, i.e., what is being done today.
From the brief survey given in *Classics for an Emerging World*,[1] one
may easily see that courses featuring the reading of classics cover a wide
spectrum of course types and purposes, from programs based solely
on the classics and taking four to five years (though with some taking a lesser number of works and years), to others of shorter duration
adapted to other methodologies or disciplinary purposes. Something
of this range was an inherent possibility from the beginning, owing to
the presumed universality of the classics themselves as embodiments

of key human concerns and values, susceptible of being extended to relevant contexts or, conversely, being looked at from different angles toward a multifaceted center.

The same was true of the intended audience. John Erskine's "Classics of the Western World" was first given as an honors course to a selected few, but it also aimed at a larger human audience—to become a required course for all undergraduates and also the basis for a program of adult education (even union workers). It sought to provide a basic literacy in the classics—"what every educated person should have read," it was said of them—works of depth and importance that merited being read and reread.

Given this large purpose, it is not surprising that the reading of the classics might become adapted to many different educational situations. The question would inevitably arise, however, in this process of adaptation: if there were no limits to its extensions or diffusion, might not the unlimited possibilities for disciplinary expansion draw the process out beyond the practical possibilities for an education meant for the sharing of common knowledge and values? The original idea of "general education" had been addressed to a general audience who would share a common cultural literacy. But once classics came to be read mainly as relevant to different cultures and academic methodologies, the danger arose that the whole process could become unhinged from the center and pursue instead the dynamic inherent in scholarly and scientific specialization. How to keep things in balance became the problem, one that called for a sustaining of the core curriculum parallel to any process of specialization. In other words, it would not just be a base point at the start but a continuing center of gravity on all levels of education.

For all this, one still needs a place to start from, and as a practical matter one is limited to the availability of adequate translations. This was indeed a question from the beginning of our effort to incorporate other major traditions in any course dealing with works variously referred to as "Classics," "Important Books," "Great Books," and now "Major Texts." Under whatever rubric they were offered, these books, it was said, were ones any educated person ought to have read—as if what it meant to be "educated" could be taken for granted in those days, even though education itself was undergoing rapid change.

In this case, the relevant change in the early twentieth century was the dropping of classical languages—Greek, Latin, and Hebrew—from the college requirements and the need felt then to preserve the reading of the "classics," long thought to be essential for educated "gentlemen," in translation. When this change occurred, defenders of the classical languages argued against it on the ground that, if the classics were not read in the original, something would inevitably be lost in translation. That there would indeed be some loss in respect to certain values inherent in the original languages and literary forms could hardly be doubted, but John Erskine, the early proponent of reading the classics in translation, discounted that loss. "How many people read the Bible in the original?" he asked, implying that the most important values in any such works could still be appreciated, as the Bible was, in translation.

Indeed, Mark Van Doren, who subsequently became a leading exponent of the "Humanities" or "Great Books" program, insisted that one test of a real classic was that it could survive translation. He meant, of course, that such a work dealt importantly with issues, concerns, and values so pertinent to and so perennial in human life that any work addressing them in a challenging way would not become obsolete.

If this is obviously so of the place of Latin and Greek classics in the English, French, or German heritages, it is no less true of the quick ascent and commanding position established by Shakespeare in European literatures and cultural idioms other than the English. Nor is this true only of the West. Confirmation of it has come likewise from Asia—from "classics" of the several Asian traditions that have survived translation from one language to another—Chinese classics translated into Korean and Japanese that have become no less accepted as "classics" in their adoptive land as were the Greek and Latin works in the "classic" traditions of Western Europe. The same has been true of Indian works translated into the languages of South and East Asia and now of Western works esteemed as classics in modern Asia.

To say this, however, is not to dismiss the question of translation as a minor issue. The standing of classical works in their own tradition may be enough to compel our attention, but the availability and quality of translations has clearly been a factor in the successful mounting of any "Humanities" or "great books" course. To a degree greater than most people today would likely be aware, enough translation had been done from Asian languages so that major works were already well-known in nineteenth- and early twentieth-century Europe and America and had long since stood as a challenging presence to leading Western writers and thinkers.

Nevertheless, the work of translation from Asian traditions was far from complete or satisfactorily done for the purposes of a core curriculum when the courses in "Asian Humanities and Civilizations" were inaugurated at Columbia in the late 1940s. Enough translations of a reasonable quality were available to launch a worthwhile program, as has been testified to by Professor John D. Rosenberg, a survivor of the pilot course. There were, however, many gaps, and there was also a major problem facing the extension of the program beyond a select few in an honors colloquium—the problem of translations suited to the general reader and accessible in forms not heavily burdened with scholarly annotation, that is, translations of the kind translators address primarily to specialists in their particular field of research.

Fortunately, competent help was soon forthcoming, in the persons of young scholars whose translations were to establish a new standard not only for scholarly excellence but for accessibility to students in general education. First of these was Donald Keene, whose *Anthology of Japanese Literature* (1955) made Japanese classic writings available in a convenient form at low cost—albeit at some cost also in the abridgement of works that would be better read as integral wholes. Keene proceeded to make up for this limitation of his *Anthology* by translating whole works only partly extracted in the earlier compilation. Most notable has been his translation of Kenkō's *Tsurezuregusa*, published under the title *Essays in Idleness* in the series Translations from the Oriental Classics launched specifically to meet the needs of general education in what is now called the Asian humanities. Next came Keene's *Major Plays of Chikamatsu* and subsequently his translation of the drama *Chūshingura*. With the follow-up work done by Keene's students Royall Tyler and Karen Brazell, Keene's translations of Nō plays in his *Anthology* have been substantially supplemented by competent translations in inexpensive paperback editions. In the meantime, another major work of classical Japanese literature, the *Pillow Book* of Sei Shōnagon, only excerpted in Keene's *Anthology*, was translated in whole by Ivan Morris, before his untimely death an active participant in the teaching of the Asian humanities at Columbia. All of these classic works have thus become available in translations that in themselves have become standard works and virtual classics of the translator's art.

On the Chinese side, although many of the Chinese classics had been translated earlier, most notably by James Legge and Arthur Waley, and had been indispensable to the early offering of the course, many other Chinese works considered classic not only by the Chinese but by all East Asians remained untranslated or else were unavailable in a form suitable for student use. A major advance in this respect was the undertaking by Burton Watson of translations from the Chinese of other classic works that convey the diversity and range of the Chinese—and what subsequently became the East Asian—tradition. Watson's early versions of alternative "classics" in Chinese antiquity—Mozi (Mo Tzu), Xunzi (Hsun Tzu), Zhuangzi (Chuang Tzu), and Han Feizi— quickly made available by Columbia University Press in inexpensive paperbacks, became standard items on our Humanities course reading lists and indeed set a new standard in the field for providing translations, both readable and reliable, for the general reader. Watson's wide range, versatility, and virtuosity as a translator has also been shown in renderings of the *Records of the Grand Historian* by Sima Qian (Ssu-ma Ch'ien); the *Vimalakīrti* and *Lotus* sutras; and his anthology of classic Chinese poetry, the *Columbia Book of Chinese Poetry*, all of which qualify for inclusion in our Asian Humanities course reading list.

Our biggest challenge with regard to readable translations has come with the major texts of the Neo-Confucian tradition, which responded to the challenge of Buddhism and Daoism. The key texts are mostly in the form of the commentaries of Zhu Xi (Chu Hsi) on the Confucian classics, and commentaries make for more difficult reading than most of the original works themselves. For this reason, many instructors prefer to avoid the Neo-Confucian texts in favor of more literary works (of which there is an almost unlimited supply). But these Neo-Confucian texts were the operative "classics" that shaped the later intellectual and ethical traditions of China, Japan, and Korea from the thirteenth to the twentieth centuries, and avoiding them is like ignoring everything in the West from Dante on. We have a similar problem with the medieval texts of the Islamic and Indian traditions, and it is not an easy dilemma to resolve, considering, as just one case in point, the lack of a suitable edition of a major work like Sankara-charya's commentaries on the *Brahma Sutras*. To some extent, this deficiency can be made up for by using translated excerpts, for Sankara in the *Sources of Indian Tradition*, and for Zhu Xi, the new translations included in the second edition of the *Sources of Chinese Tradition*. Still, this is a compromise—better than nothing but less than satisfactory.

Further, on the Indian side our program has itself produced a major contributor to the translation of Indian thought and literature. Barbara Miller got her start as a Barnard undergraduate taking the Oriental Humanities course, went on into graduate studies in Sanskrit, and eventually produced translations, in a form ideally suited for the general reader, of important texts including the *Bhagavad Gita*, the *Shakuntala* of Kalidasa, *The Love Song of the Dark Lord* (*Gita Govinda*), and the lyric poetry of Bhartrihari. Before her premature demise, Barbara had established herself not only as a prime contributor to the Asian Humanities program but as a leading figure in the field of Indian and Sanskrit studies worldwide.

Thus it may be seen that while an Asian Humanities program can rely on the inherent greatness of works that have established themselves over time—and through tough scrutiny and debate—as world classics, still their ability to "survive translation" (in Van Doren's terms) depends on having translators able to convey their contents in terms meaningful enough to new audiences in changing times and different cultures.

Teachers and students alike will continue to face the need to make choices among available translations for their own annual engagement with the Asian humanities. There will never come a time when all the work of translation is done and finished for all the eligible texts, since there will never be a complete, definitive, and final rendering of the "original" meaning of such texts. Dealing as they do with pivotal issues, subject to different interpretations, and expressing themselves in highly suggestive, expandable ways, these works may always be brought to life in new renderings. For readers who wonder how much of a gap may exist between the original text and the translation at hand, the simplest solution is to look at alternative translations and get a sense of what common ground may lie between them—or where the lines of difference lie. Recourse too may sometimes be had to such scholarly expertise as is available within easy reach. But since specialists differ among themselves as much as translations do, this is not a perfect solution either.

It remains true, however, that, though any translator is welcome to take up the challenge and offer his own interpretation, not all translations meet the need equally well, and we can count ourselves fortunate in having had an especially able group of translators, a group whose great translations almost match the great works themselves.

7

Classic Cases in Point

I n this chapter, I offer three examples of how three different Chinese and Japanese works may be read to illustrate the question asked by the preceding chapter: "What Is Classic?"

WHY WE READ THE *ANALECTS* OF CONFUCIUS

Although this section will speak mostly to why and how I read the *Analects* of Confucius, the reason I entitle it "Why *We* Read the *Analects*" is not that I claim to speak for everyone but only that my personal reading follows from what others have thought and said about it. Ever since Confucius's disciples recorded his sayings, teachings, and examples in the fifth century c.e., later generations have been inspired to pass it on, to share it with others who have read, reflected on it, and discussed it together. Thus the *Analects* are still read because they have survived this scrutiny and reexamination over the centuries, which is why we read it today—not because it became part of a fixed canon (though in some places it did) or because it was required reading imposed by one generation upon the next.

I have read and discussed the *Analects* with students in my Asian Humanities class for sixty years, and their response to it is much the same, whether they are majoring in the natural or social sciences or in the humanities. So, for practical purposes, when I speak of "Why We Read the *Analects*," it means "how I and my students have read the *Analects* together," and especially how one's first impressions are formed by the early chapters. Indeed, it is no different for other audiences of any age or at any level, including adult education. If this is what is meant by "general" education, then the *Analects* speak to the generality of human beings—to their common, perennial, "core" concerns more than to the farthest outreaches of abstract thought.

This is why I avoid speaking of what I do as "teaching" the *Analects*. No doubt, a teacher can help students with their reading and reflection upon the text, but basically students are rediscovering it and learning it for themselves. The book teaches itself, as most genuine "classics" do. Whatever may be done by a teacher is only an enhancement of the reader's own personal encounter in recognizing that the text speaks directly to him- or herself.

For me, the latest confirmation of this fact comes from the valedictory address of a Columbia College graduate in 2008 who chose to sum up his four years' learning experience by drawing on the model of the *Analects* and some of its key sayings.[1] Understandably, our valedictorian drew first on the opening lines, which read: "The Master said: To study and at times to practice what one has learned, is that not a pleasure? To have friends coming from afar, is that not a joy? To be unembittered even if one is not recognized, is that not to be a truly noble person?" If one wishes to know more of what our valedictorian made of these lines, one can refer to the *Proceedings* just cited. In what follows, despite my disclaimer of any originality or unique expertise, I shall offer my own thoughts on these lines and other key passages that mark the *Analects* as classic.

Taken together, these opening lines tell us much about the nature and context of the *Analects*. The first lines could be addressed to and understood by any literate human being, but the last line points more specifically to "the noble person" (*junzi*). Here *junzi* refers to the traditional leadership elite, an aristocratic class born to a privileged status of would-be rulers. But Confucius emphasizes the learning process for what it takes to be worthy of a leadership role or become an exemplary person; in other words, what it means to command respect as a person, whether or not one finds oneself in a position to lead or rule. Thus he reconceives the traditional concept of *junzi* from that of "nobleman" to one that emphasizes "the noble *man* (or person)" as one whose personal character, not status, establishes him as a model to be followed—a true leader in any social role whatever, even if not successful politically.

(In the context of the times, one understands that *junzi* refers most directly to male heirs of the aristocracy, but the second half of the compound, *zi*, is literally "child" and not gender specific. Thus later Japanese empresses could appropriate to themselves the expression *tianzi*, normally understood in China as "Son of Heaven" but for them clearly open to their own claim to be a "child of Heaven" regardless of gender. Still later in China, *jun* could be a suffix applied to women as well.)

The same multifaceted expression *zi* also appears as the very first word in the *Analects*: "The Master said (*zi yue*)." As "Master," *zi* could be applied to other authority figures, such as Laozi and Zhuangzi, and here it clearly refers to a teacher, but the language that follows marks Confucius as distinct from any teacher who is simply dictating or preaching to his students or disciples.

Note the rhetorical cast of all three of the statements above: they are not outright assertions, much less forceful dictates. They invite and expect an implicit response from the hearer as if one's own experience would immediately confirm the truth of what Confucius is saying— he is only telling them in a sense what they already know, without invoking any higher authority. This is not the thunderous voice of the prophet, nor is it a pronouncement from the pulpit or podium. Old Testament prophets spoke first of all to God, and then they delivered God's word to His people. Confucius speaks directly to us and asks us to recognize Heaven within and around us.

His appeal to ordinary human experience is also the ground on which he talks of studying or learning. What he says may be addressed to the individual, calling on one personally to achieve fulfillment as a truly noble person, but his hearers are learning from others as well as from their own experience and practice, and their "others" here include teachers, examples from the past, as well as "friends coming from afar" with whom one can share one's experience—it is learning that can be gained from (being open to) both the past and others able to confirm and expand on one's own knowledge.

But if I have distinguished Confucius's voice from that of the Old Testament prophet, this does not mean that there is no common ground between them. Both speak to an ideal standard by which to measure and judge the conduct of kings and rulers and, by implication, anyone else who bears a responsibility for others—which means just about all of us. In Confucius's case, however, the approach is most characteristically on the means of self-cultivation by which one can develop the virtues of the Noble Person, understood as a fulfillment of the human ideal. And most characteristic of Confucianism too is the way that the *Analects* explain this as an organic growth following the pattern of ordinary human life.

Accordingly, in the passage immediately following that quoted above, the *Analects* speak of that process as grounded in the life of the family, wherein, initially by acquiring habits of respectful conduct toward others—first of all toward parents and then to one's siblings—one engenders traits essential to human life, whether one's own—in the self—or in others. Thus the second passage concludes: "The noble person concerns himself with the root, when the root is established, the Way is born. Being filial and fraternal—is this not the root of humaneness?" (1:2).

Again the rhetorical mode—appealing to anyone's first experience of life conveys the sense that the living process is interactive and interpersonal. But here the process is identified as one by which "the Way" is born, takes life. And in the context of the preceding passages, this is also understood to be the Way that a truly noble person follows.

At the same time, this Way is centered in humaneness as the prime virtue of the Noble Person, a virtue that links the self-fulfillment of the exemplary person to the fulfillment of others. But fulfillment is the product of a sequential process for anyone and everyone. Filiality is the seed from which, with due cultivation, the growth process can be fulfilled in the flowering of humaneness or true humanity. In this respect, filiality may be considered the genetic virtue of Confucianism—important in its priority—but its full fruit or flower is humaneness (consummate virtue).

There is a widespread impression that filiality is the most characteristic virtue of Confucianism, and this notion is not just a modern misconception or misreading by foreign observers. The early critic of the Confucian school, Mozi, seized on this family virtue as almost an obsession of the Confucians he knew. And the early Legalists also took issue with the Confucians on this point, seeing a family ethic rooted in filiality as prejudicial to public-mindedness on a wider scale (as indeed Mozi had). Moreover, the powerful hold of filiality on Confucian culture was demonstrated by the resistance that it showed to Buddhism upon the latter's introduction to China.

But before we pursue this issue further, we do well to note another early reference to filiality in the *Analects*. When a disciple, Meng Wu Bo, is quoted as asking Confucius about filiality or filial piety (*xiao*), the terse answer given is somewhat perplexing in its obliqueness: "Parents' only concern should be lest their children be sick" (2:6). Traditional commentators have tended to interpret this as implying primarily an obligation on the child to take proper care of itself—attending to one's own person in bodily and moral health. No doubt this was a distinct and enduring feature of Confucian teaching and practice, and its strong sense of the person as a bodily self is what offered resistance to Buddhist questioning of the reality of any substantial self. But one should not ignore the underlying assumption here that the filial child is responding to the loving concern of his parents. Filiality is a reflection of parental love. It partakes of the basic Confucian principle of reciprocity, in the light of which filiality is to be seen not as an absolute value requiring blind obedience to parents but as a relative one to the extent that it is qualified and conditioned by a parental love that is taken for granted in the passage just quoted—one of the many natural assumptions underlying Confucian discourse.

Another later anecdote in the *Analects* underscores the same point. Confucius's disciple Zai Wo asks him about the customary three years' mourning for one's parents, expressing the thought that one year's mourning should be enough. Confucius asks him: "If you were to eat good food and wear fine clothing, would you feel at ease?" Zai Wo responds: "I would feel at ease." "If you would feel at ease, then do it. But the noble person throughout the mourning period derives no pleasure from the food that he eats, no joy from the music that he hears, and no comfort from his dwelling. But you would feel at ease and so you should do it." After Wo leaves, the Master adds: "How inhuman Yü [Zai Wo] is! Only when a child is three years old does it leave its parents' arms. The three years' mourning is the universal custom everywhere under Heaven. And Yü, was he not the darling of his father and mother for three years?"

In this case, Confucius shows a basic respect for the essentially voluntary character of ethical behavior while also upholding the standards of reciprocity that should ordinarily apply. The standard, however, presumes that natural feeling should underlie and prompt one's actions. It would do no good to make a pretense of virtue. Thus natural feelings of reciprocity engendered in the normal process of life, from birth and infancy to maturity, are the root of humaneness, as in the earlier example.

The primacy of natural sentiments born in the bosom of the family is underscored by another episode, in which the Duke of She tells Confucius: "In our part of the country there is one upright Gong. His father stole a sheep and the son bore witness against him." Confucius says: "In our part of the country, the upright are different from that. A father is shielded by his son, and a son is shielded by his father. Uprightness lies in this" (13:18). In other words, the intimacy of the family is privileged over the claims of the state, for the state cannot stand if trust within the family—the root of public trust—is undermined.

Soon after this, the primacy of sentiment or feeling over rational discourse was reaffirmed for Confucians in the *Mencius*, where Mencius defined the goodness of human nature as moral awareness (literally, "good knowing" or natural knowledge, *liang zhi*), and further when he defined the basic relationship or bond between parent and child not in terms of filiality but as one of "intimate affection" or mutual love to be cultivated (of course) in the light of reason (the sense of right and wrong, *yi*).

But since from the outset of the *Analects*, as in all the literate discourse that its readers are engaged in, there is the possibility that verbalization and rationalization might intrude on one's ordinary conduct, it is important that what one learns and says be guided and informed by both one's own feelings and one's consciousness of right and wrong (*yi*). Thus the *Analects'* early exposition of the Way of Humaneness includes the following: "A young man is to be filial within his family and respectful outside it. He is to be earnest and faithful, overflowing with love for all living beings and intimate with those who are humane. If after such practice he has strength to spare, he may use it in the study of literate culture (*wen*)" (1:6). Although the importance of study and learning had already been asserted in the opening lines—and Confucian scholarship became widely known among East Asian teachings as the most rational—here the priority of moral cultivation over literate discourse (*wen*), essential though the latter was to civilized life, is established early on in the *Analects*.

We saw in the opening lines how the process of learning started first by interaction with others but ended with the Noble Person able to stand, so to speak, on his own. He knew where he stood regardless of the approval or disapproval of others. This is not the same as a radical individuality asserting its complete autonomy but is rather a self in a state of personal balance or poise. The same conception then informs our understanding of other Confucian values connected with the Noble Person as a model of humaneness. In chapter 1:4, one of Confucius's closest disciples is quoted approvingly as follows: "Every day I examine myself on three things: In planning on behalf of others, have I failed to be loyal? When dealing with friends have I failed to be trustworthy? In receiving what has been transmitted, have I failed to practice it?"

Among each of these cases there is a connection or continuity that involves more than an obedient adherence to or following of others. "Loyalty" (as *zhong* is usually translated) is represented by the graph for "center" underlain by the graph for "mind-and-heart"; it bespeaks a centered mind and heart, one in a state of balance within the self but also balanced with others. It means being true to oneself as well as to others (not just following or obeying the latter). This then connects up with the other two values cited. "Trustworthiness" is our rendering here for *xin*, sometimes also translated as "good faith," both of which express the idea that one's actions and conduct are consistent with one's stated professions, being true to one's word. (Ezra Pound, as a poet and amateur translator playing around with the *Analects*, notes that the character for *xin* [trust] included the graph for man or person at the left and the graph for "word" or "saying" beside it on the right, which suggested to him the felicitous rendering of it as "man standing by his word.")

This same notion is implicit in Confucian "loyalty," being true at once to one's self and others, and it connects up with the faithful practice of one's professions in service to others. Another notable passage in the *Analects* speaks of the "man of service" (*shi*), here roughly equivalent to the "noble person," in the following terms: "The man of service cannot but be stout-hearted and enduring; for his burden is heavy and his way is long. To be truly humane is the burden he bears; is it not heavy? Only in death does his practice of the Way come to an end; is that not long?" (8:7).

Here the burden of humaneness is heavy because service to others that is also true to oneself can be exacting and demanding of one's own inner resources. Whether in a position of leadership or sharing in the responsibilities of government, to be truly reliable and trustworthy meant to be fully honest with oneself and unflinchingly forthright in advising others. Often, it would involve courageous honesty in counseling rulers who might resent hearing the truth, especially about themselves.

In the Confucian tradition of civil service, especially in ministerial roles, this courageous honesty was the hallmark of true loyalty on the part of those who were "stout-hearted and enduring" even to the point of martyrdom, when the true scholar-official's Way ended in death at the hands of a despotic ruler. But being true to one's word and professions had an importance beyond the individual in Confucius's whole scheme of things. A prime vocation for the man of service was the business of human governance, and the *Analects* has much to say about this. Here a few examples may suffice: When a disciple asked Confucius about government, the latter replied tersely, "Sufficient food, sufficient military strength, and the confidence (trust) of the people [are the three requisites]." When asked further "if unavoidably one had to dispense with any of these three, which of them would you forego?" the Master replied: "Let go of the military strength." The disciple next asked: If one had, unavoidably, to dispense with one of the remaining two, which should go first? The Master said: "Do without the food, for from of old there has always been death, but without such confidence (trust) a people cannot stand" (12:7).

Mutual trust among the people and their leaders is thus the most essential ingredient of any human society—a principle that underlies another response of Confucius to the question of what is essential to government: "Should you try to lead them by means of regulations or keep order among them through laws and punishments, the people will evade these and lack any sense of shame. Lead them [on the other hand] by personal virtue (*de*) and keep order among them through rites (*li*), then the people, having a sense of shame, will correct themselves" (2:3).

Here Confucius's depreciation of laws and punishment fits with his eschewal, from the passage just cited before, of coercive force ("military strength") except as a possible backup to civil action. For him, voluntarism is the basic predicate of any human society, as it had been traditionally in households cooperatively engaged in family-managed agriculture. One can rely better on a person's or people's sense of self-respect (the corollary of "the sense of shame" referred to here) to motivate people's cooperation with their leaders, just as the latter's personal virtue should exhibit exemplary self-respect combined with respect for others.

Note, however, that personal virtue and respect alone are not enough; the rites are especially involved and indispensable. This is because rites and proper customs establish practical norms of conduct that are themselves voluntaristic, cooperative, educational—and not coercive. They are the means by which the self, in the normal process of life, engages with others. They give form to things, forms and norms naturally conducive to the harmonious development of human relations or political action.

This is the basis for the "harmony" that others have seen as the keynote of Confucianism, regardless of whether they always understood its voluntarism or reciprocality in the same terms. When in seventh-century Japan Prince Shōtoku tried to incorporate Confucianism in his nation's first formal constitution, the first word that he used was "Harmony," followed by his exhortation on behalf of a consensual society. Much later, after the Communists in China recoiled from the vicious class struggle of the Cultural Revolution, they turned back, at least in name, to Confucian harmony as an essential Chinese value to undergird "Chinese Socialism."

Much more is said in the *Analects* about the rites (or ritual decorum) in daily life as they relate to personal and social health. But I am limiting myself in this section only to a few key themes that one encounters in a first reading that give us initial bearings on what follows in the text.

In the remainder of this section, I wish to focus on something no less important to one's reading of the *Analects* than the key teachings: the character of Confucius and his sense of personal vocation and mission. This image of him in the pages of the *Analects* comes through as almost more compelling and memorable than his teachings and aphorisms, to such an extent that, despite his own disclaimers of his disciples' attributions of sagehood to him, among latter-day Confucians the picture of him as he appeared in the *Analects* became the very model of the Sage (though none could hardly boast of emulating the modesty of the Sage).

The first thing to note is his becoming modesty and lack of pretension to great personal authority, which are already implicit in the conversational mode of the opening lines. He did not claim to be proclaiming any new order or teaching. "I am a transmitter, not a creator," he said (7:1). Whether he was actually creative in the process of transmitting, that is, in his interpretation and exposition of ancient ideals, is another question, but posterity has generally judged him so. One must also allow for the possibility that "in transmitting" what he had received from past tradition he was being more than just conservative. The posture of "upholding past ideals" could also appear as a critique of existing institutions that fail to measure up. Thus one episode in Confucius's teaching career portrays him, in the course of his travels, sending a disciple to ask directions from a farmer who, when he learns that the disciple's master is Confucius, recognizes the latter as a would-be counselor to rulers, going from state to state looking for one who would take his advice.

The farmer has a skeptical view of this mission; he regards the world as so unruly that the best one can do is tend to his own field. "Instead of following a scholar who distances himself from one ruler after another, it would be better to follow one who withdraws from the whole world of men" (18.6). When the disciple reports this to Confucius, the Master sighs: "One cannot herd with the beasts or flock with the birds. If I am not to go along in the company of other human beings, with whom should I associate? If the Way prevailed in the world, I would not be trying to change things" (18.6). Mere "transmitter" though he was,

Confucius did see his mission as trying to change things. Received tradition itself contained the seeds of reform, but it was Confucius who saw the need to rectify the evils that would not just resolve themselves.

Confucius was known in his time as a scholar persistent in his call to be of public service, but he was equally known for his diffidence in serving any ruler whose actions were inconsistent with his own principles. On another occasion someone asked Confucius: "Why does the master not take part in government?" The master said: "What do the *Documents* [The Classic of History] say about being filial? Be filial. Just being filial and being friendly with one's brothers contributes to governance. Why should one have to take office to do this?" (2:21).

Again Confucius's answer is somewhat terse and a little oblique, but it takes us back to where we started in the *Analects*: filiality as the value underlying all social and civic virtue. Public service is not performed only by those in office; anyone who practices and promotes such civic virtues is rendering a public service. And, indeed, the practice of such values is the precondition for anyone who might qualify for office. Elsewhere, Confucius says: "One should not be anxious about having an official position but about having the wherewithal to hold office. One should not be anxious about not being recognized [for office] but about not being worthy of such recognition" (4:14).

Again we are taken back to the starting point of our reading: the Noble Person who can stand on his own even if he is not recognized. The course that he has followed (and we in following the *Analects* thus far) is summed up in Confucius's own brief summation of his life experience: "At fifteen I set my heart on learning. At thirty I was established in its pursuit. By forty I had no great doubts [about what I was doing]. At fifty I heard what Heaven commanded of me. At sixty I could heed it. At seventy I could follow my heart's desire without transgressing" (2:4).

In the light of our previous discussion, we may be able to fill in the spaces in this spare outline of his personal history. That it starts with learning we already know. That it takes time to learn from the past and others' experience we can readily understand. Confucius's growing from adolescence to increasing security at thirty and maturity at forty—these are familiar stages in the life process. What may be somewhat unexpected is that only at fifty did he "hear" what Heaven expected of him. The language used here for "Heaven's command" is

itself not unfamiliar, but earlier it had referred to what is usually translated as the "Mandate of Heaven" (*tianming*), a claim made by rulers
or their spokesmen to justify their taking power and exercising authority, ostensibly in the name of Heaven. For Confucius, that claim could
only be considered legitimate if in fact the ruler or his dynasty ruled
virtuously on behalf of the people. And it is this sense of responsibility
attaching to the claim of legitimacy or public trust that is crucial to
Confucius's understanding of Heaven's command or charge.

Confucius himself was in no position to rule. At some point, nevertheless, he must have felt that he had some capacity and obligation to
make use of what he had learned on behalf of the public good. (Whether
or not this occurred exactly at fifty in this schematic sequence is not
the point.) More significant is that Confucius takes this charge upon
himself personally; it is not just a political concept applying to dynastic
rulers but a commission that Heaven was entrusting directly to himself.
We are already aware from other references to Heaven in the *Analects*
that Confucius felt some personal relation to it—a kind of religious
relationship between Heaven theistically conceived (a divine creator)
and its creation. Heaven spoke directly and personally to him, and he
had a filial obligation to listen.

Confucianism may not be thought of as a "religion" in the usual
sense, but Confucius bespoke a reverential attitude toward Heaven,
and the deep respect in which he held all life was a reflection of this.
In response to questions put to him by disciples about the Noble Person, he said: "He cultivates himself with reverence" (14:45), and even
more to the point here: "Without knowing (or understanding) what
Heaven has ordained (*tianming*), i.e., its charge or command, one has
no way to become a Noble Person" (20:3). Indeed, the attitude and virtue of reverence remained a key element in later Confucianism. It was
not a purely secular ethic, as some have supposed it to be.

But if Heaven charged Confucius personally with a responsibility
for public service, we know already how conflicted he was about taking
office, and we can understand the difficulty that he might face in trying
to carry out that charge. This is perhaps why it took him time (here,
another ten years) actually to "heed" what we he had heard earlier,
that is, to find a way to resolve his conscience in this regard. My own
supposition is that his resolution of the matter was in keeping with

the response that he gave to those who had questioned him about his refusal to take office: both in the given circumstances and in the larger scheme of things, taking office was not the only way to fulfill one's obligation to be of service to Heaven and humankind. Teaching was also a public service when it contributed to the individual's and people's education on behalf of the public trust.

Finally, when we are told that at seventy Confucius had satisfied his heart's desire, we are reminded that at fifteen he had "set his heart on learning," and so, in carrying out Heaven's charge to him, the outcome—his satisfaction as a scholar and teacher in lieu of an official career—fulfilled not only that early aspiration but also any political ambitions he might have had. This was not accomplished without a struggle of the kind that one who had to bear the burden of humaneness to the end might endure. But that end was, after all, marked by some measure of satisfaction and fulfillment.

To be sure, this was not exactly a supreme epiphany or sudden moment of enlightenment but rather a threshold of accumulated learning and experience. Nor does it, on the other hand, result from the sort of profound confrontation with evil and suffering that we see, say, in St. Augustine or Dostoyevsky. Including Confucius in such a range of perspectives, one can see his as a relatively optimistic or even idealistic view of life. But it is reassuring for those who have followed him in the *Analects* to believe that this good man could live out a life worthy of a truly Noble Man—the goal he set out for himself at the start.

The foregoing is just one among several ways of explaining why or how we read the *Analects*. There are others. However important it is to read the text directly and personally, the one we read always bears the imprint of the tradition that has passed it on. And if we want to know how others have received and understood it, showing a decent respect for the opinions of readers and writers before us in other places and times, we might go on to consider how it was understood by those who had a major impact on other civilized peoples.

This would be especially true of those East Asian peoples whose education was structured in the form given by the pervasive Neo-Confucian movement from the eleventh to the nineteenth centuries. Over the course of this long premodern period, the *Analects* was read as one of the so-called Four Books, a special packaging of the Confucian

classics mainly attributed to the great Neo-Confucian philosopher
Zhu Xi (1130–1200). In that form, the *Analects* was not the first thing
one read. It came after the text of the *Great Learning*, a chapter from the
Record of Rites (*Liji*) attributed to Confucius's disciple Zengzi, which
was provided with a special preface and commentary by Zhu Xi that
he thought propedeutic to any reading of the other classics included in
the Four Books. Thus how one read the *Analects* itself was conditioned
by Zhu's own way of introducing us to "How to Read a Book." The
book is still a classic, but now it is the product of a subsequent tradition, and this is not exactly the same as "reading it in the original." Zhu
Xi was now presenting it in a form adapted to his own age, in which
"new age" Confucians, that is, Neo-Confucians, responded to the challenge of Mahāyāna Buddhism by providing a metaphysical explanation
to accompany the text. The basic message remained the same, as Zhu
Xi summed it up in his preface: "Self-cultivation for the Governance
of Humankind" (*xiuji zhiren*), a memorable slogan in later literature.
Now, however, it was elaborated upon in terms of a new cosmology
and a more sophisticated philosophy of human nature (*dao xue* and
xingli xue). (Incidentally, this is how the *Analects* was reported on by
the American art critic Ernest Fenollosa, who read it in a Japanese edition of the Four Books and handed it on to people like Ezra Pound.
But this is what we all do—read it on the recommendation of someone
else in a form more or less adapted to the latest scene.)

However, it did not take long for even this Neo-Confucian version
of the traditional classic to be called into question by textual critics of
the seventeenth through nineteenth centuries, who pointed out differences between these supposed "classic" or traditional Four Books and
the versions that had been "classic" before. This led inevitably to efforts
by modern critics to rediscover or reconstruct "the original *Analects*."
If we want to incorporate any of these new versions into our own core
curriculum, however, which are we to choose? No working curriculum that tries to provide a humanities component for undergraduate
education (or even alongside graduate training) can get into all of the
complexities that this historical development entails.

There is no perfect solution to this educational dilemma, but if we
are willing to think of working solutions rather than final ones, we
can try to provide a repertoire of approaches by which one can adapt

these resources to different educational situations and different levels of learning. The important thing is that the first reading be a personal encounter with a classic text (however "classic" may be interpreted) and that it be understood as only a first reading, one to be followed up as best one can by more or other readings.

PASSION AND POIGNANCY IN *THE TALE OF GENJI*

Opening lines are usually significant clues to almost any classic work, and this is no less true of the *Genji*. Lady Murasaki's first words are uncertain but nevertheless indicative: "In whatever reign it might have been" (*izure no on toki ni ka*). Beginning on such an indefinite, questioning note (*ka*), the *Tale* could be about almost any time or place. Then, after this indefinite start comes an anonymous reference to a low-ranking court lady whose favor by the emperor exposes her to the jealousy of higher-ranking court women; in other words, instead of being introduced to a typical heroine whose noble character commands our attention if not respect, we meet a lady who simply attracts our natural sympathies. There is some necessary specificity of narrative detail, but rather than fixing our attention on that particular scene or social context, the story appeals primarily to ordinary human sentiments. In this case, the grand Imperial Court of Lady Murasaki's time simply serves as a stage for eliciting universal human feelings that provide the essential themes of the novel.

In this opening passage, the narrator shows interest in a character of somewhat marginal status. The context is courtly, aristocratic, hierarchical, and imperial (out of which contextual details professional critics or historians can make whatever they wish), but the author herself, and I think most ordinary readers, recognize the essential poignancy of the human situation being described—the conjunction of love, loss, and suffering.

My own teacher Ryūsaku Tsunoda once defined the Japanese sense of beauty in a rather offhand remark as "love touched by death." By this I think he meant "loss" in general and not just physical death. I don't think he had the *Genji* specifically in mind, but it certainly fits. Love and loss prove to be a major theme of the *Genji*. True, it is about much else as well, but given the very amplitude of the story and its diversity of incidents, we must necessarily focus here on what is most revealing of our chosen theme.

For me, one of the most telling passages is an early episode, in which Genji, at an idle moment, is casually conversing with close friends about the women they have known who have most attracted them. These include a variety of types. Physical beauty is, of course, an obvious subject of conversation, but the discussion ranges over other aspects of human affectivity that join the psychological to the physical and less often the sentimental and sensual to the practical.

In a way typical of the Japanese proclivity for indirection, the conversation that sets the tone for the whole of *The Tale of Genji* takes place as if by happenstance: on a rainy night when nothing much is going on, Genji's good friend Tō no Chūjō catches him sorting through some old letters and suspects that he might find in them some intriguing secrets of Genji's most intimate life. It ends up in an exchange of views, among them and other companions, concerning different women they have known, each of whom has some attractive features but each of whom also has some offsetting and off-putting defect.

The terms in which the discussion is couched are those given by the aristocratic court culture: categories of social class, to each of which attaches the presumption that it represents a certain standard of high-class taste or virtue. Initially at least, the question is assumed to be whether the individuals being described are truly "classy" or not, but the judgment is usually that they fall short somehow—whether by society's standards or by more fundamental human ones.

Traditionally, this episode has been spoken of in Japanese as *shina no sadame*, wherein *shina* can be understood as "quality," "qualities," or "goods" and *sadame* as "judging," "determining," or "rating." Although described here as a very casual, if not desultory, process, the scene is one that reflects the strong Japanese penchant for erecting hierarchies of qualitative judgment or standards of quality, and although the manner is loose and low key, one should not be surprised to learn, as the *Tale* unfolds, that this "idle talk" in fact anticipates much that is to follow.

Tō no Chūjō prefigures this when he leads off with the observation: "I have at last discerned that there exists no woman of whom one can say 'This is perfection,' 'This is indeed she.'" The rest of this long rambling *Tale* relates how Genji's own search for perfection brings similar results, but with a much deeper awareness of the ambiguities in these relationships.

Intimations of this appear early on in Genji's comments on a judgment offered by Tō no Chūjō, who says: "I divide women into three classes. Those of high rank and birth are made such a fuss of and their weak points are so completely concealed that we are certain to be told that they are paragons. About those of the middle class everyone is allowed to express his own opinion, and we shall have much conflicting evidence to sift. As for the lower class, they do not concern us."[2]

The completeness with which Tō no Chūjō disposes of the question amuses Genji, who says, "it will not always be so easy to know into which of the three classes a woman ought to be put. For sometimes people of high rank sink to the most abject positions; while others of common birth rise to be high officers, wear self-important faces, redecorate the inside of their houses and think themselves as good as anyone. How are we to deal with such cases?" (23).

The range of possible outcomes is further projected in a comment by Uma no Kami: "However high a lady may rise, if she does not come of adequate stock, the world will think very differently of her from what it would of one born to such honors; but if through adverse fortune a lady of the highest rank finds herself in friendless misery, the noble breeding of her mind is soon forgotten and she becomes an object of contempt" (23).

Tō no Chūjō goes on:

No doubt the perfect woman in whom none of those essentials is lacking must somewhere exist and it would not startle me to find her. But she would certainly be beyond the reach of a humble person like myself, and for that reason I should like to put her in a category of her own and not count her in our present classification. But suppose that behind some gateway overgrown with vine-weed, in a place where no one knows there is a house at all, there should be locked away some creature of unimagined beauty—with what excitement should we discover her! The complete surprise of it, the upsetting of all our wise theories and classifications, would be likely, I think, to lay a strange and sudden enchantment upon us. (23)

Here adverse circumstances may confound one's normal expectations, and we become aware that subjective factors enter into the "objective" picture to complicate and compound the judgment.

"The conversation went on. Many persons and things were discussed." Uma no Kami contends that perfection is equally difficult in other spheres:

> But when the mistress is to be selected, a single individual must be found who will combine in her person many diverse qualities. It will not do to be too exacting. Let us be sure that the lady of our choice possesses certain tangible qualities which we admire, and if in other ways she falls short of our ideal, we must be patient and call to mind the qualities which first induced us to begin our courting. (23)

If these other perspectives thus complicate the "objective" picture, this final remark suggests that the most fundamental difficulty still lies in the realm of subjectivity: the emotional complications that beset every loving relationship. Among these, jealousy is a prime factor. The games that lovers play with each other and the strategies they adopt all affect how one perceives or looks for a "perfect solution," which always remains elusive. The problem is already aired in this early conversation, but it is perhaps most vividly acted out later in the case of the young Evening Glory (Yūgao). A beauty hidden in the poorest, most unpromising circumstances, she is rescued from her shabby surroundings by Genji and installed in a more pleasant pavilion only to be struck dead by the vengeful spirit of another of Genji's lovers, Lady Rokujō, whose humiliation and embitterment, as ghostly disembodied karma (or unappeased obsession), works its own violence on Evening Glory and puts an end to this unlikely affair.

Jealousy and personal insecurity assume great prominence in *Genji*, equal almost to the intensity of love itself, because the court aristocracy is polygamous and a double standard for men and women contaminates things. The "perfect wife" is expected to suppress her own monogamous feelings and act with tolerance and forbearance toward her husband's promiscuous impulses. As Tō no Chūjō puts it: "when all is said and done there can be no greater virtue in a woman than this: that she should, with gentleness and forbearance, meet any wrong whatever that falls to her share." So obvious and unexceptional was this idea to the young gentlemen present that Genji himself dozes off in the midst of it and, as the narrator observes, takes no exception to what Tō no Chūjō is saying.

Genji, however, might well have been more alert had he not already resigned himself to the idea that perfect love was impossible to find. At the end of this long evening, the story concludes:

> All this while Genji, though he had sometimes joined in the conversation, had in his heart of hearts been thinking of one person only [his first wife, Princess Aoi] and the more he thought the less could he find a single trace of those shortcomings and excesses which, as his friends had declared, were common to all women. "There is no one like her," he thought, and his heart was very full. The conversation indeed had not brought them to a definite conclusion, but it had led to many curious anecdotes and reflections.
>
> So they passed the night, and at last, for a wonder, the weather had improved. After this long residence at the palace Genji knew he would be expected at the Great Hall and set out at once. There was in Princess Aoi's air and dress a dignified precision which had something in it even of stiffness; and in the very act of reflecting that she, above all women, was the type of that single-hearted and devoted wife whom (as his friends had said last night) no sensible man would lightly offend, he found himself oppressed by the very perfection of her beauty, which seemed only to make all intimacy with her the more impossible.   (27)

In other words, there was nothing wrong with his own No. 1 wife, Princess Aoi herself. It was rather her perfection that made her unapproachable and drove his restless heart to look elsewhere.

If we leap past the intervening incidents in Genji's subsequent affairs, much later in the *Tale* we find him taking stock of his amatory adventures in a way that he mistakenly thinks will be reassuring to Murasaki, his young protégé and later wife, who is now ailing. He reviews his affairs with other women, as if by citing their flaws he is thereby comparing them unfavorably to her. Little does he think of them as infidelities; they were simply diversions for him and imply no lack of appreciation for her. This is how he puts it to her:

> What a strange life mine has been! I suppose few careers have ever appeared outwardly more brilliant; but I have never been happy. Person after person that I cared for has in one way or another been taken from me. It is long since I lost all the zest for life, and if I have been condemned to continue my existence, it is (I sometimes think) only as a punishment for certain misdeeds that at all times still lie heavily on my mind. You alone have always been here to console me and I am glad to think that, apart from the time when I was away at Akashi, I have never behaved in such a way as to cause you a moment's real unhappiness. . . . However, you are very observant, and I cannot believe you are not perfectly well aware. (651)

To this Murasaki replies, as the ideal long-suffering wife should, by bearing with her husband: "I know that to any outside person I must appear to be the happiest of women, fortunate indeed far beyond all my deserts." Then she adds a few words that reveal her true feelings: "But inwardly I am wretched . . . every day" (651).

Try as she might, there is no way Murasaki can hold back her true feelings. All she can do is break down in uncontrollable sobbing. Genji tries to console her, but he has no idea what he has let loose within her heart. Her hero, her ideal, who should be the soul of sensitivity and sensibility, is indeed upset but still uncomprehending. He tries to divert and distract her by talking about other women he has known who did not measure up to her, as if these left-handed compliments would take the sting out of his philanderings. Instead it only makes things worse. He recalls Lady Rokujō: "Despite all that happened, I always think of her as the most brilliant creature that was at court. Never have I encountered a sensibility so vivid and profound and this, as you can imagine, made her a most fascinating companion. But there can never have been anyone with whom it was more impossible to have relations of a permanent kind." Eventually Murasaki does regain control of herself and carries on in a dutiful way. The author, however, has let us know what is really going on.

Most of this exchange is described in the language of daily life experience rather than in overtly philosophic or religious terms. Yet it should not be difficult to see in all this the underlying tensions that had arisen in Japanese culture owing to the continuing interaction between native traditions and the influx of Buddhism and Confucianism, especially Buddhism in both its original formulations and its Mahāyāna adaptations. If this early idle chat among Genji and his companions focuses on the nature of desire and the possibilities for its satisfaction, the Four Noble Truths and Noble Eightfold Path of Buddhism, with their radical questioning of desire and pessimistic view of the possibilities for its satisfaction, must have been in the back of their minds, as well, of course, as in the narrator's. Nor can the portrayal of intense passions encountered in the *Genji* have been oblivious to the turn taken by Mahāyāna Buddhism as it reckons with the qualified reality of the sensual world and concedes after all that the passions too can be a means to enlightenment. The concession to such feelings would also serve prospectively as an adaptation to the received Japanese tradition by Lady Murasaki's time.

For a classic example of the latter, we might turn to the *Manyoshū*, an imperially sponsored collection of native Japanese poetry, as much a classic for the Japanese as the Confucian *Book of Odes* was to the Chinese. As an example of how closely akin the *Genji* is in feeling to the *Manyoshū*, we may take a poem composed by an earlier court lady, Princess Nukada, in answer to a question posed by Emperor Tenji to his prime minister Fujiwara Kamatari, who had played a major role in the great Taika reform that attempted to convert the Japanese system to the up-to-date model of a unified Chinese bureaucratic state. Although the issue has nothing to do with government policy, it is in sharp contrast to some critics who read the *Manyoshū*, with its imperial sponsorship, as having a strong ideological (that is, political) subtext. In the *Manyoshū*, the poem is introduced as follows:

When the Emperor Tenji commanded Fujiwara Kamatari, Prime minister, to judge between the luxuriance of the blossoms on the spring hills and the glory of the tinted leaves on the autumn hills, Princess Nukada decided the question with this poem.

When, loosened from the winter's bonds,
The spring appears,
The birds that were silent
Come out and sing,
The flowers that were prisoned
Come out and bloom;
But the hills are so rank with trees
We cannot see the flowers,
And the flowers are so tangled with weeds
We cannot take them in our hands.
But when on the autumn hill-side
We see the foliage,
We prize the yellow leaves,
Taking them in our hands,
We sigh over the green ones,
Leaving them on the branches;
And that is my only regret—
For me, the autumn hills.[3]

If there is political significance to this, it lies in the Japanese court being "the high court" in which such "delicate" aesthetic matters would be judged. The prestige of the court is much involved in its standing as the arbiter of high culture.

As for the poem itself, it fits the pattern of the *Manyoshū*: a strong attention to the natural world, the passing of the seasons and attendant emotions, and the pervasive nostalgia for past moments of intense longing—in short, the aesthetic response to life. Later writers and critics have identified this same feeling in the *Genji* as *mono no aware*,[4] variously translated as "the sadness or pathos of things" but here rendered by me as the "poignancy of things," because it is concerned with the recollection of a momentary experience of intense beauty and deep feeling. Thus it encapsulates a spiritual experience that responds on one level to the Buddhist sense of impermanence and ephemerality and on another to the distinctive involvement with nature characteristic of Shinto as well as with the passionate response to life that becomes a hallmark of both the Japanese aesthetic and Japanese religion.

In the *Genji* itself, this aesthetic feeling appears against the background of a more traditional Buddhist conception of the religious life as "leaving the world" or "leaving home," that is, breaking one's attachments by the formal act of withdrawal to monastic seclusion. This possibility occurs to many of the principals in the story, including Genji and Murasaki. Generally, however, traditional monastic discipline is not considered a viable option. Although Murasaki thinks of the religious life as a possible surcease for her sufferings, she will not do this without Genji's permission, and he is unready to face life without her. That she obeys him, despite all the pain he has caused her, tells us that she is still bound by her primary attachment to him as a dutiful wife.

When Genji (and others like him) contemplate a monastic retreat, they doubt that they can succeed in breaking off their attachments to the world. This is not only because they are emotionally dependent on others (as in Genji's case) but because, as Genji sometimes puts it, in his own way he still feels a genuine concern for those he would be abandoning. Even in monastic seclusion, he would be worrying about them (and, indeed, from a human point of view that would not be seen as such a bad thing).

There are enough such cases in the *Tale* that we have reason to believe that the author takes the same view of formal religion as no real solution to the problem of desire. Part of the problem for Murasaki, however, is that human feelings, no matter how painful they may sometimes be, have a value that goes beyond any of the desires spoken of in the Four Noble Truths of early Buddhism. Just as in the Mahāyāna, the passions themselves can be made conducive to enlightenment; in the Japanese case, they can attain the level of a religious experience in themselves.

At this point, we would do well to consider how Murasaki deals with the matter when she has Genji speak for herself about the liberating function of literature. In another one of those casual encounters that prove to be so revealing, Genji happens to catch one of the court ladies in the midst of reading a novel, and at first he is inclined to dismiss fiction as frivolous literature. Later he qualifies this judgment and ends up taking it very seriously: "There is, it seems, an art of so fitting each part of the narrative into the next that, though all is mere invention, the reader is persuaded that such things might easily have happened and is as deeply moved as though they were actually going on around him."

He continues:

"So you see as a matter of fact I think far better of this art than I have led you to suppose. Even its practical value is immense. Without it what should we know of how people lived in the past, from the Age of Gods down to the present day? For history-books such as the *Chronicles of Japan* show us only one small corner of life; whereas these diaries and romances which I see piled around you contain, I am sure, the most minute information about all sorts of people's private affairs. . . ." He smiled, and went on, "But I have a theory of my own about what this art of the novel is, and how it came into being. To begin with, it does not simply consist in the author's telling a story about the adventures of some other person. On the contrary, it happens because the storyteller's own experience of men and things, whether for good or ill—not only what he has passed through himself, but even events which he has only witnessed or been told of—has moved him to an emotion so passionate that he can no longer keep it shut up in his heart. Again and again something in his own life or in that around him will seem to the writer so important that he cannot bear to let it pass into oblivion. There must never come a time, he feels, when men do not know about it. That is my view of how this art arose."   (500–501)

There are several points in these observations that may help us come to some conclusion about the *Genji*. First of all, in his discussion of the novel Genji is no doubt made to speak for the present author to express self-consciously what she thinks she is doing as she writes. Second is the idea that fiction, though an invention, best tells us about ordinary life; reading it, one is "deeply moved" as though these "inventions" were actually going on around one.

It is not so much that the novel may actually preserve the facts of life and history, as *Genji* concedes, and thus serve as a veritable record of a certain time and place; more important is that the author, instead of simply telling "a story about the adventures of some *other person*," writes "because the storyteller's own experience of people and things, whether for good or ill was moving him [or her, in this case] to an emotion so passionate that he can no longer keep it bound up in his heart. Again and again something in his own life or in that around him will seem to the writer so important that he [or she] cannot bear to let it pass into oblivion" (501).

"Oblivion" might satisfy the need for a kind of detachment, if one could actually put love, loss, and grief out of one's mind. But Murasaki, as Genji's creature in the novel (that is, adopted and brought up in court by him) was not free; she was only at a loss for words, sobbing uncontrollably in her grief. As the author, however, Murasaki could give voice to that grief in literature that is timeless. True liberation for her means cherishing the deepest of one's feelings as being profoundly meaningful in themselves and, by putting them into words, preserving them for, and sharing them with, all posterity.

At this point, one can relive, and perhaps even create, a reality that defies the vicissitudes of time. Impermanence and "emptiness" are overcome in a moment, and that is what gives such poignancy to the experience, which now breathes and feels with an intense reality of its own. Time stands still at that moment. "Love is touched by death," or better, "death is outdone by love," with deep pain or passion now recollected as poignantly beautiful.

THE *PILLOW BOOK*

It is notable that two of the undoubted classics of the Japanese cultural tradition have been written by women: Murasaki Shikibu's *Tale of Genji* (*Genji Monogatari*) and Sei Shōnagon's *Pillow Book* (*Makura no sōshi*). It is also striking that they appeared at almost the same early moment in history, the products of the same age, the same aristocratic society, and a culture that drew on similar religious traditions, both indigenous and imported. No less striking, however, is the marked difference between what became equally classic models; the one, *The Tale of Genji*, a narrative spread over a vast canvas of time and range of human experience, taking its time to probe into the depth of human feelings, and the other, the *Pillow Book*, no story at all but timeless in its momentary reflections on much the same life, restlessly pursuing its insatiable appetite for new aesthetic perceptions. The difference between the two, so apparent in their style of writing, was already intimated in Murasaki's unadmiring comments on Sei Shōnagon as a person:

> Sei Shōnagon has the most extraordinary air of self-satisfaction, yet if we stop to examine these Chinese writings of hers that she so presumptuously scatters all over the place, we find that they are full of imperfections. Someone who makes such an effort to be different from others is bound to fall in people's esteem, and I can only think that her future will be a hard one. She is a gifted woman, to be sure, yet if one gives free reign to one's emotions, even in the most inappropriate circumstances; if one has to sample each interesting thing that comes along, people are bound to regard one as frivolous. And how can things turn out well for such a woman?[5]

Readers of the *Pillow Book* will see enough therein of Sei Shōnagon's cockiness and her supreme confidence in her own judgments, often unallayed by compassionate sentiments, to recognize much of what Murasaki reports of her. What may be less evident is the acute irony involved in Murasaki's own boldness in passing judgment on Shōnagon—on the latter's own home ground no less—in chiding her for her incompetence in "Chinese writings," given that Sei's own family, the Kiyowaras, had long been recognized as hereditary custodians and supreme authorities in all matters Chinese.

Against Murasaki's contrarian judgment, it will seem even more ironic and unexpected that the *Pillow Book* itself should belie the fate predicted for its author by Murasaki when she says: "Things could not turn out well for such a woman." Instead, things turned out extremely well for the *Pillow Book*, and that it could survive circumstances initially quite adverse to its perpetuation tells us something of its intrinsic strengths. As a collection of random notes that did not conform to any established category of literature, the inherent appeal of its contents enabled it eventually to become a model for the informal writings known in Japan as *zuihitsu*. *The Pillow Book* appeared long before printing became available, and thus it would not have survived had it not exerted enough appeal for many individuals to have found it worth the effort to copy out by hand.

What made it worth that effort—and still makes it attractive to us as readers? The *Pillow Book* lacks many of the recognized features of the traditional classic, especially unity of time and place, plot, and sustained narrative. Yet this is, at the same time, what renders it both traditional and classic: the strong sense of place, of local color, of particularity and endless variety, to which Shōnagon responds with her own acute sensibility. It may irritate and even offend so deep a sensitivity as Murasaki's, but it is precisely the insistent self-revelation of Shōnagon herself that is endlessly attractive and impressive. Considering the formidable handicaps and disabilities that she and Murasaki both suffered in the male-dominated class system of Heian Japan, in her own way, simply by asserting herself, Shōnagon triumphed over them.

As Murasaki testifies, Shōnagon "gave free rein" to her own feelings and held nothing back, unconstrained by the polite conventions of her time or even by her conscious inhibitions. Sometimes this may seem a kind of hypocrisy on her part, as when she catches herself giving vent to feelings in conflict with the social and cultural norms of her day, which she is at one and the same time conscious of yet not bound by in her writings. This should not be taken to mean that Sei Shōnagon is engaged in social protest—that she is an early but premature advocate of women's liberation from an oppressive social system. Shōnagon is engaged in self-liberation, not social or class protest, and this is probably why she has not been claimed as a feminist by later scholars of women's resistance to the political and social discrimination so pervasive in their society.

Ivan Morris has explained Shōnagon's situation and cultural environment as one dominated by good taste, and one can understand her success as taking advantage of the predominant aesthetic culture to break through her social limitations. He writes:

> Not only did the rule of taste extend to every sphere of life and apply to the smallest details, but (with the single exception of good birth) it took primacy over all else. Artistic sensitivity was

more highly valued than ethical goodness. Despite the influence of Buddhism, Heian society was on the whole governed by style rather than by any moral principles, and good looks tended to take the place of virtue. The word "yoki" referred primarily to birth, but it also applied to one's beauty or aesthetic sensibility; the one implication that it lacked was one of ethical rectitude. For all their talk about "heart" and "feeling," this stress on the cult of the beautiful, to the virtual exclusion of any concern for charity, sometimes lends a rather chilling impression to the people of Genji's world.[6]

Here the world that Morris writes about is no less Shōnagon's than Murasaki's, but we also know that what Murasaki saw of Shōnagon left a "chilling impression" on her. Murasaki's own depth of feeling led her to perceive a certain sharpness in her opposite number. Thus despite the accuracy of what Morris says about their shared world and about Heian society in general, it may not be quite the whole truth of the matter when we see how these two react so differently to it.

Part of what needs to be considered here is the role of religion, particularly Buddhism. Morris says, this time about Shōnagon herself:

Contemporary literature suggests that for many Heian aristocrats religion had become mere mummery. The temples had become crowded with visitors, but the motives that brought them there often had little connection with the Buddhist faith. This is a subject that lends itself to satire, and . . . no one has treated it more pungently than Sei Shōnagon, whose mordant wit was, as far as we can judge, uninhibited by any religious feelings.[7]

Morris goes on to quote a memorable passage from the *Pillow Book* in which Shōnagon says: "A preacher ought to be good looking. For if we are properly to understand the most worthy sentiments of his sermon, we must keep our eyes fixed on him while he speaks; by looking away we may forget to listen. Accordingly an ugly preacher may well be a source of sin."[8]

The thing to note here is Shōnagon's frankness in admitting the actual conflict that she experiences at that moment. Her observation is psychological and confessional; she does not express any real doubt about the "worthy sentiments" she is sure the preacher has to offer but only how she may be distracted from them. It may be true, as Morris says, that Shōnagon's "wit is . . . uninhibited by any deep religious feelings," but the apparent conflict is actually obviated by the religion itself.

To understand this, we have to go back to the sources of Heian religiosity itself, and for this a well-known quotation from Kūkai (774–835) may serve our purpose. Kūkai was the leading exponent of Esoteric Buddhism in the form of the True Words (Shingon) Sect, which probably gave Heian culture its most distinctive cast as well as its inherent ambiguity. "Esoteric" signifies that it was a mystery religion, and "True Words" means that despite its inherent mystery—that it is not definable in words—words of a kind still can convey some suggestive meaning. Words may be problematic, but they still can perform some kind of magical communication.

Here the teachings of Mahāyāna Buddhism through its doctrine of expedient or convenient means (*hōben*) convert its sense of compassion into some tangible form. Thus, it could adapt itself to the traditional tastes of the Japanese. As Kūkai says:

> The law [*dharma*] has no speech, but without speech it cannot be expressed. Eternal truth [*tathatā*] transcends color, but only by means of color can it be understood. Mistakes will be made in the effort to point at the truth, for there is no clearly defined method of teaching, but even when art does not excite admiration by its unusual quality, it is a treasure which protects the country and benefits the people.
>
> In truth, the Esoteric doctrines are so profound as to defy their enunciation in writing. With the help of painting, however, their obscurities can be understood. The various attitudes and mudras of the holy images all have their source in Buddha's love, and one may attain Buddhahood at sight of them. Thus the secrets of the sutras and commentaries can be depicted in art, and the essential truth of the Esoteric teaching are all set forth therein. Neither teachers nor students can dispense with it. Art is what reveals to us the state of perfection.[9]

By Sei Shōnagon's time, Heian society was deeply involved with Esoteric Buddhism, and many of her contemporaries, accepting that Beauty is Truth, could understand how she could easily be distracted by appearances while still trying to understand what the preacher was saying. Ideally, the two should go together, but often they did not. In that situation, it would not be quite true that Shōnagon was, as Morris put it, "uninhibited by any religious feelings." She is uninhibited in expressing herself but still conflicted by the essential ambiguity of her situation, even understood in Buddhist terms, as a problematical subordination of morality to art.

What remains true in Morris's characterization of the Heian view is that "not only did the rule of taste extend to every detail of life and apply to the smallest of details, but it took primacy over all else. Artistic sensitivity was more highly prized than ethical goodness." This might also apply to Shōnagon, but it does not mean that she was unreligious, and on the contrary there are many incidents related in the *Pillow Book* that suggest otherwise.

In the incidents to be cited here, it is essential to recognize how religious ritual, whether performed at temples, shrines, or in palaces, had an aesthetic importance inseparable from its other professed functions. A common early word for governance was *matsurigoto*, the literal meaning of which was "attending to sacred rituals," which is indicative of the ceremonial conduct of government and its exercise through customary religious forms more than through open political debate. Such governance might then be noted for its lack of emphasis on what is public in the sense of stated policy or standards of public morality. In modern times, we might take this as a lack of transparency in government, which would be true of the Heian insofar as most political maneuvering was conducted in private, behind closed doors. But in a culture that responded to elegance and beauty above all, the latter, not political debate, would be the most evident, transparent, and prestigious—"public"—values.

The first illustration that I shall give of this is Shōnagon's attendance at a ritual performed at the Kamo Shrine, which combined strong natural and local features (river and mountains) with its functions as tutelary to the imperial dynasty. Shōnagon recalls her attendance at the special festival held there for the Sacred Dance of the Return.

I remember one such evening. As the smoke rose in slender wisps from the bonfires in the garden, I listened to the clear, delicate, charmingly tremulous sound of the flute that accompanied the sacred dances. The singing also moved me greatly. Delighted by the scene, I hardly noticed that the air was piercingly cold, that my robes of beaten silk were icy, and that the hand in which I held my fan was almost frozen.   (147)

It is clear that Shōnagon was caught up in a kind of transcendent experience that so lifted her out of her bodily self and senses that she was transported to a higher spiritual plane. One could regard this simply as "aesthetic," but its association with shrine rituals and the cult of the imperial house, which claimed divine origins and sanctions, suggests that some religious and political connotations are also implicit and fused in the experience.

A similar fusion of aesthetic and religious elements is found in Shōnagon's frequent mention of her experience of visits to Shinto shrines and Buddhist temples and of her attendance at palace rituals. Addicted as she was to such regular and repeated observances, she was on the lookout for impromptu happenings that could give fresh significance and charm to what otherwise tended to become familiar and dull routine. One such experience is reported on a visit to a famous pilgrimage site, Hase Temple, east of the old capital at Nara. She knows the rituals well, but she also appreciates it when something unexpected happens:

Once I went on a pilgrimage to Hase Temple. While our rooms were being prepared, our carriage was pulled up to the foot of the long steps that lead up to the temple. Young priests, wearing only their sashes and under-robes, and with those things called high clogs on their feet, were hurrying up and down the steps without the slightest precaution, reciting verses from the Sacred Storehouse or such scraps from the sutras as come into their heads. It was very appropriate to the place and I found it charming.   (126)

What was "very appropriate to the place," that is, what fitted with her own sense of place at the temple, was also reminiscent of similar experiences at the Imperial Palace. She continues:

Presently a priest told us that our rooms were ready and asked us to go to them directly; he brought us some overshoes and helped us out of our carriage. Among the pilgrims who had already arrived I saw some who were wearing clothes inside out, while others were dressed in formal style with trains on their skirts and Chinese jackets. The sight of so many people shuffling along the corridors in lacquered leather shoes and short clogs was delightful and reminded me of the Palace.   (126–127)

As Shōnagon continues her account of the temple visit, her sense of the sublime is often tinged with irony (which I would not call "satire" or "ridicule," as Morris does, since it was not actually at the expense of the religious): "On the way to our rooms we had to pass in front of rows of strangers. I found this very unpleasant; but, when I reached the chapel and got a view past the dog-barrier and right up to the sanctuary, I was overcome with awe and wondered how I could have stayed away for so many months. My old feelings were aroused and they overwhelmed all else" (127).

What Shōnagon saw looking up the stairway to the icon at the top was an image of the temple's main object of worship (*honzon*), more precisely the Bodhisattva Kannon, commonly known as the "Goddess of Mercy." As the most popular object of devotional worship and pilgrimage in Japan (not to say East Asia), she attracted innumerable devotees of all classes and kinds, which explains why Shōnagon found herself, the paragon of elite taste, in the presence of crowds she would consider uncouth, unrefined, and unpleasant. Still, if her sense of propriety and good taste dominated the social situation, it did not have the last word, as her "old feelings" toward the compassionate Bodhisattva "overwhelmed" all else.

The account of her temple visit further testifies to her genuine religiosity, again, alongside other observations prompted by her keen sense of taste and proper form:

Now the bell rang for the recitation of the sutras. It was very comforting to think that it rang for me. In the cell next to ours a solitary gentleman was prostrating himself in prayer. At first I thought that he might be doing it because he knew we were listening; but soon I realized that he was absorbed in his devotions, which he continued hour after hour. I was greatly moved. When he rested from his prayers, he started reading the sutras in a loud, fervent voice. I was wishing that he would read still more loudly so that I might hear every word; but instead he stopped and blew his nose—not in a noisy, unpleasant way but gently and discreetly. I wondered what he would be praying for so fervently and hoped that his wish might be granted.

Sometimes the booming of the temple bell became louder and louder until I was overcome with curiosity about who had asked for the readings. Then someone would mention the name of a great family, adding, "It is a service of instruction and guidance for Her Ladyship's safe delivery." An anxious period indeed, I thought, and would begin praying for the lady's well-being.

(128)

In these cases, it is not a matter of Shōnagon's being completely absorbed in her own religious feelings. She shares them with others, as she joins herself to the compassion of Kannon.

The service continued all night, and it was so noisy that I could not get to sleep. After the matins I finally dozed off, only to be woken by a reading of the *sutra* consecrated to the temple Buddha. The priests were reciting loudly and raucously, without making any effort to sound solemn. From their tone I gathered that they were traveling monks and, as I listened to their voices, which had awakened me so abruptly, I found myself being strangely moved.

(129)

These examples should suffice to show that Shōnagon was not simply a snob or a cool-headed, cold-hearted critic offering her snap judgments of others but was instead a highly cultivated woman deeply sensitive to others' feelings. What is most remarkable about her, and what renders the *Pillow Book* such a classic treasure, is the keenness of her observation and ability to capture the given moment in very precise words. Her manner of speaking is quite different from Murasaki's, but she has her own gift for making the moment memorable. As Murasaki redeemed her own sufferings by making them live forever in the *Genji*, Shōnagon had the same aspiration in the *Pillow Book*. She recalls a moment at court:

> After accompanying the Emperor, Korechika returned to his previous place on the veranda beside the cherry blossoms. The Empress pushed aside her curtain of state and came forward as far as the threshold. We were overwhelmed by the whole delightful scene. It was then that Korechika slowly intoned the words of the old poem,
>
> The days and the months flow by,
> But Mount Mimoro lasts forever.
>
> Deeply impressed, I wished that all this might indeed continue for a thousand years.   (16)

Her wish has been fulfilled with the survival of the *Pillow Book* as a classic for well over a thousand years. For all this, however, modern scholarship has not always appreciated Murasaki's and Sei Shōnagon's exceptional contributions to Japan's cultural sensibilities. In at least one recent and prominent case, these authors go unmentioned because the current trend found them irrelevant to the demand for social literature as gender protest. In a project sponsored by the Tōhō Gakkai of Japan (a highly reputable academic organization promoting East Asian studies) for "Women in Japanese Buddhism," focusing on the ancient and medieval periods, there is no mention at all of these two remarkable women who spoke for Japanese sensibilities beyond all gender limitations.[10] We may be confident, however, that this momentary neglect or oversight will fade before the *Genji* and *Pillow Book* ever do.

Part 2

LIBERAL LEARNING
IN CONFUCIANISM

8

Human Renewal and the
Repossession of the Way

Neo-Confucianism in general, and the Learning of the Way (*daoxue*) in particular, had their inception in the great reform movements of the Northern Song period (960–1127). Politically, these reached a high point in the determined efforts of Wang An-shi (1021–1086) to effectuate his New Laws (*xinfa*), which can be read also as new formulas, methods, systems, or policies. Here, however, the key word is "new," for it stands in seeming contrast to tradition as expressed in the dominant restorationist ideal of the time, that is, to the idea that the institutions of the ancient Zhou dynasty should be revived and put into practice in eleventh-century Song China. Actually, what this signifies is that tradition and innovation went hand in hand rather than going in opposite directions. When Wang An-shi invoked the Confucian classics, especially the *Rites* or *Institutes of Zhou* (*Zhou guan*), as sanction for his radical reforms, it was because tradition in this form afforded him a high ground from which to attack existing institutions, not because his new institutions would bear any close resemblance to their presumed models in the *Institutes of Zhou*.

Confirmation of this innovative use of tradition is further found in the need Wang felt to write a new commentary on the *Zhou guan*, with the revealing title *New Interpretation of the Institutes of Zhou* (*Zhouguan xinyi*). This reinterpretation of the classics employed a new criticism, by which neoclassicism was made to serve the purposes of reform. Thus "restoration of the ancient order" (*fugu*) ushered in a new day, and the "Way of the Sage-Kings" of the past was to prove in practice to be a new Way.

Though berated for his authoritarian ways and dogmatic manner in the pursuit of his goals, Wang was not alone among the great scholars of his day in believing that one could find in the ancient order the basis for a new one. Speaking in terms reminiscent of Lyndon Johnson's "Great Society," the philosopher Cheng Yi asserted no less insistently than Wang the need for a "great reform" to bring about a "Great Order" or "Great Benefit" in those times.[1] Politically at odds with Wang, he was equally dogmatic in claiming the authority of the classics for his own ideas. And this was possible for both Wang and Cheng because they shared a view of the Way as not fixed in the past but as vital and adaptable to new human situations.

One branch of Confucian scholarship in the Song that encouraged this thought was the study of the *Classic of Changes* (*Yijing*), the Great Appendix to which gave prominence to a conception of the Way as vital, creative, and life renewing (*shengsheng*). To Cheng Yi, the early proponent of the Learning of the Way (*daoxue*), this conception contrasted with the negative Buddhist view of change as impermanence and its view of the Way as deliverance from the cycle of life and death. Instead, the Confucian metaphysics of the *Changes* offered a positive view of the Way as readily accessible to human understanding and adaptable to ordinary human needs. Rediscovery and renewal then became significant values presupposed in Cheng Yi's neoclassicism. Truth was directly available in the classics and immediately applicable to the renewing of human life. As Cheng Yi quite consciously put it, the Way of the Great Learning called for the "renewing of the people" (*xinmin*), which he substituted for "loving the people" (*qin min*) in the earlier version.[2] Zhu Xi, in his own commentary on the *Great Learning* (*daxue*), greatly stressed the idea of self-renewal as the basis for a larger human renewal. In turn, the dynamism of the early Neo-Confucian movement in the Yuan and Ming periods drew heavily on this promise, for it was on Zhu Xi's new articulation of the moral nature of man and individual perfectibility that this hope of social renewal rested.[3]

One cannot take this emphasis on renewal or innovation as necessarily expressing a "progressive" view of history, if by that one would imply a linear development toward some higher stage. Its "newness" is like the regeneration of the New Year, or of spring, which may allow for an evolutionary process but is not predicated upon it. Nor can one understand "vitality" or "creativity" here as setting a high value on individual "originality," with a Western connotation of utter uniqueness. There remains a strong sense of the underlying human continuum, and Cheng Yi's "renewing of the people" implies a humanity deeply shared in common.

Nevertheless, when Cheng spoke of the advancement of the Way among men, he was quite prepared to credit certain personages with extraordinary individual contributions. Indeed, if it had not been for the insight and independent effort of a few such individuals, the Way of the Sages would have been totally lost. Among these few, of course, were Confucius and Mencius, but after the death of the latter there was a long lapse in the handing on of the Way until, according to Cheng Yi, his own elder brother Cheng Hao, "born 1,400 years after Mencius, resolved to enlighten the people with this Way. . . . He said that, after Mencius, the Learning of the Sage was no longer transmitted, and he took it as his own responsibility to restore the cultural tradition."[4]

Later in Zhu Xi's preface to the Mean (*Zhongyong*), when he was explaining the nature of the repossession or reconstitution of the Way (*daotong*), Zhu took up the same theme. After recounting how the Way had been passed down from the sage kings, he said:

> As for our master Confucius, though he did not attain a position of authority, nevertheless his resuming the tradition of the past sages and imparting it to later scholars was a contribution even more worthy than that of Yao and Shun. Still, in his own time those who recognized him were only [his disciples] Yan Hui and Zeng Can, who grasped and passed on his essential meaning. Then in the next generation after Zeng, with Confucius' grandson Zi Si [reputed author of the *Mean*], it was far removed in time from the sages and heterodoxies had already arisen. . . .

Thereafter the transmission was resumed by Mencius, who was able to interpret and clarify the meaning of this text [the *Mean*] and succeed to the tradition of the early sages; but upon his demise the transmission was finally lost.... Fortunately, however, this text was not lost, and when the Masters Cheng, two brothers, appeared [in the Song] they had something to study in order to pick up the threads of what had not been transmitted for a thousand years.[5]

In these passages, what is emphasized is not the effective imparting of the Way through some unbroken apostolic or patriarchal succession but, first, its being cut off for so long; second, its rediscovery by an inspired individual; and third, the heroic dedication required to defend it in a decadent age. Inner inspiration and personal dedication are the marks of the heroic individuals who manage to rescue the Way from oblivion.[6]

Zhen Dexiu (1178–1235), a leader of the School of the Way just after Zhu Xi's time, emphasizes the same qualities in the Song masters who had led in the resurgence of the Learning of the Way, but he underscores the extraordinary—almost supernatural—nature of their inspiration. "Man could not have achieved this without the aid of Heaven," he says. And speaking of the insights of Zhou Dunyi, the Cheng brothers, and Zhu Xi, he says: "How could they have offered such novel views and put forward new interpretations, such as their predecessors had not been able to arrive at, were it not simply due to Heaven?"[7]

Zhen uses similar language in a memoir on Cheng Hao, crediting him with the discovery of the truth concerning Heaven's principle (*tianli*). Darkness, he says, had enshrouded the Way for more than a thousand years after Mencius, when "Zhou Dunyi appeared and was able to grasp the long-lost secret. Master Cheng Mingdao [Cheng Hao], when he came upon this, recognized it immediately, penetrating the surrounding darkness and shedding further light." Further on in the same memoir, he says, "therefore Master Cheng once said to his students, 'although there are things I have learned from others, as regards Heaven's principle, what I have set forth is based on my own experience.'"[8] And in still another memoir, he expresses in vivid terms the wondrous creativity of Heaven: "Do we not have here the full revelation of the sagely learning, the dispelling of the blindnesses of this generation of men, and the correct succession to the orthodox teaching handed down from a thousand ages past? Indeed, has not Heaven shown the most extraordinary favor to this Way?"[9]

In *Neo-Confucian Orthodoxy and the Learning of the Mind-and-Heart*, I have characterized the above view as a "prophetic" element in the Learning of the Way. By this I mean to indicate an extraordinary access to truth not vouchsafed to everyone, which by some process of inner inspiration or solitary perception affords an insight beyond what is received in scripture and by appeal to some higher order of truth gives new meaning, significance, and urgency to certain cultural values or scriptural texts. Confucian tradition does not customarily speak of such a revelation as "supernatural," but it has an unpredictable, wondrous quality manifesting the divine creativity of Heaven. By contrast, I use "scholastic" to represent an appeal to received authority by continuous transmission, with stress on external or public acceptance of it as the basis of its validity.[10]

There is, of course, an obvious difference in context between this and the more theistic traditions of the Semitic world, where the prophet speaks for a God whose "ways are not man's ways" yet whose demands on man's obedience and judgments on his actions are pronounced with awful finality. Still, this difference need not keep us from recognizing the inner-directedness of the Neo-Confucian moral vision or the extent to which Heaven acts on the human conscience to maintain a dynamic tension between the ideal order and man's actual condition—that is, how it provided a leverage on the human situation that the Weberian analysis of Confucianism failed to take into account.

These contrasting attitudes, prophetic and scholastic, might also be said to differentiate liberal and conservative tendencies in Neo-Confucianism. Some caution is called for, however, lest too facile a contrast be drawn between the two. The prophetic voice, both in East and West, has often lent itself to a radical critique of existing institutions or alternatively to a fundamentalist reaction against permissive societies. In such cases, Confucian liberalism, seeking the Mean (which could correspond to Charles Frankel's description of "the liberal temperament or style as characterized by moderation, restraint, and compromise") would turn to the seasoned wisdom of the scholastic tradition and weigh the strident demands of conscience against the collective experience embodied in written texts or formal institutions.[11]

Even allowing for such countervailing tendencies, I would nevertheless point to the seminal role played in the minds of creative thinkers by this conception of the "repossession of the Way" (*daotong*) so central to the orthodox tradition of Neo-Confucianism. Again and again, recourse is had by reformers and nonconformists to the ideal of the heroic individual rediscovering and revivifying the Way. Prominent examples are found in almost every age—Zhen Dexiu in the Late Song; Xu Heng, Liu Yin, and Wu Cheng in the Yuan; Wu Yubi, Chen Xianzhang, He Xinyin, and Lin Zhaoen in the Ming. Here we shall let the better-known example of Wang Yangming suffice for purposes of illustration, as it is described by one of his followers, Wang Dong (1503–1581), in Huang's *Case Studies of Ming Confucians*:

> In the Qin period the true-learning was destroyed and when the Han arose scholars of the classics appeared who would only memorize and recite texts handed down from the ancients. From one to another they passed on a learning which became the exclusive property of classicists and literati. Lost and untransmitted was the learning which the ancient sages had intended to be understood and shared in by all men. Then Heaven gave birth to our teacher [Wang Yangming] who sprang from the eastern shore [i.e., Eastern Zhejiang]. Large-spirited and uniquely enlightened, he directly succeeded to the legacy of Confucius and Mencius which went straight to the mind-and-heart of man. Then untutored common folk and unlettered persons all could know that their own nature and spiritual intelligence sufficed for their self-fulfillment and self-sufficiency, and that it did not depend on externals, whether by oral, aural or visual instruction. With that the message untransmitted for two thousand years was restored to man's comprehension again as if in a single morning.[12]

Tinged though it is with a certain social and philosophical coloration of the Wang Yangming school, what we have here again is the mythic role of the singularly endowed individual rediscovering the Way and renewing mankind, in which Wang is now cast. Some critics would question his orthodoxy, and others would insist against him on the continuing importance of scholarship, but the claim that Wang spoke for the Way was still put in the familiar terms of the orthodox tradition as a "repossessing of the Way" (*daotong*) and a reawakening of men. The name of almost any leading Neo-Confucian could be substituted in the same formula. In the Yuan and Ming, the frequency with which this inspirational model was cited by writers of all Neo-Confucian persuasions makes clear that it served as a powerful symbol for the renewal of the tradition, which in turn kept pressing ever outward on the limits of orthodoxy.

One element that lent both color and plausibility to this claim on behalf of Wang Yangming was the key agency of the mind in the orthodox version of the transmission of the Way. By this I mean the crucial role of the mind as self-critical and self-renewing not only in the later teachings of Wang Yangming but even in the original doctrine of Zhu Xi himself. In the passage from Zhu's preface to the *Mean*, cited earlier as the scriptural source for the concept of "repossessing the Way" (*daotong*), the idea is introduced by allusions in the *Classic of Documents* to the sage-king's doctrine concerning the mind of man and the mind of the Way, which call for man to achieve utmost discrimination and oneness of mind in order to keep himself morally and spiritually attuned to the Way. In Zhu's preface, it is this state of mind that is prerequisite to perceiving the truths in the Confucian classics. Without it, the current texts are mere vehicles of classical pedantry; with it, one may perceive the special importance of such texts as the *Great Learning* and the *Mean*, which had been previously overshadowed and not fully appreciated among the extensive array of documents on ritual in the *Record of Rites* (*Li ji*).

So central was this doctrine of the mind to Zhu's thinking that it found expression in memorials to the throne as well as in classical exegesis. Thus in a memorial to the throne of 1162 he says: "Everything depends on what the ruler studies, and correctness or incorrectness here depends on his square inch [of mind-and-heart]."[13] Alluding to the steps of self-cultivation in the *Great Learning*, Zhu goes on to say: "Thus the extension of knowledge and investigation of things is like Yao and Shun's 'discrimination' and 'oneness'; to rectify the mind and make the will sincere is like Yao and Shun's 'holding fast the Mean.'

What the ancient sages passed on by word of mouth and transmitted from mind to mind was just this and nothing more."[14]

Zhu reiterated this view in a sealed memorial of 1188, presenting six matters requiring the emperor's urgent attention.

> None of these six points can be neglected, but they all have their root in Your Majesty's mind-and-heart. If the mind-and-heart is correct, then these six things cannot go wrong. But if even one iota of selfish-mindedness or selfish desire is allowed to intervene, then no matter how much mental effort or physical exertion go into the rectifying of these matters . . . the empire still cannot be well managed. Therefore this root of empire is also the most urgent of all urgent needs and cannot be put off even for a little while.[15]

Contributing to this view at the time was the rising importance of the *Great Learning* in a genre of imperial instruction, the "Learning of the Emperors" (*Dixue*), promoted in the days of the Cheng brothers and Zhu Xi by scholars such as Fan Zuyu (1041–1098) and Zhen Zhangfang (1108–1148).[16] In the latter's "Essay on the Learning of the Emperors," he again quotes the *Great Learning*: "What is called 'cultivation of the person' lies in 'rectifying one's mind.' If the person is moved by passion, he will not achieve correctness; if he is moved by fear, he will not achieve correctness; if he is moved by fondness for something, he will not achieve correctness; if he is moved by sorrow and distress, he will not achieve correctness."[17]

It is in this essay of Zhen Zhangfang that we also find one of the earliest references to the so-called method or formula of the mind-and-heart (*xinfa*), a term applied to the Neo-Confucian method of mind-rectification developed at this time. I have discussed elsewhere how this term came into use among Neo-Confucians of the eleventh and twelfth centuries.[18] Here, the point to be observed is that Zhen describes it as a method deriving from the sage-kings, Confucius and Mencius, in much the same way as Zhu Xi's *daotong*. Thus he makes an explicit correlation between the Learning of the Emperors and Kings (*diwang zhi xuewen*), the "ruler's method of the mind-and-heart" (*renzhu xinfa*), and the *Great Learning*'s method of self-cultivation through rectifying of the mind, as well as an implicit correlation with what Zhu Xi would later describe as the "repossession of the Way." In fact, in the opening lines of his commentary on the *Mean*, Zhu Xi himself made the correlation explicit when, after identifying the *Mean* as a vessel of the orthodox tradition, he quoted Master Cheng to the effect that "this work represents the method of the mind-and-heart as transmitted in the Confucian school."[19]

Simply put, these ways of learning all focused on the moral mind, but given the specifically political context in which the matter is discussed, the social conscience of the ruler is especially emphasized. Given further the heavy responsibility that attaches to the exercise of power, especially imperial power, and the consequences in human suffering attendant upon its abuse, the Neo-Confucians magnify the potentialities for good and ill in this mind, which is of course the human mind writ large in the person of the ruler. Such being the essence of the Neo-Confucian Way as it appears in these several formulations, one can recognize in it Tang Junyi's characterization of Neo-Confucianism as a "revival of the Confucian faith in man" and as an "acceptance of the need to face all the negative factors [in man's nature] and to find a way of realizing the positive ideal."[20]

There is further significance in the appearance together of the Learning of the Way (*daoxue*) and Learning of the Mind-and-Heart (*xinxue*) at this critical juncture in the development of Song thought. Not only does it suggest a correlation between the newly asserted autonomy of the mind and the claim of direct access by the individual to the Way, with the authority to speak for it implicit in the term *daoxue*, but also it implies a different relation on the part of the individual scholar to the classics. While the authority of the *Institutes of Zhou* may be invoked by Wang Anshi, or of the *Great Learning* by Cheng Yi, the individual's reinterpretation of it takes precedence over the tradition of commentary attached to the classic. Thus, though the text is still important, the individual's understanding of its significance becomes far more so. If the *Great Learning* could have lain fallow for two thousand years while classical exegetes failed to discern its true significance, as Cheng Yi and Zhu Xi said, the mere physical transmission of texts becomes far less vital than the discernment of the individual mind into its real meaning. Hence in the "repossessing of the Way," the orthodox tradition too is seen to depend less on the "handing on" of the classics and more on individual perceptivity.

During the reign of Shenzong (r. 1068–1085), the emperor was told that the Confucian Way had been taught by Hu Yuan under the aspects of substance, function, and literary expression (*wen*), with the latter providing the means for communicating and disseminating the Way.[21] Cheng Yi and Zhu Xi, for their part, emphasize substance and function but rarely mention "literature" or "texts" (*wen*) in this same connection, though texts and scholarship were hardly unimportant to Zhu Xi. And Zhen Dexiu, a prime proponent of the Cheng-Zhu Learning of the Mind-and-Heart in the early thirteenth century, substitutes "transmission" for "literary expression" or "text" in the threefold formulation of substance, function, and transmission (*chuan*),[22] as if again to allow for the crucial agency of the mind-and-heart in this process, with its own direct access to the Way (*dao*). To the extent that subjectivity was thereby granted a larger role and the objective record or formal canon was assigned a diminished one, the ground had been prepared for the individual to exercise greater autonomy in relation to received text and classical tradition. The freedom with which Cheng Yi and Zhu Xi rearranged the *Great Learning* to suit their own ideas, and the ease with which their followers accepted the change, is a good illustration of this.

Thus the concept of the orthodox tradition or "repossessing of the Way" expressed a certain ideal of the heroic individual as the reactivator of traditional values and as the agent of social reform and human renewal. Associated with this prophetic role was a view of the mind as morally and socially conscious and with a keen sense of responsibility for the consequences of one's actions and of the need this implies for the sensitization of the individual conscience—a conscience freed of excessive dependence on external authority by the Cheng-Zhu doctrine that inherent in the mind of man were all the "heavenly principles" needed to guide his conduct of life. I believe that each of these values—the importance of the individual, his duty to exercise his own conscience, and his relative autonomy in the creative interpreting of tradition—would be recognized as values in the Western liberal tradition. But before we draw any conclusions from this seeming resemblance, we shall need to explore other aspects of Neo-Confucian individualism in its social context.

9

Zhu Xi and Liberal Education

"LEARNING FOR THE SAKE OF ONE'S SELF"

The thought of Zhu Xi begins and ends with the aim of "learning for the sake of one's self," or, more simply, "learning to be oneself" (*weiji zhi xue*), a phrase that recalls Confucius's dictum in the *Analects* (14:25) that learning should be for the sake of oneself and not for the pleasing of others. This aim, which set a higher value on self-understanding and self-fulfillment than on all else, was put before Zhu early in life by his father. It was what motivated his studies under his teacher Li Tong (1093–1163), what guided him in official life, and what stayed with him to the end of his scholarly career. For many of his later followers, it was what distinguished true Confucian teaching from any other.

Confucianism was a way of learning, and Zhu Xi was a teacher above all else. Indeed, so integral was education to Zhu's philosophy as a whole that it is difficult to discuss one without the other. In this chapter, I shall try to explain Zhu's thought on "learning for the sake of one's self," his views on voluntarism in popular education, and in what sense his social and cultural definition of higher education may be seen as "liberal." In the next chapter, I shall attempt to show how he expressed a distinctive Neo-Confucian personalism in political and cultural life.

In 1148, at the age of eighteen, Zhu passed the civil-service examinations at the capital and won the advanced (*jinshi*) degree. He was already a success by the standards of the age, having achieved the goal coveted by most educated men in Song China but not often attained by them so early in life. Soon thereafter, he received his first appointment to office as a subprefectural registrar in the Tong-an district of Fujian, where his varied duties included responsibility for the local school and presented him with the occasion to address the students there. "Learning should be for the sake of oneself," he said, "but in today's world what fathers encourage in their sons, what older brothers exhort in their younger brothers, what teachers impart to their students, and what students all study for is nothing more than to prepare for the civil-service examinations." Then he urged that they should aspire to emulate the ancients' "learning for the sake of oneself" instead of "studying for the sake of others," meaning that they should aim at understanding and fulfilling their own true selves rather than let their studies be directed toward winning the approval of the official examiners.[1]

Later, in 1175, when he and Lu Zuqian compiled *Reflections on Things at Hand* (*Jinsilu*), in the important section on the "Pursuit of Learning," which sets forth the overall aims of the work, they cited Cheng Yi's amplification of Confucius' remark: " 'In ancient times one studied for the sake of oneself,' that is, Cheng said, to find it in oneself (*zide*); 'nowadays one studies for the sake of others,' that is, in order to gain recognition from others."[2] Here, Cheng Yi's reference to "finding it in oneself" echoes Mencius's doctrine that "the noble man steeps himself in the Way because he wishes to find it in himself. When he finds it in himself, he will be at ease in it; when he is at ease in it, he can draw deeply upon it; when he can draw deeply upon it, he finds its source wherever he turns. That is why the noble man wishes to find the Way in himself."[3] Here, "learning for the sake of one's self" is explained in terms of finding the Way in oneself and deriving deep inner satisfaction from it.

Later, in commenting on the original passage in the *Analects*, Zhu Xi again referred to Cheng Yi's comment that "when the ancients studied

for their own sake, it led in the end to the fulfillment of others; nowadays studying for the sake of others leads in the end to the destruction
of oneself,"⁴ an observation Zhu Xi praises highly for its aptness and
succinctness.⁵ Further, in the *Essential Meaning of the Analects* (*Lunyu
jingyi*), Zhu includes commentaries from other Song masters that
explain the meaning of "for the sake of oneself" (*wei ji*) as "being true
to oneself," "rectifying the mind and making the will sincere," and as
not ending in self-love but taking self-cultivation as the starting point
for reaching out to others.⁶ In these ways, Zhu distinguishes true self-
fulfillment from mere selfish satisfaction, identifying the latter with
self-destruction and the former with the fulfillment of others.

Zhu Xi returns to the same theme in chapter 6 of the *Things at
Hand*, which deals with the "Regulation of the Family." At the very
outset of this discussion of the family, he points to the primacy of moral
relations in learning for the sake of one's self, again quoting Cheng Yi:
"Master Yi-chuan said, 'If young people have energy to spare after the
performance of their moral responsibilities, they may study arts and literature [making reference to *Analects* 1:6]. If they do not perform their
moral duties, and study literature and art first, this is not "Learning for
the sake of one's self" (*weiji zhi xue*)." "⁷ Here, a certain tension is set up
between moral learning and the pursuit of art and literature, at least to
the extent that the latter might lead to neglect of the former.

Toward the end of his fitful and frustrating official career, on the
very eve of his official condemnation for heterodoxy, Zhu visited the
Jade Mountain Academy (Yushan xueyuan). The lecture that he gave
on that occasion later became celebrated as one of the most authoritative statements of his mature position in philosophical and educational
matters. He began it on the same theme with which he had launched his
educational efforts as a fledgling official in Tong'an many years before:

I have heard that "in ancient times one studied for the sake of
oneself; nowadays one studies for the sake of others." Therefore the sages and worthies, in teaching men to pursue learning,
did not have them patch together speeches or compose literary
pieces simply with a view to obtaining civil service degrees and
official emoluments. Only "recognizing things, extending knowledge, making the will sincere, rectifying the mind, and further

extending these to regulating the family, ordering the state and pacifying the world," can be considered correct learning.[8]

In this brief passage, Zhu summed up many of the ideals of his age and of the educational philosophy he had developed over a lifetime: the "correct learning" (*zhengxue*), which had been the dominant ideal of Northern Song reformers; the "learning of the sages and worthies," which in the Cheng Zhu school was to be increasingly encapsulated in the "Great Learning"; and "learning for the sake of oneself," which Zhu saw as both beginning and end of all the rest. Early and late, Zhu had put this moral and spiritual "learning" forward as a genuine alternative to the spurious literary learning for the civil-service examinations and had also, in citing Cheng Yi, espoused it in opposition to any pursuit of art and literature at the expense of moral learning. Later in the Yuan dynasty, when the issue of resuming the examinations arose in the court of Khubilai, those who supported the idea were known as the "literary party," while the followers of Zhu Xi who spoke in opposition to it were said to have advocated "learning for the sake of one's self."[9] It was Zhu Xi schoolmen such as these who first established his works as basic texts in the school curriculum during the Yuan dynasty, again under the banner of "learning for the sake of one's self."[10] Similarly, at the founding of the Yi dynasty in Korea, when the same issue arose with regard to the examination system, advocates of Neo-Confucianism attacked bureaucratic scholarship as "learning for the sake of others," in contrast to Confucius's "learning for the sake of one's self."[11]

"SUBDUING ONESELF AND RETURNING TO DECORUM"

Another view of the self in Neo-Confucianism, and one that at first sight seems radically opposed to the one just presented, is found in Zhu Xi's treatment of the theme "Subdue oneself and return to decorum" (*keji fuli*).

Here, Neo-Confucians understood *ji* in the negative sense of "selfishness" or "self-interest" rather than in the positive sense it has in learning for the "self," while decorum represents the objective norms governing one's relationships to society. As a member of society, the person must subordinate his selfish desires (*siyu*) to the good of the community or public good (*gong*). His true personhood is thus achieved by disciplining his desires so that they serve rather than conflict with the public good. Whether desires are seen as good or bad depends entirely on how they meet this test, just as self-fulfillment depends on how one overcomes this contradiction between the self and others.

Neo-Confucians often invoked the dictum of Confucius in *Analects* 12:1 in response to Yan Yuan's question about perfect virtue or humaneness (*ren*):

> Confucius said, "It is to subdue oneself and return to decorum. If a man can for one day subdue himself and return to decorum, all under Heaven will ascribe perfect virtue to him." Yan Yuan then said, "May I ask what it consists in?" The Master replied, "Look not at what is contrary to decorum, listen not to what is contrary to decorum, speak not what is contrary to decorum, act not contrary to decorum."

This classic definition of the concept of *ren* was given heightened significance by its central role in Neo-Confucianism and especially by the attention Zhu Xi gave to it in a key chapter of *Things at Hand*. This chapter has to do with self-examination and self-correction, the basic moral discipline that Zhu Xi focused on when he featured the *Great Learning* as a main text of instruction. The title of this chapter in *Things at Hand* is variously rendered in different versions, but as translated by Wing-tsit Chan it draws upon the edition of Ye Cai (fl. 1248), an early compiler of commentaries on this important manual of Neo-Confucian teaching. Ye's title and description read:

> On Self-discipline, 41 sections. In this chapter the effort to practice what one has learned is discussed. Having clearly investigated principles and having deeply preserved one's mind and nourished one's nature, one is about to extend one's understanding and cultivation into personal practice. At this point one should devote the utmost effort to self-discipline.[12]

Here, Ye Cai's explanation of the sequence of learning follows along the lines already given in Zhu Xi's discussion of "learning for the sake of one's self"; that is, self-understanding should be linked to one's conduct toward others and does not stop with the self. Professor Chan's translation of *keji* as "self-discipline" is in keeping with the general nature of the contents, with the emphasis in Neo-Confucianism on rational, moral control, and it is also in keeping with the tone of Ye Cai's own description. Indeed, in the text itself *keji* is often equated with *zizhi*, "self-control."

If I translate it, however, as "subduing oneself," there are, I think, good reasons for this. For one thing, "subdue" is closer to the original sense of *ke* as "to conquer or subjugate." For another, while the corollary *fuli* may fairly be rendered in the Neo-Confucian context as "return to decorum or propriety," *li* has strong residual overtones of its original religious significance in ritual sacrifice, as the ritual order by which the members of the clan, community, or state were joined together, each in a manner befitting his own rank and status, in the service of the common cult. We must not dispense too quickly with the religious overtones of this key concept or yield to the modern taste for a moral and rational humanism at the expense of the traditional religious aspect, for the latter is strongly retained in Neo-Confucianism along with the rational and moral. It is in the original connotations of the terms that *keji fuli* preserves the distinct possibility for a deeper awareness of the problem of evil and of the need for a more radical testing of oneself, for a religiosity aspiring to self-transcendence through total self-conquest.

This becomes the more pertinent when one considers the number of later Neo-Confucians for whom this religiosity had a strong appeal, as well as those others for whom it was to become an abomination. Indeed, the essential ambivalence of Neo-Confucian teaching on this score is indicated by the cases of those who exhibited both of these manifestations in one life experience, first embracing the ritual with zealous intensity and then later repudiating it.[13] Negative indications of this also came from protests in popular literature against a harsh ritual discipline prescribed in the name of Zhu Xi, which is far more repressive than simple self-discipline.

That "subduing the self and returning to decorum" could range from an enlightened practice of self-control to a religious experience of self-transcendence may be seen in Zhu's quoting of Cheng Yi in chapter 5 of *Things at Hand*:

> One's first act is to see. If one looks at what is contrary to decorum, then, as the saying goes, whenever he opens his eyes, he makes a mistake. Hearing comes next, then speaking, then action, in proper sequence. If one can "subdue himself," his mind will be broad and his heart generous, and his body will become big and be at ease. Looking up he will have no occasion for shame before Heaven, and below he will have no occasion to blush before men. We can understand how happy he will be. But if he lets up in his subduing of self for even a moment he will starve.[14]

From this it is evident that we are dealing with two selves (*ji*), not just one. There is the original, inner, and true self, and there is the self characterized by selfishness (*jisi*) or dominated by selfish intentions (*siji*). The control of the mind is not undertaken with a view to imposing some external restraint on an inherently evil self but on the contrary to liberate the original goodness of the inner self. Thus it is possible for both Cheng Yi and Zhu Xi to take an optimistic view of the process as leading to a self-enlargement and fulfillment in communion with others, and this has its outward, formal expression in the ritual order.

In the People's Republic, there has been some discussion between Fung Yu-lan and Ren Jiyu as to whether Neo-Confucianism is a religion.[15] Leaving that question aside as a matter of definition, we can say that Neo-Confucianism does speak to dimensions of human experience often seen as "religious," which are not necessarily understood in the West as antithetical to liberal education.[16] In any case, self-discipline has certainly been understood as "liberal" in the classic sense of bringing self-mastery, that is, of liberating one's powers in the very act of developing and directing them.[17]

As noted above, Cheng Yi and Zhu Xi see "subduing the self" through ritual as a process whereby the acceptance of certain limits and transcending them overcomes the distinction between self and others and joins one to a moral and spiritual community. Here, a radical individualism would seem to be ruled out, and what I would call a Confucian personalism takes its place—a concept of the person as most truly itself when most fully in communion with other selves.

SELF AND PERSON IN THE *ELEMENTARY LEARNING*

The implications of this personalism are further developed in Zhu Xi's *Elementary Learning* (*Xiao xue*), a manual of ritual conduct for the young. It is a distinctively Neo-Confucian "classic" that illustrates the concept of self and practice of self-cultivation in orthodox Neo-Confucianism. Compiled in 1187 under the direction of Zhu Xi, it consists of passages drawn from the Confucian classics that Zhu thought should guide the education of the young preparatory to the program of higher learning set forth in the *Great Learning*. Thus the scriptural authority of the classics was invoked on behalf of Zhu Xi's belief in the need for a structured education, an education that was to have a broad base among the young, extending down to the lowest levels of society. As the leading modern authority on this work, Uno Seiichi says, its underlying aim was to achieve "the governance of men through self-discipline" (*xiuji zhiren*). In other words, the ideal government is one that relies not on power but on universal self-discipline, which allows a maximum of local autonomy on the assumption that people will be self-governing. This is, of course, an extension of the central idea of the *Great Learning*, which asserts that peace and order depend on everyone, from the ruler down to the common people, taking self-cultivation (*xiushen*) as the basis of the social order. Zhu Xi develops this into one of the main themes of his own philosophy.[18]

The *Elementary Learning* consists of inner and outer portions, the former asserting basic principles drawn from the Confucian classics and the latter offering examples drawn from later history or literature. The inner portion is further subdivided into sections entitled "Setting up Instruction," "Clarifying Moral Relations," and "Reverencing the Person." Xu Heng (1209–1281), the leading Neo-Confucian teacher of the Yuan period, admired and "believed in this book as if it were divine."[19] In his characteristic fashion, Xu wrote a succinct resume of its contents for the education of laymen, excerpts from which may serve conveniently here to convey the main points:

> "Setting up Instruction" means the Way in which the sage-kings of the Three Dynasties taught men. The innate mind of man is originally without imperfection, but after birth through the interference of the physical endowment, the blinding desire for things and unrestrained selfishness, imperfections arise for the first time. The sages therefore set up instruction to help men nourish the original goodness of their innate minds and eliminate the imperfections which came from selfishness. . . .
>
> What the early kings set up, however, was not simply their own idea. Heaven has its principles and the early kings followed these principles. Heaven has its Way and the early kings carried out this Way. Following the natural course of Heaven's imperative they made it the proper course of human affairs and that was what was called instruction. . . .
>
> What then is this Way? It is the moral relation between parent and child, prince and minister, husband and wife, elder and younger, friend and friend. Therein lies the Heaven-bestowed moral nature and the Way for man. . . .
>
> "Clarifying Moral Relations"—"Clarify" means to make manifest. "Moral relations" means moral principles. In the moral nature endowed in man by Heaven each has his proper norm, as in the intimate love between parent and child, the moral obligation between prince and minister, the sex differentiation between husband and wife, the order of precedence among older and younger, and the relation of trust between friends. These are the natural relations.
>
> In the Three Dynasties when the early kings established schools to teach all-under-Heaven, it was only to clarify and manifest these relations and nothing more. Men who cannot clarify these human relations cannot bring order into distinctions of noble and base, superior and inferior, important and unimportant, substantial and insubstantial, controlled and uncontrolled

... and when it comes to this, disaster and disorder follow upon one another until everything lapses into bestiality. . . .

"Reverencing the Self or Person (*shen*)"—the preface [to this section] cites Confucius' saying [in the *Record of Rites*] "The noble man is ever reverent." To reverence the person is the important thing. The person is the branch [outgrowth] of parental love. How can one not reverence it? Not to reverence the person is to do violence to parental love. To do violence to parental love is to do violence to the trunk [of the tree of life]. Harm the trunk and the branch will die!

The sage uttered this as a warning. He who would be a man cannot for a single day depart from reverence. How much more should one reverence his own person, which is truly the trunk of all things and affairs? Err in this, and all things go awry. How could one then not be reverent?

Reverencing the person consists of four things: directing the mind, proper bearing, clothing, and food and drink. If the direction of the mind within is correct and one's outer bearing is correct, then one has achieved the most substantial part of reverencing the person. Clothing and food are meant for the service of the person. If one does not control them properly and regulate them according to decorum, then what is meant to nourish man will, on the contrary, bring him harm.

We can distinguish among these by saying that the direction of the mind and proper bearing have to do with the cultivation of virtue [the moral nature], while clothing and food and drink have to do with subduing the self. Taking them together we can say that they are all essential to the reverencing of the person. Therefore it will not do if in the conduct of the relations between parent and child, prince and minister, husband and wife, older and younger, friend and friend, there is not this reverencing of the person. That is why the ancients insisted on reverence as the basis for the cultivation of the person.[20]

Recapitulated here are many ideas concerning the self and its cultivation that we encounter in Zhu Xi's own writings and commentaries, but at least two main points stand out more clearly. The first is the interdependent character of human existence, establishing the primary human relations as the context of self-development.

This theme of the interrelatedness of human existence is reiterated in the discussion of the Five Relations of Moral Obligation, in which the self-development of the person is shown to be an outgrowth of his gradual assumption of responsibility for others with whom he has a loving relationship. This is hardly a new idea among Neo-Confucians, who had always spoken of the human mind as socially and morally conscious both in its origin and essence (as opposed to the enlightened mind of the Buddhists, which was supposedly free of personal attachments and human obligations). But Xu, following Zhu Xi, goes on to ground the process of socialization in the fundamental reality of creative love and to center it in the human person as the offspring of an intimate relation as deeply rooted and inviolable as life itself. Despite the defective logic of the opening quotation (which raised doubts in the minds of some commentators as to its authenticity),[21] the passage from the *Record of Rites* about reverencing the person is given special weight by both Zhu Xi and Xu Heng, being the lead-off quotation for Zhu and the only one cited by Xu in his précis, as if to suggest that the very circularity of the argument conveys the sense of life as a sacred continuum of affective relations, from conjugal love to parental concern and filial devotion, all centering on respect for the personhood of the individual.

Thus Zhu and Xu structure the educational process in a concept of human personhood that avoids the polarization of individual versus society. As noted above, a common view of Neo-Confucianism has it relying heavily on conformity to ritual and repression of the individual within a system of hierarchical relations preserving the status quo. Xu, however, actually makes these relations subserve the development of the human personality, while the mind that is to direct this development has acquired its moral sensitivity through the experiencing of loving relations with others, not through subjection to cognitive disciplines and rote learning.

The second point is one easily recognized. The structure of the work, though it builds on the organic sense of life developed in the first two sections, culminates in the "Reverencing of Self." Thus the *Elementary*

Learning is essentially "learning for the sake of one's self." In the word "reverencing," however, lies some significance. Aside from the supreme value it attaches to the development of the naturally good self, this concept is infused with the characteristic Neo-Confucian moral and religious spirit. Zhu Xi stresses it as an attitude of constant attentiveness to the moral and spiritual life of the individual, indispensable to the practice of mind-rectification and to "watchfulness over the solitary self." But it is also a religious attitude of reverence toward all life, one that links the self to others and to the whole life process; it thus recognizes a religious dimension in the moral cultivation of the self, bridging the active and contemplative sides of human life.

In one important respect, however, the *Elementary Learning* served poorly to represent Zhu Xi's view of the natural reciprocity in personal relations. Being addressed to the young as a primer preparatory to their taking up the higher learning, i.e., the Great Learning, it presented the parent-child relationship largely in terms of exemplary conduct on the part of the child.[22] Subsequently, this text had an inordinate influence owing to the worshipful respect in which it was held by the early Neo-Confucians in the Yuan, especially Xu Heng. Thus a more one-sided emphasis came to be put on filiality in the child than Zhu had probably intended, and certainly more than can be found in the Four Books, to which he had given his primary attention and clearest sanction. Indeed, his more typical attitude was already expressed in his *Responses of Yanping* (*Yanping dawen*), wherein Zhu conveyed his teacher's view that filiality, as explained by Confucius in the *Analects* (2:6), placed primary stress on parental love and concern as the basis for filiality, not on the obedience of the child.[23]

POPULAR EDUCATION

Before we proceed from the *Elementary Learning* to the higher education dealt with in Zhu Xi's exposition of the *Great Learning*, there is another side of primary education that deserves attention. Zhu's experience of civil administration was mainly at the local level, and he saw education as properly woven into the fabric of institutional life at that level—not only in local schools, to which he gave great personal attention,[24] but also in the organization and conduct of community affairs. He built libraries and had shrines erected to honor distinguished men of the locality who had exemplified qualities worthy of general emulation; for his students and subordinates, he provided guidance in the performance of rituals long since neglected in popular practice; he prepared proclamations for the moral edification of common people who might receive no other education. A representative example of the latter is the ten-point proclamation he issued in Zhangzhou (1190–1191). Without going into details here, the most notable general feature of the proclamation is its emphasis on mutuality and reciprocity, instead of the imposition of superior authority or law, as the basis for the proper conduct of public affairs. The appeal here is to a combination of self-respect and mutual regard among persons as the natural means of upholding a voluntaristic social order, which is seen as preferable to the enforcement of a system of state control.[25]

This same approach is built into the community compact (*xiangyue*) that Zhu Xi adapted from one of the followers of Cheng Yi, Lu Dajun, as the basic "constitution" of a self-governing community. The ideal of voluntary cooperation that inspired this system is expressed in the term *yue*, a compact or contract entered into by members of a community for their mutual benefit. Most notable is the personalistic character of the contract, which places a stronger emphasis on mutual respect for the needs and aspirations of persons than on respect for property rights or an exact quid pro quo in the exchange of goods.

The main provisions of this compact called for mutual encouragement in the performance of worthy deeds, mutual admonition in the correction of errors and failings, reciprocal engagement in rites and customs, and mutual aid in times of distress and misfortune. Under each of these headings there were detailed specifications of the kinds of actions for which members of the compact took personal responsibility. There was also provision for the rotation of leadership within the group for carrying out the terms of the compact.[26]

Here was a model for popular education in direct relation to the daily life of the community, a practical way of implementing basic Neo-Confucian principles in a context wider than kinship or personal relations. At a time that witnessed the steady extension and aggrandizement of state power, Zhu was not content simply to let public morality depend on the discipline of family life alone, or even on the five-family units of local organization (*wubao*); he sought to incorporate the principle of voluntarism into community structures that might mediate between state power and family interests.[27] Thus he recommended a social program on the basis of which one might limit the intervention of the state in local affairs and share authority among more autonomous local units, relying on popular education and ritual observance as an alternative to punitive law. Underlying this program was the idea of personal self-transformation and communal cooperation as the basis of the polity, i.e., the fusion of public and private interests (*gongsi yiti*).[28] Other expressions of this attitude are to be found in the type of local instruction based on Zhu Xi's own proclamations,[29] in the community granaries to which Zhu devoted much attention as a district official, and in the so-called Family Ritual of Zhu Xi.

Zhu's treatment of these matters was extraordinarily detailed, showing a fine grasp of practical administration. It is not surprising that they should have become models for the implementation of his teachings in later times. Because these most authentic of Neo-Confucian institutions had their importance on the local level, however, often escaping the attention of modern scholars preoccupied with affairs of the imperial court and state, their significance has not always been appreciated. Some scholars in Chinese social history, however, are aware of the long and complex development of the community compact in later dynasties.[30] It had great appeal not only because of the prestige accruing from Zhu Xi's endorsement but also because its voluntaristic and cooperative character accorded well with the emphasis on local autonomy and self-government in the Neo-Confucian doctrine, referred to above by Xu Heng as "governing men through self-discipline."

Though it experienced many vicissitudes, owing to the difficulty of sustaining a spirit of both personal initiative and collective responsibility, successive reformers, including Wang Yangming in the Ming dynasty, saw the revival and reinvigoration of the community compact as the key to local self-government.[31] In Wang's case, the voluntaristic character of the community compact accorded well with his own voluntarist and activist philosophy, and it is not unnatural that there should have been such a meeting of minds between him and

Zhu Xi on an institution of local self-governance that embodied so well their common principles. Outside of China, there was an even more impressive development of the community compact system through its widespread adoption in Yi-dynasty Korea, in the importance attached to it by leading Korean Neo-Confucians,[32] and in its continuance down into the twentieth century as a key institution for the exercise of local autonomy on the principle of "governing men through self-discipline."

Inadequate though the preceding is as an account of Zhu Xi's view on popular education, it may at least offset the tendency to think of Zhu as addressing himself exclusively to the needs of the educated elite or to the elite's control over the uneducated. In fact, few even of his writings addressed to the latter audience fail to stress popular education as the base on which higher culture rests, and it is probably only the greater difficulty of dealing with the historical details of times remote from our own that has made us slow to study and evaluate adequately the influence of Zhu's views on education at the grassroots level.

In the scholastic tradition, Zhu was better known for his views on the conduct of higher education, on priorities in the curriculum, and on which texts should be read and how. His most important writings or talks, addressed to the smaller number who would have the opportunity to advance to the higher learning (or "greater learning"), are his *Reflections on Things at Hand* (*Jinsilu*), his *Commentary on the Great Learning* (*Daxue zhangju*), and his *Articles of the White Deer Grotto Academy* (*Bailu Dong shuyuan jieshi*). The first two will be brought into the discussion of Neo-Confucian personalism in the next chapter. Here, I shall focus on the *Articles of the White Deer Grotto Academy*, presented in 1179, which became a model for Neo-Confucian academies throughout East Asia.

These articles begin with a reaffirmation of the constant moral relations that constitute the matrix of individual self-development:

"Affection between parent and child;
Rightness between ruler and subject;
Differentiation between husband and wife;
Precedence between elder and younger;
Trust between friends."[33]

The above are the items of the Five Teachings, that is, the very teachings that Yao and Shun commanded Xie reverently to propagate as minister of education.[34] For those who engage in learning, these are all they need to learn. As to the proper procedure for study, there are also five items, as follows: "Study extensively, inquire carefully, ponder thoroughly, sift clearly, and practice earnestly."[35]

The above is the proper sequence for the pursuit of learning. Study, inquiry, pondering, and sifting are for fathoming principle to the utmost. As to earnest practice, there are also essential elements at each stage from personal cultivation to the handling of affairs and dealing with people, as separately listed below:

> "Be faithful and true to your words and firm and sincere in conduct."[36]
> "Curb your anger and restrain lust";[37] "turn to the good and correct your errors."[38]

The above are the essentials of personal cultivation.

> "Be true to moral principles and do not scheme for profit; illuminate [exemplify] the Way and do not calculate the advantages [for oneself]."[39]

The above are the essentials for handling affairs.

> "Do not do to others what you would not want them to do to you."[40]
> "When in your conduct you are unable to succeed, reflect and look [for the cause] within yourself."[41]

Here the keynotes are self-discipline and consideration for others, extending into higher education the same spirit of voluntarism and reciprocity that informed Zhu's approach to popular education. Again, we note that the process begins, as in the *Elementary Learning*, with a loving relationship between parent and child, a sense of intimacy and mutual respect. The statuses are not equal, but the relationship should, taking the fact of inequality into account, look beyond this difference to the underlying bond created by a shared life.

This view of filial piety as a reciprocal relation, in which the child responds to the loving care of the parent, was not an uncommon one at the time. Lu Jiuying (1132–1180), an elder brother of Lu Xiangshan, said in a poem, "The babe in arms knows love and, growing up, learns respect."[42] It is expressed even in the writing of Buddhist masters who took filial piety seriously. These include Qisong (1007?–1072), who wrote essays on filial piety as based on parental love,[43] and Zhongfeng Mingben (1263–1323), who put it this way: "All parents nurture and love their children. Therefore the sages and worthies teach us to be filial to our parents. Filiality (*xiao*) means imitating, serving (*xiao*). Children imitate parental nurturing and repay their parents with nurturing. Children imitate parental love and repay their parents with filial love."[44]

Thus these five constant relations or ethical norms represented a widely accepted traditional wisdom for handling human relations and their inevitable frictions. In reaffirming these norms, Zhu probably sought to avoid conflict situations in which there is either a direct contest of individual wills or the threat of coercion by official intervention. Individual self-assertion, pitting one will against another, often in unequal situations, as in parent-child conflicts, could only end in damage to the self-esteem of the defeated party. Coercion would tend to destroy self-motivation. Better to foster a spirit of mutual love that recognized and attempted to transcend differences, hence better an interpersonal concept of the self than a radically individualistic one.

VOLUNTARISM AND DIALOGUE IN HIGHER EDUCATION

The social functions addressed in the first set of *Articles* give way in the second set to operations that are more intellectual and reflect the particular preoccupations of the Song scholar. One cannot say that they lack the general human relevance of the moral dicta or would be inappropriate in most human situations, yet the atmosphere of the school prevails; it would be hard to imagine peasants having much opportunity to "study," "inquire," "ponder," and "sift" in the fashion Zhu suggests. The same is true of the note Zhu Xi appended to these articles, which speaks further to the condition of the scholar:

[I, Zhu] Xi have observed that the sages and worthies of antiquity taught people to pursue learning with one intention only, which is to make students understand the meaning of moral principle through discussion, so that they can cultivate their own persons and then extend it to others. The sages and worthies did not wish them merely to engage in memorizing texts or in composing poetry and essays as a means of gaining fame or seeking office. Students today obviously do the contrary [to what the sages and worthies intended]. The methods that the sages and worthies employed in teaching people are all found in the Classics. Dedicated scholars should by all means read them frequently, ponder them deeply and then inquire into them and sift them.

If you understand the necessity for principles and accept the need to take responsibility oneself for seeing that they are so, then what need will there be to wait for someone else to set up such contrivances as rules and prohibitions for one to follow? In recent ages regulations have been instituted in schools, and students have been treated in a shallow manner. This method of making regulations does not at all conform with the intention of the ancients. Therefore I shall not now try to put them into effect in this lecture hall. Rather I have specifically selected all the essential principles that the sages and the worthies used in teaching people how to pursue learning; I have listed them as above one by one and posted them on the crossbar over the gate. You, sirs, should discuss them with one another, follow them, and take personal responsibility for their observance. Then in whatever a man should be cautious or careful about in thought, word or deed, he will certainly be more demanding of himself than he would be the other way [of complying with regulations]. If you do otherwise or even reject what I have said, then the "regulations" others talk about will have to take over and in no way can they be dispensed with. You, sirs, please think this over.[45]

Here again, Zhu's voluntaristic approach to education is evident—voluntaristic but hardly permissive. Ironically, and it is not untypical of Zhu's fate in the hands of his followers, despite all of his own disclaimers these "articles" were often spoken of as "rules" in Neo-Confucian schools, or else they were supplemented by other regulations. Yet it is abundantly clear that Zhu himself sought to put the emphasis on the person rather than on the prohibition, recognizing that without the self-motivation, without the active "taking of responsibility oneself," as he put it here, schooling would not achieve its aim of "learning for the sake of one's self."

It was natural for Zhu, addressing students, to move from the discussion of basic social relations to more scholarly concerns. In his experience, both were inextricably interwoven into the fabric of life. Yet as we follow his procedural steps, we become aware that he is also defining roles for the self that are by no means inevitable or universal. Indeed, with one exception they are not readily comprehended in the Five Constant Relations to which so much formal respect was paid. Instead, they are roles so naturally accepted within Zhu's class and his cultural tradition as to be readily taken for granted: the roles of teacher, scholar, and official, which occupied much of the lives of the educated elite. It is to these roles that Zhu speaks most often in his major works, and it is in these contexts that "learning for the sake of one's self" is given its clearest definition.

In Zhu's postscript to the *Articles* we can see how his pedagogical method establishes personal dialogue, based on mutual respect, as the proper mode of learning. Twice Zhu makes the point that learning should proceed by discussion—and not just in dialogue between teacher and student but by talking things out among the students themselves, in a collegial fashion. It is through this give and take that much of the intellectual inquiry and exploration, sifting and judging, take place, leaving the student in a position to make up his own mind and take personal responsibility for his views and actions.

These same principles apply to the education of the ruler, which is best achieved through self-education in dialogue with others. In a lengthy sealed memorial to the throne with an extensive list of policy recommendations on current issues, Zhu lists as the first requisite for the emperor to engage in the "discussion of learning" (*jiangxue*). "The business of the empire is all rooted in one man and the control of that one man's person lies in the mind. Thus if the ruler's mind is correct, all the business of the empire will be correct." To accomplish this, says Zhu, there is no better method than the discussion of all matters and issues so that their good and evil implications are brought to light before decisions are made.[46]

Dialogue and conversation had been traditional features of Chinese philosophizing, but the Neo-Confucian movement was especially note-worthy for promoting this kind of philosophical discussion. At court, Neo-Confucians placed special emphasis on the discussion of policy questions in the so-called lectures from the classics mat (*jingyan*), a practice that developed into a major institution at the Korean court of the Yi dynasty. With the rapid spread of Neo-Confucian education, a distinct intellectual uplift was felt in one country after another as new schools and academies became centers for discussion that stimulated the interest of individuals and actively engaged their energies in a com-mon enterprise.[47] At the lower end of the social spectrum, this lecture/discussion method was popular in the Middle and Late Ming, even among less-educated folk in villages and towns,[48] and in the *shingaku* schools of eighteenth-century Japan.[49] Thus Zhu's voluntaristic approach found its natural fulfillment in a social process that contributed to the individual's self-improvement as well as to the edification of the group.

The central issue of "learning for the sake of one's self" is highlighted by the reaction to these developments of the authoritarian statesman Zhang Juzheng (1525–1582), who tried to suppress popular lecturing and discussion in the local academies. In the name of "orthodoxy," he came up with the speciously plausible argument that men of true char-acter should learn for themselves and stand entirely on their own feet, without the need to muster support from scholarly colleagues.[50]

The other local "forum" availed of by lecturers at this time, using the discussion method, was the meetings of the aforementioned "commu-nity compact" groups, wherein it was most natural to have an exchange of views among the members concerning moral issues in the conduct of daily affairs.[51] In this we can see the consistency of the Neo-Confucian approach to education on both the literate and nonliterate levels, stem-ming from Zhu Xi's dual emphasis on voluntarism and reciprocity.

HIGHER EDUCATION AS BROAD LEARNING

There is one other aspect of Zhu Xi's approach to higher learning that could be called "liberal," if by that one means tolerant or broad minded.

In the *Articles of the White Deer Grotto Academy*, the starting point of the learning process was "broad inquiry" (*bo-wen*), and Zhu Xi's teaching, as it later became generally known, was distinguished by its emphasis on "broad learning" (*boxue*). Zhu's scholarship as a whole gives ample evidence of it, but this quality is especially marked in the specific recommendations he made for the curriculum that would prepare educated men for government service. In his "Personal Proposal for Schools and Examinations," Zhu argued for a curriculum that would be comprehensive and broadly representative of China's humanistic tradition.[52]

For this view, he adduced two main "liberal" arguments. One is based on the political and social responsibilities of the educated man, who, Zhu says, must be learned in all branches of knowledge lest he find himself without the means of coping with the problems of contemporary society. The branches of learning that must be mastered if one is truly to live in the present and be responsive to the needs of one's fellow man include rites and music, governmental institutions, astronomy, geography, military strategy, and laws and punishments. These, he says, are only the "major ones."[53]

Another argument given by Zhu is that the educated man cannot afford to be too exclusive in his intellectual loyalties but must take a broad, pluralistic view of the several teaching traditions that have emerged from the Way of the Sages. It is bad enough that some of the teachings survive only in fragmentary form, worse still that scholars think it right to concentrate on the study of just one classic or one philosopher. Zhu would even give consideration to Daoist and Legalist works, from whose strong and weak points he thinks one should always be ready to learn. This pluralistic approach contrasts with the more limited choice of Wang Anshi, whose educational and examination policies concentrated on just three classics, the *Odes* (*Shi*), *Documents* (*Shu*), and *Rites of Zhou* (*Zhou li*) (and for practical purposes mainly on the latter), as interpreted by himself.[54]

Compare this to Zhu Xi's curriculum, which would include the *Changes, Documents,* and *Odes,* as well as four ritual texts (the *Zhou Yili* and two versions of the *Record of Rites* by the Elder and Younger Dai); the *Spring and Autumn Annals* (*Chunqiu*) with three early commentaries; and the *Great Learning, Analects, Mean,* and *Mencius.* Among the philosophers Zhu would include Xunzi, Yang Xiong, Wang Chong,

Han Feizi, Laozi, Zhuangzi, as well as the principal Song masters. The next major division of the curriculum would consist of the major histories, to be studied for the light they could shed on the understanding of contemporary problems; these include the *Zuo Commentary* (*Zuo zhuan*); *Conversations from the States* (*Guoyu*); *Records of the Grand Historian* (*Shi ji*); the histories of the Former and Later Han dynasties, of the Three Kingdoms, the history of Jin, histories of the Northern and Southern Dynasties, the Old and New Tang histories and the history of the Five Dynasties; and the *General Mirror for Aid in Government* (*Zizhi tongjian*) of Sima Guang. A similarly copious body of literature, including the encyclopedic *Comprehensive Institutes* (*Tongdian*) of Du You, is cited for those branches of practical learning indicated above (governmental institutions, geography, etc.).

Anyone familiar with these works will appreciate the imposing character of Zhu's reading list (parenthetically, not many scholars will have mastered it, and only a few such learned scholars as Huang Zongxi and Qian Mu will actually have read them all). Zhu himself allows that they cannot be mastered all at once, and even a three-year program of study would have to be selective. Nevertheless, in principle none should be left out. "Then," he says, "there will be no classics the gentleman has not mastered, no histories he has not studied, and none of these that will not be applicable to the needs of his times."[55]

These, then, are the studies Zhu would prescribe for the gentleman or scholar-official (*shi*). They represent the culmination of an educational system to which Zhu has paid careful attention on every level. Obviously, the full burden of culture represented by this curriculum is not to be borne by every man but only by the educated elite, who must accept the political and social responsibilities that, in Zhu's mind, attach to higher education. In this respect, his system remains exposed to the danger of elitism, which attaches to any mastery of classical learning in both breadth and depth. But, as he has presented it, on both the nonliterate and literate levels Zhu's liberal education adheres to the principles of voluntarism and mutual responsibility. He has also shown a strong awareness of the differing social contexts to which these principles would have to be adapted and of the need to formulate them in terms of a continuing process of self-discovery, group dialogue, and social renewal. At the highest point in that process stands the ideal of "learning for the sake of one's self" in a form demanding enough to express the loftiest aspirations of Song society and culture. To this we shall proceed in the next chapter on Neo-Confucian individualism and personhood.

IO

Confucian Individualism and Personhood

THE CLASSIC MODEL

From the standpoint of the Chinese population as a whole, the family was the predominant social and economic institution in an agricultural society, and in many respects it furnished the theoretical model for other institutions such as the patriarchal dynastic state. But as a literate tradition, Confucianism was also concerned from the start with individuals in relation to one another, as well as with the role of the scholar-official in his relations with the ruler and other scholars, teachers, and students.

Classically, the paradigm of human relationships was stated by Mencius as:

Between parent and child there is to be affection
Between ruler and minister, rightness
Between husband and wife, [gender] distinctions

Between older and younger [siblings] an order of precedence
Between friends, trustworthiness.

(Mencius 3A:4)

Since this paradigm was strongly reaffirmed in later (especially Neo-Confucian) tradition as well as in other East Asian countries, we should note some of its implications. First, it focuses on human moral relationships and the priorities among them, particularly within the family. The setting of personal priorities and the making of value distinctions is fundamental to Confucianism. Next, it should be noted that all of these relations involve reciprocity. The obligations are differentiated but mutual and shared. Thus, for instance, the relation between parents and child is not characterized exclusively in terms of the filial duty of child to parent but in terms of mutual affection, and in other formulations of the husband/wife relationship, the same mutual affection and love is stressed.

It is also true that the respect for precedence (seniority), here identified particularly with the sibling relationship, was more broadly generalized in practice to apply to all five relationships, so that, for instance, the relationship of friends, here spoken of in terms of *xin*, mutual trust, and reliability and thus based on mutuality and equality, was often analogized to that of older and younger brother (i.e., fictively, between persons who were not actually blood relations). Similarly, the relation of ruler and minister was in later discourse often analogized to that of parent and child (though this was also disputed by leading Confucians, who saw the ruler/minister relationship as a collegial one).

Nevertheless, in this classic formulation of moral relations it is as striking that the ruler/minister relationship should contain no reference to loyalty as it is noteworthy that the parent/child relationship should lack any reference to filial piety. In later common (popular) discourse, loyalty and filial piety are often spoken of as the typical Confucian virtues, and it is to this customary Confucian formula that implicit reference is made by those today who look to Confucianism as a support for superior authority. Yet loyalty and filial piety are totally missing here. From this one can see the incongruity in the recent news from Singapore, reporting the enactment of legal processes to compel children to meet their filial obligation to support their parents. Chinese law, it is true, traditionally recognized the importance of filial obligation, and the state often honored it, but it was considered rare and abnormal for such cases to come before a magistrate. Such matters were to be settled in the home or local neighborhood. And it is clear that Confucius, as recorded in the *Analects*, would have nothing to do with mindless conformism or coercive measures to enforce filial duty. Many passages affirm Confucius's belief that a forced or mechanical conformity to the norms of filial duty was not filial piety at all.[1] Indeed, Confucius pointedly insisted on moral cultivation and consensual social rituals rather than legal compulsion as the way to deal with such human problems. This underscores how pertinent to the present situation is the historic experience of China with a genuine but neglected tradition of Confucian ritual in the authentic communitarian form, rather than in the authoritarian, law-and-order form.

Those familiar with high Confucian tradition and its finer nuances would be more conscious of the particular implications of Mencius's dwelling on the ruler/minister relation rather than on what is sometimes translated as "ruler/subject." Insofar as any subject might participate in governance, the same principle would apply, but in fact, as Mencius well understood, most "subjects" did not so participate in the political process, and what Mencius had in mind (as is the case later on with most Confucian scholarly literature) was the particular but at the same time mutual obligation of ruler and minister to adhere to what is right and to consider the relationship at an end if they cannot agree on what is right. In this case, undying loyalty attaches to principle, not persons.

In modern times, awareness of this basic Confucian teaching has often been lost, and superficial notions of unquestioning loyalty to the ruler have taken over. But as late as the Ming and Qing dynasties, Mencius was well understood by those familiar with his teachings as reaffirmed by the great Neo-Confucian scholar-teacher Zhu Xi. Spectacular cases can be cited of heroic Confucian ministers standing up for what was right against all the despotic power of Ming rulers. One of the most celebrated cases is that of the outstanding Confucian scholar/minister Fang Xiaoru (1357–1402). Fang defied the Yongle emperor, who tried to silence him by threatening death not only to Fang himself but to all his kin as far as the ninth degree of relationship if Fang did not cease his remonstrance against the emperor. Fang did not yield, and all his family paid the price—and Fang had him add a tenth degree: his disciples.

Another case is that of the Ming official Hai Rui (1513–1587), whose martyrdom was cited in the Mao era by the historian and playwright Wu Han as an example of courageous criticism of the ruler. In this instance, Hai Rui's example was taken as an oblique reference to Peng Dehuai, a critic of Mao Zedong's policies: Mao, while encouraging people to speak out, reserved to himself the right to have them punished for it, as, indeed, Peng and Wu were.

An even more revealing example of the "freedom of speech" issue is the case of the founding emperor of the Ming, Taizu (r. 1368–1398), no less of a despot for being a peasant and populist. Taizu sought to reserve to himself the prerogative of offering the ritual sacrifice to Confucius and to withdraw this privilege (with its accompanying authority) from local Confucian officials, who had performed it since at least the Tang dynasty. Then, after expurgating the text of the *Mencius* (used in the civil-service examinations) of what he considered contumacious passages insulting to rulers, Taizu sought further to have Mencius's tablet removed from the Confucian temple. When his Confucian ministers objected, Taizu threatened death to any who opposed him, whereupon the minister Qian Tang, when he next came to court, brought with him a coffin, saying: "It would be an honor to die for Mencius."[2]

Taizu's attempt to suppress ministerial opposition goes to the heart of Mencius's dictum that the ruler/minister relationship should be governed by mutual respect for what is right. It is not, then, a matter of legal rights or of free speech in general but of what Confucians would call proper respect or civility in the decorum that should prevail at court. In other words, it came under the Confucian heading of ritual decorum— of "rites" and not of legal rights or entitlements. (Indeed, in whatever ruling court or cabinet would not the conduct of such debate be a matter of personal decorum or civility rather than one of legal rights?)

The further significance of the episode lies in the specificity of the personal relations involved. This is freedom of speech in the particular context of the ruler/minister relationship. By logical and natural extension, it could apply to any subject who entered into such a personal or collegial association with the emperor (or into his official service), but ministerial remonstrance could not be taken as a right generally enjoyed by all subjects. It amounts, then, only to a restricted or limited freedom of speech, yet at the same time, asserted here as a basic human principle it is extendable to others who might assume that duty, and it could become applicable to any wider extension of people's participation in the political process. In other words, embedded here in a particular personal, historical, and institutional context is a classic case of a Confucian universal human value. One could quibble about it and say that the Confucian case does not exactly fit the modern understanding of human rights, but if instead one is disposed to respect human values as experienced and expressed in different cultural settings, one could recognize here a rough parallel to the prophetic, protesting voice in other times and places, as in ancient Israel and thereafter in the Judeo-Christian tradition. Confucian "rightness" in the ruler/minister relation does not exactly correspond to the "righteousness" of God invoked by the Hebrew prophets, with which God's "people" were to identify themselves, but as it was associated in Confucianism with the order ordained by Heaven (*Tian*), this "rightness" had a universal aspect as well as a particularistic one: it characterized the special relationship of ruler and minister as meant to serve the larger public interest and general welfare (*gong*).

On this basis, in the modern period reformers could take Confucian principles as an indigenous Chinese cultural soil in which to ground legal rights and democratic institutions. Indeed, since the Japanese in the late nineteenth and early twentieth century shared the same Confucian moral ground, they claimed it as the basis and rationale for the adoption of "people's rights" and parliamentary institutions in the Meiji period, to be followed in this shortly afterward by Chinese reformers who likewise sought to interpret Western democratic institutions in Confucian terms and transplant them to Chinese soil.

"Transplant" is a key word here because it leaves open the question of how such institutions, developed in the West, could become rooted, grow, and thrive, or perhaps not, in soil that was admittedly foreign yet at the same time recognizably human, irreducibly both common and diverse. To get a perspective on this modern adaptation, however, we must look further into the relationship of the individual and the community, so much at issue in the charge that Western human rights thinking is too individualistic for the more communitarian "Asian" traditions, then further we should consider this in relation to the Chinese historical process as it emerged from the time of Confucius and Mencius down through the imperial dynasties to the modern era. Indeed to my mind, the weakness of many discussions of China, Confucianism, and human rights is that they tend to operate purely on the conceptual level—attempting to compare or contrast values in the abstract rather than seeing how they have been observed and experienced in time, in a developing historical process.

First, let us examine the status of the "individual" in Confucian thought. Spokesmen for what is called an "Asian" communitarian position are not wrong in supposing that the concept of a radically freestanding, autonomous individual is foreign to Confucianism, but the contrast is more with the modern age than it is with some earlier Western traditions, themselves more communitarian (or even with contemporary communitarian movements in the West that react against the recent trend). Modern libertarian individualism, as a product of rapid economic development and social change, presents the individual with a new abundance of "choices" to be made, while the extraordinary power of modern technology inspires and inflates the dream of unlimited expansiveness and liberation from all constraints. However, today these are phenomena of both East and West, wherever industrialization takes place; it is not a case of East *versus* West. Moreover, advocates of a traditional Asian "communitarianism" are wrong if they suppose— as Western writers too often have done—that in Confucianism the individual's worth is found only in the group, that he is no more than the sum of the social roles he is expected to perform, or that he is content with subordination to the group and established authority.

Confucius himself in the opening line of the *Analects* sets the matter in perspective when he speaks first of learning (from past tradition) and practicing it in the present, then of welcoming friends from afar (to share experiences with them), and finally of characterizing the truly noble man as one who is unembittered even if he is unrecognized by others (especially the ruler). The first two lines express the idea of a self shaped in the process of learning from others, but the last line conveys the sense that this should produce a person able to stand on his own. Later in the *Analects*, this process is spoken of as "learning for one's self," in contrast to "learning for the sake of others' [approval]," —that is to say, for true self-development rather than to gain social acceptance or political advancement.

This concept of a fully realized personhood is reaffirmed in Confucius's concise résumé of his own life experience:

> At fifteen I set my heart on learning.
> At thirty I was established [stood on my own feet].
> At forty I had no perplexities.
> At fifty I learned what Heaven commanded of me.
> By sixty my ear had become attuned to it.
> At seventy I could follow my heart's desire without transgressing.[3]

Here Confucius characterizes his lifelong learning as centered on his own self-development and self-fulfillment in the course of meeting the demands of Heaven. If we are to judge from the rest of the *Analects*, what he learned had much to do with his relationship to others and his sense of responsibility for them, but here he describes his life experience as one of inner growth in response to the providential guidance of Heaven—Heaven as representing a higher moral authority in the universe and Heaven's Way as defining his own mission in life. In his case, "Heaven's command" (*tianming*) is not the same as a dynastic mandate, though it shares with that mandate responsibility for what Heaven ordains morally and politically. Instead, his is a very personal commission and vocation to public service that demands difficult and unexpected things of him, which is not easily accepted at first but eventually brings a sense of personal freedom and self-fulfillment.

This is no less true of the human condition and the human ideal as we see it in Mencius, for whom the Way and the imperatives of Heaven are found in the inmost depths of one's own being, just as the sense of "rightness" (*yi*) is said by him to spring from within one's deepest natural sentiments. Moreover, among the other two classic texts that for later Confucians constitute the canonical Four Books, the *Mean* (*Zhong yong*), while paying due respect to social roles and obligations, extols above all personal sincerity or integrity (*cheng*), which means being true to one's innermost self, especially when one is not observed by others or answerable to them. In the same vein, the famous Eight Items of the *Great Learning* give clear priority in the first five items to the individual's self-development, before extending this further to family or state.

It is these texts and these concepts that later became formative of Neo-Confucian self-cultivation, reaffirming the morally responsible and affectively responsive self in the face of profound philosophical challenges from Buddhism and Daoism. And it is this same sense of the Way and its rightness, deep within one's self, from which a long line of Ming Neo-Confucian scholars from Qian Tang, Fang Xiaoru, Hai Rui, and on down to Liu Zongzhou drew the conviction and courage to challenge Ming despots. When one risks one's life in order to be true to one's own inmost self, it cannot be thought of as merely performing for others, fulfilling a social role, or conforming to the values of the group. Though it would be equally inappropriate to call this self-centeredness simply a form of "individualism" (if by that one means individual freedom of choice or emancipation from social constraints), it does affirm a strong moral conscience, shaped and formed in a social, cultural process that culminates, at its best, in a sense of self-fulfillment within society and the natural order. Given its special Confucian features, one might call this a distinct "Confucian individualism," but I prefer the term "personalism" to "individualism," since it shares some common ground with forms of personalism in Western tradition as distinct from a modern liberationist "individualism." Here, "personalism" expresses the worth and dignity of the person not as a raw, "rugged" individual but as a self shaped and formed in the context of a given cultural tradition, its own social community, and its natural environment to reach full personhood.[4]

On a portentous occasion in Hong Kong, anticipating its takeover by the People's Republic of China, Professor Anthony Yu of the University of Chicago discussed some of the issues at stake there. He described one factor threatening the future of education: the view that in China the collectivity always takes precedence over the individual, which inhibits the pursuit of truth for its own sake. Characterizing the Western educational tradition as "grounded upon the supreme good of individual self-fulfillment," he contrasted this to the Chinese tradition wherein "political and moral virtues unite as an indivisible homology in which the communal and collective take precedence over the individual."[5]

This is not a new view in the West, and, of course, in China it is one the state is glad enough to accept. It remains nonetheless questionable as a characterization of the Confucian standpoint, which looked for a balanced relation between self and society. Although Confucius himself spoke for and to an educated class of scholar-officials whose sense of political responsibility was inseparable from their privileged status as beneficiaries and custodians of a civilized learning tradition, he had little success himself in government and had to reconcile himself to a life of scholarship and teaching. In the end, however, he insisted that teaching and education themselves fulfilled the obligation of public service—one need not take office in order to fulfill this duty.[6]

No doubt Confucius had something of this in mind when he spoke, in the paradigmatic account of his own life experience cited above, about how he came, albeit slowly and reluctantly, to accept what Heaven had ordained for him: that is, learning in what capacity he could conscientiously fulfill Heaven's commission (his political vocation) as he tried to cope with the specific life situation Heaven presented to him—the difficulty he encountered in trying to obtain official employment on terms consistent with his principles. Could we perhaps call this belated discovery of his true vocation (teaching, not serving in office) an affirmation of "truth" as the supreme value? In Western terms, yes, we might, but in Confucian terms not exactly congruent with our own, it would more likely be expressed as Confucius's adherence to and following of the right Way (*Dao*).

When taunted for his fastidious refusal to serve rulers if it meant being co-opted by them for unworthy purposes, while yet he persisted stubbornly in the idealistic hope of political reform, Confucius replied: "One cannot herd with the beasts or flock with the birds. If I am not to serve in the company of other human beings (i.e., act as a responsible social being), then what am I to do? If the Way prevailed among men, I would not be trying to change things."[7]

Here Confucius insists on the following of the Way as a higher duty than simply taking office, and, without abandoning the moral struggle, he persists in acting on behalf of the Way to reform an imperfect human society. Clearly, he did not take service of the state or subordination to the established order as an ultimate obligation. Rather for him, pursuit of the Way came close to what Professor Yu has called "the pursuit of truth" in the West. Yet if one considers that both "Truth" in the West and the "Way" in China open out on unlimited horizons and in some indefinable way ultimately converge, there would seem to be little use in drawing a fine line between them—much less in opening up a large chasm between East and West on this score.

The more relevant distinction to be made here is one Confucians drew between the Way of the Ruler and the Way of the Teacher. Ideally (in ancient legend), these two roles had been joined as one in the sage-kings, but by Confucius's time the Way had become split apart. For all later Confucians, Confucius as teacher and not as ruler was the personification of sageliness, the highest standard and model for anyone to follow. No later ruler ever commanded the same respect.

Another point of common confusion in regard to the issue of the individual versus the community or collectivity has been in positing the dichotomy of public (*gong*) and private (*si*) as necessarily an antithetical one—"public" as standing for the common good and "private," negatively, for individual selfishness. It is true that these concepts are sometimes found in opposition, as when individual desires are seen to conflict with the common good. This is the case in the section on the "Evolution of Rites" in the *Record of Rites* compiled in the Han dynasty, which contrasts the primordial ideal of "all-under-Heaven as shared in common" (*Tianxia weigong*) with the historical reality of people pursuing their own private interests at others' expense—a social condition Confucius himself had to face and was unable to change, sage though he was. In the same *Record of Rites*, there is also a discussion of the opposition between "Heaven's principles" (identified here with the common good) and "human desires" (understood here to be "selfish"). In the given context, however, this dichotomy refers to actions of the ruler that are selfish, when properly he should be acting in the common interest and holding himself to a higher, self-sacrificial standard of service to the public good.[8] Indeed, the implication of the passage is that the ruler should not indulge his own selfish desires at the expense of the people's legitimate desires, appetites, and material needs. It is not a question of ordinary persons sacrificing their natural desires to the group.

Thus, though "Heaven's principles" and "human desires" are juxtaposed in this case, it is not meant to suggest a necessary opposition or conflict between private and public, individual and collectivity, but rather to assert the obligation of rulers to uphold a public standard that keeps in balance individual desires and the common good. Even the great Confucian thinker Xunzi, though he is generally identified with the view of human nature as evil, subscribed to this idea that the social order should aim at the satisfaction of people's desires.[9]

The same issue arises in the famous Han-dynasty "Debate on Salt and Iron." Here the spokesmen for the state claim that their instituting of state monopolies over key resources, their maintaining of state marketing controls, and their general policy of state intervention in the economy is meant to defend the public interest against private exploitation. In this debate, however, spokesmen for the Confucians argue against this, charging that such regulation and intervention is contrary to the people's interest, which would be better served by a free-market economy and private enterprise, allowing "the people" to act in their own interest and on their own initiative. In this debate, both sides claim to speak for the public interest, but it is the Confucians who argue that this interest is better served by encouraging the people's private initiative, while the bureaucrats' claim to speak for the public interest is questioned as only a cover for the pursuit of their own vested interests.

From this it may seem again that the Confucian ideal was a balance of public and private, not an assertion of one over the other. In fact, from the Confucian point of view the state's responsibility for the public interest was to encourage legitimate private initiative. How to define what was legitimate remained an issue, and the state, historically, was not slow to assert its own authority in this respect (any more than it is today), but Confucians were just as ready to challenge any such claim on the part of the state bureaucracy (*guan*), asserting instead that the public interest (*gong*) consists in serving the legitimate desires and material needs of the people.[10] A balance of public and private (*gongsi yiti*), not the person or individual subordinated to the collectivity or state, remained the Confucian ideal.

NEO-CONFUCIAN DEVELOPMENTS

When Western notions of liberalism and individualism reached East Asia in the nineteenth century, they had no precise equivalents in Chinese or Japanese parlance, and neologisms had to be invented for them. *Geren zhuyi* (Jap.: *kojin shugi*), the term devised for "individualism," emphasized the discrete or isolated individual. This contrasts with the Confucian personalism referred to above, which conceived of the person as a member of the larger human body, never abstracted from society but always living in a dynamic relation to others, to a biological and historical continuum, and to the organic process of the Way. The term *ziyou zhuyi* (Jap.: *jiyū shugi*), which was used to represent "liberalism," emphasized the autonomy of the self, the idea that one should be able to "follow one's own inclination." *Ziyou* has appeared in many modern compound terms rendering different aspects of "liberty" or "freedom" in Western political or legal thought. The current term for "liberalization" (*ziyouhua*) in the People's Republic is an instance of this.

In these cases, while a special emphasis on the individual was perceived as the distinctive feature of these Western attitudes, East Asian translators were not completely at a loss for words to express it, nor were they forced to fall back on transliteration as the only way to represent ideas utterly strange to them. In fact, the importance of individual autonomy or being able to "follow one's own inclination" (*ziyou*) was not foreign to traditional ways of thinking, and there may indeed be a certain Neo-Confucian predilection expressed in the choice of these terms to represent the nineteenth-century Western concept of "liberalism," which put more emphasis on individual freedom than more recent definitions do. Thus the latter, though usefully broad when applied to Western or Confucian tradition as a whole, may not be as appropriate for present purposes as the definition of liberalism in *Webster's Third New International Dictionary*: "a philosophy based on belief in progress, the essential goodness of man and the autonomy of the individual, and standing for tolerance and freedom for the individual from arbitrary authority in all spheres of life."[11]

Some years ago, I noted tendencies toward individualism in sixteenth-century Ming thinkers considered radical in their own day and no less so by many modern writers.[12] Yet for all their radicalism, it seemed to me then that these thinkers in the Taizhou wing of the Wang Yangming school, and especially Li Zhi, could only be understood as products of a long Neo-Confucian development. In what follows, I will return to the Neo-Confucian sources of that individualism.

The Vocabulary of Neo-Confucian Individualism

The zi of the $ziyou$ in "liberalism" is a term for "self," frequently used in combination with ji, $shen$, or si. Like ji and $shen$, it is often translatable simply as "self."[13] In classical Chinese usage, zi also has the connotation "from, in, or of itself," much like our prefix "auto-." This sense of self-originated or self-motivated gains added emphasis when used in combination with you, "from" or "out of." Thus zi readily forms compounds corresponding to ours with the prefix "self-." For instance, in the *Great Learning* it says: "to make the will sincere means allowing of no self-deception ($ziqi$), as when we hate a bad smell or love what is good-looking, which is called self-satisfaction ($ziqian$)." In both cases, self-deception and self-satisfaction, the implication is that the source of value lies within the self and that the immediate, affective, visceral response to things is the authentic one. The Neo-Confucians proceeded on the same assumption, and one could compile a virtual lexicon of terms with the prefix zi- that recur frequently in their discussions. A few of the more common examples follow:

Ziran: "natural" in the sense of what is so of itself and not made to be or appear so (*wei*). The Neo-Daoists had made almost a supreme value of naturalness (*ziran*), in the sense of uninhibited spontaneity or an amoral, pragmatic adaptability. For their part, Neo-Confucians were unwilling to concede that moral effort and rational calculation were unnatural to man. They followed Mencius in trying to steer a middle course between a laissez-faire, value-free pragmatism on the one hand and forced effort or conscious manipulation on the other, often citing Mencius's eschewal of either "forgetting" or "abetting" the moral nature as equally prejudicial to the natural process of growth in accordance with the inner directedness of things. How to sustain a moral life that is natural, nonmanipulative, and unfeigned was a central concern of both Song and Ming thought. Thus Wu Cheng (1249–1333), in explaining the opening lines of Zhu Xi's commentary on the *Great Learning*, points out how naturally the cultivation of the moral nature leads to the "renewing of the people" because it evokes a natural response in accordance with the inherent propensity of their own natures.[14]

Ziren: "taking it upon oneself" or "bearing the responsibility oneself." This is in accord with voluntarism in the moral life and of action that is in keeping with "learning for the sake of one's self"— that is, with the idea that one must take full responsibility for one's own actions, since actions undertaken with a view to pleasing others lead, as Zhu said above, to "self-destruction." The locus classicus for the term is in the *Mencius* (5B:1), where it refers to "taking on the weight of the world." In Neo-Confucianism, this is closely associated with the conception of the moral hero and becomes a key concept in Neo-Confucian moral individualism.

Zide: literally "getting it by or for oneself." This expression was used in two important senses. One, relatively low keyed, is that of learning or experiencing some truth for oneself and deriving inner satisfaction therefrom; here *zide* has the meaning of "learned to one's satisfaction," "self-contented," "self-possessed." The other sense of the term is freighted with deeper meaning: "getting or finding the Way in oneself," as referred to by Mencius: "The noble man steeps himself in the Way because he wishes to 'get it' himself. When he gets it himself, he will be at ease with it. When he is at ease with it he can trust it deeply, and when he can trust it deeply, he can find its source wherever he turns. That is why the noble man wishes to get it himself" (4B:14). Zhuangzi also uses the term in the sense of a deep inner fulfillment in accord with the Way.[15] Zhu Xi's commentary on *zide* in *Mencius* explains it as a silent recognition and penetration of the mind, so as to find the Way naturally (*ziran*) within the self. He cites Cheng Hao's view of it as "learning that is unspoken and is acquired naturally is truly 'getting it oneself.' Learning that is contrived and forced is not 'getting it oneself.'"[16]

The centrality of *zide* in the Cheng-Zhu system is indicated by the fact that Master Cheng's discussion of it is the first cited passage at the head of the "General Introduction to Learning" in the *Great Compendium on Human Nature and Principle* (*Xingli daquan*), the Ming-dynasty compilation long accepted as the official "bible" of Neo-Confucian philosophy. Here Cheng speaks of learning as seeking within oneself and says "the most refined of principles should be sought and found in oneself (*zi qiu de zhi*).[17] Hence among the possible translations of *de* as "acquire," "obtain," "possess," any of which may be appropriate in a given context, I have in general used "get" as the most basic meaning, despite its colloquial tone, but sometimes "find," as in "finding the Way in oneself" or "finding [satisfaction, contentment, joy] in oneself."

Both *ziren* and *zide* recur frequently in descriptions of the crucial learning experiences or decisive conversion experiences of leading Neo-Confucians.

Much of chapter 4 in Zhu Xi's *Reflections on Things at Hand* on "Preserving One's Mind" is concerned with the problem of naturalness and getting the truth or the Way for oneself as a matter of practical self-cultivation. This was a particular concern of Cheng Yi. Of the many passages quoted from him on this point, the two following will illustrate the point.

Master Yichuan [Cheng Yi] said: "The student should revere and respect this Mind. He should not anxiously try to force it. Instead he should cultivate it deeply, nourish it richly and steep himself in it. Only thus can he get it for himself (*zide*). If one anxiously presses in pursuit of it, that is mere selfishness (*siji*). In the end it will not suffice for attaining the Way."[18]

Nowadays students are reverent but do not get [the Way] for themselves [*zide*]. All this is because in their minds they are not at home with reverence. It is also because they carry reverence [seriousness] too far in dealing with things. This is what is meant by "Respectfulness, without the rules of decorum, becomes laborious bustle. . . ."[19] Rules of decorum are not a body of ceremonies but natural principles (*ziran de daoli*). Because one is only respectful, without practicing natural principles, he is not at home with himself (*zizai*). One must be respectful and yet at ease.[20] Now the reason why one must be right in appearance and correct in speech is not merely to attain goodness for himself and see what others will say. It is because according to the Principle of

Nature (*tianli*), he should be so [i.e., it is both natural and proper to be so]. Basically there should be no selfish ideas but only being in accord with principle.[21]

The relevance of this to "learning for the sake of oneself" as opposed to "learning for the sake of others" need not be elaborated here. This is a familiar problem of the spiritual life in other religious and ethical traditions: how to balance or reconcile moral effort with religious awe and acceptance.[22] In Cheng Yi's case, it is complicated by the built-in ambiguity in his use of the term *jing*, meaning both "reverent" and "serious." As understood in the Cheng-Zhu school, it was meant to combine moral effort and religious acceptance in a way that was "natural" for a man of conscience.

For Zhu Xi too *zide* had a special significance in relation to finding or possessing the Way in oneself. In the *Mean* (14), the term is used in this sense in a passage that describes the Way of the Noble Person (*junzi*) as applicable to and practicable in all life situations. "The noble person can find himself in no situation where he is not himself [i.e., does not find within himself (*zide*) the Way that will enable him to deal with all circumstances]." And in Zhu's summation of the significance of the *Mean* as a whole, he says:

> Zisi relates the ideas that had been handed down to him as the basis of his discourse. First he explains that the Way originally derives from Heaven and cannot be altered. Its substance inheres in the self and cannot be departed from. Next it sets forth the essentials of preserving and nourishing this [substance in the mind] and of practicing self-examination. Finally, it expresses the ultimate achievement of sagely and spiritual men in the transforming power of their virtue. In this Zisi wished for the learner to look within and get it [the substance of the Way] for himself.[23]

From this it is understandable that Zhu's "repossessing of the Way" (*daotong*) should reflect the Cheng brothers' view of "getting it oneself" as well as Chen Changfang's linkage of the sages' learning of the mind-and-heart to "getting it oneself." Wing-tsit Chan, in discussing how Zhu arrived at his concept of *daotong*, notes Cheng Yi's central role, saying of him, "Cheng's main point was that his brother found the Confucian Way, meaning the teachings of Confucius and Mencius, in surviving Classics himself. Like most Neo-Confucianists, his emphasis was on 'acquiring for oneself' (*zide*)." In the same vein but in a quite different area of Chu's thought, Richard Lynn cites *zide* first among the qualities Zhu Xi appreciated in great poetry, along with others emphasizing naturalness, freedom, and spontaneity.[24]

The Sage as Ideal Self

Sagehood and how to attain it is the central theme of Cheng-Zhu thought, which is to say, of "learning for the sake of one's self." It was already the unifying conception of Zhou Dunyi's (1017–1073) major work *Comprehending the Changes* (*I-Tongshu*),[25] and from it Zhu Xi drew the initial selection for "The Essentials of Learning," which set the pattern for his *Things at Hand* (*Jinsilu*).[26] Cheng Yi contributed to the development of this theme with his youthful essay "What Yanzi Loved to Learn" (i.e., how to become a sage),[27] which Zhu likewise quoted early in the same chapter of *Things at Hand*. Consistently with this, Zhu's own work concludes with a discussion of those qualities in the sages and worthies that make them fitting models for the individual.

Sagehood had long been a dominant ideal of Chinese thought for classical Confucians as well as for Daoists and Neo-Daoists. What gave special significance to its discussion in the Song by the Cheng brothers and Zhu Xi was their view of the sage as not just a lofty and remote ideal but a model for their own times. They shared a conviction that sagehood could be "learned" by anyone, and Zhou Dunyi's positive assurance to this effect became one of the most quoted, and also disputed, passages in later Neo-Confucian literature:

"Can one become a sage through learning?"
"Yes."
"Is there any essential way?"
"Yes."[28]

What follows in Zhou's own work and in other major texts of Neo-Confucianism sets forth this "essential way." Thus sagehood not only was a generalized human ideal of symbolic value but became specifically a model for self-cultivation. The meaning of this is especially clear in Cheng Yi's discussion:

> The way to learn is none other than rectifying one's mind and nourishing one's nature. When one abides by the mean and correctness and becomes sincere, he is a sage. In the learning of the noble person, the first thing is to be clear in one's mind and to know where to go, and then act vigorously in order that one may arrive at sagehood. . . . Therefore the student must exert his own mind to the utmost. If he does so, he will know his own nature. And if he knows his own nature, examines his own self and makes it sincere, he becomes a sage.[29]

It is just as simple as that. The message, directed to any and all students, could not be more straightforward or matter of fact. No one lacks the essential capability for sagehood, if he will just make up his mind to achieve it.

Later, Cheng adds:

> In later years people thought that sagehood was basically due to innate genius and could not be achieved through learning. Consequently the way to learn has been lost to us. Men do not seek within themselves but outside themselves and engage in extensive learning, effortful memorization, clever style, and elegant diction, making their words elaborate and beautiful. Thus few have arrived at the Way. This being the case, the learning of today and the learning that Yanzi loved are quite different.[30]

Again, the relevance of this "learning to be a sage" to "learning for the sake of oneself" rather than "for the sake of others" is evident. The requisites for the one are the same as for the other; both are contrasted to the prevalent forms of literary learning and indiscriminate erudition. The path to sagehood, practically speaking, represents the method of "finding the way in oneself," and the sage becomes the ideal self for purposes of Neo-Confucian self-cultivation.

The meaning of this is twofold. When Zhu Xi explains the point of "Reverencing the self or the person" (*jingshen*) in the *Elementary Learning*, he says, "This section presents a basic model for emulating the sages and worthies."[31] Elsewhere, however, Zhu stressed that sagehood came from within the self. In answer to a question about relying on the teachings of the sages as a guide to one's own learning and conduct, he said, "In talking to students we can only teach them to act according to the teachings of the sages. When after making some effort they realize something within themselves, they will know naturally (of themselves, *zizhi*) what it really is to be a sage."[32] In other words, one draws on one's own experience as well as on the model put before one, and the result partakes of both individuality and commonality. The sage is the self writ large, but in both of these senses: an internalization of others' representations of sagehood (in the classics, histories, etc.) and a projection, an objectification, of one's own experience.

In this process, the experience of one's own age and the preconceptions of one's own generation enter in. Zhu Xi himself understood this when, at the end of *Things at Hand*, he drew more heavily on the personal experience and example of the Song masters than on the ancients as a guide to sagely learning. Indeed, the point of compiling *Things at Hand* was to demonstrate the contemporary relevance of sagehood by drawing on the teachings and achievements in self-cultivation of his near contemporaries. In turn, much of the effectiveness of this work and its appeal to Zhu's followers lay in its modernity or contemporaneity. Its readers could identify with the Song masters, whose experience of life was closer to their own. Thus sagehood, instead of remaining a lofty abstraction from the past, became defined, and the ideal self to some extent delimited, in ways characteristic of that age.

Some of these delimitations are more apparent to us, with the hindsight of history, than they were to Zhu Xi. He believed deeply in the perfectibility of the moral nature in all men. Philosophically, this was based on his doctrine that each man possessed the moral nature or principle inherent in all, sharing a common nature that could form a unity with Heaven and earth and the myriad things, while at the same time each had his own individuality. Zhu Xi sometimes used the metaphor of the moon and its reflection in different bodies of water to illustrate the universality and particularity of principle (or man's nature), expressed in the formulation "principle is one but its particularizations are diverse" (*liyi fenshu*). But this metaphor, drawn from Huayan Buddhism, had the defect that, since the one moon was real while its many reflections were only passing phenomena, the particular nature manifest in the individual might be taken as only an insubstantial reflection of some transcendental reality. Wishing to affirm the substantiality of the individual in his concrete humanity, morally as well as physically, Zhu later chose to express it in terms of the metaphor of growing grain:

> One substance is expressed in the myriad things, but the one substance and the myriad things are integral by themselves, while the largeness and smallness of each has its own definiteness. . . . The myriad objects embody in themselves, each and every one of them, their own principle. This is what is meant [in Zhou Dunyi's *Comprehending the Changes* (*I-Tongshu*)] by "changes in the Heavenly Way resulting in each possessing its endowed life and acquired nature. . . ." It is like a grain of millet, which gives birth to a seedling, which gives birth to a flower. When the flower bears seeds, which become millet again, the original figure is restored . . . they will go on producing like this eternally.[33]

Here the reality of principle in each individual, which is the basis of his self-perfection and his aspiration to sagehood, is made clear in a most concrete way. There is no human being not similarly endowed.

This universal principle and potentiality in all men is much in the mind of Zhu Xi as he addresses them in his written works. His preface to the *Great Learning* and the opening lines of his commentary stress universal education as the basis for renewing the people and leading each person to the perfecting of his own nature. In a preface to *Reflections on Things at Hand* (*Jinsilu*), he expresses the hope that it could serve as a guide to the cultivation of self and sagehood even for "young lads in isolated villages."[34] Likewise, when he recommended the *Elementary Learning* and its "Reverence of the Self" as a guide to sage-hood, he spoke of it as "serving for the edification of unlearned *shi*."[35] Just exactly what *shi* meant to him in contemporary terms is not clear; probably Chu thought of this class as not essentially different from the scholar-knights or scholar-officials of ancient times in regard to their basic human functions and commitments, even though he knew that conditions of life had changed since then (for instance, in regard to the conduct of education and the institutionalization of the examination system). We today would probably be more conscious of the elite status and leadership functions of the *shi* as differentiating them from the common man in the country village.

"Taking Responsibility Oneself"

The educated man, Song Confucians understood, should be prepared to serve in government and develop specialized skills where appropriate to serve humanitarian purposes. For its part, the Cheng-Zhu school held, as we have seen, that the essence of government lay in universal self-discipline, beginning with the ruler's self-rectification. This obliged the minister, in his relation to the ruler as defined in the Five Constant Relations (i.e., "Between prince and minister there is [a bond of] rightness"), to assist the emperor in his self-cultivation and in the conduct of his moral life. In other words, he is to be a minister in the sense of counselor, mentor, preceptor.

This was all the more the case with the Cheng brothers and Zhu Xi, who as court officials often served in preceptorial roles such as "lecturer from the classics mat," discussing current affairs in the light of the values and principles set forth in the classics. They directed the counsel given in their memorials and lectures toward the primary motivation of the ruler: his need to take full personal responsibility for the conduct of the Way. Often, this is expressed, as we have seen, in terms of *ziren*, "taking responsibility oneself," closely accompanied by the related ideas of learning for oneself, making up one's own mind, and making a definite decision or commitment on behalf of the Way.

Cheng Hao told the Emperor: "To rule with a sincere mind-and-heart is to be a true king. . . . Your majesty has the natural endowment of Yao and Shun, but only if he takes it as his personal responsibility (*ziren*) to have the mind-and-heart of Yao and Shun can he fulfill their Way."[36]

Here the close connection in Cheng Hao's mind between sincerity, making up one's own mind, and taking personal responsibility is evident. Cheng Yi, for his part, speaks in much the same terms and to the same point:

> The way of government may be discussed in terms of its fundamentals and of its practice. In terms of its fundamentals it is nothing but "rectifying what is wrong in the ruler's mind"[37] and "rectifying one's mind in order to rectify the minds of the officials at court." . . .[38] In terms of its practice nothing can be done if the ruler does not want to save the country.[39]

In a lengthy memorial to the throne, Cheng Yi reiterated the need for the emperor to make a definite decision and commit himself to the Way. Three things were most needful in rulership: for the emperor to commit himself, to share the responsibility he personally accepted for the Way, and to find worthy men able to accept the same responsibility.

Committing oneself means to be perfectly sincere and single minded, to take up the Way as one's own responsibility (*yi dao ziren*), to take the teachings of the sages as trustworthy, to believe that the governance of the kings can be carried out, to avoid following rigidly the advice of those nearby or being swayed by public clamor, but to be determined to bring about a world like that of the Three Dynasties.[40]

In Zhu Xi's sealed memorial of 1162, an early expression of his approach to politics, he urges the emperor not to rely on what he is told by Zhu and others but by objective study, subjective confirmation, and discussion with others, to find out and get for himself (*zide*) the truth of the Way.[41] In this and many other passages, Zhu Xi stresses mind-rectification as the essential method by which the ruler fulfills his personal responsibility for the conduct of the Way. In one sense, it can be said that this approach is derived from the view of education discussed earlier, extending it into the domain of politics. On the other hand, it is significant that the essential elements in this doctrine of the examination of conscience or rectification of mind were voiced first by Zhu Xi in this memorial, i.e., in a political context, before it appeared in his preface to the *Mean* as a more generalized doctrine for human cultivation. It was via the public man and the political function that the more fundamental human problem was first addressed.

It has often been asserted that the distinctive feature of Song political life was the increased centralization of authority and bureaucratization of dynastic rule. Sometimes this has been spoken of as "Song autocracy," a new stage in the long-term development of an increasingly autocratic dynastic system. Yet it can also be argued that the Song represented a new stage in the rise of the scholar-official class as well and in the extension of their influence in government.[42] Modern scholars have confirmed the impression given by the Song statesman and historian Fan Zuyu, who credited the Song with encouraging freer discussion and debate at court than any previous dynasty.[43]

These trends were concurrent and coexisted in a relation of complementarity as well as in a state of tension. There was an increasing centralization of bureaucratic rule, but in certain areas and on different levels of government this thrust greater responsibilities on the managerial class as well as concentrating greater power in the hands of the ruler. This power of the ruler was perceived as both an ominous threat and a promising possibility by the new class of educated, civil-oriented Confucian officials. When lecturing the emperor, they stressed how crucial it was that he use his power for good rather than ill, trying to bolster his confidence in the power to do good and impress on him the consequences of failure.

In the Northern Song especially, there had been an air of optimism concerning man's ability to accomplish great and good things by the creative use of human reason. Economic growth and cultural affluence encouraged this optimism and to some extent sustained it even through repeated frustrations and failures to achieve the idealistic goals of Song reformers. Thus with the Cheng brothers and even with Zhu Xi in more trying circumstances later there is a sense of political and cultural crisis but also a stubborn, idealistic faith that man has it within his power to meet the challenge.

No doubt the readiness, indeed resoluteness, of scholars like the Chengs and Zhu Xi to express themselves so vigorously in writing and to speak out with great frankness at court reflected some of the trends of the times and the characteristic attitudes of their class. The economic development of the country, especially in central and southern China, supported a significantly larger number of educated persons in the performance of their political and cultural functions and gave them a new sense of their own importance, a lively esprit de corps, greatly reinforcing their own self-image and self-confidence.[44] This is seen not only in the Cheng brothers but in their opponents, such as Wang Anshi and Su Dongpo.

This self-confidence cannot be compared with the more aggressive and expansive attitude of the Western bourgeoisie in later centuries, and if the scholar-officials of the Song can be thought of in any sense as performing the political functions of a middle class, it is only because as local gentry they had one foot in the land and one in the bureaucracy.[45] The "sprouts of capitalism" that have been detected in the China of this period did not grow and flower into anything like the economic and political pluralism of the West.[46] Available evidence suggests that neither the Cheng brothers nor Zhu Xi were propertied or at all well off,[47] and their later followers saw them as having led lives of great hardship.[48] This was no doubt possible, even within a generally rising trend for the gentry as a whole, because of differential rates of growth in some regions and the varying fortunes of individuals and families. Nevertheless, Song scholars did have the leisure to pursue their cultural interests, enjoyed the immunities and protections that their class had managed to win in return for its performance of essential bureaucratic functions, and were supported when in difficulty by other members of that class.

The essence of the Cheng brothers' own situation is captured in an episode involving Cheng Yi's stipend as a "lecturer from the classics mat." The convention at court was that the lecturer should submit an application for his salary to the Board of Revenue—in itself an example of the increasing bureaucratization of life. Cheng refused to do this, even though he had to borrow money to live on. When asked about this, he replied that to apply for his salary as if for a favor was demeaning, especially for the lecturer from the classics mat, who was supposed to serve as mentor to the emperor and should be treated with appropriate respect. "The trouble is that today scholars and officials are accustomed to begging," he said. "They beg at every turn."[49]

The matter was eventually handled by proxy, in typical Chinese face-saving fashion, so that Cheng did get his stipend, but for us the story registers several significant points: first, there is Cheng Yi's attempt to assert an independent role for the scholar-official at court vis-à-vis the increasing power of the ruler; second, there is his own acknowledgment that the principle or standard he wishes to uphold was not in practice widely respected; and third is the fact that he was only able to make this rather striking gesture with the help he received from his colleagues. Class solidarity supported him in this rather strained affirmation of self-respect, but the net effect, if any, was more to register a moral point than to score a political gain. Thus, when Cheng Yi and Zhu Xi urged the emperor to emulate the sages and to take full personal responsibility for the conduct of the Way, it was a projection of the same sense of individual integrity and self-respect that they wished to assert for themselves.

Much the same purpose was served by Zhu Xi's strong emphasis on the relationship between prince and minister as essentially a moral one. It tried to establish the moral equality of the two as well as their collegial solidarity, in contrast to the prevailing view of the minister as the servitor or virtual slave of the emperor. In this respect, it sought to gain moral leverage on the ruler, for want perhaps of a stronger position for the minister at court. Cheng Yi, reaffirming the stance of Mencius, insisted that the relation between prince and minister was primarily a moral one and obliged the latter to depart from the service of a ruler with whom he had fundamental differences in principle. "Unless the ruler honors virtue and delights in moral principles . . . it is not worth having anything to do with him."[50] In Zhu Xi's *Things at Hand*, Cheng Yi is quoted as saying, "When a scholar is in high position, his duty is to save his ruler and not to follow him in wrongdoing."[51] And further, "when one has resolved that 'if he can hear the Way in the morning, he will die content in the evening,' he will not be content for even a single day with what should not be acquiesced in."[52]

Julia Ching has characterized the stance of the Neo-Confucians in these terms:

> The authority to which they gave adherence was higher than the state, which saw itself as guardian of classical exegesis, higher even than the classics. They relied primarily on their own authority, as self-appointed interpreters of the sacred message. Their claim was to solid classical learning, but particularly to their own insights into the spiritual meaning of the texts. For this reason, in the political realm, they acted as moral judges of their sovereigns rather than as dutiful ministers.[53]

To this one amendment may be made, concerning the word "rather." In the view of the Chengs and Zhu Xi, it was precisely by judging the sovereign, by holding him to the highest standards of political morality, that they served as "dutiful ministers." This is what they meant by saying that the relation of ruler and minister was fundamentally a moral or righteous (*yi*) one, i.e., a relation between two individuals who had freely joined in taking responsibility (*ziren*) for the way of governing.

To assert this high standard of political rectitude may have accomplished little politically, but as embodied in the lives of the Chengs and Zhu Xi it set an inspiring example for many of their later followers, some of them scholar-statesmen who themselves manifested a great personal initiative, strength of purpose, and stalwart independence against overwhelming political odds. Fang Xiaoru (1357–1402) and Hai Rui (1513–1587)[54] in the Ming are two examples among many that could be cited. Against the formidable pressures operating to compel conformity, this side of the Neo-Confucian tradition upheld a lofty conception of the dignity, integrity, and independence of the individual scholar-official. It had a high estimate of the moral and spiritual resources of man, and while its celebration of the heroic virtues may seem hopelessly idealistic to modern minds, it aimed, like Mencius (6A:16), at the "nobility of Heaven," i.e., the moral nobility of man, judged on the basis of individual worth rather than special rank or social status.[55]

Thus far I have touched on the functional roles of the Neo-Confucian in the school, in the family and community, and in the state. Traditionally, Confucians thought of these as primary roles of the individual, corresponding to the moral duties that Confucius said (*Analects* 1:6) must have first claim on one's attention, after which, if one has time and energy to spare, he could devote himself to "letters" (*wen*). Neo-Confucians reconfirmed this priority in the Song, but as members of a class in more comfortable circumstances they also enjoyed more leisure for cultural activities than most earlier generations and with increased material and technical means at their disposal. Generally speaking, the centers of Neo-Confucian scholarship were also areas that led in agricultural production, trade, and population growth in the late Tang and Song period, i.e., modern Jiangsu, Zhejiang, Jiangxi, Fujian, Sichuan, and—for political and cultural reasons rather than economic—the capital region.[56] Whatever it may have lacked in military prowess, the Song certainly displayed brilliant cultural achievements, and it is no surprise that the outburst of individual creativity in arts and letters, especially the greater freedom of individual expression in painting, calligraphy, and other arts taken up by scholar-officials, should have expressed itself also in Neo-Confucian thought.[57]

There was a larger sense of the term *wen*, however, in which it represented something more than polite letters and aesthetic pastimes. This was the sense in which Hu Yuan was said to have spoken of *wen* as the literary expression or cultural transmission of the Way. *Wen* stood here for the highest values of the culture, for human civilization as carrying out the Way and the will of Heaven. Confucius had talked of his own mission in the world as bound up with "this culture" (*siwen*), and many Neo-Confucians likewise took it as their personal responsibility in life to make the Way manifest in the world through "this culture."[58]

By so doing, the Neo-Confucians, as an educated elite in relatively prosperous times, dedicated their new affluence and leisure to serious purposes, attempting to convert it into a higher form of culture and a better life for the people. This they did in ways characteristic of their class and time, and in particular with a sense of vocation as leaders in the society who felt keenly their responsibility to meet the social and cultural crises of their time. Led by this humane concern, they sought to revitalize tradition so that, instead of merely perpetuating antiquarian studies, it would express the highest aspirations of the Confucian elite as bearers of that culture in the Song.[59]

From this point of view, we may say that "learning for the sake of one's self" as the substantive pursuit of the Neo-Confucian was not only revealed through his functional roles in society (*yong*) but in how he related to his tradition, to his culture (*wen*), and, increasingly, to the Way (*dao*) as representing the highest values of that culture. It may well be that in all major ethicoreligious traditions some relation to the scriptures is important to the process of self-discovery and self-definition and that St. Augustine's *tolle lege* ("take up and read")—or, by contrast, the Zen master's tearing up of the scriptures—are paradigmatic acts of almost universal significance. Nevertheless, there has probably been no other tradition so clearly committed to scholarship as the Confucian, and in the absence of sacerdotal, pastoral, or monastic activities, it was book learning and literary activity that became for the Confucian even more central tasks than for the Christian, Jew, Muslim, Hindu, or Buddhist. Accordingly, it is in this cultural context that we must look for the defining characteristics of Neo-Confucian personhood or individualism.

In the writings and conversations of the Cheng brothers and Zhu Xi, this relation between the self and the Way as tradition is a central topic of discussion. Generally speaking, equal emphasis is put on (1) the need to learn the Way through the classics and histories and (2) the importance of some personal engagement and live interaction with the mind of the sages revealed therein. One of these without the other will not do. Cheng Yi and Zhu were quite methodical in their approach to the subject, and Zhu, in his *Questions and Answers on the Mean* (*Zhongyong huowen*), left a succinct statement of the procedure to be followed. It pertains to the same passage referred to in his *Articles of the White Deer Grotto Academy*—namely, the order among "studying, inquiring, thinking, sifting, and practicing":

> After one has studied extensively, he can have the principles of all things before him. He can therefore examine them and compare them to get the right questions to ask. Then, as he inquires carefully, his teachers and friends will wholeheartedly engage in give-and-take with him, and he will begin to think. As he thinks carefully his thoughts will be refined and free from impurities. Thus there is something in it he can get for himself (*you suo zide*). He can now sift what he has acquired. As he sifts clearly, he can

make his decisions without making a mistake. He can therefore be free from doubts and put his thoughts into action. As he practices earnestly, all that he has achieved from studying, inquiring, thinking and sifting will become concrete demonstrations and will no longer remain empty words.[60]

The same theme is repeated many times by Cheng Yi. He says: "Students must get it for themselves (*zide*). The Six Classics are vast and extensive. At first it is difficult to understand them completely. As students find their own way, each establishes his own gate, and then returns home to conduct his inquiries himself."[61]

In the learning process, a problem could arise too if the teacher did not take into account the need for the young to find their own way into the classics rather than accept the readymade interpretations of others:

Explaining books orally is certainly not the intention of the ancients, for it would make people superficial. A student should think deeply and accumulate his thoughts, cultivating himself in a leisurely way so that he may get it for himself (*zide*). Today a book may be explained in just one day. This is merely to teach people to be superficial.[62]

Study of the classics must be an intensely personal experience if it is to fulfill the purpose of learning the Way, which demands of the individual that he himself activate or advance the Way:

The classics are vehicles of the Way. To recite the words and explain the meanings of the terms without attaining the Way is to render them useless dregs. . . . I hope you will seek the Way through the classics. If you make more and more effort, some day you will see something lofty before you. Unconsciously you will start dancing with your hands and your feet. Then even without further effort you will not be able to keep yourself from going on.[63]

Here, and in numerous other passages from Cheng Yi's writings, the affective aspects of the learning process are greatly stressed. One should be moved by learning and not left unaffected. It is true that

Cheng Yi also sanctioned the practice of quiet-sitting as a means of achieving tranquility, composure, or "reverence," as he would most prefer to put it. But the aim here was to quiet down or curb only selfish desires while directing active emotions toward unselfish ends. The reverent man would not be lifeless and unfeeling; on a basic level, he would be experiencing the "self-enjoyment" (*ziqian*) that goes with "making the will sincere" (*Great Learning* 6); on a higher level, his affective nature would be fully engaged in the pursuit of sagehood. Study of the classics, then, if approached without ulterior motives or self-seeking expectations, should be inspirational and uplifting. It should induce a conversion experience, a natural exhilaration of the spirit over the prospect of being able to improve and transform oneself into a sage, a worthy, or a noble man. Thus Cheng Yi says of reading the *Analects*: "If, after having studied it, one is still the same person as before, he has not really studied it."[64] And again, disapprovingly, "There are people who have read the *Analects* without anything happening to them. There are others who are happy after having understood a sentence or two. There are others who, having read the book, love it. And there are those who, having read it, unconsciously dance with their hands and feet."[65]

To achieve this latter result, one must approach study of the classics through the spirit and the affections as well as the intellect. One must "taste" or "savor" the essential flavor of the texts and assimilate the nourishment that true wisdom provides to the mind-and-heart.[66] Necessary though it is to understand the meaning of the words in the text, if one tries to explain classics like the *Analects* and *Mencius* literally, he will not get the full meaning, which often goes beyond the spoken word.[67] To apprehend and appreciate this, deep thought and reflection are necessary. Yet at the same time, one should try to formulate his own understanding in words because the process of articulating one's thoughts in words helps to clarify them. "Whenever in our effort at thinking we come to something that cannot be expressed in words, we must think it over carefully and sift it again and again."[68]

Learning so understood as both active and reflective, affective as well as cognitive, also had both its critical and creative sides. It called on the scholar to doubt and to question received tradition as the prerequisite for giving full assent and active implementation to his understanding of the Way. Cheng Yi said, "The student must first of all know how to doubt,"[69] and Zhang Zai (1020–1077) also asserted the need to take a fresh approach to things: "Whenever there is any doubt about moral principles, one should wipe out his old views so new ideas will come."[70] Zhu Xi called this a "wonderful method," cited it in his methodological discussions with Lu Zuqian, and quoted it in *Things at Hand.*[71] Morohashi Tetsuji, in his monumental study of the Song school, also cited this skeptical method as a hallmark of the Neo-Confucian approach to learning.[72]

This questioning attitude toward received tradition was a major feature of Song learning as a whole. A skeptical attitude toward the "classical" learning of the Han and Tang underlay the Song scholars' wholesale reinterpretation and reformulation of the classics.[73] It was also a notable feature of Song historical studies from Ouyang Xiu (1007–1072) down to Ma Duanlin (1254–1325).[74] Further, as the more extroverted outlook of the Northern Song turned inward and as dissatisfaction with the immediate past and present became increasingly directed toward self-awareness and self-reform as the precondition for social reform, this questioning attitude and critical method became deeply embedded in the new Cheng-Zhu tradition of self-cultivation. Influential texts of the new movement like *Things at Hand* and the Four Books as formulated by Zhu Xi gave explicit encouragement to this self-conscious, critical attitude[75] and concretely exemplified that spirit at work in classical studies. Thus, later scholars who studied these texts would find their attention drawn to the self-conscious mind and its autonomous operations. In the view of Cheng Yi and Zhu Xi, nothing would substitute for the individual's inner reflection on the scriptures and reevaluation of it in the silence of his own mind.

No less importantly, along with this questioning attitude went a positive and creative approach that drew something new from its reassessment of the old. True, the established convention called for scholars to follow the example of Confucius, who had professed to be a transmitter rather than a creator. In such a tradition, complete originality would have been seen as a dubious merit. Nevertheless, while making no claims for themselves, Cheng Yi and Zhu Xi freely credited other Song scholars with making their own distinctive contributions.

Cheng Yi greatly admired Zhang Zai's *Western Inscription* (*Ximing*), with its eloquent expression of a Confucian natural mysticism, affirming man's kinship with all creation. Praising its purity and sublimity, his older brother Cheng Hao had said it was unmatched by any other teaching since the Qin and Han, and Cheng Yi went further to say that it revealed what earlier sages had never taught. As an original contribution he likened it in importance to Mencius's doctrines of the goodness of human nature and the nourishing of the dynamic power within the self that reaches out to all creation.[76]

Zhu Xi, in his turn, credited Cheng Yi with "discovering" or bringing to light (*faming*) the doctrine of the physical nature of man, which he regarded as a major contribution to the Confucian school. "With his disclosure of the doctrine of the physical nature, none of the other theories of human nature would hold water."[77] Zhu also gave credit to Cheng Yi for his new interpretation of the *Book of Changes*. Modern scholars have seen this interpretation as an unwarranted construction of Cheng's own devising, and Zhu himself acknowledged that it was not in accord with the original meaning of the *Changes*, but this did not deter him from affirming its high value.[78] Similarly, Zhu considered Cheng Yi to have developed a Confucian doctrine and discipline of the mind, in response to Buddhism, where nothing of the sort had existed before.[79] And in the generation after Zhu Xi, his follower Zhen Dexiu credited Cheng Hao with developing the philosophy of principle out of his own brilliance of mind; the classics themselves had barely mentioned it in an obscure passage of the *Record of Rites*.[80]

Small wonder, then, that Ming and Qing critics would look back on this as a revolutionary period in scholarly thought. "Classical scholarship," said the editors of the *Imperial Library Catalogue*, "as it came down from the Han, underwent a complete change in the Song."[81] And the Ming writer Zhu Yunming (1461–1527) castigated members of the Cheng-Zhu school for their claim to have rediscovered the true meaning of the classics lost in the Han and Tang and for having set themselves up as the private custodians of a supposedly new revelation without acknowledging their actual indebtedness to Han and Tang scholarship.[82]

From these examples and others given earlier, it can be seen that the Cheng-Zhu school and especially Zhu Xi saw tradition as dynamic rather than static, a living growth and not a fixed monument to the past. It consisted not only of truths revealed in the classics but also things brought to light (*faming*) by individual Song scholars, without whose contributions the Way would have been lost in obscurity. This view of the Way cannot be equated with the notion of progress underlying modern Western liberalism, but neither can it be minimized as a basis for affirming the value of individual creativity.

Later scholars, especially in the eighteenth, nineteenth, and early twentieth centuries, tended to view the Song learning historically and critically and had little sympathy with the liberties taken by Neo-Confucians in reinterpreting the classics. In their view, the new constructions of the Song masters only adulterated the supposedly pure legacy of Confucius and Mencius. But in the Song, a purely critical or skeptical approach would not have sufficed. The Cheng brothers and Zhu Xi, in an age of renewal and reconstruction, had larger needs and purposes in mind. To doubt and to adopt the questioning attitude was only the starting point, not the end, of scholarly inquiry. Repeatedly they expressed their belief in a method that would lead to some personal or social result—not perhaps to a conclusion that was final and fixed forever but to one that would give one a goal in life and enable one to make one's own contribution to the advancement of the Way. We have seen this already in Zhu Xi's *Articles* and in Cheng Yi's explanation of the learning process. In the passage cited earlier from Zhang Zai, he does not stop simply at "wiping out old ideas" but says that "new ideas will come." "Moreover, one should seek the help of friends. Each day one discusses things with friends, each day one's ideas will become different. One must discuss things and deliberate like this every day. In time one will naturally feel that one has advanced."[83]

In this passage and in others cited earlier, the individual was seen to make his personal contribution in the context of a thoughtful interaction with the classics and in a free exchange with colleagues. Thus the individual's distinctive contribution was recognized and encouraged, yet it was not for the sake of novelty or innovation or because being different was valued in itself but because the individual was expected to develop his own talent and offer his own share to the common scholarly enterprise. A delicate balance was to be maintained between self and tradition, individuality and collegiality.

With these important qualifications, then, we may be entitled to speak of a kind of individualism expressing itself in the cultural activities of the Neo-Confucian scholar, and we may observe certain values associated with the autonomous mind—self-consciousness, critical awareness, creative thought, independent effort and judgment—finding their way into the basic texts of the school. As I discussed earlier, perhaps "personalism" is a better way to describe it.

This attention to the individual and the conscious celebration of his creative faculties is most noticeable in the cultural sphere, where it would seem to be a natural outgrowth of the high degree of cultural activity sustained in the Song by the scholar-official class and by the classes supporting them. In other words, the types of personalism asserted here reflect the special status and functions of the scholar-official class, the general affluence of the times, the influence of a religious atmosphere pervaded by the Buddhist preoccupation with the problem of self, and the interaction of these with a humanistic tradition already disposed to value highly the cultural and political contributions of the individual scholar.

In conclusion—and in relation to our larger theme—we may note the similarity of these developments to characteristics of Western liberalism described by Gilbert Murray, who saw it not just as a modern political attitude but as a humane tradition linking classical antiquity to the present—the product of a leisured and in some ways privileged class, working "to extend its own privileges to wider and wider circles," aiming at freedom of thought and discussion, and equally pursuing the free exercise of individual conscience and promotion of the common good.[84]

In the Chinese case, there would be a question whether this individualism or personalism, as the product of a privileged elite, would serve simply to inflate the scholar-official's sense of self-importance or whether an active effort would be made to share these values more widely. This is a question on which some light is shed by developments in the Ming.

11

Zhu Xi's Educational Program

Zhu Xi thought of himself, like Confucius, as the bearer of tradition rather than as the founder or originator of a new doctrine. Content with the modest role of teacher and transmitter, he was a scholar who devoted himself to editing texts, compiling anthologies, and writing commentaries on the classics instead of writing treatises to advance his own theories. Indeed, by modern Western standards he would probably have to be put down as the next thing to a "mere translator." Yet, his own modesty notwithstanding, to Zhu, as to Confucius earlier, must go the credit of instigating a virtual revolution in education.

Confucius, for his part, accomplished this mainly by the force of his personal example as teacher and scholar, reflected in the *Analects* (a book *about* him, not *by* him) and in a personal following that tried to emulate his example. On this score, Zhu Xi, too, as a teacher was hardly less magisterial or commanding in influence, but if I identify him more particularly as an educator, it is because, besides being a great teacher devoted to learning, he was a thinker and an official concerned with the process of education and its institutionalization. For the title of educator in this sense Zhu qualifies by virtue of his extraordinary contributions to defining a new Confucian curriculum and a new educational process, seen in both the official schools and private academies that came to prevail throughout East Asia in the second millennium.

Zhu's aims in education, which gave that process a clear direction, coherent method, and substantial content, projected a comprehensive vision on his part. To call him visionary would no doubt be overstating or misrepresenting the case, if by this one meant looking into the future and anticipating what its new requirements would be. For Zhu, it was enough simply to face the present and its compelling needs without speculating on possibilities more remote. As he said, in stressing the need for attending to what was near at hand, "We must only proceed from what we understand in what is near to us and move from there. . . . It is like ascending steps, going from the first to the second, from the second to the third and from the third to the fourth."[1]

But if Zhu did not look to the future to redeem the past, as was often the case in the West, or put his faith in the millennium as the ultimate realization of the human struggle, he nevertheless did expect his step-by-step method to lead upward to some definite goal. This vision he put before his students and readers, offering a comprehensive view of human reality and, insofar as his reading of past and present would vouchsafe it, a human ideal to be striven for.

In this chapter, I shall try to articulate that vision and, where possible, bring out its historical significance in light of the factors that shaped his situation and defined the educational problem for him. Some of these factors Zhu himself would have been conscious of, others perhaps not. In any case, before discussing Zhu's ideas themselves, I state briefly here what I consider these factors to be. I do so only in summary form because I rely on other chapters in this volume to deal with these developments more fully.

1. The first point to note is that education, both public and private, had become a major issue in Song politics and thought well before Zhu Xi's time. It was already high on the Neo-Confucian agenda.

2. The new importance of education in the Northern Song arose in significant part from the expansion of the civil bureaucracy at the inception of the dynasty and from the increased demand this created for persons with requisite learning and skills.

3. Economic development and diversification as well as rising affluence (although perhaps regionally uneven) and increased leisure for cultural pursuits provided alternative outlets for the educated. The literati had options other than government service, and they weighed seriously the relative value and priority of the alternatives that the society and culture afforded them. Prime among these was teaching.

4. Expansion of the economy and technological advances created a wider base for the support of education, leading to an increase in the number of schools and academies. Over time, the growth of local, semiprivate academies outpaced that of public schools. With this, tensions arose, but less from rivalry between public and private endeavors than from either political pressures and literati involvement with them or resistance to state control and the distorting effects of the civil-service examinations on education.

5. Schools, especially academies (*shuyuan*), centered on teachers and collections of books. Hence the spread of printing was bound to have a significant impact on them, as on cultural activity in general. This significance is concisely stated by Carter and Goodrich in reference to the printing of the classics by Feng Dao in 953:

> The printing of the Classics was one of the forces that restored Confucian literature and teaching to the place in national and popular regard that it had held before the advent of Buddhism, and a classical renaissance followed that can be compared only to the Renaissance that came in Europe after the rediscovery of its classical literature, and that there too was aided by the invention of printing. . . . Another result of the publication of the Classics was an era of large-scale printing, both public and private, that characterized the whole of the Song dynasty.[2]

A development of such epochal proportions confronted the literati with both new opportunities for the dissemination of knowledge and new problems about how this technological change would affect the learning process. Neo-Confucians became much occupied with the nature and significance of book learning. On a wider scale, it became a question of which traditional teachings would take advantage of the new printing technology. Earlier Buddhists had been quick to do so,[3] but Chan Buddhism, the dominant form among artists and intellectuals, had declared its independence of the written word (*bu li wenzi*).[4] Two questions emerged: which of these teachings would want to reach a larger public through the use of this medium? And how would they adapt their teaching method to it? Even among Neo-Confucians there was not a single answer, but most found themselves compelled to deal with such issues as the relative importance of reading, lecturing, and discussion. "How to read books" was much discussed in the Cheng-Zhu school, and Zhu Xi's *Reading Method* (*Dushufa*) was widely disseminated. Qian Mu has said that no one contributed more to this development than did Zhu Xi—indeed, he stands out above all others.[5]

6. Song Confucians saw Buddhism and Daoism, and especially Chan, as still exerting a powerful influence on men's minds. Syncretists minimized the conflict between the Three Teachings by assigning them respective spheres of influence: Confucianism, governance; Daoism, physical culture; Buddhism, mental culture. Neo-Confucians tended to reject such formulae as too facile, on both theoretical and practical grounds. Among the latter was the educational issue: the practical impossibility of mastering three such disparate systems at once and, given the need to choose among them, the primacy of the moral imperative that claimed priority for humane learning and called for new types of scholarship to meet the increasingly complex problem of secular society.

7. At the same time, Buddhist spirituality remained a formidable challenge to Neo-Confucians, who felt a need to provide an alternative compatible with secular goals and lay life. Managing all this in one lifetime was for them clearly a matter of educational priorities.

8. Chan Buddhism had its own problems. Its masters worried about the decline of monastic discipline. Having forsworn language as an adequate means of communicating essential truth, in the Song and Yuan periods they faced a dilemma regarding the codification of monastic rules and training. In the end, leading monks compromised their own principles by compiling rules, keeping records of dialogues

and koans, and publishing them, lest authoritative traditions lapse altogether.[6] Thus, they too accommodated themselves, albeit halfheartedly, to the rising tide of printing and book learning, yet without ever addressing education as a distinct social and cultural value.

These developments touched Zhu Xi's own life and significantly affected his thought. As the son of a scholar-official, he naturally gravitated toward the same combination of scholarly activity and public service as his father. At the same time, Daoism and Chan Buddhism appealed to his religious instincts. Thus, as a young man he successfully competed in the civil-service examinations while also pursuing and actually experiencing in some vague manner a mystical enlightenment. Thereafter, searching for a way to reconcile the rival claims of scholarship, official service, and the spiritual life, he laid the problem before his teacher Li Tong.[7]

The answer, which he eventually had to work out for himself, lay in "learning for the sake of oneself." It was a Confucian answer, expressed in the language of the *Analects'* "learning for one's own sake, rather than for others'" (14:25). Zhu interpreted "learning for others" primarily in terms of the civil-service examinations and worldly success, which for him should properly be subordinated to the goal of true self-understanding. Yet the priority he gave to self-understanding in the Confucian sense represented Zhu's response also to Buddhism's insistence on giving top priority to the problem of self and no-self, or seeing one's "original face."

In *The Liberal Tradition in China*, I have discussed "learning for the sake of oneself" as the underlying theme of Zhu Xi's thought from his early years to the end of his life as a teacher.[8] In this chapter, however, I wish to distinguish between "learning" in the most general as well as the most personal sense and education as a practical, public, and institutionalized activity. In the mind of Zhu Xi, of course, the two were inseparable: education in the sense of schooling or organized instruction ought also to serve the purpose of "learning for the sake of oneself," but for my purposes here the focus will be on the public aspect.

Zhu's basic approach is made clear in the most widely disseminated of his writings—his preface and commentary to the *Great Learning*. Because later tradition followed Zhu's recommendation that the *Great*

Learning should be studied first among the canonical texts, being the gateway and guide to all learning, education in Neo-Confucian schools was almost always premised on the principles so concisely enunciated in the opening pages of that work. Here, I summarize the main points.

First, in his preface, Zhu puts forward as the basis of his educational philosophy the central Neo-Confucian doctrine of the moral nature inherent in all men, how it is affected by everyone's physical endowment (i.e., one's actual condition), and by what means the ruler should enable everyone to recover his original good nature and fulfill it.

Among relevant means, schools are most important. Zhu believed he had a model for emulation in the schools, established by the sage-kings of remote antiquity, that reached down to the smallest village and provided education for everyone from the age of eight until maturity. To modern minds, the adoption of such a system of universal education might seem an obvious course, but in Zhu's time its practicability could not be assumed. Earlier attempts to achieve it in the Song had failed, and the main factor, later cited by Mary Wright, as militating against schools in nineteenth-century China—that "the sons of peasants could seldom be spared from the fields"[9]—would have applied in the Song as well. Moreover, if economic realities and the chronic fiscal difficulties of Chinese dynasties could render such a plan unlikely to be accomplished, there were other less costly educational means to which he might have had recourse. Well-known measures were hardly uncongenial to a Confucian like Zhu: instruction in the home or through clan and community organizations, as well as the whole panoply of rituals by which "moral edification" was supposed to be achieved, especially in rural areas. Indeed, on other occasions Zhu himself had used these among the great array of persuasive means by which he would accomplish the people's uplift.

Nevertheless, in this most central of texts and most considered of arguments, Zhu puts the school system up front—not just teaching or tutoring, training in the home, official exhortation, or moral transformation through ritual observance, but quite literally and concretely the "establishment of schools" (*xuexiao zhi she*) and their operation/administration by the government (*xuexiao zhi zheng*).[10] He was not just airing a vague notion or uttering a pious hope; he was making a definite point with regard to the institutionalization of universal schooling and the commitment of resources to that end.

Second, another noteworthy feature of the educational system described in Zhu's preface is the combination of universality and particularity in its application. Because all men share the moral nature imparted by Heaven, all have a common need to perfect that nature through education. This was, according to Zhu's classical model, to be provided for the children of all under Heaven, from the king and his nobles down to the commonest of people in the smallest lane or alley. Although higher education was not similar for all but only for the more talented, these latter were again to be drawn from all ranks of society.[11]

Such being the case, there was no one without an education in those times, and of those so educated there was none who did not understand what was inherent in his individual nature or what was proper to the performance of his own duties, so that each could exert his energies to the utmost.[12]

Egalitarian though it might be with respect to education, this universalistic approach carries no necessary implication of social leveling. Zhu, like Confucius in his time, advocates equal educational opportunity but still accepts the need for a social structure and a hierarchy of authority based on merit. His point is that every individual should have the chance to realize his full human potential, given the limits of his individual endowment, situation in life, or station in society. All possess a common nature, but each has an individualized form, to be perfected by schooling and self-cultivation.

A question may arise, however, about whether this self-cultivation actually aims at an individualized result rather than at conformity to a social norm. It might be argued, for instance, that even though Zhu recognizes differences in individual capacity and disposition, the process of self-perfection is meant to bring the individual into line with some ideal type. Insofar as this might be interpreted as an idea or model external to the self to which one should measure up, practically it could mean that self-correction and self-discipline would simply subordinate one's own interest to that of the group, expressed in such terms as "subduing self and restoring rightness"(ritual decorum) (*keji fuli*) or overcoming one's own selfishness (*si*) and conforming to the common good (*gong*).

This latter dichotomy, opposing individual selfishness to the common good, was indeed a basic criterion of ethical conduct in Neo-

Confucianism, yet it has sometimes been overdrawn, as it was by early Neo-Confucians of a rigoristic bent and later by those who reacted against this ascetic extreme. The former seemed to regard any desires at all as selfish and to call for their total suppression, while the latter, on the same count, attacked Neo-Confucianism as allowing no room for individual self-expression or self-satisfaction. Enough extreme cases can be found to support this view, thus one cannot dismiss the problem of religious renunciation or even masochism as negligible for Neo-Confucianism.[13] Still, most Neo-Confucians remembered well the story of Confucius scolding Zengzi for carrying filial submission almost to the point of self-immolation: Zengzi had been weeding some melons when he accidentally cut the roots of a plant. Zengzi's father beat him for this, but when Confucius heard about it he said Zengzi should have gotten out of the way rather than submit to his father's stick. "By quietly submitting to a beating like that, you might have caused your father to kill you, and what unfilial conduct could have been worse than that!"

Zhu had in mind this reasonable and moderate view: the health and welfare of the person is primary, and human desires are good except insofar as they conflict with others' legitimate needs and wants. Like Confucius in the *Analects* (6:28), he recognized that everyone had ambitions to achieve something for himself as well as an obligation to respect that ambition in others.[14] The language Zhu uses in the passage just cited affirms as the goal of education that all should have outlets for their capacities in accordance with an understanding of both their own individual natures (*xingfen*) and their proper roles in society (*zhifen*). Here the term *xingfen* refers to the concrete, individualized nature (*xingzhi*),[15] both moral and psychophysical. Thus, for Zhu Xi's educational purposes, the individual is neither reducible simply to a social role nor wholly definable in relation to some abstract norm of conduct. He leaves room here to pursue "learning for one's own sake" as a larger reality encompassing self and others, uniting the Way within and the Way without.

It is appropriate, then, to read this passage in light of Zhu's more complete guide to self-cultivation, the *Reflections on Things at Hand* (*Jinsilu*). There Zhu quotes Cheng Hao's memorial to the emperor: "The essential training should be the way of choosing the good and cultivating the self until the whole world is transformed and brought to perfection, so that all people from the ordinary person on up can become sages."[16] Beyond this, one need only look to Zhu Xi's concluding chapter in *Things at Hand*, which is devoted to the "Dispositions of the Sages and Worthies." These "dispositions" refer to the individual natures of the sages and worthies, as does Zhu's language in the preface above, and the portraits presented are those of distinct human personalities, not totally self-effacing copies of a sagely stereotype.[17]

In Zhu's preface, the final point to be noted is how his explanation of civilization's decline since the early Zhou period fits in with his formulation of a remedy. Zhu sees the disappearance of the sage-kings and the end of virtuous rule as further aggravated by a long lapse in the teaching tradition from Mencius until the Cheng brothers in the Song. This is, of course, a view of history also set forth by Zhu in his preface to the *Mean* (*Zhongyong*), where he propounds his doctrine of the "succession to the Way" (*daotong*) and highlights the heroic role of the Cheng brothers in rediscovering the true Way.[18] Zhu reiterates the myth of the heroic teacher here to underscore the need for true education as the key to systematic reform. In dark contrast to the shining light of the Cheng brothers, Zhu paints a vivid picture of the corrupting effects of his twin nemeses: Buddhism and Daoism on the one extreme and utilitarianism on the other. The latter corrupted mankind by its pragmatism and opportunism, pursuing power and material gain at the expense of moral principles. Buddhism and Daoism, at the opposite extreme, were too transcendental and not down to earth; indeed, Zhu acknowledges that for loftiness they exceeded even the *Great Learning* yet lacked its moral solidity and practical method.[19] In this situation, only the Cheng brothers reaffirmed the inherent goodness of man's nature and recognized the true worth of the *Great Learning* as the classic par excellence, unequaled for its combination of principle and practicality in the nurturing of man's moral nature.

Throughout Zhu's preface and commentary to the *Great Learning*, this systematic, concrete, and detailed approach to learning is constantly reiterated. He believes that without specific structures and orderly procedures there can be no effective resistance to the moral erosion of Buddhist "expediency" and Daoist nihilism, which have left mankind exposed to the opportunism of power seekers and defenseless against the exploitation of autocrats.

This aim—to combine moral principles with well-defined means of instruction—leads Zhu to insist on having a school system and a sequential curriculum. Not simply because Zhu as a traditionalist reveres the classics does he find merit in a system such as was spelled out in the *Record of Rites* (*Liji*); there it says that "according to the system of ancient instruction, for the families of a hamlet there was the village school (*shu*), for a neighborhood there was the community center (*xiang*), for the larger districts there was the institute of retired scholars (*xu*), and in the capital there was the college (*xue*)."[20] Nor simply as a loyal follower of Cheng Hao does he appreciate the orderly sequence of priorities embodied in the latter's program of universal education, as quoted in *Reflections on Things at Hand*:

> Master Mingdao [Cheng Hao] said to the emperor: The foundation of government is to make public morals and customs correct and to get virtuous and talented men to serve. The first thing to do is politely to order the virtuous scholars among close attendants, and all officers, to search wholeheartedly for those whose moral characters and achievements are adequate as examples and teachers, and then seek out those who are eager to learn and have good ability and fine character. Invite them, appoint them, and have them courteously sent to the capital where they will gather. Let them discuss correct learning with each other from morning to evening. The moral principles to be taught must be based on human relations and must make clear the principles of things. The teaching, from the elementary training of sweeping the floor and answering questions on up, must consist in the cultivation of filial piety, brotherly respect, loyalty, and faithfulness, as well as proper behavior and the qualities derived from ceremonies and music. There must be a proper pace and order in inducing, leading, arousing and gradually shaping the students and in bringing their character to completion. The essential training should be the way of choosing the good and cultivating the self until the whole world is transformed and brought to perfection so that all people from the ordinary person up can become sages. Those

whose learning and conduct completely fulfill this standard are people of perfect virtue. Select the students of ability and intelligence, who are capable of advancing toward the good, to study under them every day. Choose graduates of brilliant learning and high virtue to be professors at the Imperial University and send the rest to teach in various parts of the country.

In selecting students, let county schools promote them to prefecture schools, and let prefecture schools present them, as though presenting guests, to the Imperial University. Let them come together and be taught there. Each year the superior graduates will be recommended to the government for service.

All scholars are to be chosen to serve on the basis of their correct and pure character, their filial piety and brotherly respect demonstrated at home, their sense of integrity, shame, propriety, and humility, their intelligence and scholarship, and their understanding of the principles of government.[21]

Both examples speak to Zhu's sense of the need to bring order, substance, and process into a society seen as shapeless and without moorings, drifting aimlessly between anarchic nihilism and coercive despotism.

In the opening lines of his commentary on the *Great Learning*, Zhu sounds the same keynote when he quotes Cheng Yi to the effect that only owing to the survival of this can one know the successive steps (*zidi*) and procedures by which the ancients pursued learning. Zhu then proceeds to explain the three guiding principles (*sangangling*) of the *Great Learning*. Here, too, structure and direction are emphasized: *gang* represent the mainstays of a net, and *ling* guidance or direction. The first of these guiding principles is to "clarify or manifest bright virtue," referring to the moral nature in all men, which is inherently clear and luminous but must be cleansed of obscurations if it is to be made fully manifest. The potential is innate but must be actively developed; the process is one of bringing out from within something that has its own life and luminosity rather than imposing or imprinting on it something from without. This Zhu calls the "learning of the great man" (*daren*), which has the ordinary meaning of "adult" but here suggests the fullness of self-development and the grandeur of the moral nature brought to its perfection.

The second guiding principle is to "renew the people" (*xinmin*), that is, to assist others to manifest their moral natures through self-cultivation. Here Zhu follows Cheng Yi in substituting the word *xin* (renew) for *qin* (to love, to befriend the people). Zhu specifically refers to this as "reforming the old," emphasizing active reform and renovation instead of expressing simple goodwill and generous sentiments. The political implication is that the ruler's self-cultivation necessarily involves him in helping the people renew themselves through education.

Third among the guiding principles is "resting or abiding in the highest good"; this means that, by clarifying bright virtue (manifesting the moral nature) and renewing the people, one should reach the point of ultimate goodness and stay there. "Resting in the highest good," Zhu explains, means meeting both the moral requirements of each situation and affair and fulfilling one's capability for moral action. At this point, one can rest content. Peace of mind has been achieved by satisfying one's conscience, not by transcending the moral sphere.

If I have discounted earlier any idea that Zhu Xi had millenarian expectations or looked to the future to redeem the present, it was partly in view of these three guiding principles. The impulse to renew and reform is there, but it is enough to achieve what is possible in one's own life situation and within one's own limited capabilities. "To be humane is to accept being human" (*renzhe an ren*), as Confucius said (*Analects* 4:2). However, Zhu Xi's underscoring of these three principles at the outset of his commentary has impressed on later generations the need for active renewal and reform, first with respect to oneself and then out of concern for others.

From there, the text and Zhu proceed to discuss sequential processes, ends and means, "roots and branches," and priorities in learning. Of these, the best known are the "Eight Steps" (*ba tiaomu*: items, specifications), consisting of successive steps in self-cultivation and involving a range of cognitive, moral, and social operations. These are probably the most discussed subjects in Neo-Confucian literature, but I shall confine myself to points that have particular relevance to education, differentiated above from learning in general. Much of the *Great Learning*'s text is less systematic than Zhu Xi would have liked, and he, like Cheng Yi, was at pains to rearrange it, but his interlinear note explaining this reveals Zhu's preoccupation with logical order and step-by-step procedures: "The text of the commentary [by Zengzi] is drawn at random from classics and commentaries in no particular order. It appears to be unsystematic, but nevertheless there is an underlying thread. It is most precise and detailed as regards its different levels and successive phases."[22]

Zhu draws particular attention to the first steps in the process of self-cultivation by adding a special note on *gewu zhizhi*, most commonly rendered as "the investigation of things and extension of knowledge." Zhu's commentary on these terms, however, should alert us to a possible misunderstanding. He says that *ge* (investigation) means to reach or arrive, and he indicates that in this process principles in the mind are brought into contact with principles in things, that is, made present to one another. Because our word "knowledge" is generally understood in objective terms as things known, it is well to note that in Chinese *zhi* makes no distinction between knowing and what is known. Zhu Xi comments: "*zhi* is to recognize or be conscious of, to project one's knowing, hoping that one's knowing would be fully employed (literally exhausted)."[23] The same passage can be read with *zhi* translated as "knowledge" instead of "knowing." But in that case, it should not be understood as in "a body of knowledge," for to do so would set an impossible goal for "exhausting" learning: one's knowledge would have to be complete. One would need to know everything, instead of simply developing one's learning capacity to the full.

This is a point of some significance for education because it bears on the questions of book learning and the pursuit of empirical research. To what extent should education, in the form of the reading and discussion of books, be conceived as the assimilation of principles *from* things or as the accumulation of factual knowledge? The issue has been read both ways by later Neo-Confucians, some of whom have stressed objective study and others active experiential learning. Zhu seems to have allowed for both in his special note on *gewu zhizhi*:

> "The extension of knowing lies in the investigation of things" means that if we wish to extend our knowing, it consists in fathoming the principle of any thing or affair we come into contact with, for the intelligent mind of man always has the capacity to know and the things of this world all have their principles,

but if a principle remains unfathomed, one's knowing is not fully exercised. Hence the initial teaching of the Great Learning insists that the learner, as he comes upon the things of this world, must proceed from principles already known and further explore them until he reaches the limit. After exerting himself for a long time, one day he will experience a breakthrough to integral comprehension. Then the qualities of all things, whether internal or external, refined or coarse, will all be apprehended and the mind, in its whole substance and great functioning, will be fully enlightened. This is "things [having been] investigated." This is knowing having reached [its limit].[24]

In this passage, I have translated *zhi* as "knowing" rather than "knowledge" because, even allowing for the ambiguity of the original Chinese, to render it as knowledge in the sense of something known produces an absurdity and flies in the face of other testimony from Zhu. Concerning this text, Liu Shuxian has recently observed:

When perfection of knowledge is achieved, does Zhu Xi mean that the mind actually possesses empirical knowledge of all things? This is an absurd position, as Zhu Xi freely admits that there are things even the sage does not know. Hence what Zhu Xi means is that when the mind is pure and clear without the obstructions of selfish desires, it cannot fail to grasp the principles of things and respond freely to things as concrete situations call for, and as the human mind is united with the mind of Heaven, it does not exclude anything from its scope and is in that sense all-inclusive. Moreover, since the principles are none other than manifestations of one single Principle, the realization of the substance and function of this Principle will enable the mind to unfold the rich content of the Principle without +any hindrances.[25]

As Liu suggests, Zhu Xi seems to be saying that if one pursues study and reflection long enough, one's understanding will be enlarged to the point of overcoming any sense of things or others being foreign to oneself, and the student will have achieved an empathetic insight that is both integral and comprehensive (*guantong*). One would have developed a capacity for learning and knowing to its limit and thus would be equally at home with oneself and one's world. At this point, "learning for the sake of oneself" would have overcome all distinction between self and others.

THE CONDUCT OF SCHOOLS

From the preceding discussion of Zhu Xi's aims in education, three main points emerge: (1) the need for a school system reaching the whole population, not just individualized instruction for the select few; (2) the need for a well-defined curriculum, adapted at each stage to the student's level of comprehension, maturity, and readiness to take on larger responsibilities; and (3) the importance of having a goal to the educational process that offers the individual a suitable model of the whole person, developing one's potential and exercising one's full capabilities, as expressed in the phrase "the whole substance and its great functioning" (*quanti dayong*).

I will now discuss the content and conduct of education as prescribed by Zhu Xi in different institutional settings. I will try to elicit general principles from those documents most often cited in the later tradition as authoritative guides: Zhu's *Reflection on Things at Hand* (*Jinsilu*), his *Articles of the White Deer Grotto Academy* (*Bailudong shuyuan jieshi*), his comments on the *School Rules of Messrs. Cheng and Dong* (*Cheng Dong er xiansheng xueze*), and finally his "Personal Proposals for Schools and Official Recruitment" (*Xuexiao gongju siyi*). Zhu Xi discussed learning, teaching, and schooling on many occasions, and a rich body of materials is available for the study of these aspects of his thought. But I believe the texts just cited have been most influential in Neo-Confucian schools of later times.

Reflections on Things at Hand (*Jinsilu*) centers on the self. It works out from there, through the wider sphere of social activity, toward the goal of learning to become a sage or worthy. In this it follows the basic pattern of Zhu Xi's three guiding principles: from self-cultivation, through social renovation, to attaining and resting in the highest good.

Although it has much to say about different aspects of learning, it has surprisingly little to say about schools or how they should be conducted, no doubt because Zhu Xi conceived of schooling essentially in terms of the teacher-student relationship. One can indeed say that the work exudes the atmosphere of the school; much of the text has the quality of teacher-student dialogue and conveys the impression that a scholastic tradition—a disciplined dialogue over the generations—is being perpetuated.

Nevertheless, only the brief eleventh chapter is devoted to teaching, and that is almost wholly given to the manner of instruction, not to defining a curriculum or conducting a school. I emphasize the "manner" here, not "methods," because most of what Zhu presents in this chapter concerns the example set by the teacher or the nature of the student's response to instruction rather than specific techniques of pedagogy. For Zhu, personal inspiration and motivation counted most, with more emphasis on student initiative than on how the teacher would work on or for him. With the depersonalizing and dehumanizing of education in the modern world, it may be refreshing to see how much Zhu emphasizes the personal and the human, but it may also leave one wondering about the gap between cultivation of the person and the conduct of the school system Zhu Xi had advocated.

There are, however, two exceptions to this generalization in *Things at Hand*. One refers to the organization of his school by Hu Yuan, the tenth-century master who became much admired for his combination of classical scholarship and practical studies. Supposedly, he set up two halls, one for interpreting the classics and the other for handling practical affairs.[26] This model is also cited in Zhu's *Elementary Learning (Xiaoxue)*, another highly influential text. In *Things at Hand*, Zhu quotes Cheng Hao:

When Hu Anding (Hu Yuan) was in Huzhou (in Zhejiang province), he set up a hall to study the way of government. When students wanted to understand the way of government, the matter would be discussed here, the discussion including such things as governing the people, managing the army, river conservation and mathematics. He once said that Liu Yi [1017–1086, a student of Hu][27] was an expert in river conservation, repeatedly served in government, and in all cases achieved merit in river conservation.[28]

In the *Collected Commentaries on the Jinsilu* (*Jinsilu jizhu*), Zhu is quoted in reference to this passage as giving Hu Yuan more credit for his breadth of mind and range of interests than for his precise command of technical subjects.[29] Nevertheless, the citing here, and in the *Elementary Learning* of Hu's program, with its division of studies between the humanities and technical subjects of social relevance, gave such a combination of studies the imprimatur of Zhu Xi. Moreover, the citing of Liu Yi with approval as a competent technician lent weight and respectability to such studies. In principle, such an arrangement was acceptable, even if in practice the same balance was not always maintained, with study of the classics clearly predominating among Neo-Confucians.

The second reference to actual schooling in *Things at Hand* comes in Cheng Hao's memorial, quoted earlier. Therein one finds specific reference to a school system, a distinction between elementary and advanced education, and a combination of moral and intellectual training. Significantly, however, education is for him closely linked to training officials; witness the inclusion of this memorial in the section of *Things at Hand* dealing with systems and institutions (i.e., basic governmental institutions), not with teaching, as if to emphasize education's political importance.[30] Idealistic as Cheng Hao tends to be, he sees the same values and interests as shared by all in human society; it does not occur to him that there might be any incompatibility in the schools' serving both government recruiting and general education. For him, as for most Neo-Confucians of his age, it was simply a question of converting the ruler to sagely wisdom and putting his power to humane uses through education. The idea of a separation of functions or countervailing power as between state and school was hardly thinkable at this time, although Huang Zongxi came close to it in the seventeenth century. There was only the implicit threat, if persuasion failed to gain agreement in principle between ruler and minister, of the Neo-Confucian's scruples demanding his nonparticipation in, or withdrawal from, the process.

In the Yuan period, when the issue of whether the civil-service examinations should be resumed was debated at the Mongol court, for the leading Neo-Confucian classicist Wu Cheng (1249–1333) the question was not how the bureaucratic state could be kept out of the schools but how the schools could prepare and qualify candidates for government service better than the examinations did.[31] At that time, Wu cited Hu Yuan, Cheng Hao, and Zhu Xi for their views on the school curriculum. Although one cannot be sure of his sources, Wu may well have been prompted by these excerpts about Hu and Cheng in *Things at Hand*.[32]

For Zhu Xi's views on the content of education in the schools, I turn first to his *Articles of the White Deer Grotto Academy*, so often cited as a basic charter by later Neo-Confucian academies. At the risk of repeating what will already be well known to many readers, I cite these articles or precepts for ready reference:

Affection between parent and child;
Righteousness between ruler and subject;
Differentiation between husband and wife;
Precedence between elder and younger;
Trust between friends.

The above are the items of the Five Teachings, that is, the very teachings that Yao and Shun commanded Xie reverently to propagate as minister of education. For those who engage in learning, these are all they need to learn. As to the proper procedure for study, there are also five items, as follows:

Study extensively, inquire carefully, ponder thoroughly, sift clearly, and practice earnestly.

The above is the proper sequence for the pursuit of learning. Study, inquiry, pondering, and sifting are for fathoming principle to the utmost. As to earnest practice, there are also essential elements at each stage from personal cultivation to the handling of affairs and dealing with people, as separately listed below:

> Be faithful and true to your words and firm and sincere in conduct. Curb your anger and restrain your lust; turn to the good and correct your errors.

The above are the essentials of personal cultivation.

> Be true to moral principles and do not scheme for profit; illuminate [exemplify] the Way and do not calculate the advantages [for oneself].

The above are the essentials for handling affairs.

> Do not do to others what you would not want them to do to you. When in your conduct you are unable to succeed, reflect and look [for the cause] within yourself.[33]

The significant feature of these rather prosaic articles is their attention to the basic moral and intellectual virtues applicable to one's conduct of personal life, human relations, and public affairs. Considered as the most general aims of the school, they focus on fundamental human values rather than on authority, commandments, or disciplinary rules.

Note, however, the political context of the *locus classicus* cited in the second part, that is, the Five Teachings that Yao and Shun had propagated by the minister of education, which were all one needed to learn. This makes it difficult for Confucians to conceive of an ideal state of affairs in which political and intellectual authority would be separated. To modern minds, these precepts may sound quaint, if not archaic, vague, and platitudinous. But Zhu, while consciously striving for simplicity to avoid a kind of legalistic overdetermination, had a definite structure in mind, with precise sequences, categories, and numbered sets for ease of retention or recollection by the student. At the risk of some repetition with chapter 9, I quote two relevant passages from *The Liberal Tradition in China*, I wrote:

> The social functions addressed in the first set of "Articles" give way in the second set to operations that are more intellectual and

reflect the particular preoccupations of the Song scholar. One cannot say that they lack the general human relevance of the moral dicta or would be inappropriate in most human situations, yet the atmosphere of the school prevails; it would be hard to imagine peasants having much opportunity to "study," "inquire," "ponder," and "sift" in the fashion Zhu suggests.[34]

For students, however, one could hardly find a more pithy statement of the essential values and procedures governing scholarly inquiry and reflective thought—the critical temper at work in the service of humane studies. Zhu believed so deeply, indeed, in having the student develop his own capacity to learn, weigh, and judge for himself that he encouraged the application of them even to the classics and the precepts he himself was recommending:

[I, Zhu] have observed that the sages and worthies of antiquity taught people to pursue learning with one intention only, which is to make students understand the meaning of moral principle through discussion, so that they can cultivate their own persons and then extend it to others. The sages and worthies did not wish them merely to engage in memorizing texts or in composing poetry and essays as a means of gaining fame or seeking office. Students today obviously do the contrary [to what the sages and worthies intended]. The methods that the sages and worthies employed in teaching people are all found in the Classics. Dedicated scholars should by all means read them frequently, ponder them deeply and then inquire into them and sift them.[35]

I have already spoken of this approach to learning as a kind of voluntarism that respects the essential autonomy of the self in weighing and sifting whatever is to be learned. That is not, to be sure, a radical autonomy; it does not presuppose a completely free and independent self standing in opposition to all else, but it conceives of it as engaged in a creative interaction with others, in keeping with the humaneness of man's essential nature. Nor, if one is inclined to see this voluntarism as opposed to authoritarianism, should one misconstrue the nature of authority here. Zhu shares the traditional Confucian belief in the need of men, and especially the young, for teachers, leaders, and models to serve as edifying examples. To provide the latter kind of valid authority figure, so as not to leave the young without inspirational guidance or cautionary example, is a most serious responsibility for Zhu Xi. Yet he is opposed to the coercive imposition of authority, whether in learning or politics.

This essential spirit is conveyed in the conclusion of the postscript to the "Article" discussed above:

> If you understand the necessity for principles and accept the need to take responsibility oneself for seeing that they are so, then what need will there be to wait for someone else to set up such contrivances as rules and prohibitions for one to follow? In recent ages regulations have been instituted in schools, and students have been treated in a shallow manner. This method of making regulations does not at all conform with the intention of the ancients. Therefore I shall not now try to put them into effect in this lecture hall. Rather I have specifically selected all the essential principles that the sages and the worthies used in teaching people how to pursue learning; I have listed them as above one by one and posted them on the crossbar over the gate. You, sirs, should discuss them with one another, follow them, and take personal responsibility for their observance. Then in whatever a man should be cautious or careful about in thought, word or deed, he will certainly be more demanding of himself than he would be the other way [of complying with regulations]. If you do otherwise or even reject what I have said, then the "regulations" others talk about will have to take over and in no way can they be dispensed with. You, sirs, please think this over.[36]

Zhu's disavowal of rules here is clearly not total. It would be best to dispense with prohibitions if the situation can be managed by more constructive means, but resort may well be had to rules if the alternative is disorder and destruction. This is in keeping with Zhu's consistent position on the maintenance of order in society: the guidance of rites is preferable to the restraints of law, but the latter must be invoked if rites are not respected.

In Zhu Xi's own lifetime, this question arose when he was asked to endorse the *School Rules of Messrs. Cheng and Dong* (*Cheng Dong er Xiansheng xueze*). These rules, devised by two scholars whom Zhu personally respected,[37] prescribed a school routine and conduct for which the term "rules of decorum" would be more appropriate than any term suggesting a penal code; in fact, the *ze* in the title could just as well be read as "governing principles" or "norms" instead of "rules." Its contents include many dos and don'ts, but there is no mention of punishment stronger than the following: "Choose [to associate with] those who are diligent and careful, deal with them correctly and treat them with forbearance. If someone errs in small matters, admonish him; if in more serious, make it known to the headmaster. If, when punished, he does not reform, all should ask for the headmaster to dismiss him. No one can be allowed simply to have his own way."[38]

In commenting on these rules of school decorum in 1187, Zhu Xi averred that since time immemorial there had been a need for exemplary models and methods in the education of the young, especially in village and clan schools. In preparing this text, says Zhu, Messrs. Cheng and Dong intended the rules for the edification and "renovation" of the children of their fellow villagers. This, he says, fulfills the original intention of the ancients' elementary education and should prove useful to teachers in local schools as a guide for their students. So doing, one might hope to see again in the present, as in antiquity, progress in the accomplishment of learning by the young and fullness of virtue in those of mature years.[39]

Zhu Xi is careful to describe these prescriptions as exemplary models or methods (*fa*) and not as regulations (*gui*). Later, in 1258, the scholar Rao Lu joined Zhu's *Articles of the White Deer Grotto Academy* and the *School Rules of Messrs. Cheng and Dong* as complementary manuals—"one to set forth the broad aims of education which human learning should strive to fulfill, and the other to define the constant norms of behavior to be observed in the day-to-day life of the group."[40]

These two guides, says Rao, represent the essential methods for fulfilling the original intent of Great Learning and Elementary Learning. "If the student can carry on in this manner, then root and branch will be mutually supportive, inner and outer will sustain and nourish each other, and the method for entering upon the Way will be complete."[41]

Thus does Rao express his enthusiasm for a total and balanced plan of education, while noting in conclusion that this is to be differentiated from what today are called "regulations" (*gui*), which Zhu Xi had refused to enact at the White Deer Grotto Academy.

THE CONTENT OF EDUCATION

Zhu Xi's fullest and most systematic recommendations for the content of education are found in his "Personal Proposals for Schools and Official Recruitment." Here again, as with Cheng Hao, the assumption is that there should be one program for all, so that those who serve in government may be drawn in through the same process of education as is made available to others, that is, through the schools and not a separate examination system. Zhu introduces the subject, as he had in the preface to the *Great Learning*, by proposing the model of the ancient school system, which gave priority to cultivation in virtuous conduct and moral action rather than to the polite arts (i.e., literary skills), viewing the former as solid and practical learning (*shixue*) compared to the emptiness of purely "literary" or aesthetic studies. With one pattern of education and one system of values for all, people would get their proper bearings and set a fixed course to guide their efforts in life and develop their own abilities. Note again the primary value attached here, as in the preface, to individual self-development. This contrasts with the situation in Zhu's time, when, he says, scholars engaged in empty, useless talk and followed one shifting literary fashion after another, leaving the young without a definite goal to which they can direct the cultivation of their talents.[42]

The answer to the prevailing educational confusion is to go back to Cheng Hao's proposed system of moral education, abolish the examinations emphasizing literary skills (the composition of *shi* and *fu* forms of poetry), and instate a new curriculum based on the study of the classics, philosophers, histories, and contemporary problems. Zhu also has much to say about abuses in the conduct of the civil-service examinations, especially the disparities in local quotas, but I focus here on matters most pertinent to education. If these changes are made,

Zhu says, "scholars will have a fixed aim rather than be motivated by a competitive spirit: there will be solid practical action instead of empty talk, and solid learning so that no one will lack the means to develop his talents."[43]

The basis for this confident prescription lies in the moral nature inherent in all and the need of all to find the Way in their own mind and hearts, manifest it in their own persons, and carry it out in their own conduct. "The scholar who genuinely knows how to apply himself to this can not only cultivate his own person but extend it to the governance of men and indeed to the state and the world."[44]

Obviously, Zhu's basic assumptions and aims here are the same as in his preface, showing the consistency and continuity in his thinking. Of particular significance in this proposal is the detailed curriculum it offers and Zhu's justification for the extraordinary demands it will make on the student: "The affairs of this world are all things a scholar should know about and their principles are to be found in the Classics, each of which has its own importance and none of which is substitutable for another."[45] Thus, in their different subject matters, the classics themselves embody a diversity of human experience, all of irreplaceable value. This basic pluralism, moreover, is reinforced by the fact that the classics survive only in mutilated, fragmentary condition, while the passage of time distances our experience from that of the ancients, making interpretation of the classics problematical and compelling one to supplement them by recourse to other writings. Among these are the works of the masters or philosophers (zi), whose learning, Zhu says, "also derives from the sages." Each of these philosophers, of course, has his strong and weak points, from both of which one can learn, emulating their excellences and criticizing their weaknesses. The histories, too, help fill out the picture, dealing with changes from past to present, the rise and fall of dynasties, periods of order and disorder, what is gained and lost in the course of human affairs, and so on. Then, finally, the study of contemporary affairs exists as a reflection on the truths of the classics: rites and music, systems and institutions, astronomy, geography, military planning and strategy, laws and punishments—"these are all necessary in dealing with the contemporary world and cannot be left unstudied."[46]

In *The Liberal Tradition in China*, I gave a brief summary of the contents of Zhu's curriculum, which may suffice for my purposes here, including:

the *Changes, Documents, and Odes,* as well as four ritual texts (the *Zhouli, Yili,* and two versions of the *Record of Rites* by the Elder and Younger Dai); the *Spring and Autumn Annals* (*Chunqiu*) with three early commentaries; and the *Great Learning, Analects, Mean,* and *Mencius.* Among the philosophers Chu would include Xunzi, Yang Xiong, Wang Tong, Han Yu, Laozi, Zhuangzi, as well as the principal Song masters. The next major division of the curriculum would consist of the major histories, to be studied for the light they could shed on the understanding of contemporary problems; these include the *Zuo Commentary* (*Zuozhuan*), *Conversations from the States* (*Guoyu*), *Records of the Grand Historian* (*Shiji*), the histories of the Former and Later Han dynasties, of the Three Kingdoms, the History of Jin, Histories of the Northern and Southern Dynasties, the Old and the New Tang Histories and the History of the Five Dynasties, and the *General Mirror for Aid in Government* (*Zizhi tongjian*) of Sima Guang. A similarly copious body of literature (including the encyclopedic *Comprehensive Institutes* [*Tongdian*] of Du You) is cited for those branches of practical learning indicated above (governmental institutions, geography, etc.).[47]

Further, recognizing the difficulties of interpreting the classics, Zhu believes it essential for the student to consult commentaries. "The principles of this world are not beyond the mind-and-heart of man, but the words of the sages are profound, deep and highly refined, beyond what can be reached by mere conjecture."[48] Only after one has weighed the pros and cons of what the different commentators have to say can one reflect on them in one's own mind and judge what is correct. For this purpose then, Zhu provides extensive lists of Song commentators on each of the classics. Those listed are noteworthy for the diversity of their views, including thinkers usually considered anathema to the Cheng-Zhu School of the Way: Wang Anshi, cited for his interpretations of no fewer than four classics, and

Su Dongpo, for instance. Zhu is not unmindful of the burden this imposes on the student and the danger of superficiality that extensive coverage always entails; thus, he recommends that the student be responsible for an in-depth knowledge of only one among these interpretations and enough of one other to use it as the basis for a comparative evaluation. Study of each classic would then involve a careful and thoughtful reading of the original text, the consideration of what different commentaries say, and the drawing of conclusions that are both grounded on evidence and confirmed by what seems right in one's own mind.[49]

Here one can see how Zhu applies to the study of the classics the same procedures he has recommended in the *Articles of the White Deer Grotto Academy*: to "study extensively, inquire carefully, ponder thoroughly, sift clearly, and practice earnestly"—all to the end of truly learning for oneself. Having done this, says Zhu, "there will be no classics the gentleman has not mastered, no histories he has not studied, and none of these that will not be applicable to his own times."[50] On this last point, although Zhu has not referred directly to Hu Yuan's views as he has to Cheng Hao's, the former's basic principle of combining classical and contemporary studies, principle and practicality, is incorporated into every phase of Zhu's program.

Here, then, is a conspectus of the learning to be mastered by those Zhu Xi hoped to see in government service. Indeed, he hoped for even more than this—for practical experience of family responsibilities and internship in public office, paralleling the scholarly work described above. Altogether, it would serve as the crowning achievement of Zhu's educational structure and the full fruit of a rich and varied tradition. Standing on the broad base of a universal school system, it would nurture men's talents and select for higher responsibilities those most capable of meeting them. Elitist in principle, it sought, as Zhu said quoting Mencius, "the nobility of Heaven" (true moral and educational worth) and not "the nobility of men" (social rank and privileged position).[51]

Yet this was not what would later become established, in the name of Zhu Xi orthodoxy, as the official curriculum for examinations. I say "in the name of Zhu Xi orthodoxy" advisedly. When a Neo-Confucian curriculum was adopted later as the basis of official instruction under the Mongol ruler Khubilai, the language used by its Neo-Confucian proponents was the very language of the essay just discussed, as were the arguments adduced by them in opposing a resumption of the civil-service examinations at that time.[52] It was also to be the language appropriated by other Neo-Confucians later, in 1313–1315, when they successfully established a new examination system based essentially on Zhu Xi's version of the Four Books.[53] Familiar with Zhu Xi's proposals and conscious that they were sacrificing key points in Zhu's program in order to adapt to the facts of political life under the Mongols, the Neo-Confucians still paid lip service to the importance of moral training and virtuous conduct as well as to the role of the schools in developing men of character and practical ability. At the same time, they installed a new examination curriculum vastly abridged from Zhu's, which could serve as a minimum cultural qualification for the recruitment of officials from Mongol, Central Asian, and Chinese candidates. Still later, at the founding of the Ming dynasty, when the new system was confirmed by the Ming founder in all essential respects, the edict promulgating it again drew heavily on Zhu's earlier statement of the problem, even while the latter's recommendations were being gutted in favor of a much simpler, functional approach.[54]

In the discussions and pronouncements that accompanied this historic development, effectively fixing examination form and content until 1905, the name of Zhu Xi was hardly mentioned. Neither Khubilai nor Ming Taizu had much use for Zhu Xi or Neo-Confucian philosophy as such. They were practical men, interested in recruiting competent, dependable officials and not attracted to either the higher reaches of Zhu's thought or the niceties of classical scholarship. Despite this, however, their simplified, populist version of the Neo-Confucian curriculum was to become the basis for training and credentialing a new Mandarin elite. Yet perhaps the greatest paradox of all is not that the new system should stand in such sharp contrast to Zhu's—so much indeed that it would be liable to most charges he has leveled against the previous system—but that, had it not been for Zhu himself, this new development might never have occurred.

The reasons for this are essentially two: first, the impetus Zhu Xi gave to the Neo-Confucian schools provided the principal vehicles for the spread of Neo-Confucian learning, and second, his preparation of the texts would be most suitable for use in those schools and subsequently in the civil-service examinations themselves.

Unsuccessful though Zhu was in his advocacy of a universal school system, he devoted much of his life to promoting education through academies and local schools. I wish here to emphasize only three key significances of this activity.

First, it demonstrates again Zhu's fundamental belief that human action and all hope for social reform must begin at home—in what is near at hand and on the most basic level. If Zhu had little hope of prevailing on the court at the highest level, he could at least address the problem in those communities for which he had some direct responsibility as a local magistrate or in which his scholarly reputation gave him some standing.

Second, Zhu attached great importance to education rooted in local tradition; it could invoke the authority of historical figures or local personages whose personal achievements grew out of the native soil, met local needs, and helped to share recent, presumably viable, traditions. Zhu stressed this emulation of practical examples by his efforts at the commemoration of local worthies and at reviving local schools that had fallen on hard times.[55]

Third, Zhu encouraged the building of communities of students and scholars by developing teachers who could also be leaders. This was not new—Neo-Confucians generally had attached great importance to the role of the teacher—but Zhu carried on this tradition with great personal devotion. Yet it is significant that he did this primarily by personal example, not by the explicit discussion of teaching methods.

These three factors help explain how Zhu, a political failure at court, was able to exert such a powerful influence at the grassroots level of scholarship, for there he achieved the success that later compelled the Song court to give him due recognition and led the Yuan and Ming dynasties to confirm his hold over men's minds. In this way, the academies, which grew rapidly and spread greatly in influence after Zhu's death in official disgrace, became the prime instruments of Neo-Confucian education. Against the failure of the government schools and the perversions of the examinations, in Zhu's terms, the academies served as bearers of the Neo-Confucian message throughout East Asia.

Zhu also played a large role in providing the texts and teaching guides for use not only in the schools but also in the examinations themselves. In even the extensive curriculum proposed by Zhu, numerous works he compiled himself or more often in collaboration with others, for use on several levels of instruction, do not appear. Here, I list some of the more important ones, in rough order of increasing complexity or difficulty.

1. *Elementary Learning (Xiaoxue)*—nominally addressed to the lowest and most basic level of learning; actually a social handbook dealing with a diversity of subjects.

2. *The Community Compact (Xiangyue)*—as adapted by Zhu from that of the Lu family formerly associated with Cheng Yi; contains precepts to be subscribed to by members of local communities for the conduct of basic social relations.

3. Zhu's public proclamations—as a local official, establishing guidelines for conduct in several specific fields of human activity.

4. *Articles of the White Deer Grotto Academy*—a basic charter for schools.

5. *The Family Ritual of Master Zhu (Zhuzi jiali)*—a guide to the conduct of the major ceremonies in the life of the family; represents a radically simplified version of the classic rituals.

6. *Commentaries on the Four Books (Sishu jizhu)*—a careful and concise commentary on the four basic texts featured by the Cheng-Zhu school.

7. *Memorials and Lectures on the Classics*, for the emperor or heir apparent *(Jingyan jiangyi)*—although addressed to the ruler, on a high level of importance, it is often simpler and less scholarly than other instructional works of Zhu Xi but conveys the same essential message.

8. *Reflections on Things at Hand (Jinsilu)*—sometimes referred to as a gateway to the Four Books; later sometimes so used, but in addressing fundamental philosophical issues it often probes questions of great depth and subtlety. Perhaps of greatest importance in mapping out the steps to the attainment of sagehood, a lofty ambition but one to which Zhu said any country boy could aspire.

9. *The Sources of the Cheng-Zhu School (Yiluo yuanyuan lu)*—a hagiography of Zhu's Neo-Confucian predecessors, near-contemporaries admired as among the sages and worthies.

10. *Outline and Digest of the General Mirror (Tongjian gangmu)*—structured synopsis and abridgement of Sima Guang's *General Mirror for Aid in Government*.

11. "Personal Proposals for Schools and Official Recruitment" (*Xuexiao gongju siyi*)—a brief document but proposing the most ambitious learning program offered by Zhu.

This list, far from exhaustive, may suffice to illustrate the main features of Zhu Xi's educational approach. First, it recognizes the need for an educational process reaching from youth to maturity and from the common people to the ruler. Second, it accepts the need for a plurality of means to reach different audiences on different levels, although the ultimate aim of all should be the attainment of sagehood. This is the educational implication of the interrelated concepts of self-renewal, "renewal of the people," and "resting in the highest good." Third, the path of self-development builds on successive levels of accomplishment; one cannot attain enlightenment in one leap or instant. Fourth, breadth of learning is to be balanced by concentration and precision, comprehensiveness by selectivity and structure. Fifth, applying these requisites to the classical tradition implies the need for "editing" the classics—abridging and commenting on them to highlight key principles, focusing on the concrete example or concise formula to make teachings memorable. Sixth, to repossess classical learning it is not enough simply to read the ancient texts; there must also be some continuity with the recent past and some connection with the latest scholarship, if learning is to have some organic relation to a sustained and sustaining life process. Seventh, to accomplish the foregoing aims requires cooperative, collegial scholarship in order to provide a variety of edited, graded materials for the edification of the populace at large. Virtually all the texts cited above are anthologies or reprocessed materials; whatever "original" writing they contain is mostly in the form of preface or commentary.

The results of this process may be seen in the curriculum of the Neo-Confucian academies that followed Zhu Xi's lead in the thirteenth and fourteenth centuries. *The Daily Schedule of Study in the Cheng Family School* by Cheng Duanli (1271–1345), often cited as a model curriculum, presents a schedule of readings graded according to the age of the student, with a major division between elementary and advanced education.[56] In the former, from age eight to fifteen, emphasis is placed on reading the original texts of the *Elementary Learning* (*Xiaoxue*), Four Books, Five Classics, and *Classic of Filial Piety* (as edited by Zhu Xi). In the advanced stage, from age fifteen to twenty-two, most of the same texts are read with Zhu Xi's commentary, deleting the *Elementary Learning* and *Classic of Filial Piety* but adding readings from Sima Guang's *General Mirror for Aid in Government* (*Zizhi tongjian*) and specimens of prose and poetry from Han Yu and Qu Yuan.

If one compares this list with that in Zhu's "Personal Proposals" or the list of materials edited by Zhu Xi above, the educational fare is obviously much more limited. As a practical matter, Cheng Duanli's curriculum is undoubtedly oriented to the new examination system of the Yuan dynasty. Of this John Meskill says, "Cheng Duanli devised a complete schedule for the education of a young man from childhood to the year of his examinations. The whole program provided for a very systematic progression through the classical literature and commentaries on it, culminating in diligent practice of the forms required in the examinations."[57]

From the standpoint of Zhu's "Personal Proposals" one could question, as I have above, whether the coverage of "classical literature" or the range of interpretation and alternative commentaries was nearly as broad as Zhu himself had wished. Furthermore, there is far more concentration on learning and memorizing forms and models useful for examination purposes and much less on the kind of "inquiring, reflecting, weighing, and sifting" that Zhu had recommended. An atmosphere of rote learning had prevailed, in contrast to the spirit of voluntarism and critical scholarship encouraged by Zhu.

However, the curriculum does exhibit many features of Zhu's educational philosophy: the need for selectivity, priorities, graded materials, and a high degree of specificity in study methods. By defining the reading program as he does, Cheng clearly thinks of it as a graded core curriculum to be supplemented as time and circumstances allow by further reading works that Zhu Xi had proposed or prepared in much greater variety, as the supplementary notes to this schedule indicate. Indeed, if one were to judge from Cheng's intentions alone, one would have to say that he still looked to Zhu's curriculum as the standard and expected Zhu's basic aims to be served by his own reading program. This is clear from his characterization of the classical core of the new advanced curriculum. Starting at age fifteen, he says, the student should commit himself to the pursuit of learning, "resolving to take the Way for one's aim in learning, and sagehood for one's aim as a man."[58] Then, having completed study of the Four Books and the chosen classic with its commentaries, and having faithfully followed Zhu Xi's reading method[59] with great concentration of mind and intense effort over three or four years, "all of it without exception substantial learning for the sake of oneself and none of it vitiated by even the slightest idea of selfish gain or ulterior motive, the student will have established himself in reverent seriousness and righteousness, strict in his practice of mind preservation and self-examination, and firmly rooted for a lifetime of learning."[60]

As further evidence of Cheng's intention fully to adhere to Zhu's overall aims, there are numerous writings of Zhu Xi attached to the Reading Schedule, including the *Articles of the White Deer Grotto Academy* and the "Personal Proposals for Schools and Official Recruitment."[61] Cheng did not, indeed, think of himself as jettisoning any of Zhu's program but only of modifying it for the sake of practical realization. In his preface to the *Daily Schedule*, he spoke in exultant terms of this climactic moment in history when, after centuries of failure to accomplish Confucian goals in education, the time had arrived for Zhu Xi's substantial learning (*shixue*) and practical method to overcome the preoccupation with literary composition in both the schools and the civil-service examinations. "All fathers and elder brothers have wished their sons and younger brothers to be educated, but only two or three out of them have succeeded." This, he says, is because they did not have a proper understanding of the matter and erred at the start by heading in the wrong direction. The right direction was given in ancient times when the cultivation of virtue was put ahead of literary studies, only to have this order reversed in subsequent dynasties. Of his own time (the mid-Yuan period), however, Cheng says:

In the recruitment of scholars virtuous conduct is being put ahead of all else and study of the Classics is being given precedence over literary composition. . . . In the interpretation of the

Classics the views of Master Zhu are the sole authority, uniting as one the philosophy of principle and study for the civil service examination, to the great advantage of scholars committed to the Way [as distinct from opportunistic candidates]. This is something the Han, Tang and Song never achieved, and the greatest blessing that has come to scholars throughout the ages.[62]

Nevertheless, according to Cheng, many scholars who study the classics, even if they accept the authority of Zhu Xi's interpretations, still are unaware that one must have a definite reading method, so their study is unsystematic. Hence the need for a guide like the *Daily Schedule*, which combines Zhu's study methods and other relevant writings on the subject, so that "none of the classics will be left unstudied, no principles left unexplained, no aspect of the Way of governance left unmastered, no systems or institutions left unstudied, no age, past or present, left out of one's ken, and no literary form left unmastered." Yet at the same time, says Cheng, having pursued this course of study "to the age of twenty-three, twenty-four, or twenty-five, with this he would be ready to take the examinations."[63]

More of this preface dilates on the effectiveness of this method in bringing personal fulfillment to the individual and putting the individual into full accord with the Way while also preparing the way for success in the civil-service examinations. For my purposes, however, the foregoing should be enough to suggest how Cheng expects the wisdom and practical method of the philosopher to be joined with the process of official recruitment for the transformation of state and society. Written in 1315, the very year the Yuan dynasty initiated the new examinations, his preface exudes the idealism of those who, like Cheng, went along with Cheng Jufu (1249–1318) in resurrecting the civil service–examination system and installing in it the new "Neo-Confucian" curriculum, in contrast to other Neo-Confucians like Wu Cheng (1249–1332) and Liu Yin (1249–1293), who refused to compromise Zhu Xi's basic principles in this way.[64]

Inevitably (and this is a word to be used sparingly), in this unification of power and intellectual authority the moral and spiritual aspirations of Zhu Xi are compounded with forms of learning routinized for purposes of the examinations, which tend to divert men from the moral and spiritual goals to which Zhu Xi had given the highest priority. Thus, there is more than a touch of irony in the acclaim given to the *Daily Schedule* several centuries later by Zhang Boxing (1652–1725), when he reprinted it in his collection of orthodox Neo-Confucian works, the *Zhengyi tang quanshu*. In his own preface to the *Daily Schedule*, Zhang laments the debasement of learning brought on by the examination system:

> In ancient times it was easy to develop one's talents to the full; today it is difficult. In antiquity scholar-officials were chosen for their [moral] substance; today they are chosen for their literary ability. In ancient times the village recommended scholars and the town selected them, so men engaged in substantial learning (*shixue*) and outdid each other in the practice of humaneness and rightness, the Way and virtue. At home they were pure scholars; at large they were distinguished officials. Today it is different. Men are chosen for their examination essays. What fathers teach their sons, and elder brothers their younger brothers, is only to compete in the writing of essays. It is not that they fail to read the Five Classics or Four Books, but that they read them only for such use as they have in the writing of the examination essays, and never incorporate them into their own hearts and lives.[65]

It is not difficult to see how the same system could lead to divergent results and even to conflicts within the same individual between the pursuit of worldly success and the quest for moral and spiritual perfection. Thus, a dilemma arose from even the seeming successes of the Zhu Xi school; some of these, from his point of view, could also be seen as miscarriages. For instance, successfully making Zhu Xi the centerpiece of the new examinations represented another failure for Zhu in the sense of his being misappropriated for questionable purposes. Such success, too, seems to have compromised later efforts to achieve an effective and lasting public school system of the kind he had advocated.

Meanwhile, the growth of the academies continued, amid periodic vicissitudes, to spread Neo-Confucian education in ways Cheng Duanli would have less cause to regret. For this we have testimony from the *Song History* (*Song shi*), *Yuan History* (*Yuan shi*), and *Case*

Studies of Song-Yuan Scholars (*Song Yuan xue'an*), describing the fate of the schools of Zhu Xi and Lu Xiangshan, starting first with the family of Shi Mengqing (1247–1306):[66]

> The Shi family of Siming [in Eastern Zhejiang, near Ningbo] had all followed the Lu school, but with the advent of Shi Mengqing it turned to follow Zhu Xi . . . [and] transmitted this to Cheng Duanli and his brother, who adhered purely to the Zhu school.[67]

And from the *Yuan History*:

> At the end of the Song, the Qingyuan area [near Ningbo in Eastern Zhejiang], all followed the school of Lu Xiangshan and the Zhu Xi school was not carried on. Cheng Duanli by himself took up with Shi Jing [i.e., Mengqing] in propagating Zhu Xi's doctrine of "clarifying the substance and applying it in practice" (*mingti shiyong*). Scholars came to his gate in great numbers. He wrote the "Working Schedule for Study of Books" (*Dushu gongcheng*), which the Directorate of Education had distributed to officials in the local schools to serve as a model for students.[68]

Note here the process of conversion from Lu Xiangshan's teaching to Zhu Xi's, drawing attention to the combination of principle and practice. With the latter concretely embodied in a working schedule of study and the new curriculum, in turn, officially adopted, one can see how these developments in the academies led the way for a new, officially sanctioned, system.

Last, I cite the comment of Huang Bojia (b. 1643), in *Case Studies of Song-Yuan Scholars*, concerning the underlying philosophical significance of this development:

> In the late Song the Qingyuan area was all of the Lu school and the Zhu Xi school was not transmitted there. With Shih Mengqing, however, there came a change. Following Yang Jian [1140–1125, disciple of Lu] most of the school went into Chan and pursued a form of learning without the reading of books. Departing from the source, they drifted apart. Thus, what they

transmitted from Master Lu was the very thing that made them lose Master Lu. Having studied Cheng's Daily Reading Schedule, [I find that] there is nothing missing from root to branch and there is a sequential order in its method, from which one may proceed. . . . [69]

Here Huang suggests a connection between the Lu school's lack of a reading method, reflecting Lu's own depreciation of textual study, the school's getting lost in Chan Buddhism, which "did not depend on the written word," and the contrasting growth of the Zhu Xi school, linked to its definite method of study and reading program. Since Huang, like his father, was not known for any partiality to the Zhu Xi school, this represents credible testimony to the latter's superior achievement in this respect.

More far reaching even than the spread of the Zhu Xi school through the academies was its propagation through the development of printing, which carried Neo-Confucian teachings even into homes that could afford little formal education. Whether or not Zhu Xi had any special prescience in anticipating this trend may be arguable, but Wing-tsit Chan's research indicates that Zhu was involved in the printing business as a sideline, and it is known that as a local magistrate he used printed handbills to disseminate his proclamations throughout the area of his jurisdiction.[70] In any case, his organization of thought into systematic, easily grasped structures; his concern for adapting them to different levels of comprehension; his editing and condensing of texts; his attention to the problem of an ordered sequence of readings; and the care he took in analyzing and codifying procedures for book learning all took special advantage of the new printing capability. He pronounced with finality in the *Cheng Family Schedule:* "For conveying the Way and transmitting it to later generations, the merit of books is great indeed!"[71]

It is no accident that Zhu Xi's recommendations for reading as codified by his followers in what came to be known as his *Reading Method (Dushufa)*, which addressed the what, when, and how of reading, spread with his other teachings and the publication of his books through East Asia. In its simplest form, this consisted of maxims recommending reverent seriousness and a fixed resolve in the pursuit of learning: a graded sequence and gradual progress in study, intensive reading of text and commentary accompanied by "refined reflection," reading with an open mind and without reading one's own preconceptions into the text, taking what one reads to heart and making it part of one's own experience, and making an all-out effort and keeping strict control.[72] These methods were summarized in a short piece of Zhu's entitled "Essentials of Reading," found in his *Collected Writings*. They were also discussed in Zhu's *Classified Conversations* (*Yulei*) and expounded in memorials to the throne. A large portion of the section on methods of self-cultivation in Zhu's basic textbook on *Elementary Education* is devoted to the matter of reading methods and how they relate to one's inner self-development.[73] They were further incorporated in the aforementioned *Daily Schedule of the Cheng Family School*, in the official Ming *Great Compendium of Human Nature and Principle* (*Xingli Jingyi*), and in numerous reformulations of these methods by Zhu Xi's successors, including the very pointed and detailed discussion by the recent historian Qian Mu.[74] Even the authors of a recent history of Chinese education, though not particularly sympathetic to Zhu's philosophy, acknowledge the wide influence of his study and reading methods.[75]

Other Neo-Confucians like Lu Xiangshan and Wang Yangming may well have been more popular teachers than Zhu, who seems to have been comparatively reserved, of a reflective temperament, modest almost to a fault, and not the kind who would wish to promote himself or his own ideas. Other teachings like Buddhism and Daoism, which developed substantial lay followings in these same years, also had more popular appeal than Zhu Xi's refined scholarship. But none of these, for all their charismatic, messianic, or populist features, addressed the problem of secular education the way Zhu Xi did—systematically developing schools, curricula, texts, and study methods. To the extent that the educated elite of East Asia, whatever the differences in their social and political status or functions from country to country, were identified as leaders or officials (*shidafu*) and as scholars accomplished in book learning (literally, "readers of books," *dushuren*), it was Zhu Xi who largely provided the wherewithal for their intellectual and moral formation. Thus, he became the educator par excellence of East Asia into the twentieth century.

12

Self and Society in Ming Thought

I n the three centuries since the fall of the Ming Dynasty (1368–1644) until recently, the Neo-Confucian thought of the Ming period had been held in generally bad repute. Each of the great dynasties before the Ming had been seen as making some enduring contribution to Chinese thought—the Zhou through the profusion and profundity of thought represented by the "Hundred Schools"; the Han through its synthesis of a Chinese worldview; the Six Dynasties, Sui, and Tang through the assimilation and development of Buddhist philosophy; and the Song through the great Neo-Confucian revival in humane learning and, especially, philosophy. The Ming period, by contrast, has been seen as one of general decline and aimless drifting, in the midst of which Wang Yangming stood out alone as an independent thinker. Indeed, to praise Wang was most often to deprecate Ming philosophy as a whole; to honor him was to reject the conventionality and mediocrity of most other thinkers of his age. Finally, indignities came at the hands of modern scholarship. The Song and the early Qing (under a foreign dynasty, no less) were seen by Hu Shi as periods of renaissance in Chinese thought, with the Ming as a long trough between.[1]

THE "EMPTINESS" OF MING THOUGHT

The firmness of this judgment seems to have become established very early. Few would dispute the opinion of a scholar like Gu Yanwu (1613–1682), himself a survivor of the Ming and a towering figure in the world of classical scholarship, who compared the subtleties of Ming thought unfavorably to the simple truths of Confucius's teaching:

> It is a matter of great regret to me that, for the past hundred odd years, scholars have devoted so much discussion to the mind and human nature, all of it vague and quite incomprehensible. . . . They have set aside broad knowledge and concentrated upon the search for a single, all-inclusive method; they have said not a word about the distress and poverty of the world within the four seas, but have spent all their days lecturing on theories of the "precarious and subtle," "discrimination and oneness."[2]

Cui Shu (1740–1816), another scholar who typified the finest in critical scholarship during the Qing period, confirmed this judgment when he described the Neo-Confucian philosophy of the Song and Ming:

> As scholars who valued truth none can compare with the Song Confucianists. Yet most of them concerned themselves with questions of the nature and principle of things and with moral philosophy. If one looks among them for men who devoted themselves to historical research, he will find no more than two or three out of ten. By Ming times scholarship had grown increasingly heterodox and it became so that if one hoped to write anything important he had to be conversant with Chan [Zen] doctrines and interlard his library shelves with Buddhist books.[3]

As a final example of this attitude, we have in the early years of the present century Liang Qichao (1873–1929). His *Intellectual Trends in the Qing Period* (*Qing dai xueshu gailun*) fixed in modern Chinese minds the authoritative interpretation of recent Chinese thought. He found much to admire in the early Qing but prefaced it with a severe condemnation of the late Ming, in terms that by now were almost a convention:

> When I went on to examine the substance of its thoughts, I found that the object of its study was simply too vague and intangible. A few outstanding and sincere scholars might have followed this path and achieved a state of repose for body and mind, but only rarely could ordinary mortals imitate them. It was too easy for superficial and pretentious men to pick up abstract phrases to brag about, and consequently there was a group in late Ming known as the *kuangchan* ("wild Zen") [who thought] that "every street is full of sages" and that "wine, women, wealth, and passion do not block the road to enlightenment." Their ethics hit rock bottom. Moreover, the civil service examinations and the students' curriculum to prepare for them engaged the attention of all the nation; students needed only to learn this kind of dubious and imitative language in order to be ready to jockey for position, wealth, and reputation. The whole nation indulged in it prodigally and one man after another neglected his learning and the use of his mind.[4]

Here Liang repeats the charge that Ming thought was corrupted by Chan Buddhism and adds to this an attack on the stereotyped civil service–examination system as stultifying the intellectual life of the late Ming. This too is a familiar complaint, and much support for Liang's allegation can be found among qualified critics reaching back to the Ming itself.[5]

THE VITALITY AND DIVERSITY OF MING THOUGHT

Nevertheless, the very existence of such criticism belies the common stereotype of Ming thought. If evils existed, so did opposition to them. If education tended to become subservient to official recruitment, so was there a strong countertrend among individual thinkers and in the spread of private academies disavowing such purposes and nurturing independent thought. Indeed, the irony of the situation is that many of those later described as given to empty speculation on the mind and nature were precisely those who resisted the prevailing pressures toward conformity.[6] They may appear to have been "escapists," but they sought a way out of real dangers. They were not simply avoiding troubles but looking for a way to deal with them.

Thus, whatever one's ultimate judgment of the value of Ming thought, Liang Qichao is certainly wrong in saying that the Confucians of the late Ming "neglected . . . the use of their minds." On the contrary, the sixteenth and early seventeenth centuries may well have been one of the most creative and stimulating periods in the history of Chinese thought. In those distorted times there was no lack of challenge to thought. Evils, abuses, crises, conflicts—yes. But in the midst of such difficulties creative tensions existed such as had characterized earlier periods of social decadence and intellectual ferment. What we find, then, in the extremities of the Ming situation, is anything but a dull conformity of thought to established patterns and institutions; it is rather a picture of lively controversy and intellectual diversity.

From this point of view, whether or not one views Ming speculations on the mind and nature as "empty" depends on whether or not one understands the problems to which they sought an answer and whether or not one feels the importance and the urgency of those problems as Ming thinkers did. To the successors of the Ming, whose approach was frankly "empirical" and antimetaphysical, these speculations seemed vapid and vague. Qing thinkers for the most part turned away from questions of this sort, to some extent out of a sense of disillusionment with the general failure of the Ming. The collapse of the old order and the fall of the dynasty, first to rebels and then to the Manchus, were seen as consequences of the moral decline and disorder of thought at the end of the period. Such a causal connection, alluded to by Liang Qichao above, may be difficult to establish and no doubt reflects a typical Confucian predilection for the moralistic interpretation of history. Nevertheless, whether as cause, symptom, or both, the apparent failure of Ming thought and nerve loomed large in the minds of those who sought to explain this catastrophe.

A notable exception to this line of thinking is found, however, in the studies of Huang Zongxi (1610–1695). He had suffered as much as anyone from these tragic events and was deeply moved to comprehend their meaning. Indeed, in his *Mingyi daifang lu* Huang was unsparing in his exposure of the failings of Ming rulers and institutions. Loyalty to his own dynasty did not stand in the way of a most searching analysis of its weaknesses and evils. Yet when he came to compile his monumental survey of Ming Confucian thought, the *Mingru xue'an*, Huang sought to preserve its contributions from the neglect and indifference, if not the contempt, of the subsequent age. In his foreword, he explains:

> It is often said that the literary and practical accomplishments of the Ming did not measure up to former dynasties. Yet in the philosophy of Principle it attained what other dynasties did not. In everything Ming scholars made the finest of distinctions and classifications, as if they were sorting the hair of oxen or picking silk threads from a cocoon. They thereby discovered what other scholars had failed to discover. Though the Chengs and Zhu Xi [in the Song] spent many words in refuting the Buddha, they never got beneath the surface. Buddhism's specious reasonableness and confounding of truth they failed to point out. But Ming scholars were so precise in their analysis that the Buddhists were completely exposed and trapped.[7]

What is important here is not Huang's evident hostility to Buddhism. It is true that his survey is motivated by a desire to uphold the orthodox Confucian tradition, but for the most part it is not marked by an unreasoning rejection of all things Buddhist, and in later life his attitude grew increasingly tolerant of heterodox thought. What stands out is his claim that Ming thought came to grips with the challenge of Buddhism by a more precise clarification of issues rather than by simply rejecting it out of hand. It acknowledges that Ming thinkers were concerned with the subtleties and refinements that his contemporary Gu Yanwu had so little use for but affirms that these enabled a more precise analysis of the fundamental problems at issue in the encounter of Confucianism and Buddhism. For ourselves, likewise, the mere fact

that Qing scholars took little interest in such questions is not a sufficient basis for regarding the Ming attempt as vain. We must try to
understand, rather, why and how these questions assumed such importance in fifteenth- and sixteenth-century China.

THE SITUATION OF THE MING INTELLECTUAL

From the comments above, we are aware of two problems facing the
Ming Confucian scholar. One had to do with public service and the
examination system. The other involved his confrontation with Buddhism and Daoism. Of the two, the former was the more pressing, for
intellectually Buddhism and Daoism were in a state of relative decline
and institutionally in a weakened condition. They could not have compelled his attention except that, in wrestling with his own Confucian
conscience, he could not ignore what they had to say to his inner self.

The question of first priority, then, concerns the Ming Confucian in
his dual role as scholar and official. With his traditional commitment
to public service, it was natural that the scholar should be drawn to
the business of government and that this in turn should subject him
to great political pressures, if it did not actually expose him to grave
dangers.[8] But in the Ming, to an extraordinary degree, the Confucian
found himself overshadowed by the power of the state and, whether in
or out of office, felt his social conscience under great strain. Most historians, whatever their differences in other matters of interpretation,
acknowledge the unprecedented concentration of power in the hands
of the emperor and its despotic uses by those who acted in his name.
It is not for us here to review the entire question of Ming "despotism"
but simply to emphasize two related points: one is that autocratic and
bureaucratic power existed in the situation, and the other is that men
still attempted to defend themselves against it.[9]

Awareness of these conditions will help us to avoid a common error.
We shall not mistake the seeming introversion of Ming thought and
its apparent quietistic tendency as indicating that it had strayed from
the "real" problems of life or lost interest in practical matters. Nothing
was more real and practical for the thinker and scholar in that age than
the preservation of his life, his integrity, and his fidelity to essential

Confucian values in the face of such overwhelming odds. If to with-draw into reflective contemplation or solitary pursuits helped achieve this, then, even if the withdrawal has the connotations of escapism, we must not think of it as useless or sterile. From this process of introspec-tion and reexamination emerged not only the most deeply committed and personally effective of Confucian activists, Wang Yangming, but also at the end of the dynasty the most searching critique of political and social institutions China had ever known.

But let us consider, more concretely, the effects on Ming Confucians of the civil-service system—an old problem in a new situation. Earlier, in the late Tang and Song, there had been protests against the type of Confucian scholarship encouraged and rewarded by the examinations. The integrity of Confucian teaching had constantly to be defended against the danger of debasement through its use as an official ideology or as a mere professional qualification. But if Liang Qichao and others, like Jiang Fan, the historian of seventeenth- and eighteenth-century thought, stress the particularly deleterious effects of the civil-service examinations on Confucian thought in the Ming,[10] it is because dur-ing this period the system presented a more serious problem than ever before, and paradoxically so, since it was in many ways better organized and more widely effective.

The founder of the dynasty had sought to broaden the avenues of official recruitment, to extend the official school system so as to train more scholars, and to simplify the examinations so that men of practi-cal ability need not demonstrate great erudition in order to qualify.[11] A concomitant of this effort at "democratization," however, was a further routinization and standardization of both training and recruitment. Simplification of the examinations resulted in a limiting of the scholar-official's intellectual horizons and placed almost no value on his com-mitment to Confucian ideals. Little more was demanded of him than rote memorization of the classics (especially the Four Books), a mind-less assimilation of the commentaries of Zhu Xi, and a technical mas-tery of the required essay and poetry forms.[12]

More thoughtful men naturally questioned whether this was true Confucian learning and whether official service on this basis could be considered a fulfillment of the Confucian sense of duty to humankind. But the much larger numbers of candidates recruited under the new system, with all the implications of social leveling and a lowering of scholarly standards that implied, greatly intensified the strain on the Ming Confucian. The tension increased between his egalitarian ideals and his elite standards, between his commitment to public service and his revulsion at careerism on a mass scale among supposed Confucians devoid of genuine intellectual and moral worth.

And, quite apart from his own interior struggles in these matters, there was the constant political and social pressure to conform, to yield his scruples and high ideals in the service of a questionable master. To refuse was to find himself in an embattled minority. What was worse, it was a minority without status and with almost no cohesion as a group. In a sense, it lacked even a *raison d'etre*. Within Confucianism, the concept of a "minority" had no place.[13] The scholar stood alone, with comfort and support coming only from personal friends and distant admirers. He could only retire to his home ground, strive for economic self-sufficiency on the land (like Wu Yubi), or devote himself to teaching.

Under such circumstances, independence or resistance to the dominant power tended to be manifested in individualistic ways rather than through some interest group. In the early Ming, Fang Xiaoru is an excellent example of this. Rather than being a spokesman for the scholar-gentry as a class, he is representative of them in the sense of exemplifying the only kind of independence possible for them— individual heroism and individuality of thought—rather than in the conscious assertion of their interests as an opposition group.

It was among such individuals, thrown back upon themselves, that Ming thought in the true sense was born. Their inner conflicts, however, were of many sorts. It was one thing to defend one's own sense of the authentic Confucian tradition against a debased official "orthodoxy," as did even the Cheng-Zhu school (e.g., Wu Yubi and Hu Juren) of the early Ming in holding itself aloof from the establishment. This was a conflict between the philosopher and the state as to what truly constituted orthodoxy. This was another thing that the philosopher felt within himself: the stresses of time and change as they affected his understanding of the Confucian Way. This was a conflict with the past, and, again, even those who cherished orthodoxy experienced it. They suffered not only alienation from the established regime but also, in a more complex and indefinable way, estrangement from received tradition.

THE BURDEN OF CULTURE IN THE MING

This tradition Ming scholars received largely from the Song (960–1279). Indeed, Ming China may be seen as the second phase of a far-reaching cultural development that had come to its first apex in the Song. The Confucian revival in that period had been stimulated by forces that continued and were greatly intensified in the Ming—the strengthening and enlarging of the civil bureaucracy, expansion of commerce and industry, increasing urbanization and the growth of an urban culture of great diversity and refinement, the development of printing and the comparatively wide distribution of books, and the great extension of education, partly occasioned by increased social mobility and the participation of larger numbers of people in the competition for office if not in the civil service itself.[14]

The effect of this was not felt immediately in the democratization of learning on any large scale or in a breaking down of the traditional distinction between the Confucian educated elite and the uneducated masses—though something of this was to come. The most direct effects were felt within the educated class itself—those who carried the burden of high culture and would be most sensitive to changes in the cultural situation. Until Zhu Xi, it had been possible for the Confucian to conceive of himself as potentially a master of the arts, though even by his time signs of strain had appeared between interior moral cultivation and excessive involvement in external culture.[15] The enjoyment of arts and letters—aesthetic pursuits such as landscape painting; gardening; the collecting of bronzes; the furnishing of the scholar's studio with fine paper, brushes, and ink stones; and scholarly hobbies of an antiquarian sort—could sap completely the will of the Confucian to put the world in order. Still, somehow the Song giants had found the energy to impose order on this fascinating diversity instead of denying it. Zhu Xi's all-embracing system had reunited the rational and moral orders; Sima Guang had encompassed all history in a sweeping panorama of recorded fact and moral example; and encyclopedists such as

Zheng Qiao, Wang Yinglin, and Ma Duanlin had traced the development of social and cultural institutions from the primitive past to the complex present.

Yet they may have done their work too well for the Ming. Who could compete with such masters? Individuals found the problem too staggering; its magnitude now required large-scale cooperative effort such as was embodied in the massive *Yongle Encyclopedia* (1407). Printing and the dissemination of books, which made education more widely available, rendered mastery more difficult. To pursue the "investigation of things" and their principles in one thing or affair after another, in book after book, seemed an endless procedure. Indeed, the Ming scholar was already confronted by the typical modern dilemma—how to keep up with the proliferation of literature and how to cope with more and more specialized branches of learning while not losing the sense of human relevance. Was he not threatened with a loss of the intellectual and spiritual integration that had always been the aim of Confucian study?

Those who set the tone and direction of Ming thought, such as Chen Xianzhang and Wang Yangming, often voiced concern over the harmful effects of excessive involvement in book learning and belles-lettres. This was indeed a crucial issue between Wang and his great predecessor Zhu Xi. The latter, Wang believed, had even learned to regret his own overindulgence in bookish pursuits:

[Zhu] all along . . . directed his efforts only to intellectual investigations and writing. Naturally he would have had no time for these if he had given priority to self-cultivation with a sense of genuine and personal concern. . . . If he had really worried lest the doctrine not be made clear to the world, and, following the example of Confucius' retiring to edit the Six Classics, had eliminated superfluous works and confined himself to the simple and essential in order to enlighten later scholars, in general it would not have required him to do much investigation. When he was young he wrote many books and then repented doing so in his old age. That was doing things upside down.[16]

Reflected in this passage is the overpowering figure of Zhu Xi as a prodigious scholar whose written work had left a monumental legacy to later generations. One might have thought that Zhu's philosophy and his writings had been most impressive for their comprehensiveness. They had achieved the same remarkable balance of concern for philosophical inquiry, moral self-cultivation, cultural endeavor, and public service that had characterized Confucius himself. Yet it is that very comprehensiveness and complexity that disturbs Wang. He longs for the simplicity of the ancient sage and puts forward his "innate knowledge" (*liangzhi*) as a return to the irreducible essence of Confucius's teaching:

> In learning to become a sage, the student need only get rid of selfish human desires and preserve the principle of nature (*tianli*), which is like refining gold and achieving perfection in quality. . . . Later generations [however] . . . seek sagehood only in knowledge and ability . . . and merely cripple their spirit and exhaust their energy scrutinizing books, investigating the names and varieties of things, and imitating the forms and traces of the ancients.[17]

Thus, through man's instinctive moral sense, based on Mencius's doctrine of the goodness of human nature, Wang seeks to redress the Confucian balance in the direction of moral cultivation in practice, as opposed to cultural activity and the accumulation of learning. He is saying that the sage must be more a man of action than a scholar.

It would thus be possible to interpret this development within the context of Confucian humanism alone. Wang Yangming in his own experience of life is the Confucian as the man of action, the scholar who devoted more of his life to active official service than almost any other Song or Ming thinker did, much of that activity being of the most strenuous and demanding sort. Indeed, the official *Ming History*, which categorizes him as a statesman rather than a scholar, credits him with the greatest military achievements of any civil official in the Ming period.[18] Zhu Xi, by comparison, saw little active service. For the most part, he either held sinecures involving cultural activities and very little active administration, or else he was out of favor at court and living in "retirement" as a scholar.[19] Wang Yangming complains in the quotation above that Zhu wrote too much. And it is true that he devoted his life mainly to intellectual inquiry and writing rather than to the active expression of his Confucian concerns in public service. In terms, then, of the traditional function of the Confucian as both scholar and official, or of Confucianism as upholding both culture and morality, there is some basis for saying that Wang Yangming manifests the instinct within Confucianism to restore this balance in the direction of moral action.

But what Wang expresses here is what other Ming thinkers before him had also sensed. The emphasis on interiority rather than intellectuality is already found in his predecessors, Wu Yubi, Hu Juren, Chen Xianzhang, and Lou Liang. Chen in particular had stressed the dispensability of book learning and even the obstacle it might put in the way of achieving sagehood.[20] Yet their roles in life were quite different from Wang's. They tended to be reclusive and not to engage in active official life as he did.[21] Hence we know that this fundamental difference between Zhu Xi and Wang Yangming arose not simply from the former's more scholarly way of life and the latter's more activist approach but more broadly from a heightened awareness of the burdens of culture that was common in the Ming, as well as from that deeper preoccupation with the true nature of the self to which both political and cultural pressures drove the Ming thinker. In other words, the tensions that existed in Confucian thought between morality and culture, action and quiescence, political involvement or disengagement all focused on the underlying problem of man's nature: was it static or dynamic, metaphysical or physical, an abstract ideal or an active force, a moral norm or a transmoral perfection? How was the individual to understand that nature in relation to his actual self and his society?

THE MING EXPERIENCE OF THE SELF

In a concrete sense, Ming thought proper originates in an experience of the self. Chen Xianzhang and Wang Yangming, generally acknowledged to be leaders and exemplars of new thought in the Ming, each underwent a personal experience that had a decisive effect on his thinking. In both cases, there is an atmosphere of intense spiritual crisis surrounding the event. Chen had returned from Peking, having failed twice in the metropolitan examinations, and entered upon a prolonged program of concentrated study and meditation, broken only by a brief

period of study with Wu Yubi in Jiangxi. Extensive reading characterized the earlier phase of this program; later, the emphasis shifted
to quiet-sitting in meditation as Chen became convinced that self-
realization could not come from books. Finally, his solitary effort
resulted in an experience of "enlightenment," described in terms of seeing his essential self and its identity with all things and drawing from
this realization a sense of unlimited power in dealing with the world.
A feeling of overflowing joy and unshakable self-confidence ensued.[22]

Wang Yangming's experience came after his banishment to
Guizhou, a period of extreme hardship less significant for its physical
difficulties than for the intellectual and spiritual isolation he suffered.
A man of tremendous energy and strong commitment to public service, he found his activities severely restricted. With a brilliant mind
and a fondness for intellectual discourse, he had little company among
the aboriginals, exiled criminals, and emigrés of little education who
surrounded him. In such circumstances, Wang was pushed to the limit
of his spiritual resources. His *Life Chronology* (*Nianpu*) reports how he
was driven in upon himself: "He had already given up and put behind
him all thought of personal success or failure, honor or disgrace, and
only the question of life and death remained to be overcome. Thus day
and night he stayed in silent, solitary meditation." Then late one night
as he was pondering what a sage would do in such circumstances, he
suddenly had a "great enlightenment." In it was revealed to him the real
meaning of "the recognition of things and the extension of knowledge"
that earlier had eluded him as he tried to apprehend the principle of
things through contemplation of the bamboo in his father's garden.
Transported by his discovery, he called out exultantly, and his feet
danced for joy. His companions, awakened from sleep, were amazed at
his behavior. Thus he first learned, it is said, "that the way to sagehood
lies within one's own nature."[23]

Such experiences were common in the Ming, but recent historians
have treated them with considerable reserve. Those of a rationalistic
and critical bent tend to dismiss such accounts as conventional hagiography, and others who find that they do not fit the picture of Wang
Yangming as a "pragmatic" philosopher or man of action have preferred
not to emphasize the religious overtones. The similarity to Chan experience was also disturbing to find in a supposedly proper Confucian.

But a phenomenon so widespread, or even a convention so well established, requires some explanation. No doubt, the lingering influence of Chan helped to produce an atmosphere in which some extraordinary experience of "enlightenment" lent authority to one's views. In Wang Yangming's case, the references to his confrontation of "life and death" and his prolonged absorption over many years with "recognizing things (gewu)," almost as if this were a *kōan* for him that awaited some flash of illumination, lend some plausibility to this interpretation. But if Wang was not unfamiliar with the ways of Chan and Taoist meditation, he had long since repudiated his own experiments with it, and while feeling no compulsion constantly to attack Buddhism, he made clear his rejection of it as incompatible with Confucian principles.[24] There are, moreover, indications that his experience and that of other Confucians in the Ming falls into a broader category of mysticism that need not always be labeled "Chan." Indeed, the possibility of a distinctive Confucian mysticism can by no means be ruled out.

On this particular occasion, Wang Yangming was preoccupied not only with the problem of apprehending "the principle of things" but in an intensely personal way with the question of how to become a sage. In his pioneering work, *Chūgoku ni okeru kindai shii no zasetsu* (*The Frustration of Modern Thought in China*), Shimada Kenji has drawn attention to the special urgency with which Ming thinkers felt this need.[25] What for Zhu Xi and the Song school had been seen as an ideal for all, though achievable in fact by only a few, had become for them— and this includes Chen Xianzhang, his teacher Wu Yubi, and Wang's teacher Lou Liang, as well as Wang Yangming himself—an overriding necessity. It was, one might say, as if their salvation depended on it. Men had become persuaded that sagehood should no longer be thought of as a remote, lofty, and awesome ideal exemplified by a few great figures in the past. It must be something realizable here and now by anyone.

THE EXPERIENCE OF ONENESS WITH ALL CREATION

One key to the Ming experience of the self and of sagehood is the Neo-Confucian doctrine that "the humane man forms one body with Heaven-and-earth and all things." A development from the earlier

Confucian idea of the unity of Heaven and man, this doctrine had been put forward by Cheng Hao and was often associated with Zhang Zai's mystical vision of man's essential harmony with the universe expressed in his celebrated *Western Inscription*.[26] According to this view, man in his essential nature (*xing*) is identical with all nature (*tiandi*) and of the same substance as all things. Theoretically, this identity is based on the equation of humanity or man's nature with life itself. The fundamental characteristic of the universe or Way is seen as its creativity or productivity, and man too is seen as creative in his very essence.

It was especially in relation to Buddhism that Neo-Confucians stressed the importance of this doctrine. As they saw it, Buddhism identified life with suffering and illusion; it insisted that man could discover his true identity only by negating and then transcending his ordinary humanity, that is, recognizing it as an illusory distinction in a transient world. For the Neo-Confucian, on the other hand, self-transcendence should be attained not by denying one's humanity but by affirming it, by overcoming selfishness in one's daily life, identifying with others, and coming to an awareness of man's ethical and cultural activity as participating in the creative process of Heaven-and-earth.

In the Ming, the importance of this conception is evident in the frequency with which it is employed to describe both man's role in the world of action and his experience in the life of contemplation.[27] Overtones of it are found in Professor Ren's discussion of Chen Xianzhang, particularly in the lines "Standing between Heaven-and-earth, what dignity this body of mine possesses," and "This body of mine, small though it is, is nevertheless bound up with ethical principles. The pivot is in the mind."[28]

Man's bodily self and his moral mind are at the center of the creative process and therefore play an exalted role. "Man forms one body with Heaven-and-earth," Chen says. "Hence the four seasons proceed and all things are produced. If one gets stuck in one place how can one be the master of creation?"[29]

To be a sage, then, was to be the master of all creation. For Wang Yangming and many of his followers, the sagehood to which any man might aspire was no less cosmic in its significance. With a belief in the direct attainment of sagehood and a vision of man standing at the center of creation, the ingredients of a spiritual revolution were at hand.

In some ways, this development is comparable to the proclamation of universal Buddhahood through the Mahāyāna in China, Japan, and Korea centuries earlier and especially to those forms (Zhenyan and Chan) that emphasized the attainment of Buddhahood in this life and this body. There is a difference, however, in the Ming exaltation of life, creativity, and the potentialities of the human individual.

QUIETISM AND ACTIVISM

If the mystical quality of Ming thought is inspired by this sense of man's oneness with all creation, it has important implications for both self-cultivation and man's proper activity in the world. This is an ethical mysticism, of which the natural expression is an impulse toward action on behalf of all mankind. As we have seen in the case of Wang Yangming's experience of sagehood, there has been a tendency to interpret such mystical phenomena, especially where they involve the cultivation of "quiescence" (*jing*) or the practice of "quiet-sitting" (*jingzuo*), as showing the influence of Buddhism and Daoism. Nor can there be much doubt that, in a general way, Buddhist ideals of non-attachment and peace of mind along with Taoist meditative practices exerted a strong attraction on Neo-Confucians of both the Song and Ming. Quiet-sitting was approved and encouraged by Zhou Dunyi, the Cheng brothers, and Zhu Xi. Though a practice without precedent in earlier Confucian tradition, its sanction by these Song masters was sufficient to justify and encourage its use among orthodox scholars from Wu Yubi in the early Ming to Gao Panlong in the late Ming. Thus it seems indisputable that the Buddhist-Daoist example exerted a magnetic pull on the growth of Neo-Confucianism, causing it to develop along lines that would have been improbable except in a climate permeated by such influence.

On the other hand, as we have just seen, Neo-Confucianism from the start had felt compelled to reject the basic assumptions of Buddhist nonattachment or Daoist vacuity. A detached attitude toward things might be admirable, but the Confucian conception of human life and the self did not allow the individual to be seen in isolation from his social environment or the moral imperatives of Heaven. It was unrealistic, wrong, and selfish to conceive of human existence apart from the concrete relationships and obligations inescapably involved in the production and sustaining of human life. One could not renounce these obligations and cares even if to do so brought peace of mind. Anxiety, as Fan Zhongyan had implied, might be a higher state of mind than the peace of Nirvana.[30]

Confucian detachment, therefore, was sought in another direction. Virtue, humaneness, love, in their fullness and perfection, could express detachment in the midst of human involvement. Unselfish performance of duty to others was a discipline of ordinary life leading to both self-transcendence and self-fulfillment. An example of this is found in the case of Chen Xianzhang. The latter is said to have abandoned the wearing of silk after the death of his mother, to whom he had been deeply devoted. One might have taken this as a sign of utter desolation over his loss: Chen had become so identified with his mother and emotionally dependent upon her that the rest of his life was overshadowed by his sense of mourning. Yet Chen's own explanation was of another sort. His preference in dress, he says, had always been for the utmost simplicity. He had put on finer robes only to please his mother and, though he continued for years to humor her, with her passing he was free to please himself. We may have doubts today as to how well Chen understood what he was doing or the extent to which hidden compulsions operated here. Yet such doubts are in one sense irrelevant. In his own mind, he had no consciousness that subordination of self to filial duty involved the loss of his own identity. His own preferences, though submerged in hers for so long, remained intact and unimpaired, awaiting the proper time for their expression.

Thus, in most Neo-Confucian methods of cultivation, even those characterized by "quiescence," the object was to root out not desire itself but only selfish desires—desires that set one apart from others, from things, from the world, from Heaven. Zhang Zai's *Western Inscription* is the most eloquent statement of this ideal, and its enduring popularity suggests how central to later Confucian thought was this mystical vision of man harmoniously united to all forms of life.

In the formulation of this view, Neo-Confucians could draw upon the legacy of classical Confucian teaching for most of the essential ingredients, if not for the practice of quiet-sitting. Among these is the idea that involvement in life, the active cultivation of moral man, can lead to true repose. As we have seen in Confucius's memorable summation of his own experience of life:

> At fifteen, I had my heart set on learning.
> By thirty, I had established myself (in its pursuit).
> By forty, I had no perplexities.
> By fifty, I knew the will of Heaven.
> By sixty, I was ready to listen to it.
> By seventy, I could follow my heart's desire without transgressing.[31]

Here we find a confidence that human life can follow a meaningful pattern and by ordered stages of growth and maturity attain a freedom wherein one's spontaneous desires are naturally in accord with Heaven, the moral order and vital power in the universe. This is a freedom in which one's own desires have been brought into perfect relation to the means of their fulfillment, the desires and needs of others, and the creative purposes of Heaven as the source of all life. In the Ming, it is an ideal and an aspiration intimately bound up with sagehood, and, as the latter came to be thought more readily attainable, so did this freedom. What it meant, however, to be able to "follow one's heart's desire without transgressing" depended greatly on one's understanding of the heart-and-mind of man. Hence the lively discussion of this problem—the mind and nature—throughout the Ming and especially of this freedom among the existentialist followers of Wang Yangming.

At the same time, the ideal of freedom-in-action implied that active involvement in the world and personal commitment to doing Heaven's will need not require constant and compulsive action in the world. Obedience to Heaven's will called for quiet acceptance and resignation as often as it did for effort in behalf of right. The *Book of Changes* proffered a kind of moral science in which the conditions for "advancing" and "withdrawing," engaging and disengaging, were specified. Here too Ming scholars were more attracted by these "signs" as a guide to action than they were to the *Changes* as a cosmological system, as is shown, for example, in Professor Huang's study of the utilitarian thought of the late Ming statesman Ni Yuanlu. The essential notion, however, is quite implicit in the *Analects* and *Mencius*. Mozi saw it and condemned it as fatalism, but (as Professor Tang Junyi has brought out in his studies on the Will of Heaven in early Chinese thought) the Confucian conception was far more profound than Mozi appreciated.[32] The decree of Heaven manifested itself in various forms and on different levels. One could not identify it wholly with a single course of action. One's moral nature, which was the endowment of Heaven, might prompt one to take action in a good cause, but Heaven's decree, as made known through the circumstances surrounding this action, might nevertheless thwart the accomplishment of one's objective or force a redirection of one's efforts before success could be achieved. Alertness was required to all the promptings of Heaven, whether internal or external, in a constant process of reexamination. There were times for action and times for quiescence.

Beyond this, moreover, there was a need for quiescence in action. This was an attitude of mind that not only took into account the circumstances favoring engagement or disengagement at any given time but also accepted the necessity for continual striving in the face of continual disappointment. Confucius described himself as one who kept on trying even when he knew it was of no use. In other words, he could be engaged in what he thought to be right yet disengaged so far as his own expectations were concerned.

To sum up, then, Confucian cultivation was alert to the external signs that suggested whether to "advance" or "withdraw" and sensitive to the promptings of one's heart as to what was right in some circumstances, but not necessarily in all, or what one must hold to under any circumstances. Thus there could be stability of purpose and composure of mind in the midst of action, and there could also be active mental or spiritual contact with the world even when circumstances dictated a period of inactivity.

As applied to the Ming, therefore, or indeed any other period in Chinese history, we cannot expect from the Confucian active involvement only of a kind that is highly visible or outwardly effective. Wang Yangming was outstanding as an active statesman and general, and some see this as exemplifying his doctrine of the unity of knowledge and action. Others cite it further as illustrating the more dynamic and active spirit of the Ming. But Wang was a most exceptional figure for his or any other age. For many Ming thinkers confronted by difficult political choices, right action consisted in political disengagement. They chose deliberately to live in what would be known as official retirement, pursuing a life not dissimilar to that of Confucius as a teacher and scholar. Thus, if the spirit of Ming thought is to be considered "active" and "dynamic," the basis for it must be an involvement with life not exclusively political in character.

MIND, BODY, AND SELF

In the Ming, as its critics complained, there were as many ways of viewing the mind and nature as there were schools and thinkers. There were differences, for example, as to whether the substance of the mind (the nature) was static or dynamic, whether its cultivation should be active or passive, and, if active, whether the effort at cultivation (*gongfu*) should be applied to the substance of mind (*benti*) or to its functioning (*yong*). Most Ming thinkers agreed, however, that Confucian teaching in these matters differed from Buddhism in taking actual life as its starting point. For the Neo-Confucian, life (*sheng*) is the basic value. He is ever conscious of the intimate connection between it and man's nature. The nature is what fosters life, and action or conduct conforming to the true nature of man conduces to his total well-being—physical, emotional, spiritual—and ultimately to the welfare of all things. Thus a truly moral life builds one's morale and spirit but also contributes to one's bodily health. Conversely, one's mental and moral capacities greatly depend on one's physical powers and drives for their development. Even the so-called School of the Mind does not see this mind as a disembodied spirit but rather as a vital power manifested through the physical aspect of man, his material force or ether (*qi*). Likewise, this school rejects the tendency in Cheng-Zhu thought to distinguish an abstract essence of mind or moral nature, on the one hand, and an emotional, sensual self identified with the body, on the other. The nature as principle is neither an immutable norm by which one judges the propriety of one's impulses and desires nor a purely rational law standing over against man's physical drives and passions. The life-fulfilling nature and the vital power of material force are inseparable.

When we refer to the School of the Mind (*Xinxue*), then, we must remember that *Xin* represents both the heart and mind of man, his affective as well as his rational nature. To think of this school as a form of philosophical idealism or Neo Platonic mysticism is misleading. The mind here represents man's actual nature, and a major tendency in the school is undoubtedly existentialist. At the same time, the very effort to overcome or to embrace the antithesis between ideal and actual, the spiritual and the material, the static and the dynamic creates its own ambiguities and precludes simple characterization. We do well to note the range of possibilities inherent in these concepts. Insofar as our word "spirit" designates the breath of life, its original and basic meaning in the West, it must be identified not with reason or principle but with the Chinese *qi* ("material force" or "ether"), which is constantly active in the universe, constantly emerging from an invisible state into a visible. So too in the mind the creative power of material force is constantly manifesting itself.

The moral nature, which is spoken of also as the "substance or essence of the mind" (*benti*), is the principle of unity and harmony between man and things. And the impulses, desires, and drives that arise in the mind are not necessarily evil unless they impair or destroy that harmony. The problem of self-cultivation is to observe these impulses and ideas as they emerge from the formless state and to insure that their expression (or functioning) conforms to this total harmony. Mind culture in the more orthodox thinkers consists in identifying these impulses at the point of inception (*ji*) and acting on them in such a way that the fundamental composure or harmony of the self is preserved and sustained. On the other hand, if one assumes, as Ming existentialists do, that the essential mind or nature is transmoral in its perfection, then self-cultivation becomes a matter of true self-expression rather than of moral judgment or self-restraint.

In either case, the School of the Mind focuses on the active, living subject in contact with others and with things seen as one body with oneself. Self-understanding, an apprehension of one's true self, or insight into the substance of the mind does not require withdrawal from the senses or from contact with the world. Knowledge and action involve a constant interaction between the self and others, the nature and the senses, the individual and the environment. Rightly or wrongly (and I cannot deal fully with the issues here), most Ming thinkers felt that this distinguished Confucian self-cultivation from the type of Buddhist contemplation that sought withdrawal into an inner self or a higher self, in which the flow of ideas, thought, and desires had been stopped.

This view of the mind or self was holistic in the sense that man and his universe were seen as an organic unity, whereas Buddhism asked man to disavow his distinctively human nature and establish his true nature in a state of nondependence on the world. According to Wang Yangming, this destroyed the essential unity of things by creating higher and lower spheres of existence, a transcendental and a mundane order. It did not help that Buddhism ultimately reconciled the two through insight into the identity of Nirvana and Samsara. Such a mystical insight afforded no way of dealing with the world in rational, human terms.

If, however, this life-affirming view was seen as opposed to Buddhism and Daoism, there were in Ming thought other tendencies toward reconciliation. The intuitionist and existentialist trend in the Wang Yangming school led close to Chan Buddhism, even if their original premises differed. There were points of convergence in the belief in sagehood and buddhahood being inherent in all men and in the experience of enlightenment as the recognition of one's true selfhood being identical with the actual self. Further, the affirmation of the physical and affective side of man's nature opened the way to Daoist concepts and practices of self-cultivation through both physiological and psychological means.

A NEW "LIBERALISM" AND "PRAGMATISM" IN THE LATE MING

In the widespread trend toward "Unity of the Three Teachings," so marked in the sixteenth century, there is no doubt a large element of traditional Chinese syncretism. But syncretism of this sort had usually operated on a low intellectual level as an aspect of popular religion. The striking feature of the new humanitarianism that developed out of the Wang Yangming school was that, drawing on the latter's liberal view of man, it brought together the upper and lower classes, deepening the level of social consciousness in the former and raising the level of moral consciousness in the latter, while also releasing new political and cultural energies throughout the society. In other words, this was not simply a popular religious phenomenon but one that tended to unite and activate new forces on several levels, with leadership coming from an important segment of the educated elite. This is particularly apparent in popular literature and painting. Evidences of it are found in the new "morality books" discussed by Professor Sakai, on one hand, and in a very different way by Professor Hsia's discussion of the romantic trend in the dramatic literature of Tang Xianzu.[33] Both of these developments arose partly out of contact with the so-called left wing of the Wang Yangming school. The morality books drew upon its view of the autonomy of the moral self, and romantic literature drew upon its recognition of the passionate and appetitive nature of the individual. The present writer's discussion of individualism in the late Ming brings out further the possibilities inherent in the optimistic and liberal view of the self found in this school.[34]

There is still other evidence that what we find in the sixteenth century is a near-revolution in thought rather than simply a passing mood of eclecticism. The new view of the self, stressing the actual nature of man and especially his physical life and concrete needs, tended to generate a new "pragmatism" that gave increasing attention to "practical" realities in statecraft and fiscal administration.

Since this kind of thinking centered, philosophically speaking, around the concept of *qi*, it has been described as a kind of materialism. If we recall, however, the dual aspect of *qi* as both matter and "spirit," we are not surprised to find that its proponents in the late Ming are as readily drawn to Chan Buddhism as to anything resembling Western materialism. It is also significant that among Confucians upholding a monism of *qi* the emphasis on realism and practicality finds its concrete expression within the domain of the traditional Confucian concern for society, that is, primarily in government, rather than in the development of a thoroughgoing empiricism in either the physical or social sciences. At the same time, it is more an expression of Ming "activism" than it is of the kind of detached, theoretical speculation important to the development of science in the West.

It is for these reasons that I have spoken of a near-revolution in thought during the latter part of the Ming, recognizing both the new potentialities and opportunities it presented and also the failure of these to develop fully. By and large, the new trends were confined during the seventeenth century to the established areas of Confucian concern: self and society as understood essentially in humanistic and moralistic terms. Nevertheless, this could not mean simply a return of Chinese thought to the *status quo ante*. If a new empiricism and positivism failed to develop fully, still the Ming left its successors at a new stage. The antimetaphysical tone of Qing thought is clearly the product of the increasing Ming emphasis on practical action, physical reality, and empirical study. In other words, Qing thought is the direct heir of the Ming, even though it prefers not to acknowledge this indebtedness. Like the Ming itself with respect to the Song, the Qing attacks in its predecessor what the latter had taught it to be dissatisfied with. It washed its hands of the Ming in Ming water.

13

The Rise of Neo-Confucianism in Korea

Despite its modest size and marginal situation on the edge of Asia, Korea has played a key role in the development of East Asian civilization. Without challenging China's claim to be the Central Kingdom or dreaming, as Japan at times has done, that it could become the dominant power in Asia, Korea has afforded again and again throughout its history not only a meeting ground and sometimes a battlefield for its larger neighbors but also cultural achievements to rival those of China and Japan. It is only recently, however, that its stellar contributions to East Asian culture have gained the recognition they deserve.

Three personal experiences, on visits to disparate points in East Asia, have impressed upon me the unpredictable ways in which this Korean contribution has been made. The first occurred in 1960, when I visited the Confucian Society, in what was then known as Saigon. Officers of the society showed me, with a sense of real achievement under difficult circumstances, a new publication of theirs. It was a bilingual edition, in romanized Vietnamese and Chinese characters, of a traditional

Confucian primer that had been highly regarded in their country, the *Minh-tam bao-giam*. On examination it proved to be not a Chinese work but the *Myŏngsim pogam*, a "classic" compiled by the Korean scholar Ch'u Chŏk (Nodang) at the end of the thirteenth century. Much admired as a primer in Korea down into modern times,[1] its diffusion throughout East Asia and the high regard in which it was held for summing up the wisdom of the East even led to its translation into Spanish and introduction to Europe in the seventeenth century. Clearly, the ascending star of Neo-Confucianism in the late Koryŏ and early Yi dynasties had shed its light far beyond what Westerners have called the Hermit Kingdom.

My second visit was to the library of Yi T'oegye, the Tosan Sŏwŏn, in the mountains near Andong, Korea, where I found the writings of the scholar Zhen Dexiu (1178–1235), a Neo-Confucian scholar-statesman of the next generation after Zhu Xi (1130–1200), the great synthesizer of Neo-Confucianism. Though widely influential in the early centuries of the Neo-Confucian movement, these writings had been largely ignored by modern scholarship. Once recognized, however, for their importance to Korean philosophers and kings in the thirteenth to eighteenth centuries, these works and their historical significance for China itself could be recovered and appreciated.

My third visit was to the Cabinet Library (Naikaku Bunko) in Tokyo. There one could examine the charred and smoke-soiled remains from Edo fires of works studied by the Hayashi family mentors to seventeenth-century Tokugawa shoguns. Among them were Neo-Confucian texts, written or commented on by Korean scholars like Yi T'oegye (1501–1570), and reprinted or recopied with handwritten comments in the margin by their Japanese understudies. Here one could see in textual transmission the process by which the seed of Neo-Confucian discourse was propagated from one fertile soil to another across East Asia.

Neo-Confucianism has usually been thought of as a scholastic teaching and philosophy, but as it spread in the thirteenth to seventeenth centuries it carried a new form of cultural and religious contagion—a dynamic way of life that only later settled down into more fixed patterns. To the restless, impatient eyes of the nineteenth and twentieth centuries, Neo-Confucianism has appeared stuck in a rut—an immovable mass of tradition and rigid dogma. Yet viewed from the other end, as it arose in the thirteenth century, the new movement is most striking for its burgeoning vitality and reformist zeal.

True, Neo-Confucianism was far from a *mass* movement. Its first signs of life appear in the relative seclusion of schools and academies in South China, where Zhu Xi's disciples quietly propagated his teachings. In those early days of the thirteenth century, the odds were against their achieving any wide success. Zhu Xi's doctrines had been proscribed by the state as heterodox, and when this inquisition abated, China found itself locked with the Mongols in what seemed to be a life-and-death struggle for the survival of Chinese civilization.

Of this the surprising outcome was that the Mongols themselves, though hardly dedicated to the propagation of Chinese culture, became the unpremeditated sponsors and purveyors of Neo-Confucianism. To them it was a secular teaching not necessarily in conflict with their adherence to Buddhism or with Khubilai's patronage of Daoist masters. Once the Grand Khan had reconciled himself to governing China through a dyarchy of Mongol tribal and Chinese bureaucratic institutions, he became persuaded by the scholar-statesman Xu Heng (1209–1281) that Neo-Confucianism could serve as the ideological basis for the new hybrid state. Thus Xu became entrusted with organizing a new educational system based on Zhu Xi's texts and teachings. Thereafter, its successful propagation led in 1313–1315 to the adoption of a Neo-Confucian curriculum for the civil-service examinations—a system that would largely channel the energies and intelligence of educated Chinese down into the twentieth century.

If this were all that Khubilai and his Mongols had done, it might explain how Chinese ideas and institutions endured in their homeland but would not account for the almost revolutionary impact of Neo-Confucianism on the rest of East Asia. What differentiated his situation from the typical dynastic order was that Khubilai's ambitions and power reached well beyond the traditional limits of China proper. His was a conquest regime, and Peking served as the capital not only of China but of a larger empire comprising other Mongol dependencies. A cosmopolitan city, it housed residents from Central Asia, Korea, Vietnam, and elsewhere who participated in the cultural life at the hub of a universal empire. Among them were kings and heirs-apparent to the Korean throne, who were obliged to reside in Peking as virtual hostages of the Mongols. They and a retinue of scholarly compatriots had access to the new learning from the South, first brought to the Yuan capital in 1235 by another captive of war, Zhao Fu (c. 1206–c. 1299), who lectured on Zhu Xi's teachings and his commentaries on the Four Books at the recently opened Academy of the Supreme Ultimate. Until then, for years before the Mongols extended their conquest to the South, North China and Korea had been largely (though not totally) cut off from the Southern Song. There was a pent-up interest in the latest of Song scholarship and philosophy, especially among Confucian activists like the charismatic Xu Heng (himself a student of Zhao Fu). As an advisor to Khubilai and rector of the Imperial Academy, Xu was in a position to direct the cultural policies of the Yuan state and to manifest his missionary zeal in teaching not only Chinese but Mongols, Central Asians, and Koreans as well.

When eventually Neo-Confucian texts were incorporated in the new civil service–examination system, Koreans were among those eligible to take part in the ethnically diverse and highly cosmopolitan field of candidates. Among the non-Chinese, the Koreans were no doubt the best prepared and the most adept of students as well as the most avid collectors of books for transmission back home. It was from these expatriate subjects of the Koryŏ dynasty that a new generation of scholars was to come, and they would, with the introduction to their homeland of the new "Learning of the Way," first stir up an intellectual and educational revolution and then help bring down the Koryŏ dynasty itself.

The Neo-Confucianism thus introduced to Korea was highly specific in form and in its historical development. It drew, of course, on a large body of tradition, and in much of its content could simply be described as Confucian. Nevertheless, its history begins with Zhu Xi and can be traced in precise detail (as Yi T'oegye and more recently Wing-tsit Chan have done) from Zhu's disciples down into the Yuan period[2] and then to Koryŏ. It spread through identifiable academies, pursuing a well-defined curriculum. Its texts, largely from the hand of Zhu, contained new doctrines concerning human nature and the social order, which at a certain point in time began to displace the traditional subjects in schools and examinations, first in China, then in Korea.

Indeed, one can trace its rise in the course of ideological and political struggles at the Yuan court, from which the new teaching emerged triumphant over older forms of Chinese learning.[3]

This, then, is not just a case of the old Confucianism reaching maturity, developing a comfortable middle-aged spread, and then slumbering off into dreams of China's ancient glories. It is rather a new offspring, one full of energy and ambition to take on the world. Not content simply to reclaim the Central Kingdom for Chinese culture, it reached out to embrace a multicultural world extending beyond even the Mongol empire.

SPEAKING OF NEO-CONFUCIANISM

In the historical instance just described, the new movement had a quite specific content and character as the Cheng-Zhu Learning or School of the Way (*daoxue*). This was itself, however, just part of a larger process, and even its centrality in the mainstream of the new social and cultural trend can be appreciated only in relation to the whole enterprise known as Neo-Confucianism. Though of Western coinage, this term has gained some acceptance even in East Asia to designate the groundswell of new thought that arose with the Confucian revival in the Song period (960–1279) and flowed down into modern times.

Much of this term's currency in the West may be attributed to its use by scholars including Fung Yulan, Carsun Chang, and Alfred Forke, whose historical surveys were among the first to draw attention to the later development of Confucian thought.[4] Fung's translator, Derk Bodde, adopted "Neo-Confucianism" as a rendering for *daoxue*, the Chinese term used by Fung in volume 2 of his *History of Chinese Philosophy* (*Zhongguo zhexue shi*).[5] In the latter work, as also in his later *Short History*, Fung took a comparatively broad view of *daoxue*. He did not restrict it to the so-called Cheng-Zhu School, as the *Song History* (*Songshi*) had done, but included within its scope such independent thinkers as Lu Xiangshan (1139–1193) and Wang Yangming (1472–1529). Further, Fung extended the discussion of Neo-Confucian developments down into the Qing period (1644–1911), viewing even critics of the Cheng-Zhu school as variant expressions of a philosophical dialogue initiated in the Song. In his treatment of *daoxue* in the Song, on the other hand, Fung was less inclusive. No doubt constrained by the selectivity demanded in writing a general history of Chinese philosophy, he focused on the metaphysicians who contributed to the synthesis of Zhu Xi and neglected large areas of Song thought that earlier had been represented in *Case Studies of Song and Yuan Confucians* (*Song Yuan xuean*), the classic account of Song thought by Huang Zongxi (1610–1695) and Quan Zuwang (1705–1755).

Beside the fact of its having come into general use in the West, the name "Neo-Confucianism" has the advantage of being broadly inclusive of different schools and successive phases in the later development of Confucian thought rather than being narrowly identified with one particular view of it. At the same time, as one aspect of the larger Confucian tradition Neo-Confucianism includes much that is basic to Confucian thought as a whole. Thus some scholars may well question why elements identifiable with the ethical and political core of a perennial Confucianism should not simply be called "Confucian" rather than "Neo-Confucian." Why not indeed! The coexistence of old and new, of perennial "fundamentalism" as well as of distinctive new elements in later thought, must be allowed for.

Among the latter, Neo-Confucians often invoke ancient phrases or traditional concepts while putting them to new uses. Thus, for instance, the ancient virtue of "reverence" or "respect" (*jing*) became supercharged in the Song with a new moral and intellectual "seriousness" as well as with a sense of religious awe and mindfulness or "concentration," each reflecting a different side of Neo-Confucianism's flanking attacks on Buddhism. This is also the case with the central Confucian concept of humanity or humaneness (*ren*), the interpretation of which was greatly amplified by Zhu Xi and others. There are, too, such formulations as the "five moral relations" (*wulun*) and "three mainstays" (*san gangling*) among other expressions from the classics especially dear to Neo-Confucians and invested by them with a new importance. One can, of course, identify any of these as Confucian in the larger sense, but often their significance in the context of later thought lies in how and why they were singled out for special emphasis by Neo-Confucian thinkers. In such cases—and others will be cited below—one is warranted in underscoring the "Neo-Confucian" character of even traditional values.

The appropriateness of such distinctions varies from period to period. In the late Song and Yuan, there was open conflict between old-style, conservative Confucians and liberal Neo-Confucians who were quite free in their interpretation of the classics. Later in the Ming and Qing, after specifically Neo-Confucian formulations had become institutionalized and sometimes officially sanctioned, these recently established interpretations themselves became subject to a still newer brand of criticism that exposed the license taken by Song thinkers in their reading of the classics. As to whether such purist or fundamentalist criticism in the late Ming and Qing should be called Neo-Confucian or Confucian, it is perhaps a case of six of one or half a dozen of another, depending on whether one views this scholarship as a further extension of the Neo-Confucian's critical reinterpretation of received tradition or whether one sees it as a fundamentalist return to an original and supposedly "pure" form of Confucianism that should remain a fixed standard of literal interpretation for all times.

One would underestimate the actual complexity of the problem, however, if one did not take into account the ways in which the great neoclassicists of the seventeenth century, among them Huang Zongxi and Gu Yanwu (1613–1682), were heirs to, as well as critics of, Song-Ming Neo-Confucianism. It was no doubt in recognition of this that Fung Yulan spoke of Qing learning as

> a continuation of Song and Ming Neo-Confucianism, the major contribution of which lay in new answers and interpretations to the latter's traditional problems and texts.... Hence those adherents of the Han Learning [in the Qing] who concentrated on philosophy should, despite outward opposition to Neo-Confucianism, properly be regarded as its perpetuators and developers.[6]

To point out these nuances in the use of terms is also to acknowledge that Neo-Confucianism underwent successive modifications from its very beginning. Neo-Confucians differed among themselves as to whether the Way or Dao should be conceived of as a mainstream of fluid thought, with many tributaries and side currents, or whether it should be seen as a fixed legacy to be handed down intact to later generations. Demonstrably, Neo-Confucianism first struggled and then flourished as a dynamic intellectual movement before it settled down to become an established tradition. When finally it did assume scholastic form, the tradition survived primarily as a dialogue or body of discourse built up by citing earlier texts and historical cases as a way of defining issues for discussion. An example of this, and also of the Confucian/Neo-Confucian dichotomy referred to above, is the new attention given to the so-called Four Books. These texts were "Confucian" in the sense of being drawn from the earlier Confucian classics, but interpreted and repackaged as they were by Zhu Xi, they came to have a new meaning and significance in Neo-Confucian discourse. Unless one is quite familiar with Zhu Xi's commentaries on the *Great Learning* (*Daxue*), for instance, as well as with the intense discussion that his interpretations aroused in ensuing generations, one might miss the specific point of later references to Zhu Xi's views (as in Wang Yangming's *Inquiry Into the Great Learning*) and fail to recognize in what way the Neo-Confucian dialogue was being advanced.

A scholar's identification with tradition depends not only on his avowed loyalties or antipathies but also on which earlier writers he chooses to converse with over time, and which texts we must be conversant with if we are to comprehend him. He may be more or less of a "traditionalist" and more or less "orthodox" according to current definitions of that term, but he would be working within, or out of, Neo-Confucian tradition as long as it provides him with his basic frame of discursive reference and he does not call into question its underlying assumptions.

A case in point is the Japanese philosopher of the Tokugawa period Miura Baien (1723–1789), who has been cited in recent years as a highly original thinker, one who departed from orthodox Neo-Confucianism and anticipated modern scientific thought. Yet on more careful reflection in the perspective of East Asian thought as a whole, Professor Shimada Kenji finds little in Miura's thought that is not already anticipated by Song and Ming Neo-Confucians. Miura's philosophy, he concludes, "was hardly anything more than a variation on the philosophy of *qi* formulated by Song philosophers."[7] It is ignorance of the latter, more than a failure to recognize Miura's distinctive achievements, that distorts the picture.

Philosophically speaking, what may be considered irreducibly "Neo-Confucian" in these cases will vary according to one's reading of

Zhu Xi's or the other Song masters' thought as a whole. Yet as a system of thought undergoing historical development, Neo-Confucianism was a tangible body of discourse with definable characteristics; we are not without signposts by which to gauge directions or to measure continuity and change in the system. Among these reference points internal to the tradition itself are the new names scholars themselves coined to designate the Confucian Way and the new concepts with which they explained it—names and concepts not previously identified with Confucian tradition, which I shall discuss below. Another set of indicators is the texts accepted by them as authoritative, the shared basis of their common discourse. A third consists in institutions closely identified with the life of Neo-Confucianism, either those that promoted the discourse or those promoted by it—i.e., that were produced by Neo-Confucians themselves as a means of giving practical shape to their ideas. Finally, there are the specific interests served by Neo-Confucianism, or those interests it was made to serve through its official adoption by the state, etc.

Neo-Confucian Designations for the Way (*dao*) or Learning (*xue*)

Daoxue/tohak

Although the term "Neo-Confucianism" embraces many trends of thought, it was used in the Fung-Bodde translation to render *daoxue*, which in Chinese (indeed, in East Asian) usage has generally been identified with the Cheng-Zhu school and often with a narrow definition even of that. Literally translatable as "the Learning of the Way" or "School of the Way," depending upon whether one emphasizes its thought content or its scholarly transmission, this term has had a special importance in the history of Neo-Confucianism. As used by the Cheng brothers and Zhu Xi, it conveyed the sense of ultimate value and the commitment to it that we usually associate with religion. Not surprisingly, this claim to ultimate truth and its followers' intense dedication to it evoked a comparably strong reaction from those who rejected the claim. Hence the ironic use of the term among the critics of the Cheng-Zhu school or the characterization of it as false or spurious learning (*weixue*) during the Song period, when *daoxue*, far from constituting the officially approved learning, was on the contrary ridiculed and officially condemned.[8] It was only later, at the end of the Song and during the Yuan period, as a reflection of Zhu Xi's increasing influence in the scholarly community, that official acceptance of Zhu's teaching gave *daoxue* the connotation of an established orthodoxy.[9] This is the sense in which the term appears in the *Song History* (*Song-shi*), wherein a special section is devoted to Neo-Confucian thinkers who qualify as bearers of the True Way, with the implication of their being a breed apart from other Confucian scholars treated in the *Rujia* section of biographical accounts.

Given this usage of *daoxue*, I suggest that it be translated as "Learning" or "School of the Way" and that it be understood to represent orthodox Neo-Confucianism insofar as this would differentiate a subset of those thinkers officially considered "orthodox" from the larger numbers of those who accept the basic terms of, and participate in, the wider Neo-Confucian discourse. One must bear in mind, however, that many thinkers claimed to represent the authentic Cheng-Zhu teaching, though not all had official support for their claim.

In the *Unfolding of Neo-Confucianism* and in *Principle and Practicality*, I have pointed out that even those who resist official orthodoxy, or a narrow definition of it, rarely go so far as to reject any standard for "true teaching" at all.[10] A radical skepticism of this latter sort may sometimes be found in Daoist or Buddhist thought, but Neo-Confucians, for their part, hold to a belief in the existence of "real" values (*shi*), the possibility of knowing and communicating them, and the correlative obligation to follow a definable Way. One can understand this as "orthodoxy" in the broadest and most liberal understanding of the term, or one can think of it as "Neo-Confucian tradition" in contradistinction to "Orthodox Neo-Confucianism" in the more limited *daoxue* sense. Huang Zongxi's conception of the unity and variety of the Way, set forth in his discussion of *Yiben wanshu* in *Case Studies of Ming Confucians* (*Mingru xue'an*),[11] conveys his idea of Neo-Confucian thought as carrying on a Way (distinguishable from Buddhism and Daoism) with its own basic integrity and coherence, while at the same time it generates innumerable differentiations in individual schools and thinkers. It is this broad conception of the Confucian tradition, as well as its inherent power of creative diversification, that Huang celebrates in the sweeping panorama of Song, Yuan, and Ming thought presented in *Case Studies of Song and Yuan Confucians* and *Case Studies of Ming Confucians.* Objective though Huang tried to be in his exposition of Neo-Confucian thinkers, it would have been inconceivable to him that such objectivity could be altogether "value free" or noncommittal. The Way still provided a definite guide or standard for human life, and Huang decidedly rejected the notion that one could be all things to all men.

Shixue/sirhak

A less frequent characterization of Neo-Confucianism than *daoxue* is *shixue*, meaning "solid," "real," "substantial," or "practical" learning. This differentiated Neo-Confucianism from the "emptiness" of Buddhism and Daoism. It asserted the substantiality and knowability of Confucian values, in contrast to the mutability and uncertainty that governed all ordinary existence and cognition in the Buddhist view. For Neo-Confucians, *shixue* was the study of enduring moral, social, and cultural values, together with the practical benefits that could accrue from acting upon them or from studying their role in the historical process. It is noteworthy that Zhu Xi especially employs this term in his advocacy of an education that would be truly rooted in humane values and be of practical benefit to human society, and in Korea Chŏng Tojŏn (1342–1398) echoes this when he refers to Neo-Confucianism as "the real learning of the ancients which manifests the moral nature and renews the people."[12]

As the social and cultural context changed, so too did the view of "reality" in this tradition. This was particularly true in the field of learning, a matter that involved virtually all Neo-Confucians, and in the political and social affairs that concerned many of them. Here the processes of steady differentiation in human affairs produced a "reality" of increasing complexity. From a view of "real learning" that had focused on the human mind as embodying value principles and performing an integrative function in the conduct of life, there was a gradual shift toward the other pole of Neo-Confucian scholarship, the study of principles in things and affairs, with emphasis on their concrete particularity. The later stages of this process then converged on forms of Western learning that produced a utilitarian view of reality or a pragmatism much in contrast to the earlier holistic conception of Zhu Xi.

Xinxue/simhak or xinfa/simpŏp

The Learning of the Mind-and-Heart (*xinxue*) and the formula of the Mind-and-Heart (*xinfa*) are terms developed in the eleventh and twelfth centuries to characterize the Neo-Confucian doctrine of the mind and its proper discipline. They appear in the writings of Shao Yong (1011–1077), the Cheng brothers, and Zhu Xi and refer to a Neo-Confucian view of the mind, distinct from the Buddhist, which was in turn key to the Neo-Confucian political doctrine that the way to govern men was through individual self-discipline and that the key to self-cultivation was mind-rectification. I have discussed this development in *Neo-Confucian Orthodoxy and the Learning of the Mind-and-Heart*.[13] Here I wish only to stress that these terms were applied to the Neo-Confucian philosophy of mind as a whole and especially to the Cheng-Zhu school's central teaching concerning the "Mind of the Way" (*daoxin*) and the "Mind of Man" (*renxin*). In the thirteenth and fourteenth centuries, this Learning of the Mind-and-Heart spread through China and into Korea as an integral part of the Learning of the Way, i.e., orthodox Neo-Confucianism. Students of Neo-Confucianism in Korea will be familiar with this aspect of the tradition, so clearly echoed in writings of Yi T'oegye (Yi Hwang), for example, the *Ten Diagrams of the Sage Learning* (*Sŏnghak sipto*), of which the seventh is entitled "Diagram of the Learning of the Mind-and-Heart"[14] (*Simhak to*). Coming from a sharp critic of Wang Yangming, this Learning is unquestionably of the Cheng-Zhu School and not the so-called Lu-Wang School.

In the latter case, there has been some confusion because of the recent tendency to speak of the "School of the Mind" as something passed down from Lu Xiangshan to Wang Yangming and opposed to the Cheng-Zhu school as the School of Reason or Principle (*lixue*). To some extent, this is reflected in the treatment of the subject in Fung Yu-lan's *History of Chinese Philosophy*, where the Learning of the

Mind-and-Heart is most prominently identified with Lu Xiang-shan and Wang Yangming in chapter 14.[15] Actually, Fung himself cautions against drawing too sharp a dichotomy between Zhu and Lu in this respect. In his comparison of the two Fung says, as Bodde has translated it: "A popular way of contrasting Zhu Xi with Lu Jiuyuan is to say that the former emphasizes the importance of study, whereas the latter emphasizes the 'prizing of one's virtuous nature.' . . . What it overlooks, however, is that the final goal of Zhu Xi, no less than of all other Neo-Confucianists, is to explain the nature and functioning of the inner self."[16] This last expression, "the nature and functioning of the self," is actually a quotation drawn from a key section of Zhu Xi's discussion of the method of the *Great Learning*. It appears in the *Words and Phrases from the Great Learning* (*Daxue zhangju*) and *Questions on the Great Learning* (*Daxue huowen*), in a context that refers to the formula of the Mind-and-Heart (*xinfa*).[17] What Bodde has rendered as "the nature and functioning of the inner self" might be translated more literally as "the whole substance and great functioning of our mind-and-heart (*wu xin zhi quanti dayong*).[18] This is a central concept in Zhu's thought and assumes the importance of a "technical term" much discussed in the later Zhu Xi school. Here, it underscores the significance of Fung's observation in the Chinese text that "the final goal of Zhu Xi was to explain the nature and function of the mind-and-heart." In early Neo-Confucianism and even in much of the later school, there would have been no disposition to concede this crucial area to Lu and Wang as their special property. To avoid further confusion, it may be wise to translate *xinxue* as "Learning of the Mind-and-Heart" when it is used in this most general Neo-Confucian sense and to recognize "School of the Mind" as an attempt retroactively to link Wang Yangming's teaching to the thought of Lu Xiangshan. In this latter case, it would be seen as one significant outgrowth of the earlier Learning of the Mind-and-Heart, along with others like Chen Xianzhang's, which reflect a changed perception of the mind during the Ming period.

Another consideration here is that our term "school" may only be equated with the Chinese term *xue*, "learning," in a very loose sense. In fact, "Lu-Wang School" can only mean a loose affinity of ideas, not an intellectual lineage from teacher to disciple or scholar to scholar. Wang Yangming's "learning" or "thought" is akin to Lu Xiangshan's, but Wang did not receive it from a line of teachers coming down from Lu. In the case of the Cheng-Zhu "Learning of the Mind-and-Heart," however, there is usually some scholastic filiation, some personal link involved. By this criterion, Wang would have to be identified more with Cheng-Zhu.

Shengxue/sŏnghak

"Sage Learning" (*shengxue*) has several different connotations. It is, of course, the learning that comes from the sages of the past, i.e., "the Learning of the Sages," but Zhu Xi particularly emphasized it as the Way of learning to be a sage, or learning for sagehood. For him, the important thing was that sagehood could be a practicable ideal in the Song, that one could transform one's wayward mind-and-heart into a Way-ward one, through a definite process of self-cultivation. Zhu Xi's lifework and much of Neo-Confucian literature is premised on this idea. Unless one renders it as something like "Learning for Sage-hood" rather than simply "Learning of the Sages," one misses perhaps the most dynamic element in the Neo-Confucian version of this traditional conception.

The alternative rendering, "Way of the Sages and Worthies" (*shengxian zhi dao*) conveyed the idea that worthies of recent times, like the Song masters, came close enough to achieving sagehood as to be spoken of in the same breath with the ancients. It suggested the possibility that such attainment remained within anyone's reach. Inscriptions still hanging in the Royal Confucian College (*Sŏnggyun'gwan*) in Seoul today bear witness to the power of this ideal among the early Neo-Confucians in Korea.

Sagehood was understood in two principal forms. Classically, it had strong associations with the sage-rulers of the remote past and with the Way of the Sage-kings. This perennial political concern of Confucians is still prominent in the minds of Neo-Confucians, whether as proponents of programmatic, institutional reform or as advocates of the intellectual and moral self-reformation of the ruler. Many Neo-Confucian leaders also served as ministers to the ruler, counseling him on how he might revive and follow the Way of the Sage Emperors and Early Kings. From this a new kind of "traditional" learning arose in the eleventh century, along with the Learning of the Way (*daoxue*), which was known as the "Learning of the Emperors and Kings" (*diwang zhi xue*) or, for short, "Learning of the Emperors" (*dixue*). Scholars who propounded it, often in the lectures on the classics at court, were active in the same scholarly and official circles as the adherents of the Learning of the Way. Important among them were Fan Zuyu (1041–1098), a colleague of Cheng Yi (1033–1107) and Sima Guang (1019–1086), and Zhen Dexiu, a leader of the School of the Way in the generation after Zhu Xi.[19]

Sagehood was also conceived as the ideal form of, or model for, the self. Not everyone could expect to be a sage-ruler, but anyone could aspire to sageliness in virtue and wisdom. When Zhou Dunyi, the Cheng brothers, Zhu Xi, and other Neo-Confucians talked about learning to become a sage or transforming oneself into a sage, they were said to be pursuing "learning for the sake of one's self" (*wei ji zhi xue*), as Zhu Xi had put it using the language of the *Analects* (14:25): "The ancients pursued learning for one's own sake; nowadays they learn for the sake of [pleasing] others."

Whether as sage-ruler or as ideal self, the Neo-Confucian concept of sagehood exhibited certain perennial Confucian features as well as others particular to the Song. As Neo-Confucian ideas made their way into the Ming and other periods, problems of continuity and discontinuity arose with both conceptions. Some of these will be discussed later, but for illustration's sake one can imagine the difficulties that would arise with a "learning for the emperor," intended to activate the consciences of Song rulers, if one tried to apply it to Japanese emperors, who reigned but did not rule. Differences between Chinese and Korean monarchies would no doubt present their own problems.

Lixue/ihak and xinglixue/sŏngnihak

In the later development of Neo-Confucianism and in modern works, the Learning or School of Principle (*lixue*) has been one of the most common terms for Neo-Confucianism. *Li*, as principle, order, inner structure, was unquestionably a central concept in Neo-Confucian metaphysics. Yet its full significance only emerged with the passage of time. The Cheng brothers and Zhu Xi do not refer to their doctrine in this way, probably because they saw such a concept as only explanatory of, or instrumental to, the study of the Way and pursuit of sagehood. Zhen Dexiu, fully appreciative of the historic contributions of the Chengs and Zhu to the philosophy of principle, also recognized that the concept of *li* itself had little standing in classical Confucian literature and was not even mentioned in the original text of the Cheng-Zhu school classic, the *Great Learning*.[20]

When it came into wider use during the Ming and in Korea, *lixue* was closely associated with the Learning of Human Nature (*xinglixue*) and the Learning of the Mind-and-Heart. It stressed principle as human nature and principles as inherent in the mind. The imperial Ming *Compendium on Human Nature and Principle* (*Xingli daquan*), widely circulated in Korea, reinforced the idea that Cheng-Zhu teaching was to be understood as a philosophy of "human nature and principle." In the first general accounts of Ming Neo-Confucian thought, the *Authoritative Transmission of the Learning of Principle* (*Lixue zangquan*) by Sun Qifeng (1585–1675) and *Case Studies of Ming Confucians* by Huang Zongxi, references to *lixue* were understood to include *xinxue* within its scope. Yi T'oegye, as mentioned before, also speaks of *lixue* and *xinxue* as complementary terms, although by his time he felt the need to exclude Wang Yangming from the company of orthodox Neo-Confucians, which neither Sun nor Huang were prepared to do.[21]

There may be no harm in identifying *lixue* with reason or rationalism so long as this does not imply a merely logical ratiocination or conjure up a Western-style antithesis of reason versus intuition or emotion. According to Cheng-Zhu teaching, the moral principles that constituted the nature of Heaven in the mind of man were humane feelings and impulses. It was the ordered structure and inherent rationality of these natural feelings that gave the Learning of the Mind-and-Heart its confidence in men's spontaneous intuitions, and it was the reliability of basic human instincts—their universality and predictability among all peoples—that underlay the rationalism of the Learning of Principle.

A somewhat similar problem is met in describing the relation between principle (*li*) and ether (or material force, *qi*) in Neo-Confucianism. The language used for this by Professor Takahashi Tōru in his early accounts of Korean Neo-Confucianism has an aptness that is difficult to reproduce in English usage. The Japanese *shuri-ha* and *shuki-ha* can be understood as tending to put a relative emphasis on principle or ether (material force) respectively, without implying a necessary antithesis between monism and dualism.[22]

It is significant that no such term as *qixue* came into use among either Neo-Confucians or the critics of Cheng-Zhu *lixue* despite the rising importance of *qi* (material force) in later Neo-Confucianism. In the twentieth century, great attention was paid to what in seventeenth- and eighteenth-century Chinese thought has been called by "Marxist" writers "materialism" or by Japanese scholars such as Yamanoi Yū the "*qi* philosophy" or "*qi* thought" (*ki no tetsugaku* or *ki no shisō*).[23] Traditionally, however, it would not have been considered appropriate to view learning as primarily aimed at the study of matter or ether apart from the reason or principle inherent in it.

Daotong/tot'ong—The "Orthodox Way"

Daotong was a term widely used among Neo-Confucians after Zhu Xi applied it to the orthodox Way that he believed had been revived by the Cheng brothers. In *Neo-Confucian Orthodoxy*, I have already pointed out significantly different uses of this term in the Cheng-Zhu school depending on whether one stresses, as Zhu Xi did, the inspirational and prophetic elements in the revival and reinterpretation of the Way or authoritative transmission and scholastic filiation. Both of these have an important role in later Neo-Confucianism, but it is significant that when Neo-Confucians wish specifically to express the idea of transmission, *daotong* alone is not seen as sufficient, and therefore *daotong chuan* has been used to specify the "transmission of the orthodox Way."

Tong itself does not necessarily imply direct succession. In the related use of *zhengtong* as "legitimate succession," there is no necessary implication that legitimate dynastic rule is something handed on or directly conferred by one dynasty on its successor. Similarly, when Zhu Xi spoke of *daotong*, he emphasized the lack of continuous succession and stressed rather the repossession of the Way after a long lapse in transmission. In both of these cases, *tong* has the primary meaning of "control," "bring together," "coordinate." With Zhu Xi, it is effective repossession or reconstitution of the Way that is conveyed by *daotong*, just as *zhengtong* meant effective repossession or reconstitution of the empire, often after a period of disunity. For Zhu Xi, *zhengtong* constituted a recognition of a dynasty's political legitimacy without necessarily conferring on it the moral legitimacy of *daotong*. In this respect, Zhu Xi remained true to the earlier Song view that the Han and Tang, though great dynasties in asserting their effective political control of the empire, had failed to fulfill the Way of the Early Kings. Thus the purity of the Sages' Way was upheld while political common sense was not flouted.

In *Neo-Confucian Orthodoxy*, I have stressed *daotong* as the active repossession of the Way partly in order to bring out the significance of Neo-Confucian orthodoxy's being promoted under Mongol rule in ways that had no precedent during the Song or Jin dynasties. The Yuan dynasty's achieving of legitimate rule by actively reintegrating the whole empire after long years of division had a seeming analogue in the "repossessing of the Way" (*daotong*), achieved when the Learning of the Way (*daoxue*) became the established teaching in the Yuan schools and examination system.

Some acceptance of this idea would seem to have been implied when Korean converts to Neo-Confucianism sought to establish it as the orthodox teaching of Korea in the fourteenth and fifteenth centuries. Yet this same conception of the Way as "broken off" for centuries and only regained late in time by the Cheng brothers and Zhu Xi meant that Koreans too could think of it as something they were capable of repossessing directly without the need for any intermediation by the Chinese. Indeed, some Korean writers would think of their own active reconstituting of the Way as retrieving a long-lost Dao originally implanted in Korea by the sage-statesman Kija (Ji Zi), variously identified in classical sources as a survivor of the Shang dynasty who either came to northern Korea as a vassal of the Zhou or chose exile there rather than serve under a new dynasty.[24] In this view, the Koreans could be seen as resuming an indigenous "broken" transmission of the Dao, sharing in a larger world order based on Confucian values, while developing their own authentic version of the Way. Here there was room for a Korean identity to assert itself, eventually claiming for the Yi dynasty that it was more orthodox than the Ming itself in fidelity to that shared Way.

Concepts Conveying the Essence of the Way

Along with the foregoing names for the Way or for Neo-Confucian learning, there were other terms taken to express central truths or values in the Neo-Confucian teaching. Many ideas could be included here that individual thinkers and schools advocated as, in their eyes, keys to all others in the system. Humaneness, reverence, filiality (*xiao*), and innate knowing (*liangzhi*) are typical examples. Other concepts or doctrines may be identified with individual thinkers as their own distinctive contribution to the development of Neo-Confucian thought: e.g., Zhou Dunyi's "Nonfinite and yet the Supreme Ultimate" (*wuji er taiji*) or his "stressing quiescence" (*zhujing*), teachings that might be taken by some as central to Neo-Confucian metaphysics or spiritual praxis but accepted by others only with reservations.

Korean thinkers, no less than Chinese and Japanese, held diverse views on these matters. Certain ideas and practices were seen to have a special meaning for individual scholars and teachers depending on their own life experience; indeed, their learning would be thought superficial if it conformed simply to one model and did not reflect some personal struggle to "get" or find the Way for one's self (*zide*). This idea is not uncommon among Korean Neo-Confucians, but it is most evident in Yi Yulgok's (Yi I, 1536–1584) frequent reference to "getting it oneself" (*chadŭk*, for the Chinese *zide*). Yulgok particularly emphasized the Korean role of Kija as a sage comparable to Confucius and Mencius and, by equating Korea with the native states of the latter sages, Lu and Qi, he naturalized the Way of the Sage Kings with Kija as its spiritual patriarch. Kija thus served paradigmatically to demonstrate that "getting the Way oneself" was not finding it outside and internalizing it but finding the Way within and affirming it as universal.

Beyond these core ideas and individual concepts, however, there are formulations that attempt to characterize the tradition in a broader and more balanced way. Such formulations represent the Way as a comprehensive process or pattern in which it is vital to maintain a balance between polar values. "To abide in reverence and fathom principle" (*jujing qiongli*) expresses the idea that learning should link scholarly study and moral/spiritual cultivation. "To spend half the day in quiet-sitting and half in the study of books" (*banri jingzuo, banri dushu*) conveys the same idea in more concrete terms. In a similar vein, there is the classic formulation taken from the *Mean (Zhongyong)*, which speaks of "honoring the moral nature and pursuing intellectual inquiry" (*zun dexing, dao wenxue*). There has been some tendency recently to dichotomize these values in such terms as intellectualism versus anti-intellectualism or to identify one with Zhu Xi and the other with his "antagonist" Lu Xiangshan, but traditionally both elements were seen as equally necessary, and indeed complementary, aspects of the Way.

Each of these formulations conveys a sense of the Way as embracing certain universal values or developing basic human faculties, while at the same time each can be associated with the particular moral and intellectual concerns of the Song scholar-official (*shidafu*). Thus "abiding in reverence" may take the form for the Song scholar of quiet-sitting, since he is heir to Buddhist and Daoist meditation techniques (whether professedly so or not) as well as to Confucian ritual. For him too "fathoming principle" is more often pursued in bookish learning than in systematic observation of nature. As it happens, the Korean *yangban* aristocracy, also scholar-officials with Buddhist influences deeply embedded in their native tradition, inclined toward many of the same pursuits as Song scholars, e.g., office holding, "quiet-sitting," and classical studies. In principle, however, the expression of religious/moral concern or intellectual inquiry need not, and did not, adhere strictly to Song models, for Zhu Xi himself had acknowledged that such practices would vary with individual circumstances.[25]

On a more theoretical level, there is the expression of Zhu Xi referred to earlier, which is found in his *Words and Phrases from the Great Learning* and his *Questions on the Great Learning:* namely, "the whole substance and great functioning [of the nature as expressed in the mind-and-heart (*quanti dayong*)]." This formulation appears frequently in the writings of the early Cheng-Zhu School in the late Song, Yuan, and early Ming and conveys the sense of Neo-Confucian Learning as completely integrating the ideal of man's moral nature with its practical realization in fulfilling the needs of mankind.

As Zhen Dexiu explained it, there could be no separation of principle and practice, no discussion of "substance" that did not take human needs into account, and no resort to practices (functions) that did not conform to the moral nature of man and the Way.[26] Here the concept is broad enough to implicate the entire Cheng-Zhu system of metaphysics as the basis for one's understanding of the moral nature as well as to connote a large body of historical and social experience considered relevant to the "functioning" of that nature in particular human situations.

Professor Kusumoto Masatsugu has written a long essay on this recurrent theme in Chinese Neo-Confucian thought, which also had its Japanese proponents.[27] Korean Neo-Confucians too were familiar with this doctrine, and for them also it tended to define the essential tradition. Clearly, "substance" and "function" would have to be understood in terms of the Neo-Confucian discourse and are not comprehensible in classical terms alone.

On the same level of theoretical abstraction is the formula of Cheng Yi: "principle is one, its particularizations diverse," or "the unity of principle and diversity of its particularized functions" (*liyi fenshu*).[28] This served especially to distinguish Neo-Confucian teaching from Buddhism and Daoism, affirming the reality both of the immutable principle or substance of the nature—in man, his "humanity"—and the innumerable forms of action in which this virtue was given concrete expression. One could also view it as a way of emphasizing the unity of substance and function.

Some persons held that there was no essential difference in principle between Confucianism and Buddhism, since Confucian "humaneness" could be equated with Buddhist "compassion." According to this view, the only significant difference between the two teachings lay in the functional aspect, i.e., Buddhism's lack of a practical program such as Confucianism offered for dealing with the needs of human society. Li Tong (1093–1163), Zhu Xi's teacher, contended that the difference in practice also pointed to a difference in principle. One could not expect Confucian practice to follow from Buddhist principle, nor could one accept as true principle what did not lead to Confucian ethical practice. Hence there could be no dichotomizing, as in Buddhism, of principle and practice to represent two different orders of reality, principle real and undifferentiated and practice less real because it pertained to the world of differentiation and discrimination. To substantiate principle, one must realize one's humanity in the midst of practice, i.e., by fulfilling one's individual lot (*fen*) or station in life with its differentiated duties. This is what was meant by realizing "the unity of principle and the diversity of its particularizations."

For Neo-Confucians, this doctrine served to distinguish their "real or practical learning" from the "empty learning" of Buddhism, which viewed the world of moral action as a secondary or qualified order of reality in contradistinction to the essential Truth of Buddhist Emptiness.[29] Li Tong was unwilling to concede either the Buddhist bifurcation of reality on two levels of truth or the need for transcendental enlightenment as the precondition for coping with the world. For him, on the contrary, true spiritual freedom was to be attained in the performance of the moral task. In Yi T'oegye, such ideas resurfaced with special intensity, as he held Li Tong in even higher respect than Zhu Xi had done.

"Principle is one, its particularizations diverse" was much discussed by Xu Heng, the leading Neo-Confucian teacher of the Yuan period in China, who was a seminal force in the spread of the Learning of the Way.[30] Since his influence was strong in Korea as well as in seventeenth-century Japanese Neo-Confucianism,[31] one may take frequent reference to Li Tong, Xu Heng, and this concept as confirming the underlying continuity from Chinese Neo-Confucianism to the Korean and Japanese versions. It is understandable that a doctrine linking universal values to particular applications and recognizing the differentiated expression in social and cultural life of one underlying Way would have special significance for Koreans and Japanese, whose adherence to Neo-Confucian teaching was not taken to entail a loss of their own cultural identity.

Still another expression for the same basic idea is Cheng Hao's (1032–1085): "Humaneness which forms one body with Heaven-and-Earth and all things" (*tiandi wanwu yiti zhi ren*).[32] According to this holistic view, one's self-fulfillment was achieved by engendering a state of mind and following a way of conduct in which there was no longer any consciousness of a distinction between self and others. Such a view was quite prominent in Ming thought and in Tokugawa Neo-Confucianism. Professor Shimada Kenji, in his early studies of modern thought in China, saw an essential link between this ideal of Song-Ming Neo-Confucianism and late nineteenth-century reformers like Tan Sitong (1865–1898)—a continuity running down through almost a millennium of Neo-Confucian thought in China. More recently, in comparing the differing outlooks of the seventeenth-century Japanese thinkers Kaibara Ekken (1630–1714) and Yamazaki Ansai (1611–1682) in relation to Cheng-Zhu thought, Professor Okada Takehiko cited this doctrine of the "Humaneness which forms one body with Heaven-and-Earth and all things" and its importance in Ekken's thought as the crucial element of continuity in Neo-Confucianism and the key criterion by which to distinguish Ekken's essential orthodoxy from the skepticism of Ancient Learning [Kogaku] thinkers, which in some other respects Ekken shared.[33]

As a last example of this type of formulation, I offer the doctrine of "self-cultivation for the governance of men" (*xiuji zhiren*) or "ordering the state through self-discipline" (*xiushen zhiguo*). This was an outgrowth of the ethicopolitical thought developed during the Song in connection with the *Great Learning* and particularly in the lectures on the classics at the Song court. The appeal of this idea lay in its utter simplicity and rich ambiguity. Its primary meaning was that the responsibility for self-discipline fell first of all on the ruler (or his surrogates), who had to set the model for others' self-cultivation, but its plausibility rested on the idea that truly to govern men was not possible except through their voluntary cooperation and self-discipline.[34] *Xiushen zhiguo* was shorthand for the eight steps (*batiaomu*) of the *Great Learning*, and one might refer back to the latter for a fuller idea of what "self-cultivation" consisted in. But shorthand lent itself to oversimplification, and problems could arise from simplistic thinking about governmental administration. Perhaps in periods of decline or transition, when institutions failed, there was some advantage in putting everyone on their own and something hopeful about making a virtue of necessity in the midst of rapid political and social change. At any rate, this may have been the case in the late Song, Yuan, and early Ming, when the idea of "ordering the state through self-discipline," especially as advocated by Zhen Dexiu and Xu Heng, seems to have played a large role in gaining acceptance for Neo-Confucianism as the dominant public philosophy.

A similar phenomenon is observable in the writing of Fujiwara Seika as a proponent of this philosophy in Japan during the transition from the Warring States Period to the founding of the Tokugawa shogunate.[35] From my own reading in the thought of early Neo-Confucians in Korea and from the work of Martina Deuchler,[36] I conclude that this aspect of Neo-Confucianism had much the same appeal: it was par excellence an answer to the need for an explicit political philosophy flexible enough to be adapted to varied circumstances. Yet by the mid-Ming period in China and by Yi Yulgok's time in Korea, the idea was wearing a little thin; one sees a groping for something less moralistic and more substantial, more concrete, to work with. In response to this, there developed the institutional studies and "solid learning" (*shixue*) that became identified with "practical statecraft" (*jingshi zhi yong*). In Korea, too, this seems to have prepared the way for the practical learning known as *sirhak*.

To conclude this discussion of key concepts, I offer as a contrasting example of ostensible continuity in Neo-Confucianism what may, in the end, prove to be a case of discontinuity, the Japanese expression *taigi meibun*, or *meibun taigi*, which asserted that the "highest duty is to perform one's allotted function (i.e., to fulfill the obligations of loyalty to one's lord or ruler)." This doctrine was developed among the followers of the school of Yamazaki Ansai, especially Asami Kei-sai (1652–1711), citing Zhu Xi's writings on the threat of foreign conquest in the Song. By the nineteenth century in Japan, *taigi meibun* had come to be regarded as a cardinal teaching of Zhu Xi and indeed the very essence of Neo-Confucian teaching on duty and loyalty. Today, one can read through any number of Chinese works on Neo-Confucian thought and philosophy without finding any mention of it. From this one might adjudge *taigi meibun* to have been a peculiarly Japanese appropriation of Neo-Confucianism. Elsewhere, I have suggested that it may be more reasonable to "take it as a distinctive Japanese formulation of an ethicoreligious attitude which finds diverse expression within and among the cultural traditions sharing the Neo-Confucian legacy."[37]

This would seem to be confirmed in the Korean case. Korea was threatened, to an even greater degree than were China or Japan, with the danger of foreign conquest and the loss of its national identity. There, however, a heightened sense of loyalty and resistance to foreigners elicited from Neo-Confucians an intense feeling of fidelity to principle and a self-sacrificing devotion, often spoken of in terms of *chŏri*, "integrity and righteousness," which inspired many acts of self-martyrdom. This was not clearly identified with supreme loyalty either to one's own ruler or one's own nation but would present itself, for instance, as resistance to the Manchus out of loyalty to the Ming[38] or resistance to the ruler in the name of fidelity to principle. For all the acts of heroism one might cite in the name of *chŏri*, however, it remains only an intense Korean expression of a concept and an ethicoreligious attitude shared among Neo-Confucians in China and Japan as well. *Taigi meibun*, on the other hand, seems not to have been known or at least much talked about in Korea until modern times, when the Japanese repaid, in their own coin, some of Yamazaki Ansai's debt to Yi T'oegye.

Authoritative Texts

Another measure of continuity in a tradition is the transmission of texts that establish the terms of the ongoing discourse and are generally accepted as standard or canonical works. Views on which texts can claim primacy vary with individual participants in the Neo-Confucian dialogue, even when they accept in general the authority of the tradition. An illustration of this is given in the paper by Yamazaki Michio for the "Conference on Zhu Xi's Philosophy and Korean Confucianism" in Seoul, September 1980, wherein he presents the differing views of Yi T'oegye, Yamazaki Ansai, and Miyake Shōsai on the priority to be assigned to the *Elementary Learning* (*Xiaoxue*) and *Reflections on Things at Hand* (*Jinsilu*) as basic texts.[39] Neither of these works compiled under Zhu Xi's direction would have been thought canonical by Zhu himself, but among his followers they became virtual "classics" with a social and educational importance far beyond their derivative status as "scriptures." The *Elementary Learning* served, for instance, as the proximate scriptural authority for the adoption of the community compact and village wine-drinking ceremony widely practiced in rural Korea. Indeed, there were times in the political history of the Yi dynasty when the standing of the Neo-Confucians at court was closely correlated to the status of the *Elementary Learning* and its acceptance as a basis for economic and social reform.[40]

Competing in these same circles for priority as an introductory text or primer was a third neoclassical work, Zhen Dexiu's *Classic of the*

Mind-and-Heart (*Xinjing*), which I have discussed in *Neo-Confucian Orthodoxy and the Learning of the Mind-and-Heart*. This *Heart Classic*, as I learned after a chance encounter with the text in Yi T'oegye's library at the Tosan Sŏwŏn had set me off on the path to a rediscovery of its roots in earlier tradition, had once carried great weight in the Learning of the Mind-and-Heart transmitted from China to Korea and Japan.

Another new classic of the greatest practical importance was the *Family Ritual of Master Zhu* (*Zhuzi jiali*, or *Wen gong jiali*). Compiled under Zhu Xi's direction but left unfinished at his death (he had hoped to do more refining and polishing of it), the *Family Ritual* reflected Zhu's sense that the ancient ritual texts, prescribing elaborate ceremonial observances for the Zhou aristocracy, were unsuited to the life situations of scholars in the Song. The rites needed to be simplified and their costs brought within the considerably reduced means of the Song literati. For this purpose, Zhu sought to synthesize writings of Song masters such as the Cheng brothers, Zhang Zai (1020–1077), and Sima Guang, believing that their recommendations on ritual would serve as a more practical guide in the contemporary circumstances than would ritual classics literally adhered to. Of all the East Asian peoples during the Neo-Confucian age, the Koreans seem to have embraced this approach most enthusiastically. They made the *Family Ritual* virtually the law of the land and "ritual studies" (*yehak*) a major field of Confucian studies.

Apart from helping us to fill in the early history of Neo-Confucianism, the *Family Ritual*, *Heart Classic*, and similar works illustrate how this school of thought was constantly creating and recreating its own past in the attempt to remake the present. In a basic sense, it made up "classics" as it went along—partly with pieces of old fabric from the ancient canon and partly out of the whole cloth of new commentaries lacing these fragments together. This was of course true of the Four Books, which owed their existence as such to Zhu Xi, and especially true of the *Great Learning* and the *Mean*, to which he gave a new interpretation and a central position. Another example of a popular classic, though one of less consequence to the canonical tradition, is the aforementioned syncretic work of the Korean Ch'u Chŏk, the *Precious Mirror for Clarifying the Mind-and-Heart* (*Myŏngsim pogam*;

Viet.: *Minh-tam bao-giam*), which appeared to sum up the wisdom of the ages in regard to mind-cultivation and the conduct of life.

It would be misleading, however, to suggest that this improvisation knew no limits and that there are no objective tests by which to ascertain the consensus of tradition in respect to its core curriculum. Though this was still a tradition in the making, already by Xu Heng's time the *Elementary Learning* had won a place as a text virtually on a par with the Four Books and Five Classics in the basic curriculum of the Imperial College and other state schools during the Yuan dynasty. Indeed, Xu spoke of it as sacred scripture.[41] This only reflected a consensus already established in the local academies, where instruction in the new teaching was flourishing well before its acceptance by the state.[42] When the Yuan dynasty, after much debate, finally resurrected the examination system and installed the Four Books with Zhu Xi's commentaries as required texts for the first time, the *Elementary Learning* did not make it into this official company, perhaps because it was regarded as something to be studied on the elementary level. But in the eyes of Wu Cheng (1249–1333), the leading classicist of his day, it was eminently worthy of inclusion in the curriculum that he unsuccessfully proposed for adoption at that time.[43]

Against this background, it becomes relevant to ask whether there was much debate over the content of the examinations later adopted in Korea and what selectivity, if any, was shown in the fixing of curricula for state and local schools. Did these tend to follow lines already laid down in China? The Ming dynasty, certainly, followed the Yuan system almost to the letter, without any questions being asked worthy of mention in the record. Having once become fixed in the Ming "constitution," i.e., in the official enactments of the dynasty's founder, the content of the examinations was of course not readily subject to change by his heirs, but even the succeeding Qing dynasty did not exercise a new regime's normal option to install different texts.

In Korea, the examination system underwent many changes, but if the *Great Statutes for the Governance of the State* (*Kyŏngguk taejŏn*) may be taken as a standard for Yi-dynasty Korea, the Five Classics and Four Books became required texts for one part of the examinations (the other part being the various literary styles) for both the lower and higher civil-service degrees. No candidate could successfully complete either stage of the exams without showing his mastery, at the lower level, of the *Family Ritual* and the *Elementary Learning*, and at the higher level, of the *Family Ritual*.[44]

Another kind of official certification is found in the *Great Compendia on the Five Classics, Four Books, and [the Philosophy of] Human Nature and Principle (Wujing, sishu, xingli daquan)*, compiled in 1415 on the order of Ming Chengzu (r. 1403–1425). This went beyond simply confirming the position of the Five Classics and Four Books. It strongly endorsed many writings of the Song philosophers and gave the imperial imprimatur to such texts as Zhou Dunyi's *Diagram of the Supreme Ultimate Explained (Taijitu shuo)* and his *Penetrating the Book of Changes (Tongshu)*, Zhang Zai's *Western Inscription (Ximing)*, *Correcting Youthful Ignorance (Zhengmeng)*, and many writings of the Cheng brothers and Zhu Xi. In 1426, a set of these *Compendia* was given by the emperor Xuanzang (r. 1426–1436) to the Korean king,[45] and to judge from the frequency with which they were reprinted and appear in the classical collections of Korean libraries, they would seem to have had wide influence.[46]

As is well known, the Qing dynasty not only reprinted these compendia but sponsored an official abridgement of the *Great Compendium on Human Nature and Principle* under the title of *Essential Ideas of Nature and Principle (Xingli jingyi)*, published in 1715.[47] Comparing the comprehensive scope of the original version (seventy *juan*) with the later one (twelve *juan*), one can see two rather different approaches to the perpetuation of the tradition: the earlier one expansive and comprehensive, the later one much more selective and trim. Contrary to the conventional view, traditions do not simply accumulate heirlooms from the past. From time to time, they feel the need to sort out their possessions and clean house to get some room to live and work in. In the process, they reveal what adjustments are being made in their own priorities. Sometimes, too, there is a need to adapt to the level of practical comprehension on the part of a new master in the house, like the non-Chinese rulers of the Qing (Manchus), just as had been done by Xu Heng in educating the Mongols to Neo-Confucianism.[48] Thus there was ample precedent within the tradition for such adjustments on the part of the Koreans. Even before the *Great Compendium on Human Nature and Principle* was abridged under the Manchus, it had been reduced to more manageable proportions by the Koreans. As Martina Deuchler reports, "The famous symposium of Song philosophy, the *Great Compendium on Human Nature and Principle* was printed several times during Sejong's reign (r. 1418–50) but seems to have reached its full significance for the development of Neo-Confucian thought in Korea only after it was excerpted by Kim Chŏng-guk (1485–1541) at the beginning of the sixteenth century."[49]

If historical circumstances warrant such adjustments, however, we must remember that Zhu Xi himself set a prime example of how one consolidates and encapsulates a tradition for educational purposes, as he did in his commentaries on the Four Books, his simplification of the ritual in the *Elementary Learning* and *Family Ritual*, his concise anthology of the Song masters in *Reflections on Things at Hand*, and his condensation of Sima Guang's history, among other projects.

In Japan, the nature of the "official orthodoxy" (what I call "Bakufu orthodoxy" in contrast to the Mandarin orthodoxy of China)[50] was much looser, with the state less directly involved in education, with no civil-examination system comparable to the Chinese, and with individual scholars taking more independent initiatives. Accordingly, the ruling regime rarely got into the business of defining and publishing an approved canon of Neo-Confucian literature. Indeed, the contrast is so sharp between the Japanese and Chinese cases as to raise similar questions about the Koreans. In the matter of approved texts, is there anything to establish the "official" content of the canon? And among independent scholars, or in the libraries of their academies, is there any consensus concerning the standard works that are seen to represent the core of tradition?

Such questions are not easily answered on the basis of existing scholarly studies, but judging from the holdings of academy libraries (mainly post-1590s and the Hideyoshi invasions) the indispensable texts would appear to have been the Four Books, Five Classics, Chinese dynastic histories, Zhu Xi's works including the *Basic Structure and Selected Details of the General Mirror* (*Tongjian gangmu*), Zhen Dexiu's *Heart Classic* and *Extended Meaning of the Great Learning* (*Daxue yanyi*), and the aforementioned *Great Compendium of Human Nature and Principle*.[51]

In the early days of the Neo-Confucian movement in Korea, scholars and officials drew freely on a considerable body of classical and historical literature for whatever sanction it might offer their plans for reform. They invoked especially the three ritual classics of the Confucian tradition: the *Record of Rites* (*Liji*), *Rites of Zhou* (*Zhouli*), and *Ceremonial Rites* (*Yili*). But they did not stop there. Zhu Xi's *Family Ritual* had almost greater authority for them, not despite but indeed because of its being a recent adaptation better suited to their own times than the classic rites prescribed for Zhou aristocracy, which had long since disappeared. As precedents for governmental institutions, classically subsumed under the concept of religiosocial liturgies (i.e., "rites"), Korean Neo-Confucians did not hesitate to cite later historical encyclopedias such as the *Comprehensive Institutes* (*Tongdian*) of Du You (735–812) and the *Comprehensive Inquiry Into Recorded Institutions* (*Wenxian tongkao*) by Ma Duanlin (1254–1325) in the scholarly lineage of Zhu Xi and Zhen Dexiu. Also, more for historical precedents than institutions, they consulted Zhu Xi's *Basic Structure and Selected Details of the General Mirror*.[52] In this process, by consensus among scholars rather than by official prescription, the Koreans participated in the identification of Neo-Confucian classics that would have as much effective authority as the original classics in the actual conduct of affairs and of life.

Neo-Confucian Institutions

In the corporate life of Neo-Confucianism, political institutions loomed large. This was not because scholar-officials had effective control over them or had much opportunity to impress on them a specifically Neo-Confucian character but simply because, with the Confucian commitment to public service, they had to live with them and make the best of it. Institutions of state tended to follow the persistent patterns of dynastic rule; for the most part, they remained typical of the centralized bureaucracies of the past, much at variance with Neo-Confucian ideals of a Zhou restoration and return to decentralized feudalism.

To this generalization, the new civil-service examinations of the Yuan dynasty stand as only a partial exception. Neo-Confucian reformers at Khubilai's court resisted plans to reestablish the examinations, preferring to recruit, train, and bring up leaders through a system of public schools. When, in a later reign, they finally compromised, accepting a system in which the examinations' content, and to some extent the form, were of Neo-Confucian authorship, the concession was rather typical of the Neo-Confucian's adjustment to the hard facts of political life and the stubborn persistence of dynastic institutions.

Another partial exception, yet only a qualified success by the Neo-Confucians' own standards, is the institution at court of "lectures from the classics mat." These constituted a serious effort to promote Neo-Confucian ideas of rulership, giving leading scholars an opportunity in the presence of the emperor to discuss classical principles in relation to contemporary affairs. We know that Zhu Xi seized this opportunity to stress the importance of the *Great Learning* as a manual of imperial self-cultivation, often in direct reference to urgent political problems of the day. We also know that Fan Zuyu's *Learning of the Emperor* (*Dixue*) and Zhen Dexiu's *Extended Meaning of the Great Learning* are byproducts of this kind of imperial instruction and that recourse was had in these "imperial seminars" (as Robert Hartwell has called them) to manuals of statecraft and political histories that became classics in their own right, offering a practical wisdom for the guidance of rulers rather in contrast to the Four Books. These included the *Essence of Government in the Zhenguan Era* (*Zhenguan zhengyao*), the *Imperial Pattern* (*Difan*) of Tang Taizong (r. 627–650), the *General Mirror for Aid in Government* (*Zizhi tongjian*) of Sima Guang, and the *Mirror of Tang* (*Tangjian*) of Fan Zuyu.[53]

The importance of these works in the political literature of early Neo-Confucianism has not been well recognized in recent times. Perhaps a realization that the classics mat as an institution and these texts as political classics, along with Zhen's *Heart Classic* and *Classic of Government* (*Zhengjing*), played a prominent role at the Korean court will direct new attention to the Chinese prototypes. As it is, there has been some disposition to believe that Neo-Confucian political thinking was largely limited to well-worn clichés of self-cultivation drawn from the Four Books.[54] One cannot dispute this view altogether, inasmuch as the latter texts were basic to the intellectual formation of scholar-officials in later centuries, and the idea of "self-cultivation for the governance of men" or "self-discipline for the ordering of the state" certainly led in this direction. Nevertheless, Zhen Dexiu's *Extended Meaning* covered extensive historical ground and went into many political problems never dealt with in the *Great Learning* itself. Zhen did this by embracing a great deal of practical political lore under the rubric of "the investigation of things and affairs" and the "learning to be pursued by the ruler." Thus it is significant that Chŏng Tojŏn (1342–1398), in proposing a new constitutional order at the inception of the Yi dynasty, should identify the lectures from the classics mat as one of the most essential institutions of the royal court and should specify Zhen Dexiu and his *Extended Meaning of the Great Learning* as the model for these discussions.[55]

Zhen's scholarly enterprise in this connection reminds us that "broad learning" was one of the twin aims of Neo-Confucian cultivation, along with moral and spiritual discipline. For Zhu Xi to stress "self-cultivation" did not necessarily imply a moralistic reductionism on his part, for he was equally emphatic on the need for intellectual inquiry. And even though Zhu, like Mencius, spoke disparagingly of the pursuit of "systems" or institutions in a utilitarian sense, he did not neglect institutions intended to serve "humane" or "righteous" causes. Zhu himself devoted much attention to the workings of institutions that could benefit people on the local level. The community compact (*xiangyue*) and local granaries (*shecangfa*) became classic Neo-Confucian examples of this.[56]

It may be that such institutions do not loom large in the thinking of scholars for whom practical statecraft is almost entirely an affair of the court and central government and who look somewhat indifferently on problems of lower-level administration. But Zhu Xi's brand of realism and practicality accepted the need for grassroots organization and for dealing with people in their actual condition. Thus he pursued this interest in the only way feasible to him (given his nonparticipation for most of his career in service at court), that is, through statecraft practiced on the local level. In this way, Zhu remained true to his own belief in the importance of "great functioning" or "great usefulness" (*dayong*) as a necessary complement to the cultivation of the "whole substance" of the mind. This "great usefulness" may be seen as all the more complementary to self-cultivation if we consider that one of the implications of "ordering the state through self-discipline" was a recognition that the only practical way to administer a vast and teeming empire was to allow for a large measure of local autonomy or self-governance.

It should be no surprise to us that this kind of practicality took diverse forms among Zhu's followers. For some, like the historians Wang Yinglin (1223–1296) and Ma Duanlin, it meant directing their "broad learning" to the study of social and political institutions in their historical development. For others, like the Neo-Confucian reformers at the court of Khubilai, it meant strengthening Han Chinese institutions under Mongol rule, even those of a traditional dynastic sort, for which they became known as exponents of "practical statesmanship" (*jingshi zhi yong*).[57]

Among such institutions in the Yi dynasty the censorate may be cited as one that Neo-Confucians powerfully reinforced as a means of restraining royal power. Recognition of the Confucian censors' right and duty to censure the king became such a feature of Yi politics as to effect a real sharing of power. According to Edward Wagner, this equilibrium of power "at its finest point of balance represented a constitutional monarchy."[58] For others in the Ming dynasty, practical statecraft meant grafting the Neo-Confucian "community compact" onto the local system of collective security (*baojia*). And in Korea, too, the practice of Neo-Confucian statecraft on this level apparently proved adaptable to local conditions and of "great usefulness" in meeting practical needs. The community compact was for many Neo-Confucians in Korea a key institution widely practiced on the local level. Curiously enough, the authority often invoked on its behalf was Zhu Xi's *Elementary Learning,* which cited the community compact as an "exemplary practice" (*shanxing*).[59]

Another set of distinctively Neo-Confucian institutions were the four major rituals prescribed in Zhu Xi's *Family Ritual:* "capping" (coming of age), wedding, funeral, and sacrifices for the ancestors. For the perpetuation of these rituals it was essential in the eyes of Cheng Yi and Zhu Xi that each family set some land aside to support an ancestral shrine, where filial respect would be shown to the dead and gratitude expressed for the blessings of life received through them. This was to be a modest approximation of the shrines and rites prescribed in the ancient ritual texts for the Zhou aristocracy; by Tang times, these could be maintained by only a few great clans, and by the Song period they were only a vestigial memory of scholars concerned over the fragmentation of property by equal inheritance and the consequent atomization of the social and political structure before the growing power of the state. In China, it remained difficult for any but a few clans to keep up the appearances of the aristocratic lineages (*zong*) of the past or even to preserve the simplified version Zhu had adapted to the situation of the Song family or household (*jia*). But in Korea, the hereditary prerogatives and propertied status of the *yangban* scholar-aristocracy put them in a better position to practice this system and fulfill Zhu Xi's intentions.

For all this, Korean use of the *Family Ritual*, according to Martina Deuchler, remained quite selective. The parts most faithfully followed were the ones on ancestor worship (although there were long and, in the end, inconclusive debates about the number of ancestral generations that should be venerated) and on funerals. Capping was most often performed, if at all, as a preliminary to the wedding ceremony, and the latter remained Korean into modern times (just as weddings in Japan have kept to Shinto rites).[60]

One of the most discussed institutions in Neo-Confucian literature is the well-field system. It appears also to have been one of the least practicable as a system of agricultural organization, though its "utility" may from the beginning have been more symbolic and pedagogical than practical, i.e., it was a vivid illustration of the principles of economic equality and communal cooperation rather than a workable system of land management. Already by Zhu Xi's time he had tended to belittle Zhang Zai's attempt to recreate a well-field system as rather idiosyncratic and ineffectual.[61] One does not hear much of it thereafter as an actual institutional form in China. In Korea, too, it was often held up as a model for reform but never, it seems, actually instituted in its classic form. Curiously, in Japan there were symbolic reenactments of the system in feudal domains of Neo-Confucian-minded daimyō, and one can still see vestiges of nine-squared plots in public parks that had once been gardens of the daimyō[62]—nostalgic evocations of an Arcadian ideal somewhat reminiscent of the rustic cottages of the Bourbons at Versailles. Perhaps the ultimate adaptation of this idea to the aesthetic tastes of the Japanese is the miniature well field incorporated into a few square feet of the garden at the Zen temple of Tōfukuji in Kyoto.

Of more practical significance in the corporate life of Neo-Confucians was the academy (*shuyuan*), in which Chinese Neo-Confucian thought first germinated, was then earnestly cultivated, and eventually came to full flower. Several features of Neo-Confucianism reflect this "academic" provenance. Academies (as the name *shuyuan* indicates) were for the keeping and study of books. Thus book learning and the preservation of the cultural heritage were central to the Neo-Confucian enterprise even before it became known for its speculative philosophy. Second, academies were for teaching and played a large part in the spread of education in the Song, taking up some of the slack from the failure of state schools to fulfill the need for public education. Third, academies were local institutions. Though sometimes winning a wide reputation and attracting students from a considerable distance, they depended essentially on local initiative and support. "Private" in the sense that they were not part of the official state system and had the voluntary support of the community, academies still needed the cooperation of local officials and occasionally received grants from the state. Thus they had somewhat less independence from officialdom than the word "private" would suggest in the West. So far as I know, no Neo-Confucian championed academies as "private," in contrast to "public," schools. Universal education through state-supported schools remained the ideal, as Zhu Xi's writings clearly implied. In both China and Korea, however, academies provided the institutional base for Neo-Confucian scholarship and teaching; they afforded a measure of intellectual autonomy, if not financial independence, and kept alive a spirit of both voluntarism and community involvement in the life of learning.

As a typical social and cultural institution of the Chinese scholar-official class (*shidafu*) in their home setting, the local academy could well serve a similar function for even the more aristocratic *yangban* class in Korea, who identified themselves in the same terms as Confucian *sadaebu*. In Japan, however, the ruling elite or *samurai* class had military functions, feudal allegiances, and often religious loyalties, much in contrast to the Chinese and Korean cases. Hence the academy could not function in the same way as a meeting place of an upper class conscious of upholding its traditions and position vis-à-vis the ruler. In such circumstances, it is not surprising that the *shoin* (equivalent term for the Chinese *shuyuan* and Korean *sŏwŏn*) should be transmuted into a cultural adornment of the Japanese aristocracy, known best as an architectural feature in a new style of residential villa (*shoin tsukuri*), and thus assimilated, like the "well field," as an aesthetic element in the new culture of the Edo period. Meanwhile, the educational functions of the local academy were served by private schools (*shijuku*), including schools for townspeople (*chōnin*), as well as by schools (often known as *gakkō*) maintained by Japanese daimyō as domainal (*han*) institutions. This difference did not, in the end, prevent such schools from serving many of the same cultural services as the academies, yet they could not quite stand as the embodiment of a class-conscious culture in the way the latter had done during the Ming and Yi dynasties.

As regards the Korean case, the role played by local academies in the development of Yi-dynasty education and culture was perhaps even greater than that of their Chinese counterparts. Moreover, Korea is probably unique in having preserved the academies so well, with their collections of books largely intact.

For all that, the full significance of the academies can only be measured against the failure of the Neo-Confucians to achieve their stated objective of establishing a universal public school system. Neo-Confucians in the Song, Yuan, and early Ming stressed education as a prerequisite to good government and called repeatedly for rulers to establish official schools on all levels from the court down to the village. Yet actual measures to accomplish this under all three dynasties eventually lapsed into ineffectuality. Thus, by default, the local academy was left to perform a function it had limited capacity to fulfill. This too was a pattern to be repeated in Korea.

The Uses of Neo-Confucianism

In its long Chinese life, Neo-Confucianism has served many purposes—educational, political, social, philosophical, and ideological. At its inception in the Northern Song, it was a movement among scholars and would-be officials of a regime strongly oriented toward civil-bureaucratic rule. Hu Yuan (993–1059), an early leader of the movement, was particularly known for his commitment to the education of scholar-officials in both classical learning and practical governmental skills.[63]

This was well after the Song dynasty had established itself, so the new thought and scholarship, instead of ideologically spearheading the drive to power of a new dynasty, responded rather to the needs of a centralized civil administration following a period of contentious warlordism.

In this situation, Neo-Confucians tended to take power for granted and were more concerned about its legitimate uses. Their scholarship celebrated the civil virtues, their culture the arts of peace. Already by the time of Li Gou (1009–1059), a scholar patronized, like Hu Yuan, by the statesman Fan Zhongyan (989–1052), Li could complain about the failure of contemporary scholars to give due attention to power factors and especially to military affairs.[64] This state of affairs was not untypical of Neo-Confucians in later times. Rarely did they give much thought to the seizing and organizing of power or the founding of new dynasties, yet often they found themselves serving as custodians of a power and managers of a state they had not themselves created.

Historically speaking, Neo-Confucianism was a class phenomenon in several important respects. Its rise in the Song was concomitant with the rise to new heights of power of a professional scholar-official class whose scholarship and cultural activities were the beneficiaries of the new affluence, material means, and leisure enjoyed by that class. Its concerns reflected their heightened sense of responsibility for political leadership and for preserving the essential values—"this culture"— on which they believed the polity should rest. With one foot in the land as a kind of landed gentry and the other in the halls of power as bureaucrats, they had a measure of independence from the ruler and fought hard to maintain their own status and integrity, with the alternative of repairing to their home base if need be. Yet often it was not much of a propertied base they returned to. Many Neo-Confucians were not well off, and to maintain their independence required heroic struggle of the kind Confucius spoke of when he said, "Poverty and low estate are what every man detests, but if they can only be escaped at the expense of the Way, [the Noble Man] will not try to escape them" (*Analects* 4:5).

To a degree, Neo-Confucians functioned as buffers or mediators between dynastic power and the common people. But the insecurities of both property and power were such that scholar-officials could only act as a countervailing force, a kind of political "middle class," because of the solidarity maintained among the *shidafu* as sharers in a common mission and culture. Education was a crucial factor in developing that sense of common identity. In the case of the leading Neo-Confucian thinkers, who sometimes experienced great hardships, they could sustain themselves in poverty or dismissal from office only because of the moral and physical support of their own class.

On this basis, they tried to express in their philosophy the highest ideals of that class and their common aspiration for self-fulfillment. As a program of self-cultivation, Neo-Confucianism gave meaning and direction to their individual lives; as institutionalized instruction, first in schools and then in government, it became the public philosophy of the educated elite. As philosophy, it was subscribed to by generations of later scholars; as ideology, it was resorted to by dynasty after dynasty, irrespective of ethnic and even cultural differences among them—by Mongols in the Yuan, Chinese in the Ming, and Manchus in the Qing.

Perhaps the most remarkable thing in the extension of this system to other lands and peoples is its ability to transcend the limitations of the class that produced it. Its first purveyors to Japan were Zen monks, whose social and political role contrasted sharply with that of the scholar-officials of China and whose interest in Neo-Confucianism was cultural in the narrow sense (if not actually commercial, as a commodity in the China trade engaged in by Zen monasteries). Truly transmitters of the teaching rather than its proponents or creative interpreters, the Zen monks were superseded as sponsors of Neo-Confucianism by professional Confucian advisers to the Tokugawa aristocracy, a military elite whose social circumstances differed markedly from the Chinese mandarins. So little did the Tokugawa military government have in common with Chinese civil bureaucracy that it strains credulity to think of Neo-Confucianism as offering explicit ideological support to established institutions in cases as dissimilar as the Ming and Tokugawa. In fact, Neo-Confucianism lent little to the ideological justification or legitimization of Tokugawa rule itself,[65] though ethically and philosophically it contributed much to filling a vacuum left by the silence of Zen and Pure Land Buddhism in the social arena. Yet, adapted as it was to the way of the warrior, to the new cultural needs of a reunified Japan, and to the native religious traditions of Shinto, Neo-Confucianism was able to play a substantial role in the social and cultural life of premodern Japan.

More significant in this process than political or economic structures was the spirit of voluntarism and self-determination implicit in much of Neo-Confucian teaching. Here the emphasis lay on individual initiative and local autonomy. It did not renounce formal structures but saw them as growing from within rather than being superimposed from without. This allowed the Koreans and Japanese (and I would suppose Vietnamese too) to adjust Neo-Confucian views on the primacy of moral relationships to their own social and political structures and adapt Neo-Confucian concepts of self-cultivation to indigenous traditions of moral and spiritual discipline.

NEO-CONFUCIANISM IN KOREA

In its own historical development Korean Neo-Confucianism appears to be unique. The case of the Yi dynasty would seem to be a singular instance in which Neo-Confucians played a large role in the creation of a new regime and in the formulating of its institutions. For any comparative study of continuity and change in Neo-Confucianism, the founding of the Yi dynasty and remolding of Korean society at this time offer a fascinating test case for some of the generalizations offered above.

Though unique in the depth of its political involvement, the role of Neo-Confucianism in fourteenth-century Korea is not without significant parallels in other dynastic situations close at hand: e.g., in its relation to the Yuan state and then to Koryŏ. Here, Neo-Confucian social values, as appropriated by both dynasties, may have afforded them some degree of legitimacy, but in the not-too-long run rationalistic and idealistic tendencies in Neo-Confucianism probably worked as a leaven to undermine these regimes and hasten their replacement.[66] This reflects an ambivalence in Neo-Confucianism toward any ruling power; i.e., whether one's primary loyalty should be to one's royal masters or to higher ideals often at odds with the status quo. Indeed,

Khubilai himself seems to have sensed this ambivalence. He had his own suspicions and premonitions concerning the dependability of Confucian support. When urged to adopt Confucianism, he pointedly asked if the weakness of the preceding Jin dynasty and its defeat by his Mongols were not attributable in part to the softening effects of Confucian humanistic teachings.[67] In the end, there were committed Neo-Confucians who gave their service to the Yuan, and others to the Ming, some to Koryŏ and others to the Yi. In such cases, too, Neo-Confucianism survived the demise of its official sponsors.

The issue, of course, is not solely one of Neo-Confucian influence. Both Yuan and Koryŏ remained deeply involved with Buddhism and were also heavily dependent on structures of authority, imposed by conquest, which would be jeopardized by reformism of any kind. In this respect, these dynasties faced the classic dilemma of authoritarian regimes that are never so endangered as when compelled to accept a measure of liberalization. There are parallels here to the late Tokugawa shogunate, undone in the midst of its own efforts to reform and modernize in the 1850s and 1860s, and to the reforms of the declining Manchu dynasty in the early twentieth century. How to manage change without letting it get out of hand is a problem for military regimes whose rule has not actually been predicated, as Confucian theory requires, on the consent of the governed.

As regards coexistence or conflict with Buddhism, there is more than one parallel: to the Confucian revival in the Northern Song period; to the intellectual and political ascendance of Neo-Confucianism in Yuan China, the early Ming, and early Tokugawa Japan; and to a concurrent pattern of ideological syncretism drawing on Buddhism as well as Neo-Confucianism for purposes of dynastic legitimation in these same settings. We are not yet in a position to handle, in more than a suggestive manner, the complex questions that arise in the comparative analysis of such cases, but it is perhaps significant that Neo-Confucians in the early years of the Yi dynasty revert to the persisting influence of Buddhism as an important challenge to Neo-Confucian reform efforts.

Regardless, however of the allowances made for prevailing religious attitudes, Korean Neo-Confucians did not conceive of the problem as a matter solely of translating Zhu Xi's ideas into Korean terms. From the start, they took most seriously the transplantation of

Neo-Confucian institutions as well. This is shown, as in the cases of Chŏng Tojŏn and Kwŏn Kŭn, by the readiness to espouse radical reforms, to adapt selectively major Yuan or Ming institutions, and beyond that to put into effect many of Zhu Xi's practical proposals not even widely adopted in China itself.

During the Early Yi dynasty, education in the capital and the provinces was reformed, first according to the Yuan system and then in ways thought to be more in accordance with Zhu Xi's own ideas. The twists and turns of successive reforms and counterreforms suggest that even a fundamentalist and literalist approach to the reading of Zhu's intention was not proof against different interpretations being drawn to serve divergent power interests. Schools and examinations, playing a key role as avenues to power and influence, quickly became subject to partisan controversy and strife.

A special feature of the Korean situation was the *yangban* aristocracy's almost exclusive prerogative of admission to the examinations, in contrast to the more open, egalitarian, and meritocratic system in China. Zhu Xi himself, like other Neo-Confucians before him, had not set much store by the civil-service examinations as such. He preferred to train up talented persons through the schools, observe their conduct and moral character firsthand, and then have meritorious candidates personally recommended for government service. A similar rationale seems to have lain behind the substitution of oral, for written, examinations in Korea—a practice never sanctioned in China. Written examinations were favored by scholars at the capital, oral by candidates from the countryside. The latter might lack literary skills and intellectual sophistication, but their moral character could be discerned in personal interviews. Understandably sharp cleavages developed along these lines, as oral examinations were alleged to be too subjective and liable to favoritism, while written exams were said to favor those highly literate in the Chinese tradition.

In education, on the other hand, there were marked similarities between China and Korea in the gradual decline of the public schools and the rise of private study halls (*sahak*)[68] and later local academies as centers of learning and social influence among the *yangban*,[69] a role academies had also served among the local gentry in China. Here too the contest for power between the king and the *yangban* aristocratic bureaucracy was reflected in the king's support for public schools as a counterweight to *yangban* influence, while the latter supported academies as bastions of local power and culture.[70] Ironically enough, one would be hard put to find any endorsement in Zhu Xi's writings for academies versus state schools. The rise in importance of the former simply reflected the failure to carry out what Zhu had urged be done for the latter.

One of the most distinctive Neo-Confucian institutions at the Chinese court during the Song, Yuan, and Ming dynasties were the "lectures from the classics mat," in which distinguished scholar-ministers lectured to and carried on discussions with the ruler concerning lessons to be drawn from the Confucian classics for contemporary affairs. This role had been performed by several of the great Neo-Confucian teachers who had the greatest influence on the Koreans: Cheng Yi, Zhu Xi, Zhen Dexiu, and Xu Heng.[71] For their part, Korean Neo-Confucians went even further in the systematic conduct of these lectures, which emphasized the importance of the scholar-minister as mentor to the throne and sought to enhance the latter's influence vis-à-vis the increasing concentration of power in the hands of the ruler.

A natural corollary to this kind of royal education in Korea was the provision for the education of the heir apparent. Dr. JaHyun Kim Haboush, who has reported on the conduct of the royal lectures under the Yi dynasty,[72] has undertaken to study the education of the crown princes of the Yi dynasty during the fourteenth to eighteenth centuries. The significance of the subject lies in the key Neo-Confucian doctrines on which the instruction was premised: the goodness of man's nature and his potentiality for sagehood, the special responsibility of those who exercise great power to learn how to use it well and commit themselves to becoming sage-rulers, and the importance of the ruler's self-cultivation as setting an example for others to follow (i.e., fulfilling the basic aim of Neo-Confucian political doctrine: to govern men by "renewing" them through exemplary self-cultivation).

Since adequate studies have not yet been made of the Chinese counterpart to this system of education at court, we are in no position to make comparative assessments. Judging from Dr. Haboush's evidence alone, which includes many striking individual cases, the results in

Korea were at best mixed. She suggests that three special factors may have affected the outcome. One was the lack of significant motivation on the part of princes whose future seemed assured simply by hereditary right. A second was the lack of real leverage on the part of the tutor in dealing with such a privileged student. The third consisted of the attractive diversions from study that were readily available to the crown prince. No doubt other considerations pertaining to the content of instruction played a part. The more his preceptors stressed the heavy responsibility of the ruler, the greater could become the prince's resistance to this kind of moral overload. In any case, Dr. Haboush's detailed case studies provide us with fascinating illustrations of the problems encountered at this crucial juncture in the relations of the king and his Neo-Confucian mentors.

The golden age of Korean Neo-Confucian philosophy in the sixteenth century followed upon a period of substantial progress in the development of Neo-Confucian institutions and culture in the fifteenth century, especially during the reign of the renowned King Sejong. Sejong was responsible for marked advances in several areas of cultural life. One of these was the devising of the Korean phonetic alphabet, a unique creative achievement that contributed to the growth of vernacular literature. This development shows how Neo-Confucian influence, though always implying some measure of sinicization, did not necessarily inhibit the growth of native traditions. In fact, it sanctioned and stimulated cultural activity in general and encouraged a people's natural self-expression.[73] In keeping with its central conception of "the unity of principle and diversity of its functional applications," Neo-Confucianism accepted cultural diversity and, rather than insisting simply on conformity to things Chinese, helped to strengthen the Korean people's sense of themselves and encourage their distinctive expression of the Way (*zide*).

The philosopher Yi T'oegye has attracted much attention in East Asia. Professor Wing-tsit Chan, a leading authority on Chinese thought and Zhu Xi in particular, has examined the scholarly work of Yi T'oegye in regard to Zhu Xi's life and writings. He finds that Yi, while holding Zhu in the highest respect, was most thorough and critical in his scholarly annotations of Huang Gan's (1152–1221) account of Zhu's "conduct of life" (*xingzhuang*), being particularly attentive to details of Zhu's movements and whereabouts, his relationship to his teacher Li Tong (1093–1163), his deep interest in religious and ritual matters, and his serious concerns over national defense—matters relatively neglected by other writers. In the last three respects, Professor Chan's observations have heightened significance in that these particular emphases in Yi's scholarship may well have had a part in shaping Japanese perceptions of Zhu Xi.

In a similar vein, Tu Weiming has discussed the centrality in T'oegye's thought of the famous "Four-Seven Debate." This concerned the relation of principle and material force (or ether) in the issuance of the Four Beginnings (feelings or impulses that constitute the inherent tendency to goodness in human nature), on the one hand, and the Seven Emotions, which may work for either good or evil, on the other. Professor Tu analyzes in detail the views expressed by T'oegye and a junior colleague in a continuing exchange on this question. Out of this developed T'oegye's more mature and refined views on the active or dominating character of principle and the crucial agency of the mind in coordinating reason and emotion. This dialogue in Korea, according to Professor Tu, represented an authentic, independent development of the Neo-Confucian discourse, notable for its thoroughness, frankness, and civility, "a model of scholarly communication for [later] generations.[74] From it Professor Tu suggests there emerged a clarified perception of the human feelings, one marked by a precision and finesse not often matched in China.

Not long after T'oegye's time, the dialogue was resumed by Yi Yulgok, a powerful thinker and worthy rival of T'oegye in the interpretation and propagation of Zhu Xi's philosophy. Yulgok stressed the primacy of material force in the dialogue he carried on with a friend about the "Four-Seven" issue. Julia Ching, in "Yi Yulgok on the Four Beginnings and Seven Emotions," emphasizes the complementary relationship or dialectical unity of the "beginnings" and emotions rather than their opposition. Professor Ching concludes that Yulgok, like T'oegye, has detected and clarified certain ambiguities in Zhu Xi's thought and "has made a real contribution on an issue that Chinese thinkers had not clearly settled."[75] Further, we note that this clarification, though it sometimes has the appearance of hairsplitting, actually deals with a central issue for Neo-Confucians engaged in self-cultivation, whose conscientiousness in regard to moral imperatives and the disciplining of selfish desires was still meant to express the spontaneous goodness of man's moral nature. It also demonstrates the intellectual and moral seriousness that Koreans brought to their practical realization of Neo-Confucian principles.

Another indication of the Koreans' active pursuit of Neo-Confucian goals is found in the attention both T'oegye and Yulgok gave to Zhu Xi's recommendations for the setting up of community compacts—voluntary local charters in the nature of social contracts, by which people subscribed to a code of conduct and various forms of cooperation and mutual aid. Zhu Xi had recommended a model compact worked out in 1076 by Lu Dajun, whose family in Shoanxi had been associated with Cheng Yi. It was one of several schemes for self-governing communities experimented with by such early Neo-Confucians as Zhang Zai. Zhu Xi had written a modified version of the Lu family compact, adapted to his own time and situation, the text of which was included in his collected works. The Lu version was also reproduced in the official early Ming compilation *Great Compendium of Human Nature and Principle* (1415).

This is an aspect of Zhu Xi's thought that seems not to have attracted much notice in the early days of the Neo-Confucian movement in Korea, when reform centered on the organization of central government, schools, and examinations; the land system; and the conduct of family affairs according to the prescriptions of Zhu Xi's *Family Ritual.* According to Sakai Tadao, interest in the community compact arose after the text became available in Korea during the early fifteenth century,[76] and the actual institution of the system was not officially sanctioned until the early sixteenth century. In China itself, adoption of the compact had spread from the mid-fifteenth into the sixteenth century. Thus the Korean development could possibly be seen as an extension of the compact's propagation in China. If this is so, however, it is more a matter of stimulus than of substantive replication, since the early form of the compacts in Korea follows, if anything, Song models and only later incorporates certain Ming adaptations. In other words, the Korean phenomenon followed its own internal lines of development from shared premises.

In the compacts devised successively by Yi T'oegye and Yi Yulgok, the detailed specifications are based on community consultation and adapted to local conditions, especially to the existing social structure and the tradition of covenant associations, which had deep roots in Korea. Professor Sakai speculates that the community-compact idea in China had sprung from similar roots in local covenants and that in Korea too an attempt was made to ground the compact organization in such indigenous structures and practices. Organizationally, the Korean compacts were fitted into the pattern of *yangban* leadership in the local community, though Sakai sees Yulgok as more egalitarian than T'oegye and more progressive in emphasizing education in the vernacular for commoners and in linking the administrative direction of the compacts to that for the communal granary and local school, as Zhu Xi himself had done. However, for Zhu Xi the local school had been the official or public school in the districts, whereas by Yulgok's time in Korea the public schools had seriously declined and been largely superseded by local academies, quasi-private schools maintained by the *yangban*. Nevertheless, according to Sakai, where T'oegye had tended to buttress *yangban* authority and uphold class privilege, Yulgok promoted the upward mobility of commoners and cooperation between the upper and lower classes. This he sees as reflecting Yulgok's more pragmatic and realistic approach, which in turn is linked to his empirical philosophy of material force or ether.

However this may be, we should not fail to note the normative, didactic content of the compact texts and the natural association of the compacts with schools. This shows the strong continuing interest of these major Korean thinkers in education and in the plurality of means by which this was to be accomplished on different levels of society. In this T'oegye and Yulgok were carrying on a major and indeed central commitment of the Neo-Confucian tradition as it came down from Zhu Xi. There may be differences from one Neo-Confucian to another as to their elitism or egalitarianism, but none in respect to the fundamental need for the "renewal of the people" (as Chu Hsi had put it) through education.

This, then, provided the background for the flowering of Neo-Confucian culture, as expressed especially in the teachings of T'oegye and Yulgok and in their personal involvement with the community compact. Finally, this development is linked to the flourishing of the local academies as centers of *yangban* culture.

If in these respects Professor Sakai draws attention to progressive features of the Neo-Confucian movement, he concedes that more than one class, party, or faction sought to exploit Neo-Confucian ideas and institutions for their own purposes, some of them certainly protective of their own interests and often conservative of the status quo in the midst of economic and social change. In such circumstances, it was only natural that controversy would arise as to who could legitimately claim to speak for Neo-Confucianism as either authoritative teaching or official ideology.

Thus political struggle, factional rivalry, and disputes concerning orthodoxy and heterodoxy may be seen as inseparable concomitants of Neo-Confucianism's rise to dominance in Korea. Along with this, there was a change in the way "orthodoxy" was conceived or asserted over the course of Neo-Confucianism's becoming the established teaching.

For Chŏng Tojŏn and Kwŏn Kŭn in the late fourteenth century, the problem had been how, in order to achieve their social goals, the positive values or "correct learning" of Neo-Confucianism could be propagated in the face of entrenched Buddhist influence. The Neo-Confucian scholar Kim Koengp'il (1454–1504), following after Chŏng Tojŏn and Kwŏn Kŭn, felt a need to press the case for a public philosophy centered on a view of the self defined in rational, moral, and social terms, as opposed to the nonrational and essentially private experience of "nothingness" or "emptiness" in Buddhism.[77] By the sixteenth and seventeenth centuries, however, with the new teaching firmly established, the question had become, rather, which brand of Neo-Confucianism could claim to represent itself as the authentic heir of Confucius and Zhu Xi.

Further, there was the vexed issue of the Korean relationship to China and the extent to which political loyalty required Korean acceptance of the latter's ideological authority. Koryŏ had identified closely with the Yuan at a time when the Yuan court stood as the principal sponsor of Neo-Confucianism to such an extent indeed that the Mongol collapse in 1368 undermined Koryŏ's own authority. The Yi dynasty, though initially identified with the Ming, experienced repeated difficulties in its relations with the latter and, while professing loyalty to its suzerain, strongly implied that the exemplary virtue of the Koreans in this respect showed them to be the truer of the two as custodians of the Confucian heritage. Thus total devotion to Zhu Xi became a badge not only of Korean fidelity to the Way but of its independence from the decadent Ming—a form of subtle nationalistic self-assertion worthy of the Neo-Confucian claim to have "gotten" the Way for oneself.

Further advances in Korean thought during the fifteenth and sixteenth centuries, discussed by Dr. Deuchler, confirmed this autonomous capability. Yi T'oegye developed his own orthodox "learning of the mind-and-heart," which preempted much of the ground taken up in China by Wang Yangming, while Yulgok's dual emphasis on the creative mind and concrete reality kept within the orbit of the Zhu Xi school's tendencies that in late Ming China veered off from the Neo-Confucian center of gravity. T'oegye thus became the great symbol of a conservative orthodoxy and Yulgok of a more liberal one—both claiming fidelity to Zhu Xi and both exemplifying the autonomy and authenticity so central to Neo-Confucianism. Official confirmation of these claims came in 1610, with the enshrinement in the Confucian temple of leading Korean Neo-Confucians who symbolized Korean independence of China and rejection of the corrupt, heterodox thought that allegedly permeated the late Ming.

Dr. Deuchler points to the idea of individual inspiration in both T'oegye and Yulgok.[78] T'oegye acknowledged no single teacher as the direct source of his views but rather thought of himself as the true successor to Zhu Xi. In this respect, he was casting himself in the same role as Zhu Xi had cast the Cheng brothers (and, by implication, himself), who had discerned the true meaning of the Way after the tradition had lapsed for more than a thousand years after Mencius.

Elsewhere, I have identified this view of tradition as a "prophetic" one, stressing the unique insight of one who rediscovers and repossesses the long-lost Way, as contrasted to the "scholastic" or apostolic emphasis on lineal transmission from teacher to disciple.[79] Typical of the prophetic role is its powerful self-assurance, its sense of direct access to truth, as well as dogmatic conviction of its own hold on the Way and its rejection of any other. This was as true of their Song predecessors as of their Korean emulators, and since there could be no inherent limit on such claims, rivalry and partisanship were the almost certain consequences.

Ironically, Yulgok availed himself of the same privilege by declaring his independence of T'oegye, whom he accused of being too slavish in his devotion to Zhu Xi. For Yulgok, the key to authentic possession of the Way was "getting it oneself."[80]

In this light, many of the leading Korean Neo-Confucians would appear to be acting out roles already modeled for them by their Song predecessors, though no doubt doing it their own way and reacting to situations in Korea for which there could be no exact parallel in China. The outcome, while an autonomous development within Korea and not merely a response to external stimuli, was in significant part, as Dr. Deuchler has put it, a "result of the intellectual challenge inherent in Neo-Confucian philosophy."[81] Hence, while further research may well differentiate the historical conditions or social forces impinging on this process, there would seem to be nothing in the Neo-Confucian discourse itself to mark the Korean sense of orthodoxy as unique, except in the Neo-Confucian sense that all human activity partakes of both commonness and distinctiveness, i.e., the underlying unity of principle and diversity of its manifestations.

For all that, at least some tentative conclusions may be arrived at. One is that the Koreans showed a remarkable capacity for assimilating both Neo-Confucian thought and institutions, as well as their social and cultural adjuncts. Another is that the process of assimilation was not merely one of skilled copying but from the beginning involved creative adaptation to Korean needs and conditions. Individual thinkers and statesmen achieved a thorough grasp of different aspects of Neo-Confucian thought as well as their historical antecedents in China and the relevant background in Korea. Early on, a statesman like Chŏng Tojŏn, and later on a scholar like Yi Yulgok, could make highly original contributions to Neo-Confucian statecraft thought that bear favorable comparison to, and often anticipate the handling of similar problems by, leading Chinese thinkers. Because of their native versatility and the range of fields they were prepared to deal with, Koreans at the end of Koryŏ and the inception of the Yi dynasty were able to undertake ambitious reforms in their national life beyond anything attempted in China. Though many of these were subject to later modification, the experience gained in a massive program of political and social engineering, as found in the record kept of it, must be considered one of the richest chapters in East Asian, if not world, history. This is especially true of the efforts to implement Zhu Xi's political and social thought, which often go beyond anything attempted in China and Japan, e.g., the implementation of his *Elementary Learning* and *Family Ritual*, his recommendations for the community compact, communal granary, village ceremonies, schools, etc. Truth to tell, in many instances little attention has been given to their counterpart ideas or institutions in China, and it is only their inescapable importance in Korea, once one gets around to looking at them, that compels us to reexamine these neglected areas of Chinese—and perhaps Japanese—intellectual and social history.

14

Confucianism and Human Rights

To many contemporary observers, Confucianism and human rights would seem to be an unlikely combination, if not a completely incompatible couple. As far away as Africa, the *New York Times* reports, authoritarian regimes restrictive of human rights are looking to an Asian model of development based on Confucianism rather than to a Western one.[1] The presumption is that Confucianism spells authority and discipline, limiting individual freedom and strengthening the state. How, then, could it be reconciled to a view of human rights fundamentally premised on the dignity and autonomy of the individual? Moreover, anyone familiar with the Confucians' reservations about law as an inherently defective instrument for dealing with conflicting human interests would wonder how they could make room for a Western conception of human rights so bound up with legal guarantees and dependent on constitutional protections.

The negative view of Confucianism on these scores owes much to critics of the Chinese tradition earlier in the twentieth century, as we can see from these words by one of the prime Chinese advocates of liberation from Confucianism:

> The pulse of modern life is economic and the fundamental principle of economic production is individual independence. Its effect has penetrated ethics. Consequently the independence of the individual in the ethical field and the independence of property in the economic field bear witness to each other, thus reaffirming the theory [of such interaction]. Because of this [interaction], social mores and material culture have taken a great step forward.
>
> In China, the Confucians have based their teachings on their ethical norms. Sons and wives possess neither personal individuality nor personal property. Fathers and elder brothers bring up their sons and younger brothers and are in turn supported by them. It is said in chapter thirty of the *Record of Rites* that "While parents are living, the son dares not regard his person or property as his own" [27:14]. This is absolutely not the way to personal independence. . . . In all modern constitutional states, whether monarchies or republics, there are political parties. Those who engage in party activities all express their spirit of independent conviction. They go their own way and need not agree with their fathers or husbands. When people are bound by the Confucian teachings of filial piety and obedience to the point of the son not deviating from the father's way even three years after his death and the woman not only obeying her father and husband but also her son, how can they form their own political party and make their own choice? . . .
>
> Confucius lived in a feudal age. The ethics he promoted are the ethics of the feudal age. The social mores he taught and even his own mode of living were teachings and modes of a feudal age. The objectives, ethics, social norms, mode of living and political institutions did not go beyond the privilege and prestige of a few rulers and aristocrats and had nothing to do with the happiness of the great masses.

These words were written in December 1916 by Chen Duxiu, who subsequently became a founder of the Chinese Communist Party—

though he was later disowned by the party and thus, for all of his efforts on behalf of individualism, became a nonperson.

Now consider what was said even earlier by a leading feminist who championed a blend of anarchism and communism for the liberation of women:

> Almost all of the writings since the Qin and Han dynasties have followed Confucianism, and Confucian learning is marked by its devotion to honoring men and denigrating women. . . .
>
> Later generations of Confucians respected what the founders had to say and followed their example in venerating men like gods while condemning women to the hells. They felt that as long as it was of benefit to men, then it was fine to twist the truth around in any way to gain advantage. . . .
>
> The learning of Confucianism has tended to be oppressive and to promote male selfishness. Therefore, Confucianism marks the beginning of justifications for polygamy [for men] and chastity [for women]. Confucians, representing the ancestral learning of the Han dynasty, felt free to twist the meaning of the ancient writings as they pertained to women in order to extend their own views. . . .
>
> Just as men loyal to a fallen dynasty went into hiding, women should die faithful to their deceased husbands like a loyalist giving his life to his country. . . . Thus are women driven to their deaths with this empty talk of virtue. We can see that the Confucian emphasis on propriety is nothing more than a tool for murdering women. . . .
>
> This proves that women have duties but no rights. Household responsibilities cannot be assumed by men but all the tasks of managing the household are given to women. Out of fear that women might interfere with their concerns, men said women had no business outside of the home. This deprived women of their natural rights.[2]

Clearly, these writers saw Confucianism as an obstacle to the adoption of Western standards of individual freedom, with which they had become acquainted through the new Western-style education in

China and the so-called New Culture of the early decades of the twentieth century. But even a scholar like Kang Youwei, widely recognized in his time as a leading modern exponent of Confucianism, believed that China (and even Confucianism itself) had to be liberated from a Chinese family system intrinsically repressive of the individual. Hard though it is to conceive of Confucianism stripped of its family system, this is what Kang had to say about it:

> We desire that men's natures shall all become perfect, that men's characters shall all become equal, that men's bodies shall all be nurtured. [That state in which] men's characters are all developed, men's bodies are all hale, men's dispositions are all pacific and tolerant, and customs and morals are all beautiful, is what is called Complete Peace-and-Equality. But there is no means by which to bring this about this way without abolishing the family. . . . To have the family and yet to wish to reach Complete Peace-and-Equality is to be afloat on a blocked-up stream, in a sealed-off harbor, and yet to wish to reach the open waterway. To wish to attain Complete Peace-and-Equality and yet keep the family is like carrying earth to dredge a stream or adding wood to put out a fire; the more done, the more the hindrance. Thus, if we wish to attain the beauty of complete equality, independence and the perfection of [human] nature, it can [be done] only by abolishing the state, only by abolishing the family.[3]

Kang Youwei envisaged a universal order, the Grand Commonality, in which the traditional Confucian value of public mindedness would be fulfilled by the dissolution of virtually all traditional forms of particularistic loyalty and obligation. The state (if it existed at all) would have few functions, and in the absence of any significant social infrastructure regulating human activity, there would be almost no limit on individual freedom.

If, however, Kang was ready to go this far in modernizing Confucianism, it is hardly surprising that the authors of our first two quotations above should have gone further to promote violent revolution, aiming at total liberation, rather than to rely on a shaky parliamentary democracy as the vehicle for achieving individual rights. Nor, given this powerful liberationist impulse (later enshrined in the official declaration of the year 1949 as marking China's "Liberation"), is it surprising that Mao's Great Proletarian Cultural Revolution in the late sixties should have urged young Red Guards to press on to final "liberation"— only revolutionary zeal and one last campaign of unrelenting class struggle were needed to make it a complete reality.

As is well known, the outcome of this new revolutionary struggle was not the anarchist utopia dreamed of earlier but a kind of disorderly freedom that Deng Xiaoping and his colleagues found necessary to suppress, first by putting down the Cultural Revolution and later by cracking down at Tiananmen Square. Yet we can understand this as a not unexpected consequence of the revolutionary élan generated earlier and the violence it would work on China. Moreover, if Confucianism, seen all along as essentially conservative, had been a main target of such attacks, early and late, we can understand too how the more moderate or conservative elements under Deng, having put a stop to these revolutionary excesses, would have taken a second look at Chinese tradition and found a conservative version of Confucianism to their liking—not only a potential force for stability but also a work ethic that could be supportive of Deng's modernization program.

Although the views of Confucianism cited above have swung sharply from contra to pro in the protracted revolutionary process, a key line of continuity persists through it all: the promise of total liberation bore within it the need to accept total revolutionary mobilization, and in the end, total political control by the revolutionary party has survived the demise of liberation and individual rights. Success in unifying the country itself now suffices to justify the party's long-term monopolization of power, and in this light even anarchy—or rather the threat of it—has become a pretext for withholding many of the human rights that the anarchist ideal had once been meant to foster and serve.

Which of the alternatives outlined above speaks for the Chinese people—the rejection of Confucianism in the name of human rights, or the denial of human rights in the name of a conservative Confucian tradition—remains an open question. Either view is open to challenge; both are still held and propagated. Among the poster writers of the Democracy Wall movement in the early eighties and the activists in the

Tiananmen demonstrations, there were (and still are among the sur-
vivors) heirs to the May Fourth Movement and Cultural Revolution
who, even though long cut off from any informed contact with Confucian teachings, distrust Confucianism, as it is now associated in their
minds with the repressions of the current regime. And among the current spokesmen for a Confucian revival there is enough involvement
of officialdom to warrant the suspicion that the government as sponsor
has its own vested interests and illiberal ends in mind.

Meanwhile, we do well to note that the alternatives so characterized by no means exhaust the available approaches to human rights
in China. Alongside the more extreme liberationists quoted above,
there were more moderate advocates of liberal reforms, "people's
rights," and "human rights," who saw these as lacking in China but
did not see Confucianism as necessarily, or in all ways, an obstacle to
their adoption. Among these perhaps the most influential spokesmen
were Liang Qichao (1873–1929) and Hu Shi (1891–1962). Others,
including some who continued to identify themselves as determined
defenders of Confucianism, supported liberal democratic reforms,
most often in diaspora or exile. Indeed, enough of these later spoke for
China in concert with representatives of other Confucian-influenced
cultures, so that when the Universal Declaration of Human Rights
was adopted by the United Nations in 1948, Chinese delegates saw to
it that Confucian sentiments found expression therein, in support of
human rights. This makes it awkward now, if not actually specious, for
opponents of human rights in Asia today to dismiss these as merely
culture-bound "Western" concepts incompatible with "Asian communitarian" values.

The purpose of the present chapter is neither to endorse nor to discount any of the views characterized above but to take them all into
account and especially to consider what has been said on the subject in
China—not just in agonizing moments of extreme national travail and
cultural disorientation but in the larger perspectives of past, present,
and future.

For these purposes, we take as our working definition of human
rights the abovementioned Universal Declaration of Human Rights
adopted by the United Nations in 1948—which is not to adopt it as
the final or definitive statement on the subject but only to accept it as

the going one—universal to the extent that it was ratified formally by representatives of many world regions and cultures and not thereafter repudiated by any official body but only confirmed and added to in subsequent protocols. Thus it represents a growing consensus on an expanding body of human rights concepts.

Moreover, many of these "rights" have been incorporated in the constitutions of nations the world around. This suggests that there is less disagreement on the concepts themselves than one might suppose, which belies the notion that irreconcilable cultural values or cleavages are the basic issue. Rather, the problem is, as it has been all along, what material and political resources are available for their implementation, how effective are the processes of enforcement, whether or not there is a supporting cultural environment, and whether there may not lie in Confucianism other resources, as yet not fully developed, for the further enhancement of human rights. Hence this chapter attempts to deal with both concepts and practices, seen in historical, institutional, and evolutionary perspectives.

It is obvious enough that Confucianism itself did not generate human rights concepts and practices equivalent to those now embodied in the Universal Declaration; it is not obvious that Confucianism was headed in an altogether different authoritarian or "communitarian" direction, one incompatible with the rights affirmed in the Declaration. Our aim has not been to find twentieth-century human rights in Confucianism but to recognize therein certain central human values—historically embedded in, but at the same time restive with, repressive institutions in China—that in the emerging modern world could be supportive of those rights. In this our concern is not so much to render judgment on the past record as to clarify the bases on which past judgments have been made—those that could inform our understanding of human rights as still in the process of formation.

In accepting as our working definition of human rights the Universal Declaration adopted by the United Nations in 1948 and amended in the mid-1970s by a covenant on Civil and Political Rights and another on Economic, Social, and Cultural Rights, we conform with the general practice in human rights studies today, i.e., we refer to a consensus statement ratified by an international body and to a public document widely available.

Apart from this, definitions and understandings of human rights vary greatly. Indeed, such disagreement is apparent in the essay of Sumner B. Twiss ("A Constructive Framework for Discussing Confucianism and Human Rights") and Henry Rosemont Jr. ("Human Rights: A Bill of Worries").[4] The latter considers that human rights, as commonly known, are based on a belief in the radical autonomy of the individual, which Rosemont takes to be a false and unrealistic premise. Thus in Rosemont's eyes the whole human rights project is misbegotten. Whether in fact the original signatories to the Universal Declaration or human rights advocates championing it have made the same assumption regarding individual autonomy is, for Twiss, questionable but not a crucial point. No matter how long debated, such philosophical issues are unlikely to be resolved. Meanwhile, it is better to leave such questions open to diverse and even revisionist interpretations rather than predicate the human rights program on any one set of philosophical assumptions. Indeed, for just such reasons, Twiss argues that a pragmatic approach is called for, starting with the initial consensus of the Universal Declaration and amending it as new understandings are arrived at.

Here we might note that if Rosemont believes that liberal democratic notions of individual autonomy were unduly influential in the formulation of human rights concepts, in the history of Western liberalism itself one may observe an evolution from the early emphasis on individual liberty in the nineteenth century to a greater concern for social and communitarian values in twentieth-century liberal movements. It was precisely on this account—their socialist leanings—that liberals were often characterized as "leftist" or "pinko" in midcentury America.[5] Thus the evolution of liberal thought in the United States provides a parallel to that of the Universal Declaration and its protocols, with their increasing emphasis on social, economic, and environmental rights.

Twiss believes that in this process it is possible for new understandings of human rights to develop out of different moral and cultural traditions and for these to help in identifying both common grounds among these traditions and different appropriations of rights concepts among them. An early example of this is seen in the very process leading up to the formulation of the original Declaration itself. Since this occurred just after World War II, in what might be thought the heyday of Western liberalism and internationalism, it could easily be suspected that concepts of radical individual autonomy might have dominated the framing and terms of the Declaration, yet in fact Confucian and Mencian concepts of humanity and humaneness (*ren/jen*) were accepted, at the insistence of the Chinese delegation, as keynotes to the Declaration, to be enshrined in its preamble in the family-centered language of the Confucian *Analects*, e.g., the saying "All men are brothers."[6] Curiously, it was only after admission of the People's Republic of China in place of the Nationalist delegation that objection was raised to these Confucian sentiments by PRC spokesmen on Marxist-Leninist grounds (i.e., arguing from doctrines of European provenance), that Confucian universalistic humanism, as expressed in the quotation from the *Analects*, was obsolete if not wholly reactionary. Having been superseded in Communist China by an ideology of continuing class struggle that left no room for a classless humanism, the offending Confucian sentiments, it was argued, should be stricken from the document.

A further irony in the course of this continuing evolution is that a member of the earlier Chinese delegation, instrumental in the framing of the original preamble, later became head of the institute that sponsored the Confucian revival in Singapore during the 1980s and subsequently promoted the same revival in Beijing after the eclipse of Mao's anti-Confucian movement in the People's Republic.

A central point of Twiss's argument is that a moral consensus was arrived at pragmatically in the original Declaration—"a common vision of central moral and social values compatible with a variety of cultural anthropologies." Even if the latter had not conceived of these rights in the same way, as living traditions they could find the internal moral resources to recognize the validity of these rights and generally abide by them, each culture interpreting them in ways most congenial to it, which others who do not necessarily share in them could still respect. Rights so recognized do not depend on any one epistemological position or philosophical theory but can draw support from many.

Twiss offers a variety of evidence from Confucian tradition supportive of human rights, even if not couched in the current idiom of human rights. One such example is a passage from the text of Mencius that is often cited (as it is by several writers in this volume) as express-ing "the people's right of revolution." The passage reads:

> King Xuan of Qi asked, "Is it true that Tang banished Jie and
> King Wu marched against Zhou?"
>   "It is so recorded," answered Mencius.
>   "Is regicide permissible?"
>   A man who mutilates benevolence is a mutilator, while one
> who cripples rightness is a crippler. He who is both a mutilator
> and a crippler is an "outcast." I have indeed heard of the punish-
> ment of the "outcast Zhou," but I have not heard of any regicide.[7]

When considered in its own terms and in the larger context of Mencius, the passage does not support the popular modern interpre-tation of a "people's right of revolution" but does, I believe, confirm Twiss's main line of argument. First, one should note Mencius's central point: the proper exercise of kingly power and the likely consequence of its abuse—that a ruler forfeits his claim to kingship and exposes himself to being overthrown. Nothing at all is said about "the people" or "revolution," much less a people's "right" to revolt. As a matter of fact, elsewhere Mencius makes it clear that, while the people's welfare should be a prime concern of the ruler, he does not expect, over the normal course of things, that the people should take an active part in the political process. The common people, engaged in heavy labor, are in no position to do so—lacking the education, training, or time nec-essary to become well informed about governmental matters (*Mencius* 3A4). Instead, Mencius lays this responsibility on scholar-officials who serve the ruler. If the ruler misbehaves, it is the duty of his ministers to remonstrate with him. Then, if repeated remonstrances fail, they are to leave his service in silent protest (4B4). Should enough of them leave, it is a signal that the king has lost legitimacy and is due to be removed.

Does this, then, call for revolt? No. For Mencius, the next move is to have the responsible members of the ruling house depose the errant ruler (5B9). Failing that, it is understandable that some other leader will overthrow him, punish his misuse of power, and replace the defaulting dynasty. While recognizing that unchecked misrule may well provoke rebellion, Mencius recommends a process entirely consistent with his—and the general Confucian—view that violence is to be avoided at all reasonable costs. Revolt is only a last desperate recourse for an exasperated people, one that is understandable but not to be commended. Mencius is well aware that violence often prevails, but the point of his teachings is to replace the use of force with a well-considered civil process and above all with due process (what is right, fitting, and orderly in the circumstances). It is in this sense, then—that the observance of human rights is dependent on civility and due process—that Mencius and the Confucians can be said to offer what Twiss calls informed moral resources in support of human rights.

Twiss's paper, characterizing the human rights movement as an evolving one that potentially draws on the resources of diverse cultural traditions, is followed by that of Henry Rosemont Jr., who presents a sweeping critique of the whole Western human rights concept. He argues that the purposes of the movement would be better served by disassociating it from a rights-based conceptual framework and from notions of individual autonomy; better, instead, to turn to a Confucian conceptual framework for the expression of moral sentiments, preferably one defining people in terms of kinship relations and community.

In Rosemont's view, the rise of human rights concepts in the West, as well as of views of individual autonomy and liberal democracy with which it has been closely associated, was concomitant with the rise of industrial capitalism and a legal system protective above all of individual property rights. He believes further that a rights-based approach is incapable of dealing with the conflicting claims and contradictions generated within the liberal capitalist West. Thus his title, "Human Rights: A Bill of Worries."

One can share his concerns and most of his Bill of Worries, including the increasing inadequacy, if not bankruptcy, of policies based on individual autonomy and property rights, to deal with the social dilemmas and ecological challenges of the contemporary world (whether Western or Eastern, it makes no difference today), yet still believe that human rights concerns are among the legitimate "worries" of us all.

As one who from the 1940s was "worried" like Rosemont over the effects of industrialization in both America and East Asia and convinced that Confucian personalism (with the self and society seen in an indivisible, balanced relation to each other) had much to recommend it over the "rugged individualism" of the American West, I can see the human rights movement as embodying humane concerns that would be shared even by great Confucian reformers like Fan Zhongyan (989–1052) in the Song period, who said that the Confucian noble person (*junzi*) should be "first in worrying about the world's worries and last in enjoying its pleasures." Confucian personalism, family ideals, and social conscience do have much to offer the contemporary world and in key respects may provide a better grounding for both human rights and environmental rights. Yet it is also true that Confucianism had its own problems adapting in later times to the complexities of a society and state that had grown beyond (but not necessarily "outgrown") the homely truths of Confucius and Mencius. Increasingly, the concerns we refer to as "communitarian" were overshadowed by a dynastic state that proved far more intractable than the rulers of the relatively decentralized late Zhou city-states. And, as I argue in my discussion of "constitutionalism" in *Waiting for the Dawn*,[8] Confucian noblemen like Huang Zongxi were already "worrying" about the dynastic Leviathan, while others were worried about the state of the community, in an age when their counterparts in the West were just beginning to worry about laws and constitutions that would restrain despotic power.

I shall pursue this question of socially and culturally diverse, but in some respects convergent, evolutions later. Here, having made a case earlier for a Confucian "rites-based" approach as compared to a "rights-based" one,[9] I would like simply to register the increasing awareness among Confucians themselves that "rites" alone had proved insufficient to cope with the realities of power in late imperial China, and when informed Confucians of the late nineteenth and twentieth century in China became aware of constitutional law and "people's rights" in the West, some recognized it immediately as having relevance to the "worries" of earlier Confucians.

As do Twiss and Rosemont, other contributors to the same symposium, depending on how they define human rights or interpret Chinese tradition, come up with somewhat ambivalent responses to the question: "Are human rights concepts alien to China and Confucianism?" Julia Ching concedes immediately that human rights as expressed in the Universal Declaration are largely a modern Western creation, but she sees them as products of earlier developments in the West for which rough counterparts existed in traditional China ("Human Rights: A Valid Chinese Concept?"), hence it was not difficult for cultured Chinese to recognize, appreciate, and accept these values as they did when the Universal Declaration was ratified. Not only have several East Asian countries—Japan, South Korea, and Taiwan—claimed and made these their own, finding them not incompatible with their own Confucian values, but they have demonstrated by their economic success and rising standard of living that there is no necessary conflict between individual rights and economic/social/communitarian rights. Rather, these are seen as in many respects complementary. To assert otherwise—that in underdeveloped countries individual rights must be subordinated or even sacrificed to so-called group rights—may well be specious, serving not the advancement of society but some one party's monopolization of power.

Daniel W. Y. Kwok ("On the Rites and Rights of Being Human")[10] poses a similar question for himself—whether human rights existed in traditional China—and he comes up with a similarly qualified answer, but in rather different terms from Julia Ching. To him, individual rights of the modern type could not exist because there was no room for a free-standing, completely autonomous individual. Rather, the self was always seen, and acted, within a network of socially differentiated human relations governed by rites, wherein rights and duties were always interconnected and similarly differentiated. "Being human," which was for Kwok the aim of Confucian self-cultivation through the rites, always subordinated personal rights to the duties and responsibilities of the person within the network of social relations.

In this context, something like rights as legitimate expectations did exist, but not for the isolated individual as an anonymous cipher but only in a form that subserved the interdependence and harmony of the social group. Too often, according to Kwok, this meant subordination to the interests of the stronger party in the relationship, especially parents, husbands, and rulers. Given the fact of unequal power relationships, even today, after almost a century of revolutionary change, one hears, as Kwok says, amid protests against despotic rule, "Cries for laws and rights that safeguard human decency."

In contrast to Kwok's emphasis on the socially differentiated aspects of Confucian ethics, Irene Bloom ("Mencius and Human Rights") places herself squarely on the side of Mencius's belief in the moral equality of a common humanity (whether understood as the human species or the human potential). This common humanity, she argues vigorously and with impressive evidence from Mencius, is "the single most important connecting link between traditional philosophical and religious ideas and contemporary human rights documents." Indeed, the thrust of Bloom's argument is to call into fundamental question whether, in Mencius or the influential Mencian tradition in East Asia, it is true, as Kwok avers, that human equality is always subordinated to the unequal relations embedded in the rites.

This view of natural equality by virtue of a common human nature, though rooted in shared human sentiments of sympathy, shame, and respect and less exclusively identified than in the Western Enlightenment with the human capacity for reason, bears marked resemblances to the views of seventeenth- and eighteenth-century thinkers whose natural law philosophies were influential in the rise of human rights thinking in the West. The principal difference between the West and China lay in the rapid assimilation of these sentiments into public declarations and legal enactments in Western Europe and America— especially in such formulations as "equality before the law" and "equal protection of the law."

Mencius's view of natural equality, Bloom argues, is closely allied to his view of the inherent natural dignity of all human beings, which for Mencius is primary as compared to all social distinctions, including "aristocratic dignity." One can even affirm, she says, this natural equality as fundamental to all of the distinctions and differentiations associated with ritual relations and social roles. Whatever the status distinctions to be observed, all human beings are entitled to an irreducible measure of respect. Thus Bloom emphasizes that "there is a consistent sense in the *Mencius* that the claim to receive respect from others and the disposition to behave respectfully toward them, are both psychologically and morally correlative. This is as true of ordinary people, including wayfarers and beggars, as it is of ministers and kings." The reference to "wayfarers" and "beggars" in the *Mencius* is especially pointed and poignant; even the most transient and least substantial of human lives manifest something of this dignity.

These two basic elements in Mencian thought, human moral equality and natural dignity, did not, for reasons having to do with other factors in the evolving Chinese tradition, directly generate democratic ideas or human rights thinking of the modern Western variety, as Bloom readily concedes, but they "are consistent with, and morally and spiritually supportive of, the consensus documents [on human rights] that figure importantly in our emerging modern civilization."

Wejen Chang's essay, entitled "The Confucian Theory of Norms and Human Rights,"[11] includes an extensive examination of many of the same Confucian moral relations, or norms, referred to by Daniel Kwok, analyzing in some detail the references to them in key Confucian texts such as the *Analects*, *Mencius*, *Xunzi*, and *Record of Rites* (*Liji*). He finds that most of those having a bearing on political matters, especially the ruler/people and ruler/minister relationships, emphasize reciprocal obligations, mutual respect, and the repayment of boons or benefits received. He stresses that if anything—if indeed there is any imbalance in these mutual obligations—the heavier burden lies on the side of the ruler's obligations to the people and his responsibilities for their welfare.

The closest thing to the Western notion of human rights according to Chang is the Chinese concept of *fen*, "share." Whereas "human rights" are grounded in the natural order and seen as innate (in the way that Mencius and the *Mean* see the moral nature as an innate endowment from Heaven), shares (*fen*, understood variously as "role," "function," or "duty") are defined in some proportion to the role or function performed—a connection of "shares" with "duties" that corresponds to some extent with Western views of rights as going together with duties and responsibilities.

Chang believes that these two different approaches to the problem, "rights" and "shares," each has its advantages and limitations. The particular virtue of "rights" is the confidence they give to the individual in claiming, and even struggling for, his own entitlements before state and society. On the other hand, this can lead to contentiousness and conflict. The virtue of "shares" is precisely in the sense of sharing, based on mutual respect and reciprocity. Where the latter qualities are encouraged and developed, contentiousness can be reduced.

Nevertheless, if genuine reciprocity does not prevail, the individual may lack the confidence to assert himself, or the people may be without the means to claim their legal rights; hence resentments deepen. For this reason, Chang believes that the two approaches, rather than being mutually exclusive, may complement the other and offset each others' weaknesses.[12]

In Chung-ying Cheng's paper on "Transforming Confucian Virtues Into Human Rights," he argues that in Confucianism virtue and duty go together and that the duties of rulers carry the implication that they also possess the authority or right to perform these duties for the benefit of humankind. Further, in the other Confucian moral relations a similar power or right is implied for the carrying out of the duties appropriate to each. Since, however, it is only in the relationship of friend and friend that we find relations of equality, it is on this basis, and as an extension from it, that one could see the possibility for grounding the rights of the individual in a Confucian theory of correlative duties among members of a community. "The only thing lacking," he says, "is an explicit assertion of these rights as the basis for their political recognition."

Cheng recognizes that in the absence of such explicit recognition in the past, as well as in the modern period (especially in the May Fourth Movement of 1919), there has been a strong need for "rational liberation" to achieve a more open, more explicit, and more orderly procedure for public policy making. In his view, such a process could well be grounded in the Confucian values of equality, self-respect, and mutual respect for personal dignity, predicated on the Confucian conception of the mutual coinherence of self and society.

As a Confucian basis for the exercise of democratic political rights, Cheng cites a passage in *Mencius* wherein Mencius enjoins the ruler from taking any action to appoint or dismiss an official, or to execute an offender against public order, without fully consulting the people as a whole. This is a most significant claim on Mencius's part, but a real difficulty also attaches to it: though the passage in question clearly implies that there should be a careful and deliberate process of consultation—a sense of due process in governance—the agent throughout is the ruler, and nowhere does Mencius explain how the people themselves would become active in the process. One can easily conjecture that in a relatively simple agrarian society, processes of local consensus formation could be assumed to exist and thus be taken for granted. However, the nature and extent of such participation in higher policy formulation becomes a serious question in the changed circumstances of the later imperial dynasties.

Cheng acknowledges this problem; given the failure historically to articulate individual rights and the people's political rights, ruling dynasties have dominated the situation, asserting their own interests as in effect representing the public interest. When this domination has become too oppressive, revolution has been the inevitable consequence. This too, Cheng says, is justified by Mencius in what has become known as Mencius's "right of revolution," as discussed above.

In this case, Mencius, consistently with views of his expressed elsewhere in the text, favors due process and not the resort to force. At another point, he says one should not wish to take power if to do so meant committing even one unrightful act, which has always been understood as avoiding the taking of life. Moreover, it is consistent with a longstanding, widely accepted view among Confucians that force should be resorted to only after all other remedies have been exhausted, i.e., when it has been made clear that a ruler or criminal is incorrigible.

When Cheng suggests, in his conclusion that after almost eighty years of revolutionary and republican history in twentieth-century China, that resistance to oppressive rulers may still have to take the form of revolution, it is doubtful whether he would have Mencius on his side. Revolutions may be understandable when all else fails, but they have come and gone in modern times without solving the problem. No one was more conscious of this than Mencius, i.e., that violence breeds violence and in the long run proves counterproductive. The power organized to lead revolutions, which mobilizes the force to prosecute them, remains thereafter to fill the power vacuum with its own, now entrenched and coercive, methods.

For the most part, the papers discussed above address human rights questions as they relate to classical Confucian conceptions, based on evidence in the prime early Confucian texts. Yet most of our contributors acknowledge that the subsequent Chinese tradition hardly bespeaks, or well exemplifies, these classical values. Thus even while one might grant that these Confucian values are compatible with certain modern human rights ideas, there remains a question as to why Confucianism did not develop along these lines in later times. A common answer to this question is that China's subsequent historical development, especially in the political sphere so crucial to Confucian concerns, was dominated by an imperial dynastic system in many ways at odds with Confucianism. This does not, in itself, suffice to answer our question, however, since, while other systemic and ideological factors could be held accountable for the actual result, Confucians too were involved in the process. Hence, to assess the respective roles and relative weights of these factors in the developing Chinese tradition, we must consider the contending elements and alternatives to Confucianism that may have affected the outcome.

Yu Feng does this for the so-called Yellow Emperor tradition ("The Yellow Emperor Tradition as Compared to Confucianism"),[13] based on a recently discovered document known as *The Four Texts*, which represents a distinctive mix of Daoist and Legalist ideas known to have played a prominent role in the earlier period of Chinese dynastic history. Feng believes that this tradition, known as the "Way of Might" (rather than "Right," as with the Confucians), upheld certain universalist conceptions of law and political practice that contrast with the particularism inherent in the Confucian rites. Hence if one considers that the rites may serve as a plausible Confucian ground for human rights, one must also consider those ways in which the Yellow Emperor tradition offered viable alternatives to, and pointed to certain limitations of, the Confucian approach.

Where Yellow Emperor theorists agreed with the Confucians was in the principle of providing for the people's livelihood as fundamental to rulership. They also shared the idea that the ruler's power should be limited, in the Yellow Emperor's case by subordination of the ruler to the law as truly universal and applicable to all. For this purpose, the latter tradition advocated Daoist nonaction or "doing nothing" (*wuwei*), with the ruler restraining himself as much as possible from interfering in the people's conduct of their own affairs. In this view, the people's pursuit of their own interests would eventually redound to the material advantage of the ruler himself. Feng goes further to assert that this laissez-faire political policy also implies that people, managing their own affairs, would be entitled to their own opinions and even to express them as a way of informing the judgments made by the ruler who, holding to no preconceived opinion of his own, would be completely open to them.

This approach to rulership, characterized by Feng as "covert" because the ruler conceals his own inclinations, is nevertheless supposed to yield a more "public" process of policy formulation inasmuch as it would "objectively" reflect people's opinions. It remains unclear, however, as to just how these opinions are to find expression and how influential they could be when, in the end, the ruler, as the unquestioned locus of all power and authority, makes the sole decision.

Feng believes the influence of this school of thought was beneficial in the early years of the Han, as manifested in its laissez-faire policies, and in the early Tang, as embodied in a process whereby the emperor instituted several stages of policy review before making his decisions. This Feng calls "mild autocracy," in contrast to the strong autocracy that prevailed in the Song and after. Feng does not, however, speculate as to why, in the continuity of dynastic rule, the milder form, if so successful, should have given way to even stronger autocracies.

In the end, Feng credits the Yellow Emperor tradition with promoting the idea of the people's right to subsistence and also the idea of universal law as, ideally, limiting the ruler's exercise of his power. He concedes, however, that it is deficient in respect to other human rights that would be better served by Confucianism.

Unfortunately, while this gives us a fuller picture of the conceptual resources available in Chinese tradition, it does not get us far in explaining an outcome, in the later dynasties, acknowledged by almost all to be deficient in political and legal rights of the Western variety. That outcome has to be considered, however, in the perspective of the continuing contest between laws and rites and the further development of Confucian thinking in regard to both.

The nearest equivalent to constitutional law in China is found in the great law codes of the Tang and Ming, widely emulated throughout East Asia. Parallel to this, however, was a continuing development of Confucian thinking about rites, which often at the Chinese court involved a serious contestation between imperial authority and Confucians at court who saw the rites as an important means of challenging that authority.

Ronguey Chu calls attention to four episodes, of which two are particularly dramatic, at the court of the Ming-dynasty founder, Taizu (r. 1368–1398), which illustrate how Confucians contested imperial power by invoking the superior authority of the Confucian classics.[14] In the first of the instances to be cited here, Taizu, overriding a centuries-old tradition, decreed that the performance of the sacrificial services to Confucius should be reserved only to the emperor himself and Confucius's own family in Qufu; they should not be allowed to Confucian officials and schools elsewhere in the empire. Ritually speaking, the implication was that the emperor stood above all others in speaking for Heaven and the Confucian Way. Despite the harshness with which Taizu was known to deal with his critics, prominent Confucian ministers remonstrated with the emperor against this, and eventually he rescinded the edict.

The second incident has to do with Taizu's expurgating of passages in *Mencius* he considered contumacious of rulers and Taizu's banishing of Mencius from the Confucian temple. Again courageous ministers protested, and after Taizu threatened death to anyone who opposed these actions, one minister brought his coffin with him to court saying, "It would be an honor to die for Mencius." Again Taizu, as powerful and cruel a despot as any China has seen, backed off in the face of this heroic defense of Confucian tradition.

Incidents such as these demonstrate that there was indeed a moral culture in traditional China that could stand up in certain spectacular cases to abuses of power—a moral culture that served, in its own day, some of the same function as the moral culture, or "constitutional culture," spoken of by Louis Henkin, who attributed the fall of Richard Nixon to the moral pressure exerted on him by a constitutional culture that constrained even a supreme commander of the armed forces and head of law enforcement agencies.

Individually impressive as were these heroics of Confucian ministers, they were more the exception than the rule, and while they testify to a moral culture compatible with human rights sentiments, something more was needed. That "something more" as perceived by Huang Zongxi in the seventeenth century was what might be called a civil society protective of political freedom and of public discussion at the Chinese court. Huang's father had died a martyr to the cause of outspoken criticism at the Ming court, and Huang believed that a truly humane government should not depend for its workings on such extreme self-sacrifice of honest, conscientious Confucian ministers. Whereas the keynote of the great Neo-Confucian Zhu Xi's political doctrine—widely accepted in Neo-Confucian East Asia—had been the self-disciplined, dedicated service of the Confucian noble man, who was totally at the service of the public good and defiant of all despots, Huang discounted the idea that the heroics of such noble men could accomplish much without strong constitutional supports of a structural, institutional character. The Confucians had the moral culture; what they lacked was a legal structure that would do more for the Confucian than the rituals of the imperial court. The systemic details of Huang's constitutional plan for a balancing of powers, so as to make the people (*min*) masters in their own house, are given in my *Waiting for the Dawn*. True, this was only one man's plan, but before one dismisses it as no more than that, one should recognize that other leading scholars in the seventeenth century (Ku Yanwu, Lu Liuliang, Tang Jian, and Wang Fuzhi) were thinking along the same lines, and although Huang's ideas could not circulate freely in the seventeenth and eighteenth centuries, they became an inspiration to reformers in the late nineteenth and early twentieth centuries, providing them with an indigenous resource to be invoked in support of the constitutional movement. Moreover, as further evidence that Confucian culture at large might be compatible with constitutionalism, we should note that at the founding of the Yi dynasty in Korea, a leading Neo-Confucian statesman, Chŏng Tojŏn (1342–1398), drew up a monumental constitutional plan including many features similar to Huang's, but almost three hundred years earlier!

By this point it should be obvious that the implementation of Confucian principles in imperial China was greatly conditioned by the structure and processes of bureaucratic administration, and this was true both early and late, from the Han down to the Qing. It is also true that the administrative system, which combined both executive and judicial functions, for the most part recognized levels and areas of social activity in which the Confucian rites were respected by the state and thought to be the most effective means of maintaining social order in localities beyond the effective reach of the mandarinate. Likewise, on levels and in areas of governance where Legalist-type laws rather than Confucian rites were thought to be more applicable (i.e., beyond the normal reach of family or village control), it was still Confucian-educated officials who administered legal procedures. Thus Confucian values and Legalist systems were inseparably involved with each other, while, as we see with Huang Zongxi, they coexisted in some degree of tension with one another.

One consequence of this was a judicial system oriented more toward upholding of administrative law and order than to defending the interests of the individual, as Alison W. Conner's article ("Confucianism and Due Process") confirms, but it was at the same time influenced both in its stated procedures and actual practice by Confucian humane concerns.[15] Thus, in regard to the use of torture, which is universally condemned in theory (as in the Universal Declaration of Human Rights), though it was legally allowed down into the Qing period, its practice was clearly circumscribed by explicit due process, as Conner argues. Thus the Qing system of confession by the use of torture was one, as she says, "based on detailed rules, even if bureaucratic ones; it was neither arbitrary nor unregulated, and it embodied a clear conception of what constituted a fair trial." The best of this system, she is inclined to think, reflects Confucian influences, and in the present situation it could well be in order to review and reappropriate "the best of that tradition."

Although by the seventeenth century important Confucian thinkers like Huang Zongxi, Gu Yanwu, Lu Liuliang, Tang Jian, and others had made progress in their critique of dynastic rule, the success of the Manchu conquest and the preoccupation of most scholars with relatively nonpolitical (e.g., philological, text-critical, and bibliographical) projects directed attention away from ideological issues. Not until the later years of the dynasty, especially under pressure from the West and Japan, did both reformers and revolutionaries take renewed interest in broad constitutional issues of the kind that Huang, Gu, Lu, and others had addressed.

When they did, it was in an atmosphere of increasing crisis and soul searching. Radical alternatives were being considered, including some from the West transmitted through Japan (and these somewhat transmuted into Chinese terms). In both Japan and China there was a tendency to interpret the Western conception of natural rights in Neo-Confucian terms as "Heaven's endowment" (*tianfu*), which is Zhu Xi's explanation of "Heaven's imperative" (*tianming*) in the first sentence of the *Mean* (*Zhongyong*): "Heaven's imperative" is called the moral nature (*xing*).[16] Here, "Heaven's imperative" (commonly rendered politically as Heaven's Mandate) has the broader meaning of "what Heaven has ordained." "Heaven" had always had a sense of the "natural," but this included a moral aspect, i.e., not an amoral, "objective" view of nature but one that included the subjective element revealed in the human moral sentiments associated with *xing*. "Natural law" so interpreted was thus, for Confucians, grounded in human moral sentiments more than in some abstract universal construct.

A related problem was the tendency for Confucians to think of human relations in terms of mutual obligations or duties. In this conception, rights and duties necessarily went together, but if "rights" were grounded in the inborn moral nature and understood in this sense as an inalienable endowment from Heaven, they would achieve a certain dignity and priority over duties, i.e., not contingent on recognition by the state or the performance of duties incurred in society. This was a question of serious concern for those who believed, as a practical matter, that the most urgent priority of the day was the building of an effective, functional state, without which no individual rights could be guaranteed.

Joan Judge's "The Concept of People's Rights (*minquan*) in the Late Qing: Classical and Contemporary Sources of Authority"[17] illustrates the process of adaptation by constitutional reformers in the late Qing who sought to incorporate "people's rights" in a movement that asserted the "people's powers" without directly challenging the monarchy. In these circumstances, it was natural for Chinese writers to reformulate new political ideas in the vocabulary of earlier Chinese discourse—as the Japanese themselves had done and were continuing to do. And while evocations of the past sometimes led to revisionist misconstructions and to some misconstruing of Western ideas as well, one cannot discount the importance of this effort to deal with fundamental issues of the cultural encounter between East Asia and the West. Although sometimes dismissed by Western observers as sentimental effusions or nostalgic reveries of the past—essentially conservative, if not reactionary—this is to underestimate the depth and persistence of the issues at stake, to which subsequent discourse and debate have repeatedly recurred.

It should have been no surprise that, after the high tide of the twentieth-century revolutionary movement had been reached in the Great Proletarian Cultural Revolution of the late 1960s and 1970s, in its backwash would reappear with renewed—and indeed heightened—significance several of the figures referred to in Peter Zarrow's discussion of "Citizenship and Human Rights in Early Twentieth-Century Chinese Thought."[18] In this process there are notable elements of both continuity and discontinuity. Both reformers and revolutionaries, even those powerfully moved by new currents from the West, are affected in their selection and adaptation of new elements by both cultural predispositions and indispositions, both dissatisfactions with a present seen as seriously handicapped by its past and by worries over the effects of too rapid and abrupt an intrusion of new ideas and practices from the West.

Zarrow focuses on two leading thinkers of the early twentieth century, Liu Shipei, the leader of a significant anarchist movement who anticipated many of the revolutionary changes to come, and Liang Qichao, probably the most influential intellectual figure of the first three decades. Both Liu and Liang represent a scholarly capability for bridging past and present that became increasingly rare after the major shift to Western-style education post-1905 rendered it difficult for Chinese to acquire the command of the classical tradition that still stood Liu and Liang in good stead (and the virulent antitraditionalism that prevailed from the New Culture and May Fourth movements down through Mao's Cultural Revolution only added to this difficulty).

Liu's anarchist ideas were marked by a basic commitment to the value of equality—a prime value in Chinese tradition as well, but one historically held in some balance with the need for expertise and structured authority as the meritocratic bureaucracy attempted to reconcile them. In Liu, however, equality was pushed to the limit, circumscribed only by a totalistic, cosmic/human holism that, paradoxically, gave little attention to the definition of individual human rights. It is understandable that this unstructured utopian idealism should lend itself eventually to communism, wherein the egalitarian ideal, governed only by emphatic political authority, would eventually prove inimical to individual rights.

Liang Qichao, by contrast, was far more concerned with both structure and due process. Initially, an advocate of constitutional monarchy during the late Qing, after 1911 he accepted republicanism but held firmly to constitutionalism and to the promotion of "people's rights." The latter he conceived, however, not so much as "individual" rights but as rights necessary to the exercise of citizenship in a nation-state.

Liang's strong adherence to constitutionalism could be seen as consistent with his early admiration for Huang Zongxi as a kind of Confucian constitutionalist; moreover, his concern for developing the kind of civil infrastructure associated by him with the people's participation in citizenship, while it set a certain limit on the interpretation of people's rights as individual rights, was not inconsistent with a Confucian view akin to Huang's. Where Liang decidedly departed from tradition was in his acceptance, under Western and Japanese influence, of the nation-state (rather than the professedly universalist or cosmopolitan dynastic state) as the primary form of political organization and in his reformulation of Confucian self-cultivation to serve the roles and duties of citizenship. In this respect, he could be said to have advanced beyond both Zhu Xi's concept of the self-cultivation of the leadership elite and Huang Zongxi's conception of a constitutional infrastructure still largely in the hands of Confucian scholar-officials.

If several of our writers believe it possible to ground the practice of human rights in the Confucian concept of rites, Randall Peerenboom, who both practices law in Beijing and has written on ancient Chinese legal philosophy, seriously questions this. For him, Confucian rites may have a value in establishing a moral consensus and promoting beneficial customs within a community, but this does not protect the individual or the minority from the tyranny of the dictator or the majority.[19] Moreover, since rites place a premium on the ideal of social and political harmonization, they, and rites-based views of sound order, lend themselves to authoritarian rule and to conformity, rather than freedom, of thought. Thus in his opinion, a revival of Confucianism in a conservative form emphasizing "harmony" as the supreme value (as currently is the case among its sponsors in the PRC) would be prejudicial to the protection of individual human rights and to the freedom of thought essential to political democracy.

Generally, Peerenboom believes that the Confucian rites and Western conceptions of rights serve different purposes but may be, to some extent, complementary. "In most instances rites can complement rights, providing a moral dimension to interpersonal actions, suggesting possibilities above and beyond the legal relations defined by rights. . . . The rites may remind us of our moral obligations, our duties to others." Nevertheless, he also sees a danger in it: "to the extent that rites represent the moral consensus of the community, they exert pressure to conform one's thinking to others." Then, too, according to him the emphasis in rites' thinking on social solidarity has contributed to "the enduring appeal of the utopian myth of harmony, thereby blinding rulers and reformers alike to the realities of disharmony."

Peerenboom is on strong factual ground when he says that historically Confucianism did not produce liberal democracy, popular sovereignty, democratic elections, civil liberties, and the like. Nonetheless, his argument leans heavily on a theoretical model of Confucianism and may not take into account the developing historical awareness of later Confucian thinkers that moral cultivation and ritual norms were insufficient, in themselves, to cope with the excesses of authoritarian rule, as for instance Huang Zongxi and Liang Qichao correctly perceived the matter, or even as an orthodox Neo-Confucian like Lu Liuliang (a prime exponent of Zhu Xi in the seventeenth century) came up with a radical critique of Chinese despotism, in the context of the rites.

No doubt Peerenboom is correct theoretically and to some extent practically when he sees the ruler as cast by Confucianism in a supreme leadership role, harmonizing divergent views and interests in the society; there are, indeed, abundant examples of courtly, if not utterly sycophantic, officials who credited emperors with such sagelike authority. This is not, however, the whole story. There is evidence also, as early as the *Mencius*, the *Zuo Commentary* (*Zuozhuan*), and *Discourses of the States* (*Guoyu*), that contests the legitimacy of rulers who do not listen to criticism and remonstration. And if Peerenboom sees the ruler as the unique interpreter of, and authority on the Way, this was not undisputed; there was the alternative tradition, abundantly recorded in Neo-Confucian literature, that saw the custody of the Way as divided, from the Zhou on down, between the ruler who held power and the wise Confucian mentors, without whose advice and the ruler's acceptance of it, the latter lost authority and legitimacy.

Among prominent twentieth-century spokesmen for Confucianism, such as Tang Junyi, Mou Zongsan, Carsun Chang, and Xu Fuguan, one finds a readiness to acknowledge that this dissenting Confucian tradition, unable historically to prevail over the politically more dominant dynastic tradition, has welcomed Western constitutional democracy as a support for the more liberal Confucian tradition as they espouse it.[20]

Our final two papers present different views among Chinese intellectuals with regard to the continuing influence of Confucianism. Merle Goldman[21] sees a considerable residue of that influence among leading intellectuals down into recent years, but it is a Confucianism having mostly to do with how intellectuals perceive their role in relation to the state, which bears many resemblances to the role of the traditional literati, especially in their sense of obligation to serve in government out of a responsible concern for the welfare of the people.

The efforts of Wu Han, a scholar and writer as well as vice mayor of Beijing under Mao, is illustrative of this idealistic strain of Confucian-inspired resistance to despotism. What aroused Mao's ire and resulted in Wu's martyrdom as a target of the Cultural Revolution was Wu's play, *Hai-Jui Dismissed*, in which a sixteenth-century Confucian minister paid with his life for criticizing the emperor. It dramatized the Confucian concept of true loyalty consisting in honest remonstrance to the ruler, i.e., in true dedication to the public interest. Besides making thinly veiled references to Peng Dehuai's criticism of Mao, it prefigured Wu's own martyrdom for challenging Mao.

The historical case and Wu's play illustrate some key features of how the Confucian legacy has operated in the post-Confucian setting. First of all, history has uses in serving as indirect political criticism when circumstances preclude more direct reference. This has not only been a traditional Confucian use of the past for very present purposes, but it also shows in what way Confucian values may live in popular art (here the drama) long after they have ceased to be taught in doctrinal form—which is as much as to say that, no longer being taught, Confucianism does not survive in its traditional form, as an articulated doctrine, but now lives on in forms more subtle yet still palpable in the popular imagination—in poetry, song, and drama, as the moral grounding and tone of a whole culture rather than as the philosophy of the elite. In such circumstances, the influence of Confucianism may be inchoate and almost impossible to estimate, but it is there, exerting an immeasurable power of attraction.

It may indeed be true, as Jeremy T. Paltiel reiterates, that younger generations in post-Mao China know little about and think less of Confucianism.[22] Rather, they perceive it either as a "feudal" remnant being revived and reimposed by an oppressive regime or else as an idealistic, even romantic evocation of the past, mainly by foreigners, that is being adroitly manipulated by the current regime for its own conservative purposes. To some degree, this view may hold for a supposedly "liberated" generation, long since cut off from any knowledge of Confucianism except for the vague, negative impressions they formed of it from the repeated anti-Confucian campaigns of the twentieth century. It must be admitted too that recent advocates of human rights and liberal democracy see little relevance of Confucianism to their own cause. Meanwhile, writers like Wu Han, rare in their own time, are still rarer today. Wu was the product of an education and scholarship under the Guomindang that was at least liberal enough for Wu Han, as a scholar, to learn something of Chinese history and become aware of its traditional moral and political resources. This has been far more difficult since 1949, and thus far less typical of the present generation—many of them unschooled Red Guards—whose political activism in the 1980s and 1990s is more informed by the libertarian May Fourth Movement and by China's belated opening to the West as part of Deng's modernization program than it is by anything Confucian. The same is largely true of the developing Chinese legal community in recent years, as is evident from the debates over human rights in legal journals, of which Paltiel gives a most revealing account.

For all this, the exposure of the more recent generation to intellectual trends outside China will make them aware of the importance increasingly being attached to Confucianism abroad, both as a newly recognized—or at least imputed—factor in the successful modernization of other East Asian states and as a serious object of scholarly study outside China. If the new generation expects to live in this larger world, it will have to reckon with these currents abroad, and with more of an understanding of them than May Fourth allowed for. Moreover, if Jeremy Paltiel is right that problems of "national identity" persist in all East Asian countries historically under Confucian influence, and there is ample evidence pointing in that direction, it is unlikely that these can be resolved without the Chinese becoming better informed than they are now of the contents, historical development, and wide cultural extension of Confucianism. If no people can ignore its own past or fail in some way to come to terms with it, it is no less true that Chinese, like other East Asians, will have to deal with such problems in a better educated and thoughtful way, lest this cultural battle be lost by default to those busily appropriating Confucianism for their own regressive—and sometimes repressive—purposes.

In arranging this symposium, I wished to open up a dialogue, as wide ranging as possible, between China and the West—a dialogue that would go beyond the immediate political confrontation over human rights demands and accusations, in order to get at some of the deeper cultural issues that underlie the claims and counterclaims now being made in the political arena. This dialogue was meant to be open and open ended, exposing issues without necessarily settling them. In clarifying them, however, one could, I believe, say that a rough consensus emerged on some points that may serve to advance future dialogue:

1. Confucian values and Confucian discourse over the centuries have been involved with many of the same issues that have concerned Western human rights thinkers, though in somewhat different language.

2. Thinking about human rights, in the form recognized by the Universal Declaration of 1948, is a relatively recent development in the West, which, however, emerges from a long historical development of humanitarian concerns expressed in different religious, ethical, social, and legal traditions. Human rights as currently understood have deep and diverse roots in the West, are hybrid in cultural character, and are still evolving in practice.

3. The same is true with regard to Confucian values in China, and more broadly in East Asia as a whole, to the extent that East Asian countries otherwise culturally diverse have shared in certain common

Confucian values and in the modern period have faced a similar challenge from Western ideas and practices. It is significant, however, that several East Asian countries (Japan, South Korea, Taiwan) have not found their Confucian past an obstacle to the acceptance of Western-style constitutions and guarantees of human rights. Cultural diversity did not prevent Chinese representatives from actively participating in the formulation of the 1948 Declaration of Human Rights, as they found no incompatibility between the essential humanistic values of Confucianism and these new human rights initiatives.

4. Although some contrast may be drawn between a greater emphasis on individual autonomy in modern Western conceptions of human rights and a greater emphasis on social and communitarian values in Confucianism, the contrast is often overdrawn at the expense of shared concerns and understandings. Social and communitarian values have by no means been lacking in traditions that have contributed to human rights thinking in the West, while respect for the dignity of the self and person have been central to Confucianism from its inception.

5. Key to these questions is the linking in Confucianism between the primacy of the morally responsible self and the social norms embodied in Confucian ritual decorum, as compared to the "Western" coupling of individual rights and legal protections. To some extent, the Confucian reliance on ritual norms was at the expense of legal protections for the individual, but in the long-term evolution of Confucian thinking there was an increasing consciousness of the need for law in a constitutional sense and in the sense of due process. This rendered it possible for at least some prominent Chinese thinkers in the early twentieth century to view the advent of Western constitutionalism and human rights legislation as quite congenial to their own sense of need in this respect. At the same time, some Westerners concerned with social and communitarian values have been ready to find in Confucianism a remedy to what they see as an excessive individualism and libertarianism in the West.

6. One could look, as some scholars do, for a reconciliation of the two in a complementary relationship, but the picture is complicated by the legacy of anti-Confucianism in the successive liberationist, revolutionary movements in China from the early twentieth century down to recent times. Thus there are cleavages today, cutting across China,

East Asia, and the West, as between divergent understandings of both Confucianism and human rights and whether priority is to be given to individual rights, social duties, or communitarian needs. Should these indeed be seen as anything but mutually implicated and equally necessary? Is it not specious to assert that subsistence needs and economic progress in underdeveloped countries should come before political freedoms? Can either be achieved without the other? What gauge could there be for a satisfactory level of subsistence as a precondition for the granting of civil rights or for the level of economic progress to be achieved before human rights are recognized?

7. The foregoing are all questions that bear further investigation and discussion, but at least two others have a major bearing on the outcome of human rights issues. One is the question of civil society: Could any kind of human rights program, whether conceived in individual/social or legal/ritual terms, be effective in the absence of both a civil-political infrastructure and a moral culture supportive of them? The other question is whether the urgent industrial, technological, environmental, and ecological problems that confront us today— and China in some respects more urgently even than most others— do not demand new human rights conceptions and practices, with a humane concern extending beyond the human to the earth and all forms of life. These cannot but concern us all, East and West, in equal measure today. Thus the dialogue must go on.

15

China and the Limits of Liberalism

On the first day of my return to Beijing in the spring of 1979, two things in particular struck me. At the airport, as we left the plane for the terminal, there were portraits of the great authority figures of Communist China hanging over the entrance—monumental in scale, heroic in style: Mao Zedong and Hua Guofeng, and then the patriarchal figures of Marx, Engels, Lenin, and Stalin—the latter especially impressive in his Soviet marshal's uniform. Today, many of these portraits have been removed, but the picture of Stalin, so long after he had been put out of sight elsewhere, remains, which typifies the reluctance of even a more "pragmatic" regime to scrap the authority structure on which it continued to depend.

The second spectacle was an opening-night performance, that same evening, of a celebrated play by Wu Han[1] concerning the upright Ming-dynasty official Hai Rui (1513–1587), who had challenged corruption in high places and risked death in the endeavor to rectify injustice and the abuse of power. The play *Hai Rui Dismissed*[2] was being performed for the first time since its banning during the Cultural Revolution. Its revival was one step in exposing the crimes of the Gang of Four and rehabilitating those who had been persecuted by them. Thus, back to back that day, we had Hai Rui and Stalin as symbols of two contrasting sides of contemporary China.

When first performed in 1961, the play was widely interpreted as an indirect criticism of Mao and a defense of Peng Dehuai, who had spoken out against Mao's policies during the so-called Great Leap Forward and had suffered martyrdom as a result. Whether this was Wu Han's specific purpose or not, as a competent historian of the Ming period from his precommunist days, Wu Han had a strong predilection for historical figures who manifested a noble, self-sacrificing spirit in the service of the people. Among them he chose Hai Rui as the personification of human intelligence, courage, and unyielding determination in the righting of injustice.

Among the features of Hai Rui's character and career as an official, Wu emphasized his rugged independence of mind; his clear insight into the shams and hypocrisy of bureaucratic officialdom; his intolerance of favoritism, bribery, and corruption; his condemnation of the illegal annexation of property by powerful officials and of the concentration of wealth in their hands; his exposing of the polite conventions by which officials acquiesced in or collaborated with wrongdoing; his positive efforts to rectify the system and make fundamental reforms to equalize landholding and taxation; and above all his personal conscientiousness and dedication, his uncompromising integrity in the struggle against abuses of power.

One aspect of Hai Rui's life and thought that is not underscored by Wu Han is his Confucianism (or Neo-Confucianism, the later, mature form in which it reached Hai Rui). In the repressive atmosphere of his own time and given Mao's powerful hostility to Confucianism, for Wu Han to have taken this up would have risked misunderstanding. Wu knew that he would be exposed to ideological attack for seeming to glorify a kind of humanistic reformism rather than emphasizing the need for class struggle. Such reformism, it would be charged, actually served to buttress the existing order of that time. It ignored the realities of class conflict and, by offering palliatives to ameliorate the old order, delayed its inevitable overthrow through revolutionary struggle. Another likely objection would be that Neo-Confucian reformism tended to glorify the role of the individual rather than the group or class. No doubt anticipating these objections, Wu gave particular emphasis to Hai Rui's "progressive" stance: his close identification with the people, his contempt for bureaucratic officialdom, and his awareness of the need for fundamental changes in the economic and social system of his time.

Even so, from the controversy that broke out over Wu's play in May 1964, the Confucian background of Hai Rui's reformism could not be kept out of sight. Indeed, it may well have been one of the issues that precipitated the anti-Confucian campaign that became such a prominent feature of the Cultural Revolution. Over the course of this campaign, Confucian reformism was cast as the ideological bedfellow of bourgeois revisionism, which had its own historical associations in Mao's mind with Western liberalism. As a proponent of revolutionary change, he no doubt saw in Confucianism the same traits of tolerance, moderation, and compromise that he attacked in his essay "Combat Liberalism" as impediments to ideological struggle and direct action.[3] Moreover, Wu Han had had scholarly associations with Dr. Hu Shi, the American-trained philosopher widely regarded as the epitome of liberalism.

Yet if Mao saw liberalism and Confucianism as having something in common, it was because for him they both belonged to a discredited past, not because they shared anything of genuine value. And this in turn owed much to Western perceptions of China's past that Mao received from Marx and Stalin—perceptions of traditional China as hopelessly retrograde and without any capacity of its own for renewal or fundamental reform.

That China had any such capability was widely doubted in the nineteenth-century West. In the seventeenth and eighteenth centuries, a more optimistic view of China had prevailed in Europe, based in part on the favorable accounts of Jesuit missionaries and in part on the idealizations of China as governed by rational *philosophes* in the eyes of Enlightenment thinkers. In the nineteenth century, however, the West encountered limits to its own expansion in the East and some disenchantment over its expectations for enlightened government in China. In contrast to the West's growing belief in human progress during the nineteenth century, China seemed resistant to change and improvement. Hegel and Marx expressed this pessimism in regard to the backwardness of Asian societies, and the liberal economists of Britain felt disappointment over the failure of India and China to measure up to the material progress of the West and its hopes for freedom of trade and intercourse. James and John Stuart Mill contributed to Marx's view that Oriental despotisms—powerful, managerial bureaucracies—inhibited economic development and condemned the major agrarian civilizations of Asia to unending stagnation. Increasingly, the view became established that Confucianism too was an essentially reactionary force, an instrument of ideological control in the hands of a predatory dynastic state. In that view, there was no hope of reform from within or of an internal evolution that would bring China abreast of the modern world. Mao's own experience of the disintegration of the old dynastic order, coupled with the exposure of his generation to revolutionary doctrines from the West, persuaded him that nothing short of violent revolution and the total exposing of Confucianism's reactionary influence would suffice to break China out of the age-old pattern of repression and stagnation. Mere reformism would not do it. Many Western writers shared the same view.

Against the background of this earlier impatience with reformism and, by contrast, high hopes for revolution, one can more readily appreciate the significance of Wu Han's work. Contrary to these earlier expectations for Mao's revolution, it not only experienced failures of its own but proved highly resistant to criticism of them; hence the example of Hai Rui as an outspoken critic of those in power might still fit the repressive situation in which China found itself post-"liberation." Wu Han, of course, was not the only one to notice despotic elements of a traditional kind in the new order. One line of such analysis in the West has been represented by scholars including K. A. Wittfogel and more recently Marvin Harris, who have noted the appearance in Mao's China of a state communism that in Harris's words "may actually be nothing more than a new and more highly developed form of managerial despotism"[4] greatly restricting the options available for freedom of action and expression by either the individual or the group. Yet even within China under the new dispensation (post Mao) the persistence of repressive features from the past has been widely acknowledged. Whether these are described as "despotic," "totalitarian," or, in Stalinist/

Maoist terms, "feudalistic," the one-party dictatorship and its manage-rial bureaucracy present problems similar to earlier dynastic regimes. In fact, it is probably this resemblance to dynastic rule that leads people to characterize these features as "feudalistic," even though old-style rule in the name of one family disappeared in the 1911 Revolution.

With Mao gone, a new approach is being tried, less militant, less intense and severe, and possibly less repressive. Nevertheless, contra-dictory signals have been given of alternate encouragement and repres-sion of dissent. There are striking reports of outspoken criticism as well as well-publicized cases of dissenters being put on trial. As everyone knows, there has been a campaign to expose the alleged crimes of the so-called Gang of Four, in which many defects in Communist rule have been exposed that were previously well hidden, but there has been continuing repression of those critical of the system that allowed such crimes to occur.

Under these circumstances, we can sympathize with Arthur Miller's frustration, recounted in his recent book *Chinese Encounters*,[5] over the seeming passivity of the Chinese in the face of these admitted outrages and the lack of any apparent outcry against them. To the student of China, Miller's reaction evokes the memory of nineteenth-century Western observers in China who were similarly struck by the apparent passivity of the Chinese and their "fatalistic" acceptance of such situa-tions. From this we know that we are up against a perennial problem in the understanding of China. The reviewer of Miller's book in the *New York Times* noted this in commenting on Miller's perplexities:

> In the end the answers to Miller's questions suggest a fundamen-tal difference between our two worlds, but Miller is never able to explain it. What his book lacks (understandably since Miller is not a student of China) is a sense of the unique confluence of history, culture and Western values which has flowed together with Maoist doctrine during the last 50 years to create the "New China."
>
> Perhaps if we could know more, for instance about the histori-cal role of individualism or the notion of what it meant to be an intellectual in traditional Chinese culture, both we and Miller would end up less perplexed by what he encounters.[6]

In earlier essays, I have described something of the "historical role of individualism" and "what it meant to be an intellectual in traditional China." Before attempting to relate this to the current scene, I should like to consider further the case of Hai Rui, since Wu Han himself saw it as especially pertinent to the present situation.

In his play, Wu Han focused on Hai's principled conduct as an official who was willing to risk offending higher authorities by exposing the corruption in which they too were implicated. This role as official critic was a recognized one in traditional China, since the ruler had his own interest in seeing that his officials enforced the law in conformity with the higher interests of the state. In historical fact, however, Hai Rui's criticism went much further than this: in a memorial to the throne, he directly censured the emperor himself for his delinquencies as a ruler: his extravagance and self-indulgence, his inordinate exactions from the people, his indulgence of sycophants, his terrorizing of worthy ministers, his neglect of his own sons, his inattention to affairs of state, his refusal to heed honest criticism, his acquiescence and complicity in the crimes of corrupt officials, and so on.

It was a long and relentless attack. In conclusion, Hai Rui expostulated that his sense of indignation over these outrages impelled him to speak out, even though he risked death for it. According to the official history,[7] when the emperor finished reading the memorial, he flew into a rage and ordered Hai Rui to be put under house arrest. "Don't let him escape," he ordered. But a eunuch attendant responded: "When Hai Rui prepared the memorial he knew that he would have to atone with his own life for his insults and disobedience. He bade farewell to his family, prepared his own coffin, and now is awaiting punishment in the court. His servants have all scattered and he is left alone. Indeed he is making no attempt to escape."

This gave the emperor pause. He remained silent for a long time. Visibly shaken, he could not come to a decision on what to do with Hai Rui. Though recognizing the essential truth of what Hai had said, he remained bitterly resentful toward him and later had him thrown in prison, where he almost died from tortures used to extract a confession that his memorial was all part of a plot against the emperor. When another court official dared to propose clemency for Hai, the emperor had him flogged with a hundred lashes of the heavy bamboo, thrown in prison, and interrogated under torture day and night to make him confess his being party to the plot. In the end, however, the emperor himself wasted away and died without having approved the sentence of death, which willing servitors in the Ministry of Justice had sent up to him. Hai Rui, by contrast, was released from prison by the new emperor, lived out a noble career as an official, and died a natural death in honest poverty. Here in one episode, you have the epitome of both Ming despotism and Ming Neo-Confucian heroism.

Wu Han knew all this but left it out of his play, no doubt as too directly provocative of the ruling power. Nevertheless, he knew too that he put much at risk in merely writing his play, and he must, in a sense, have had his own coffin ready and waiting. Attacked by Red Guards during the Cultural Revolution, he died in circumstances that have not, to my knowledge, been fully explained.

Among historians, the Ming dynasty has been known as perhaps the most despotic of all in its repression of opposition. Much of the basis for this view lies in the numerous cases of outspoken critics upon whom were visited official degradation, beatings, torture, imprisonment, death in prison, and summary executions. In the Ming for the first time officials were stripped naked and thrashed publicly at court. One of Hai Rui's predecessors, Fang Xiaoru,[8] was celebrated for his fearless opposition to the third Ming emperor. The latter not only had Fang executed for this but extended the punishment to his family by exterminating Fang's kin to the tenth degree of relationship. In this period, eunuchs at court and their secret police raised repression to a new level of intensity and viciousness.

But, looked at another way, for each instance of repression there had to be someone willing to resist the abuse of power, someone ready to stand in opposition regardless of the personal consequences. It is true that many of these were acts of lonely heroism—exceptions to the rule—yet, on the other hand, it cannot be said that they were wholly unique or unprecedented. Indeed, we have enough successive instances to constitute a virtual tradition of principled dissent.

Though not expressive of an organized political movement or systematic opposition, neither were they, on the other hand, simply cases of idiosyncratic nonconformism. Custodians of Confucian tradition and historians of thought have placed Hai Rui (and the earlier martyr

Fang Xiaoru, who defied the third Ming emperor) squarely in the line of Neo-Confucian orthodoxy. They were indeed "squares" (the Chinese too refer to rectitude in this rectangular way), and they were conscious of upholding a tradition of resistance to despotism which was central to Neo-Confucianism. It is significant that the lives and works of both Fang Xiao-ru and Hai Rui are recorded in orthodox Neo-Confucian compilations.[9] At the same time, lest one perhaps think of them as representing solely the high or elite tradition, they are remembered as living legends in popular literature.

In the memorial of Hai Rui cited before, he associated himself with a tradition of outspoken Neo-Confucian scholars who as mentors to the throne counseled the emperor against ill-considered and improper actions. Even Hai Rui's sovereign acknowledged this (according to the official history) when he likened Hai Rui to a virtuous minister in ancient times who had tried to warn the wicked last emperor of the Shang dynasty against his own follies. The further implication of this analogy, that he himself resembled that vicious and depraved ruler of ancient times, the Ming emperor rejected. It is probably to this that Hai owes the sparing of his life: the emperor did not wish to lend credibility to such a tyrannical image of himself among the Confucian keepers of the historical record.

The emperor Shizong's consciousness of these historical analogies arose from a tradition of scholarly discussion that had come to be incorporated in the formal instruction of heirs apparent and in the lectures and discussions held at court on the significance of the classical humanistic texts for the conduct of rulership. The "lectures from the classics mat," as we have observed earlier, established the principle that such criticism should not only be protected but encouraged. It may sound paradoxical that this sanctuary of free criticism could have managed to become established in the heart of the imperial institution precisely in those periods, the Song and the Ming, when the power and control of the ruler had grown to unprecedented proportions. Such was indeed the case, however, thanks to the unremitting efforts of distinguished Neo-Confucian scholars who asserted the need for this function to be served at court. Indeed, the rise of Neo-Confucianism in the Song and Yuan periods is inseparable from the rise of this type of reformism.

One such institution could not have been effective without others supportive of it. Another important restraining influence was the institution of court historian, entrusted with the function of keeping impartial records of proceedings at court. To this we owe the full text of Hai Rui's memorial and detailed observations on the emperor's reaction to it, which give us much insight into the human factors operating in this situation. This, in turn, we owe to the traditions of impartiality and inviolability, which had become established around this official historiographical function.

The skeptic today might still question how effective such institutions could be in restraining imperial despotism as long as the emperor held unchallenged final authority. Yet the exercise of such authority, whether in traditional dynasties or modern totalitarian states, is never absolute. It is always modified in some degree by the human instruments through which it must work, just as those instruments themselves are modified in their effectiveness by the total systemic environment in which they operate. Thus, a pertinent question to ask here is whether in the case of Wu Han anything similar to these Ming institutions acted to protect Wu's exercise of even implied criticism (much less the direct criticism of a Hai Rui). We do not know the answer to this because the record is not available to us, and it is possible that we shall never know. There is no longer any independent office of court historian, and there is not even any lip service paid to the idea.

When Charles Bettelheim, the director of studies of the Ecole Pratique des Hautes Etudes in Paris, resigned in 1977 as president of the Franco-Chinese Friendship Association, he complained that those who had seized power and ousted the Gang of Four never offered a plausible account of the ideological issues at stake nor a fair statement of the case against the Maoists for their alleged crimes.[10] Without that, he said the campaign against the Gang of Four could not be seen as anything but a cynical self-justification for a coup d'etat carried out by unprincipled revisionists. On the basis of the record as we have so far been given it, one could not dispute that view, yet exactly the same could be said of the so-called radicals who dealt even less generously with their enemies; certainly they provided no impartial forum, court, or record for the charges made against their enemies: Peng Dehuai, Liu Shaoqi, Wu Han, and so on.

In this brief discussion, I have dwelt on just two institutions at the center of dynastic power that helped to protect freedom of discussion—the discussions of the classics and the work of the court historian. With more time, I could extend the analysis to other institutions, such as the censorate, whose function was to investigate and report on abuses of official authority or violations of the law by those in power. Their function was, quite literally, to "speak out," and Hai Rui was just such a censor who spoke out. Then too there were the schools, in the form of local academies, which supported independent, critical thought. Their growth and spread in the eleventh to the sixteenth centuries, as we have seen earlier, paralleled the rise of the Neo-Confucian movement, for it was through these schools that the teaching was disseminated when it was banned as heretical by the court. Among other things, these academies served as libraries where the historical, philosophical, and literary record could be preserved beyond the direct control of the state.

By some it might be argued that these forms of dissent or opposition were flawed or limited by their class character; that is, they reflected the interests and concerns of a relatively small elite of educated scholar-officials. It might also be claimed that the heroic ideal of this movement expressed a kind of individualism akin to the middle-class individualism of the West and therefore could not ultimately serve the interests of the people as a whole. Moreover, these spectacular acts of individual heroism might be seen by skeptics as at best accomplishing little more than their own martyrdom.

Such assertions would not be without some basis in fact, and indeed there was a reaction to this moralistic idealism in later centuries. Even by Hai Rui's time, there were scholars who had come to believe that this brand of Neo-Confucianism made inordinate and unrealistic demands on the individual for the total sacrifice of self to duty and principle. From this there gradually developed a trend of more realistic Neo-Confucian thought, which recognized the limited power of the individual to affect the course of events in the absence of more fundamental institutional reforms. In *Waiting for the Dawn*, I offered Huang Zongxi as an example of this trend. Thus Neo-Confucians had already come to an awareness of how importantly individual actions like Hai's were conditioned by the institutional or systemic environment in which they operated. In other words, the supposed class background and individualistic tendency of the Neo-Confucians did not prevent them from recognizing the limits of individualism in that historical situation.

Not surprisingly, Huang's critique of dynastic institutions was suppressed by the Manchus and only reappeared in the late nineteenth century, when reformers and some revolutionaries hailed Huang as a native apostle of democracy. Westerners tended to be skeptical. They were not impressed by the claim that Huang was "China's Rousseau," nor were they able to appreciate the liberal Confucian tradition upon which Huang drew and for which he spoke. To them he was at best a freak, a will-o'-the-wisp in the bogs of Chinese despotism, and, to increasing numbers of alienated young Chinese in the twentieth century, the messianic appeal of Western revolutionaries was far more alluring than the seasoned wisdom of a Huang Zongxi expressed in a classical language many of them could no longer understand. Yet as I have listened to Chinese scholars in mainland universities describe the tyranny of the Gang of Four and the horrors of the Cultural Revolution, I could not help but think of what Huang had said about the need for the protections of law, for the decentralization of power, and for the independence of schools.

At the same time, it should not be overlooked that Mao, in his own way, was trying to cope with some of the most persistent realities of Chinese political life. Proverbially, it was said of China's conquerors that they might win the empire on horseback but could not rule it from horseback; that is, they had to recognize that China could only be administered by a civil bureaucracy. Mao himself had waged a revolution to destroy the old order only to find that a massive, intractable bureaucracy reappeared under the aegis of the dictatorship of the Party. Unable to reconcile himself to this, he fought this nemesis from the past through the Cultural Revolution, resorting to the tactics he was most experienced in: mass mobilization for the conduct of protracted guerrilla warfare. Now it was in the form of "guerrilla politics" as practiced by the militant Red Guards, whom he threw against his own illegitimate offspring in the state and party bureaucracy.

That he could succeed in this without destroying China was a dream more vain than those of the Neo-Confucian idealists. Bureaucracy and technology are here to stay, and the question for the Chinese, as for us, is what ends they should serve and what ethos should guide them. On this score Mao was not wrong in sensing the threat that a purely technocratic education and pragmatic policy offered to the kind of revolutionary egalitarianism he had sought to propagate. Yet revolutionary violence having failed, gradualism and reformism acquired a new relevance as the only practicable alternatives. The violent revolutions in 1911, 1927, 1948–1949, and more recently the Great Proletarian Cultural Revolution have only intensified, not altered, the basic syndrome.

Thus after thirty years of revolutionary change, the new regime finds itself, ironically enough, talking about the need to reform and modernize. It is sending groups, delegations, and numbers of students abroad to catch up with the latest Western methods. It is inviting innumerable experts from abroad to share their expertise in many fields. All this testifies to the continuing need of the Chinese state for an educated leadership class, a need that in the traditional society had created the functional base for the Confucian scholar. And if we are to look today for some institutional base in which more liberal attitudes and values could become established, it is in this same area, especially in educational and legal institutions, that the crucial issues will most likely be faced.[11]

Allowing for the built-in resistance to change of both Communist and traditional Chinese regimes, one cannot be optimistic about the long-term prospects for liberalization, but neither need we be wholly pessimistic. Even without a strong economic or social base for a more pluralistic political order in China, the common experience of the Chinese people under the terror of the Cultural Revolution aroused a widespread desire for the protections of law, a feeling not confined to the masses but shared by many among the leadership who suffered at the hands of the Gang of Four.

Unfortunately, in the absence of even a court historian today, we have no adequate account of the individual or collegial stands that must have been taken among the leadership in order to bring the revolutionary terror to a halt and achieve the limited liberalization that has taken place. Yet if authorities in Beijing thought it worth resurrecting the case of Hai Rui and the play of Wu Han, it must have been because Hai's personal example spoke to their own experience of life, no matter how many years or how many "revolutionary" changes had intervened, and because it was still more natural for them to turn to native models than to remote Western ones. The play would never have been written had not Wu Han been able to identify himself with this sixteenth-century Neo-Confucian scholar-official and find in his courageous example the inspiration for his own daring protest. And Hai Rui, we know, looked to similar models in his own past, while his effective advocacy at court depended on institutions built up over the centuries to protect honest criticism as a form of loyal opposition.

This may be a tenuous thread, one too precarious to be called a "tradition" of liberal thought, but we recall that the succession to the way (*daotong*) was itself a precarious, "sometime thing," yet, if only people had access to books and plays, the ideas in them could still have vital effect, even in circumstances quite different from those of their original creation.

Today in China, there is strong interest in both the outside world and China's own past. Since much of that past was off-limits during the Cultural Revolution, retrieving it today offers some of the thrill of a new discovery, even for the Chinese, and also for them some of the satisfaction of reclaiming their natural inheritance.

In this process, historians and philosophers are reexamining many matters that were previously tabooed or were subject to such rigid ideological interpretation as to preclude serious study of the facts. Now the slogan is "to seek truth through facts" (*shi shi qiu shi*), a motto that itself goes back to seventeenth-century Confucian scholarship.[12] And the subjects being reexamined in a more open spirit include both Neo-Confucianism and the first stirrings of modern liberal thought in the May 4th and New Culture movements, which arose in the late 1910s and 1920s of the twentieth century.

Many of the liberal tendencies of which I have spoken had lapsed or become obscured by then. (How and why this happened is a complex historical problem beyond my scope here.) In any case, these liberal tendencies stand in obvious contrast to the view of Neo-Confucianism as a repressive, reactionary system held by many young Chinese of the May 4th generation. Proponents of the New Culture movement in the 1920s, whose newly Westernized education had made a sharp break with classical Confucian learning, were often left ignorant of the thinkers and works cited above. Nevertheless, their own thought processes may well have remained unconsciously subject to lingering Neo-Confucian influences. As members of what was still a privileged intellectual elite, they easily identified Western-style liberalism with the autonomy of the self, which had already been a value in the earlier literati culture. The new trend from the West promised to expand a freedom they knew something of, whereas the implicit Western accompaniment of that freedom—some concept of laws and rights guaranteeing those freedoms on a wider basis—was more foreign to their thinking. The result among many young Chinese in the late 1910s and 1920s was a heady mixture of radical individualism, often romantically linked to an anarchist philosophy, which then turned on Neo-Confucianism as a social system standing in the way of progress—an incubus burdening the individual with old-fashioned ideas about social responsibilities, which his new education did not dispose him to accept or equip him to fulfill.[13]

Yet this was only part of the new picture. Sun Yat-sen saw China's problem not as a lack of individualism but as an excess of it. To him, as a would-be nation builder, China seemed to be a "heap of loose sand" and the Chinese a people whose individualistic ways proved the despair of anyone trying to construct modern democratic institutions.[14] Whether Sun would have thought to attribute this inveterate weakness to Neo-Confucianism is doubtful. It is even less likely that he would have known of the criticisms that had already been made of Neo-Confucian individualism in the seventeenth and eighteenth centuries—not obviously with nation building in mind but on the ground that its radical assertion of the autonomy of the mind would undermine any basis for political authority or social order.[15]

At the present moment, brakes are being put on the so-called liberalization process, but my own reading of the situation is that this spells caution in—and not a complete reversal of—current trends toward greater openness of inquiry and discussion. In the longer run, I would see both tendencies—liberalization and repression—continuing to be engaged in mutual struggle, as was the case, I believe, in traditional China. One type of "realism" in China today will stress the threat of anarchy if liberalization gets out of hand and individualism runs rampant. Some will identify this danger with alien influences from the West, perhaps as a way of banishing ideas they would prefer not to recognize as natural and indigenous. On the other hand, another type of "realism" or "pragmatism" will point to the high costs of repression in destroying people's motivations for work and to the danger of intellectual stagnation in handicapping the Chinese ability to fulfill the goals of "modernization."

Realism here may require us to take another look at certain stubborn problems of China's past and present. Education, for instance, may be seen as an area of crucial importance, then and now. Yet for all the optimism earlier in this century about the renovation and democratization of education in China, today higher education, even of a quality that leaves much to be desired, is still limited to a small percent of China's high school graduates and is still essentially geared to producing a technically qualified elite to serve the interests of the state. Would not the present system, then, still be exposed to the kinds of criticism leveled at traditional dynasties by Chen Xianzhang and Huang Zongxi? Are we not compelled to reckon both with the persistence of such features of Chinese life (at least on the mainland of China) and perhaps the continuing relevance of earlier critiques?

In addressing such questions, we have an opportunity, as scholars today reappraise Neo-Confucian reformism along with the reform movements out of which the new China was born, to reexamine some of our own assumptions about liberalism and liberal education. For Westerners to adopt too narrow or culture-bound a definition of "liberalism" will be as self-defeating as was the attempt in China to limit Neo-Confucian orthodoxy to one particular school of thought. To see liberalism as having roots only in a Western past means confining and condemning it to an increasingly attenuated future. For Chinese, on the other hand, to see it as a foreign body, inassimilable to their own lives and culture, may likewise inhibit a natural growth from their own roots or by the process of cultural hybridization that today is the natural outgrowth of living together in the modern world. It is better to look at this the way Confucius would—as an opportunity to learn from one another's strengths and weaknesses, hoping to enhance the one and remedy the other. Or perhaps even as the Neo-Confucians would—finding the Way in oneself, corroborating it in discussion with others, and accepting the responsibility for sharing it with a larger world.

As I said some years ago, in the early days of the Cultural Revolution:

The Chinese have thought of the Way (or Dao) as a growing process and an expanding force. At the same time, following Mencius, they have felt that this Way could not be real or genuine for them unless somehow they could find it within themselves, as something not external or foreign to their own essential nature. The unfortunate aspect of their modern experience has been the frustrating of that healthy instinct, through a temporary loss of their own self-respect and a denial of their right to assimilate new experience by a process of reintegration with the old. To have seen all value as coming solely from the West or as extending only into the future, and not also as growing out of their own past, has hindered them in recent years from finding that Way or Dao within themselves. The consequences of that alienation and its violent backlash are only too evident in the Cultural Revolution. We may be sure, however, that the process of growth is only hidden, not stopped, and that the new experience of the Chinese people will eventually be seen in significant part as a growth emerging from within and not simply as a revolution inspired from without.[16]

I believe that what is said above accords with the spirit expressed by Professor Qian Mu himself, in his introductory lectures at New Asia College, when he called for a larger, continuing dialogue on the meaning of Chinese history and culture in relation to the contemporary world. Professor Qian insisted that each people had the first responsibility for understanding and preserving its own culture, and the first task in accomplishing this was to characterize Chinese culture in its own terms, without superimposing Western categories on it. Thus the basic Chinese approach to life should be distinguished from the Western. The latter, he said, was marked by a tendency to differentiate, to analyze and separate things out. Hence the West became particularistic and individualistic. The Chinese way, by contrast, sought to see things whole, to achieve harmony, accommodation, consensus, and unity. It prized collective action, family solidarity, and continuity with the past above the "heroic" achievements of single individuals.

In my own discussion of Neo-Confucian individualism, I have made similar observations about differences between it and the modern Western variety. Indeed, since I only saw Professor Qian's published lectures after I had finished my own, it seemed uncanny how often we touched on the same points. Nevertheless, his emphasis and mine have been different in some predictable, and also some unexpected, ways. Professor Qian, in affirming continuity with the past, presents a somewhat conservative view of Chinese tradition and differentiates it from the Western emphasis on innovation and individuality. By contrast, I have pointed out what was new and liberal in Neo-Confucianism and how importantly the heroic individual figured in it. The contrast, no doubt, is more apparent than real; each of us recognizes what the other talks about as part of the total picture. But Professor Qian's great contribution has been to defend the integrity of the Chinese vision against an aggressive invasion of Western influences. For my part, in furthering the dialogue he has begun, I have tried to point out certain common values in Chinese and Western traditions underlying the cultural differences.

There is something ironic in this seeming reversal of roles. Professor Qian has said that the Western way is to differentiate, while the Chinese way is to seek the underlying unity and continuity, yet here he is sharply differentiating China from the West, and here I am looking for common ground between the two. It seems as if he has adopted the Western mentality and I the Chinese.

If Lu Xun were here, he might be tempted in his sardonic way to say that one of us is putting on Western airs and the other Chinese. But in the end, I think Professor Qian himself points the way to a resolution of this dilemma. After identifying such concepts as "individual freedom" (*geren ziyou*) and "human rights" (*renquan*) as typically Western,[17] he says we should set these aside and try to describe the Chinese experience objectively in its own terms. That being done, each of us can then make his own subjective evaluation of the phenomenon so characterized. "I do not oppose," he says, "each individual's bringing his own viewpoint to bear in evaluating what is right and wrong, good and bad; this is the individual's own free choice (*zhe shi geren de ziyou*)."[18]

If I have made my point above, the terms Professor Qian speaks in are not simply "Western" but have become "second nature" for the

Chinese as well, precisely because they were not so alien in the first place. Today, with increasing contact and convergence among peoples, the seeming reversal of roles between us is a natural consequence of the effort to understand one another. In that process we discover not only the distinctive qualities in one another but also something of our common humanity.

Part 3

TRIBUTES AND MEMOIRS

16

Huang Zongxi and Qian Mu

When I was invited to give the Qian Mu Lecture for 1982 at the Chinese University of Hong Kong, the honor of being asked to participate in such a distinguished lecture-ship was enough to compel my acceptance, whatever the doubts I had about being able to meet the expectations aroused by so great a name in Chinese scholarship. I had, too, strong personal reasons for taking up this charge. For many years, Qian Mu had been a teacher of mine through his writings, and though others also have taught me in this way, he was one of the earliest and most influential in guiding my studies of Chinese thought. If a request comes in the name of a teacher to whom one is so indebted, it cannot be refused.

Qian Mu's impressive scholarly contributions are linked in my mind to the name of an earlier scholar, the seventeenth-century Huang Zongxi, who attracted my attention soon after I first ventured into Chinese studies. That was in 1937–1938, when most people would have thought that only missionary connections could draw one to such an out-of-the-way field. But in New York and at Columbia then, the interest in China was just as likely to be political as religious, and I soon found myself in a Chinese class with the singer Paul Robeson and others of a radical persuasion, sharing with them socialist leanings and a youthful enthusiasm for Mao Zedong's revolutionary exploits. Later, there was to be some disenchantment on my own part, as I and others of my generation watched the course of events in Europe—the betrayal of revolutionary idealism in Stalin's purges; the Hitler-Stalin pact, which let loose the violence of World War II; the division of Europe between Nazi and Soviet forces; the spreading holocaust and Soviet gulag; etc. Less optimistic about Western-style revolution as the way out of China's difficulties, I began to search for something in the life and history of the Chinese people themselves that might offer grounds for hope in a future less torn between revolution and reaction.

Casting around, I lit on Huang Zongxi, about whom not much was then known in the West. At the turn of the century, he had been something of a hero—some called him "China's Rousseau"—to Chinese reformers and anti-Manchu revolutionaries, who looked to find some sanction in the past for democratic values, though they rarely pursued the comparison very far or examined Huang's ideas closely in the context of his own times. Later, the revolutionary tide swept all such Confucian reformism aside, as a "brave new world" burst forth that saw total emancipation from China's past as the only solution.

It was here that Qian Mu came into the picture for me, his approach to Chinese history and thought offering a larger perspective in which to view these disjointed times. As he later reaffirmed this view and articulated it more fully in his inaugural lecture for this series, China's true liberation would not be achieved in the manner of the Cultural Revolution, by trying to root out all vestiges of the past and destroy them, but only by coming to terms with Chinese culture, whatever its virtues and deficiencies, and seeing the future of this great people as authentically rooted there. While some Chinese might emigrate to other countries and adapt to different cultures, this was not possible for the great mass of Chinese, who had to live with one another in a condition, and with an outlook, very much shaped by their common past.[1]

As a rare and accomplished historian of Chinese thought, Qian Mu earlier had reopened the Neo-Confucian record and established the context of Huang Xongxi thought in the intellectual history of the Song, Ming, and early Qing periods. I discovered Professor Qian's work, especially his *History of Chinese Thought in the Last Three Centuries* (*Zhongguo jin sanbainian xueshu shi*), just at the time (after my World War II service in the Pacific theater) when I was digging into Huang's own studies in intellectual history. Professor Qian prefaced his history of seventeenth-to-nineteenth-century thought by reminding his readers of its roots in Song Neo-Confucianism.[2]

Huang's best-known work, the *Mingyi daifang lu* (*Waiting for the Dawn: A Plan for the Prince*), had been written in 1662, not long after his retirement from years of struggle in the resistance movement against the Manchus. His frustrations as a participant in reform efforts at the end of the Ming and then as a member of remnant Ming forces holding out against the invader were given powerful expression in this critique of Ming despotism and decadence. As a loyal minister of the Ming, he rendered his penultimate service to it (in the Confucian sense) by offering forthright criticism of its weaknesses, and as a Neo-Confucian with a broad grasp of history he extended his analysis of these evils back into the earliest of the imperial dynasties.

The outcome of this scholarly effort stands as probably the most sweeping and systematic critique of Chinese despotism in the premodern period. It was indeed a radical attack on traditional imperial institutions, and the succeeding Manchu dynasty, notwithstanding Huang's excoriation of the Ming, saw his work as no less threatening and subversive to them. To me it remains a major landmark of Confucian political thought, remarkable for its breadth of historical scholarship, depth of moral passion, and power of trenchant expression.

In these respects, then, Huang's work is almost in a class by itself, yet one would be mistaken to think of it as wholly unique or exceptional. Huang was no solitary genius, breaking with his past and at odds with the scholarship of his time. Rather, his protest only gave more pointed expression to political views that other thinkers of the day shared with him, and his radical manifesto, though sharpened by the crisis of dynastic upheaval and foreign conquest, was but one culmination of a liberal Neo-Confucian tradition he was glad to acknowledge and reaffirm.

Huang's essay was not, however, to be his last word on the Ming. He did not just expose its bankruptcy and divest himself of a bad business. Most of the remaining years of his life he devoted to preserving the record of Ming Confucian scholarship in thought and literature. Representative of this later work is his *Case Studies of Ming Confucians* (*Mingru Xuean*), a critical anthology of Ming Confucian thought that has come to be recognized as a major monument in the writing of Chinese intellectual history and one much emulated (even by Chien Mu himself, in his *Zhuzi xinxuean*). In an explanatory note at the beginning of this magnum opus, Huang asserted that whatever the other failings and shortcomings of the Ming, in the central domain of Neo-Confucian thought (*lixue*), Ming scholars had won unprecedented achievements.[3]

It is a claim with more than one significance for us. On the surface, Huang's massive work of compilation could be seen as a conservative effort—a typical example of Confucian scholarship conserving tradition. But since Huang was so critical of the Ming in other respects, his expressed admiration for its philosophical achievements cannot be taken for granted or dismissed as conventional praise. Moreover, Huang's generally sympathetic approach to the subject and his insistence on the positive importance of preserving Ming thought contrasts with the prevailing judgment against it in the latter half of the seventeenth century, when it was seen as empty, decadent, and best left interred with the ashes of the fallen Ming. Indeed, Huang had to buck a tidal wave of reaction against Ming thought, one that was to carry down into the present century. From this standpoint, in his effort to "conserve" the Ming Neo-Confucian legacy, Huang was adopting an independent stance vis-à-vis the dominant intellectual trend and certainly one counter to the official view in his time.

I shall have more to say later about the deeper significance of this commitment on Huang's part. Here it may not be out of place for me to suggest that the more recent scholarship of Qian Mu, likewise, has had to withstand some of the same hostility to Neo-Confucianism and, even more, violent political attacks against Confucianism as a whole. Qian was one of a very few distinguished scholars who resisted the prevailing trend in his own time and thus effectively emulated, in my view, the earlier example of Huang Zongxi in preserving, though not uncritically, his Neo-Confucian heritage.

When Huang spoke for Ming *lixue*, he referred to a distinctive phase in the development of thought trends that had first appeared in the Song period (960–1279). Later, having completed his anthology of Ming thought, he extended his survey backward in time to cover the Song and Yuan periods as well, leaving at his death an unfinished anthology, the *Song Yuan xuean* (*Case Studies of Song and Yuan Confucians*). These works covered the whole broad movement of Confucian thought that was traceable from the Song period, as its formative phase, down through the Yuan and Ming. Clearly, he still hoped in the late seventeenth century that the flowering of thought he so admired in the Ming would bear further fruit in his own time and thereafter.

The modern Western expression "Neo-Confucianism" as it has been used by Fung Yulan, Derk Bodde, Carsun Chang, and in our *Neo-Confucian Studies Series* at Columbia is generally coextensive with the new trends covered by Huang. This means that it embraces a range of schools and thought currents stemming from the Song masters of the eleventh and twelfth centuries, including *lixue* in the form not only of the Cheng-Zhu school but also of the so-called Lu-Wang school (so-called because of a certain affinity of thought between Lu Xiangshan and Wang Yangming, though the latter actually emerged from the Cheng-Zhu school of the early Ming and was linked to Lu by no line of scholastic filiation coming down from the Song). For Huang Zongxi, and for other historians of Neo-Confucian teaching like Sun Qifeng, the school or learning of principle (*lixue*) included Lu Xiangshan and Wang Yangming,[4] and the Learning of the Mind-and-Heart (*xinxue*) was as much identified with the Cheng-Zhu school as with Lu and Wang.

Recently, certain Western writers, falling in with one particular claim to orthodoxy, have identified Neo-Confucianism exclusively with the Cheng-Zhu school and with what the latter spoke of as the School or Learning of the Way (*daoxue*). But Huang Zongxi explicitly rejected the claim of Cheng-Zhu adherents to an exclusive hold on the Way and refused to confine *lixue* to *daoxue*.[5] The latter term has a valid historical basis as a designation for the Zheng-Zhu school, since both Cheng Yi (1033–1107) and Zhu Xi owned up to the name. Moreover, since this school's claim to orthodoxy was accepted by many later Neo-Confucians in China, Korea, and Japan, there is a sense in which one can legitimately speak of the School of the Way (*daoxue*), or the Cheng-Zhu school, as "orthodox Neo-Confucianism." However, to limit the term *lixue* or Neo-Confucianism to the Cheng-Zhu teaching alone would run contrary to historical fact in respect to *lixue* and be a departure from established usage regarding "Neo-Confucianism."

The terminological issues faced here are not trivial. They go to the heart of the matter I shall be addressing. For Huang Zongxi fought on two fronts against a narrow conception of Neo-Confucianism. He rejected the conservative, proprietary, and authoritarian claims of a narrow orthodoxy and, with equal vigor, the antipathetic reaction of those who, repudiating that "orthodoxy," would dismiss the whole tradition as moribund and irrelevant. In other words, as both historian and philosopher he argued for a broader, more liberal, and more vital interpretation of Neo-Confucianism.

In using the word "liberal," I must of course anticipate other possibilities for misunderstanding. There will be objections from those who adhere to a narrow, purist view of liberalism as defined within a specific Western context (as identified, say, with John Stuart Mill) and others too who, reacting against certain libertarian features of the presumed Western prototype, would reject it as alien and inapplicable to China. To me, these are small risks to run. Indeed, I welcome the fullest possible discussion and delineation of differences in historical experience between China and the West, as long as this does not preclude the finding of some common ground between the two and thus arriving at a deeper understanding of each other.

A few years ago, in a symposium held at Columbia, my late colleague Charles Frankel, well known as an articulate spokesman for both liberalism and the humanities in America, defined six senses of the term liberalism, which I summarize as follows:

1. Cultural liberalism, as opposed to parochialism and fanaticism: "An affirmative interest in the promotion of diversity and qualities of mind which encourage empathetic understanding and critical appreciation of the diverse possibilities of human life";

2. Political liberalism: "emphasis on procedures for the legitimation of peaceful change";

3. Economic liberalism: "policies designed to correct imbalances of economic power";

4. Philosophic liberalism: "belief in the supremacy of rational methods of inquiry";

5. The liberal temperament or style, characterized by moderation, restraint, and compromise;

6. Liberal education: "commitment to long-term moral ideals, long-term ideals of culture, long-term ideals of civilization," and to "compromise without complacency."[6]

It is not difficult to cite aspects of the Confucian tradition corresponding to each of those just listed, though any satisfactory treatment of them would also have to qualify the comparisons substantially and deal with significant differences between what we might call Confucian liberalism and the Western variety—for instance, under number 4, in how one would understand the supremacy of rational methods of inquiry—differences equally illuminating with regard to the limitations of both.

Confucian teaching was humanistic in the sense that it saw man as playing a central, creative role in the transformation of the world. Insofar as Confucius viewed human life and experience as the focus of all valid learning, "humanistic" here means "this-worldly." It was not, however, seen as opposed to the divine order of things; rather, Confucius conceived of the human order itself as revelatory of the divine ("Heavenly") order.

The enduring value of human experience was affirmed by Confucius in his efforts to conserve what was best in traditional culture. In this sense, he could be called conservative. But Confucius was, at the same time, liberal in viewing past ideals and models as the basis for a critique of existing institutions and as a reminder of the greatness to which man was called by Heaven. "Liberal" here could stand for "reformist" vis-à-vis existing unjust governments, which denied men the opportunity to fulfill their legitimate wants and aspirations. As Gilbert Murray has said of conservatism and liberalism in the West, they are not contrary principles but complementary. "The object of conservatism is to save the social order. The object of liberality is to bring that order a little nearer to what . . . the judgment of a free man—free from selfishness, free from passion, free from prejudice—would require and by that very change to save it the more effectively."[7]

Confucians in later centuries were also reformist in their advocacy of humane social-welfare policies. Revolutionary Maoism, or "leftism" as it might now be called in the People's Republic, acknowledged the existence of this kind of liberal reformism among Confucians but criticized it as a misguided, meliorative approach to social infections that should have been allowed to fester and erupt into revolutionary action. Confucian reformism, according to the Maoist view, temporized or compromised by pursuing methods of peaceful change rather than insisting on radical surgery.

Nevertheless, Confucius himself was far from complacent or content with the status quo. He spoke of himself as struggling on with his efforts to change things even when these efforts seemed to be getting nowhere, and he lamented it when, with advancing age, he could no longer conjure up visionary dreams of his political ideal as a spur to reform. Men had a positive obligation to respond to the needs of others; for their leaders to be unresponsive was to be less than human. Thus Confucian reformism was inspired by a positive commitment to human welfare and informed by a critical attitude toward established institutions that reflected an awareness of alternative possibilities for improvement.

The Confucian revival in the Song, which had given birth to Neo-Confucianism, brought it to a new stage of development in ways characteristic of that age. In what follows, I call "Neo-Confucian" those elements in this movement that have a distinctive quality of their own, though they are not without some precedent in the Confucian past, and I shall continue to call "Confucian" perennial values or attitudes that, though inevitably different in some ways from the past, are not markedly so. Among the new developments I would point to are some that draw upon traditional Confucian values yet move in a "modern," "liberal" direction. I shall refer to certain key concepts of Neo-Confucianism representative of these general trends. My method follows the history of ideas, much in the style of Qian Mu himself, citing central concepts prominent in the Neo-Confucian discourse of the Song and Ming periods but with occasional reference to Korean and Japanese uses of the same in the extended East Asian dialogue. Neo-Confucianism, as a whole, in the broad sense of Huang Zongxi's *lixue*, provides the larger context for the discussion of these ideas, but the concepts themselves will mostly be drawn from the mainline of Neo-Confucian thought usually identified with the Cheng-Zhu school or "orthodox" Neo-Confucianism.

One last point of resemblance between Qian Mu and Huang Zongxi: Huang spent much of his early adult life in diehard resistance to the invading Manchus, retreating with the Ming loyalist forces into the southeastern coast and offshore islands. It was only in his late middle age that he gave up the struggle and returned home to study, teach, and write his major works.

Much later, when Mao's forces overran the mainland, Qian Mu took refuge in Hong Kong, where he helped set up New Asia College and later carried on his scholarly work in Taiwan. It was there that I last saw him, on a most memorable occasion for me when he thanked me for making his work better known in the West. Qian Mu had experienced the vicious anti-Confucian campaign of the Maoists but finally witnessed the thawing of that campaign in the late 1970s and after, just as Huang survived long enough to witness the official Manchu recognition of Confucianism and Huang's work in the late seventeenth century. One trusts that Qian Mu's work will likewise gain increasing recognition in his homeland.

17

Tang Junyi and New Asia College

I t is a pleasure and a great privilege for me to be asked to address this distinguished gathering, which is meeting to honor the memory of Professor Tang Junyi and to discuss the future of Chinese philosophy. I regret that my wife's health prevents me from attending in person (a fact and a reason which I think Professor Tang himself would appreciate because he and his wife were greatly devoted to each other).

First, let me speak to my personal association with Professor Tang, which was in some ways a happy accident of what was otherwise a misfortune in the disruption of our lives by the violence of revolutionary times. Although that history in the twentieth century was generally prejudicial to Confucianism, in my own case the early reaction to Confucianism, prematurely judged to be an obstacle to China's modernization, aroused a response in my early student days, a skeptical response based precisely on my own doubts about the adequacy of Western understandings of both China and modernization.

In some ways, I was a singular beneficiary of the displacement of traditional Chinese studies during the 1920s, 30s, and 40s. It was an extraordinary turn of world history that brought to Columbia in the early twentieth century such a cohort of distinguished Chinese scholars/officials as Dr. Hu Shi, Luo Longji, and Feng Yulan, and the anthropologist Fei Xiaotong, to name just a few, who were at Columbia, off and on, during my early years there.

My further education in Chinese studies, however, was much deepened by my research in Beijing in 1949 as a Fulbright scholar, which gave me the opportunity to read intensively the works of Tang Junyi and Qian Mu that bore on my doctoral research in the works of the seventeenth-century scholar Huang Zongxi: When Beijing was besieged later that year, it was a wrenching experience for me to have to break off from this satisfying immersion in such rewarding studies, but when the U.S. ambassador Leighton Stuart sent his private plane to Beijing to evacuate the Fulbright scholars before the impending takeover of Beijing by Mao's forces, I left for the south.

I could not have imagined that my eventual relocation in the Guangzhou region would have the unexpected benefit of my meeting up with some of the very scholars whose works I had been studying earlier. It was an extraordinary time not only for me but for the future of Chinese philosophy and Confucianism, since the dislocations of Tang Junyi and Qian Mu led to their relocation in Hong Kong and the revival of Confucian studies in New Asia College. For me, it was a great privilege to witness the small beginnings and travails of this great educational center, the founding of which we now celebrate today, sixty years later.

That meeting for me had two major significances, one scholarly, the other educational. First, let me speak of the scholarly side, which was primarily in the domain of intellectual history. In the case of Huang Zongxi, his historical interests and intellectual concerns went beyond the merely intellectual to include a wide range of economic, political, social, literary, and educational fields, but enriching as it could be to explore such a range and depth of Chinese history, still what counted most for me in Tang Junyi's case was his addressing the same issues as Huang did in his massive, monumental studies of first Ming and then Song-Yuan scholarship.

When I started my own studies in the 1940s, the attempts to revalidate the Chinese tradition tended to focus on those aspects that might approximate the dominant tendencies in modern Western history—in other words, to discover in the later Chinese tradition those developments that could be seen as resembling the progress of modernity in the West. In this vein, scholars like Hu Shi and Feng Yulan quite understandably and legitimately drew attention to the critical thought of eighteenth- and nineteenth-century scholars whose work resembled the enlightenment of the early modern West. In doing this, however, they tended to interpret it as reformist and revolutionary, replicating the dynamics of the modern West, with China following the same unilinear pattern of history, rather than following its own pattern of development, both similar to and different from the West in some respects.

Some forty years ago, I described this development and Tang Junyi's relation to it in the following terms:

> The seventeenth century, which serves as the focus of this book, stands at about the midpoint in the long period of Neo-Confucian dominance and, if our interpretation is correct, this century may also represent a turning point in its development. How to interpret that turning, however, has been disputed. A prevalent view in the earlier decades of the twentieth century saw Neo-Confucianism as having lost all genuine vitality by the seventeenth century. New trends of thought were breaking away from Neo-Confucian dogmas, and an era of intellectual enlightenment was dawning which only the dead hand of the past, supported by the political repression of Manchu conquerors, held back. In these terms, the seventeenth century could be pictured by some as a kind of watershed in the development of Chinese thought, marking the emergence of the Chinese mind from a dark age of introspection and metaphysical escapism—into a new day of robust empiricism, scientific criticism, and materialism. This general view has had many adherents, but its most prominent spokesmen have been Liang Q'i-chao, Hu Shi, and more recently Hou Wai-lu. An opposing view, as expressed by Tang Junyi, does not dispute the historical facts but seeks to give them a different meaning. For Tang the change that took place represented a falling-away from the highest levels attained by Chinese thought. He considers the greatest achievements of Neo-Confucianism to

have lain in the spiritual realm depreciated by Hu. To him the "super-moral ideas" of the Neo-Confucians, especially in the sixteenth century, "should be taken as expressions of their highest moral experience." The shift in thought from the beginning of the Qing dynasty, in the mid-seventeenth century, he sees as the start of a long decline: "Chinese thought from the end of Ming to recent years has gradually left the spirit of Neo-Confucianism, which paid more attention to the spiritual values of human life, and now pays more attention to social, utilitarian, technical and natural values of human life."[1]

I shall not attempt to explain further the more positive view of Ming Confucian thought that fills out Tang's conception of its proper place in the evolutionary process. This is found in numerous works of his in Chinese already known to scholars in the audience here today and for readers in English may be found in two substantial articles of his contributed to conferences on Chinese thought to which I invited him in the 1960s, as an outgrowth of his earlier participation in my seminar on Neo-Confucianism at Columbia in 1964.[2]

I think it is important to recognize Tang's contribution to these early overseas developments in the study of Chinese philosophy because they were a natural extension of his purposes in the establishment of New Asia College here in Hong Kong. The very title of the college itself is indicative of his recognition that Chinese and Confucian studies could not be sustained simply in a Chinese context or as a matter just of Chinese national survival. It is true that he went into exile in order to preserve the true Chinese tradition when it was undergoing brutal suppression at home. But he had no illusion that Chinese tradition could endure in solitary splendor, nor did he see Confucian tradition as standing alone in the world. Early on, he recognized the importance of Indian thought as a vital counterpart to Chinese studies, and even the main focus of his own Neo-Confucian studies recognized how much was "new" in it that responded to the earlier challenge of Buddhism. In the twentieth-century world, Confucianism could be expected to respond generously and positively to the challenges of Western thought. But China would be doing this alongside other Asian civilizations as well, so the best of Chinese tradition could only be sustained in recognition of and cooperation with other Asian traditions. This was reinforced for me later when we spent weeks together at the guest house of Kyoto University sharing our reactions to key features of Japanese tradition. Thus "New Asia" was essential to the name of this new college even while it was primarily dedicated to the survival of Chinese culture.

There is significance too in the choice of a traditional Chinese term for what would be known in English as a "college," here called a *shuyuan*, rather than the more common *daxue*. *Shu yuan* was the expression common to Neo-Confucian academies from the eleventh to nineteenth centuries. "Hall of Books" would be a more literal translation of the term, but "academy" comes close enough to conveying that it was a meeting place for scholars whose culture was based on the preservation and study of books among communities of scholars, sustained by local support. A key feature of these academies was the promotion of open discussion (*jiangxue*, "discursive learning" or philosophical discussion). It was not simple indoctrination. *Shu yuan* were centers of private local education, independent and distinct from state-supported and controlled schools. To me, it is significant that Tang Junyi and his colleagues (especially Qian Mu) must have made this choice consciously in order to emphasize its intellectual independence and autonomy. This, of course, remains a crucial issue now that New Asia College has been incorporated into the state-supported Chinese University of Hong Kong.

Another key feature of *shu yuan* culture was its core curriculum. Because of the local nature of the academy, the curriculum was usually set at the option of local gentry and the presiding teacher, but its general character tended to follow the model set by Zhu Xi and his immediate disciples. The essential feature was that it be based on a set of classics selected to provide a proper starting point for higher education and therefore graduated at every stage to build toward intellectual maturity.

What is most relevant to the present occasion is the question of how the future of Chinese philosophy and a core of Chinese classics bear on each other. Here I think the most important point is how the classics as we receive them are not just the products of the age that produced them. Of course, we do have to read classics in their original contexts just as a first reading, and this initial reading is called for and warranted by the fact that they have continued to be meaningful in age after age. But they are not just validated by their antiquity. They have become foundation stones for subsequent structures, built as memorials to the old that have achieved a monumentality of their own.

This is precisely what Zhu did in his time and what Tang Junyi did in his—drawing on ancient texts to deal with current issues. And this I believe is what New Asia College was founded to do. As a consequence, we can see the establishment of its core curriculum as integrally involved in the discussion of Chinese philosophy's present and future.

The Chinese University is to be congratulated for taking a leadership role and for assembling such an international gathering to address the problem today as one of both contemporary philosophical research and of its bearing on the future of world education. Serving the latter, in my opinion, without addressing the core, nor the core without the classics, is building on sand. The core, however, today will certainly reflect the outcome of a new interplay between past, present, and future, just as it did in Zhu Xi's case. In compiling his *Jinsilu* (*Reflections on Things at Hand*), he anthologized the new philosophy of the Song in such a way as to serve his curriculum based on the method of the *Great Learning*. And his new commentaries on the *Four Books* were informed by the new concepts developed by his Song predecessors in response to the challenges of their own day.

Thus I hope that those gathered here today will follow the example of both Zhu Xi and Tang Junyi. In addressing the future of philosophy East and West together, they should be able to identify "classic" texts that have a bearing on contemporary philosophical issues. They will then be reassessing and redefining what it means to be "classic," which would include both ancient and neoclassical texts.

Today, among some influential writers who want to validate classic traditions, there is a tendency to reaffirm the relevance of the early classics to contemporary problems. This is fine, but this should not stop with the ancients. It is important to include neoclassical texts that tell us how later writers revisited the classics in response to the challenges of the evolving civilization. In so doing, they produced modern classics for their own time. We can further the same process by reexamining recent works that have been thought almost canonical in the nineteenth and twentieth century: Immanuel Kant, Adam Smith, John Locke, Rousseau, Alexis de Tocqueville, Charles Darwin, John Stuart Mill, Karl Marx, etc., are such candidates in the West. Their counterparts in Asia should be considered at the same time, and I leave it to you to take your own pick. As you discuss the future of Chinese philosophy, I trust you will be reassessing both ancient and modern classics as candidates for a core common to East and West. It would be a fitting tribute to the memory of Tang Junyi.

18

Ryūsaku Tsunoda, Sensei

Ryūsaku Tsunoda, retired curator of Columbia's Japanese Collection and former lecturer in the Department of Chinese an Japanese, died in Honolulu on November 29, 1964. It was an appropriate place for him to take his departure—where he had first set foot on America and where he still had family, friends, and former students. It was also an appropriate time; though he had hoped to spend his last days in Japan, in retirement at home, one could hardly imagine such an active life dragging slowly to an end. And it was in an appropriate manner—in transit between America and Japan. Had he not, in body, mind, and spirit, been a constant voyager between his native land and his adopted home in America?

I say "adopted home" because he adopted America in a way that America could never adopt him. From first to last, Ryūsaku Tsunoda was a son of Japan, never a refugee or an expatriate. He had come here to learn "the meaning of America," a modern representative of those pilgrims who, from Japan's earliest history, ventured overseas in search of whatever new learning, new arts, new truth the outside world could offer Japan. His predecessors were scholars, statesmen, artists, and monks, mostly traveling to China but some hoping even to reach India. Mr. Tsunoda told their stories often, and their resemblance to his own could not have escaped him.

But more especially, Ryūsaku Tsunoda was a son of Meiji Japan, born within the decade following the Restoration of 1868, which plunged Japan headlong into the modern world. His was a remarkable generation—eager to learn, adventurous, facing the future with great hopes, yet still close enough to its peasant roots to draw strength from the soil, taking its first breaths from an atmosphere still permeated by samurai ideals of self-reliance and self-sacrifice, and surrounded still by an ancient culture that prized creative intelligence and refined sensibility.

All this is reflected in his early education. The youngest son of a farmer in the Tone River country, he was sent to Tokyo for advanced schooling at a new Western-type college later to become Waseda University. That he alone in his family received this opportunity is a tribute not only to his promise as a scholar but also to the industry, thrift, and cooperative spirit of his family. But the next step after college was not, as one might suppose, study abroad. As an undergraduate, his introduction to the scholarly study of Buddhism came from a Western missionary, Arthur Lloyd. It was a shock and a challenge to him that the Japanese should have to depend on a foreigner for instruction in their own religious traditions. He turned back, then, to rediscover Japan, before going on to explore the West. For him, the route to America lay through Kyoto, the traditional seat of Japanese culture. There he spent years in study and teaching at Buddhist seminaries. Significantly, his first published work was a study of the popular seventeenth-century novelist Saikaku, whom he judged rather severely according to the categories of Tendai Buddhism. It is as if an American critic of the early twentieth century had chosen to evaluate Henry Fielding in terms of St. Augustine's philosophy or Dante's structuring of human life. But later, in America, he was able to draw on this experience to convey an appreciation of both Saikaku and Tendai.

And here we see one important difference between Ryūsaku Tsunoda and his pilgrim predecessors. He came not only to learn but to teach. He came with something of Japan to give and at the same time a greater capacity to receive. Having absorbed the best of his own culture, he was better able to appreciate what was best in ours. Thus to Hawaii and New York he brought his knowledge, his books, his search for truth, and his love for other seekers of learning. On one of his trips from Japan he brought to New York a valuable collection of books, contributed by Japanese friends, businessmen, and the imperial family, with which he founded in 1928 the Japanese collection at Columbia, the first of its kind in America. This pioneering work reminds us again of those early Japanese monks Saichō, Kūkai, and Ennin, who brought books back from China and with them founded the great centers of monastic learning in Japan. Let us hope that his work endures as theirs did. His collection has continued to grow, under the care of devoted students, but to the end of his life it remained an intimate concern of his. As he set out on his last homeward journey, Mr. Tsunoda expressed the wish that he might with such strength as he had left do something more for that collection. I am glad to say that others have volunteered to help fulfill that last wish. Professor Keene will be heading a committee to establish a book fund in his name.

As a teacher, Mr. Tsunoda was known to all as "Sensei." It is a common enough term in Japanese, and there are thousands of senseis in the world, but there was only one Sensei at Columbia. In him, this name for teacher found unique expression. You can put away the thought that it meant, in his case, something like "Master" or the Indian "guru." This unpretentious, undogmatic teacher had no special message, claimed no special authority, demanded no obedience to his person. Like Confucius, he forgot himself in his wholehearted devotion to study. There was never a class or lecture that he did not spend hours in preparation for. There was never a student in whom he did not take a personal interest, though he could be severe as well as sympathetic. There was hardly a day on which he did not make some intellectual discovery for himself and joyfully share it with anyone around the office or library who might understand. His prodigious memory held not only facts and ideas but persons as well in its tight embrace. My own memory has failed the test he put it to at our last meeting, as he recalled student after student to whom he would have liked to say farewell and in some cases offer a final word of advice. "Tell Miss So-and-so," he said of a student who had written on the affinity between the Chinese poet Du Fu and the Japanese poet Basho, "not to forget what a difference it makes that Du Fu was a Confucian and Basho a Buddhist." A typical comment from a man who had such a holy respect for both sameness and difference.

By ordinary academic standards, Tsunoda Sensei was no great scholar. He produced no monument of original research. He wrote much but published little. Though kindly and constructive in judging the work of others, he could not satisfy his own high standards. Part of the difficulty, I suspect, lay in the fact that his natural medium of expression was poetry. His poetic eloquence came through as he talked and lectured; it came through in hundreds of haiku and tanka as he walked and traveled through life. But it rarely pleased him to find what he had said in print, after the moment of inspiration had passed.

Professor Goodrich, chairman of our department during much of his long tenure, recalls the near tragedy that occurred in December 1941, when Tsunoda Sensei suddenly found himself an enemy alien, herded off with other Japanese to Ellis Island and possible internment. When his case came up before the court, Columbia people were there to speak for him, but it was probably Tsunoda who spoke best for himself. Midway in the interrogations, after he had been asked several questions requiring extended replies, he was interrupted by the chairman of the court with a question that needed no answer: "Mr. Tsunoda," he said, "you are a poet, aren't you?"

In the light of what was to follow, this experience was perhaps the least of the sufferings that came with the war between Japan and the United States. One can imagine the conflicting emotions of a loyal Japanese who thought himself also a true friend of America. Tsunoda Sensei could only suffer helplessly as he watched his students go off to do their military duty, destroying the land he loved. At his age (in 1942 he was already sixty-five), there was little he could do, while others donated blood and rendered similar noncombatant services. With his extremely modest means, what contribution could he make? He resolved to give up his only luxuries in life, smoking and drinking, for the duration of the war. But the "duration" for him ran well past August 1945. While Japan lay prostrate and devastated in the postwar years, he felt no less deeply the sufferings of his people. Did he perhaps wonder if, after all, internment might not have been a better way to share their sufferings? If so, we can only be grateful that he did not choose this way out but stuck to his duty as a teacher and thereby redeemed much that was lost.

It is comforting to think that, while he could never be an American, his being a Japanese did not prevent him from becoming a true New Yorker and a loyal Columbia man. True, of course, in the sense of being truly and uniquely himself in these surroundings. Was there ever a more devoted fan of the New York Giants? Who but this Japanese gentleman would regularly sit alone in the bleachers, so that he could weep freely and anonymously when they won and lost? What resident of Washington Heights was so faithful to his early morning walk in Fort Tryon Park? Who else knew every tree and flower there as intimately as did this nature-loving son of the Tone River country? Who else at the end of his morning rounds stopped outside St. Elizabeth's Hospital in salutation to the statue of the Virgin Mary? Who but he knew where to hike across the George Washington Bridge and find the tender *warabi* ferns growing atop the Palisades?

And who knew better than he all that Columbia could mean to an insatiable student? From the days when he first came to hear the lectures of John Dewey to his last years on the campus, he was constantly slipping into the classrooms of other teachers. Though he may never have taken a course for credit and certainly earned no degrees, he had unquestionably learned more from one great teacher after another than anyone else I know. But, then, it was knowledge assimilated and recreated by him in his own fashion. And it was quite in order that this achievement should have been recognized in a special way, two years ago, by the university's conferring on him the honorary degree of Doctor of Letters. He coveted no such award or rank. The man who had always been content as just plain "Sensei" or "Mister" must have experienced some kind of identity crisis on finding himself suddenly a Doctor. But surely it pleased him that his love for Columbia was fully requited. And surely it was good that we had the chance, at the convocation in his honor, to tell him before his death what so often is only said after.

I turn finally to the religious significance of his life's work. Unquestionably, his teaching had such a significance, though he was no missionary in the traditional sense. He was his own kind of Buddhist, unaffiliated but not disaffiliated. His independence and skepticism were a sign not of rebellion but of a deeper religious commitment. He used to say that he was not a Buddhist, but what he meant was that few men could claim really to meet the demands of the Buddha, to live the life of the Buddha. He hated the gimmickry and satori salesmanship of the popular purveyors of Buddhism in this country. A man of the strictest moral standards, he was indignant that Buddhism should be degraded by the Beats in behalf of self-indulgence and sensuality. A gentle and kindly man, he nevertheless identified himself with the Bodhisattva Fudō, the fierce avenger of sin and injustice.

But he continued to ponder the true meaning of Buddhism and to wonder how it would survive in the modern world. He wondered, for instance, if *madhyamika* skepticism were not too negative a basis for Mahāyāna Buddhism and if this negativism had not fundamentally impaired Buddhism's response to modern life. On the other hand, like John Henry Newman, who was led by that "kindly light amidst the encircling gloom," he had great faith in the "inner light" of Buddhism. In one of his few published lectures, delivered as the Mary Keatinge Das Memorial Lecture on this campus, Tsunoda Sensei explained that this "inner light" consisted of the three L's: Love, Law, and Labor. "Love," he explained,

> is the core of religion. Law is the basis of government. Labor is the backbone of industry. As religion, government and industry are inseparable and equally essential to the well-being of civilization, so are the three L's for the peace of our life. Love without law is madness, and without labor it is a midsummer night's dream. Law without love is tyranny, and without labor it is a scrap of paper. Labor without love is servitude, and without law it is warfare. Only together and in harmony will the three L's be the light of life.

Let all men here mourn the passing of their friend, Ryūsaku Tsunoda. But let Buddhists rejoice that the *dharma* was transmitted in these halls dedicated to the glory of Almighty God, and let Christians thank God that the inner light of this Bodhisattva has shone among us. *In lumine tuo videbimus lumen.* In thy light we see light. The Columbia motto.

19

Thomas Merton, Matteo Ricci, and Confucianism

I'm not sure when I first met Tom Merton. It was probably in the middle of my college years at Columbia. Merton had graduated a few years before (1938), but as a part-time English instructor and half-serious graduate student he continued to hang out with other former and current editors of *Jester*, the college's humor magazine, in their office on the fourth floor of John Jay Hall. The "*Jester* crowd" included the poet Robert Lax; Robert Gerdy, later an editor at the *New Yorker*; and Edward Rice, who created *Jubilee*. Robert Giroux, who went on to the publisher Farrar, Straus, later published Merton's *Seven-Storey Mountain*. Together this lively, fun-loving crowd liked to clown around in John Jay and do "stunts" they could write about in *Jester*. We shared a strong enthusiasm for the jazz then thriving in nearby Harlem—at the Apollo Theater, the Savoy Ballroom, in midtown at the Roseland, and in the Village at Nick's. The college quad echoed to the jazz emanating from Rice's phonograph in the first floor of Livingston Hall.

I was of a somewhat different sort—active in the debate council and later one of its presidents and active also in student government. In that connection it was Bob Gerdy, as a leader of the Fusion Party and my political mentor, who listed me on the *Jester* masthead even though I did not actually write for it.

In this group, what probably recommended me as a freak along with the other *Jester* clowns was the fact that I had started learning Chinese, one of just two undergraduates in a Chinese language class that included two missionaries, the singer Paul Robeson, and a German spy who used her studies at Columbia as a cover for her espionage. This was in one of the few American colleges that offered Chinese in the 1930s. It was only much later that Merton got around to studying Chinese—and then mostly the mystics.

What Merton and I shared early on was an admiration for Dorothy Day, the editor of the *Catholic Worker*, a religious, communitarian, pacifist, and anti-industrialist supporter of the craft movement (à la Gandhi). In high school, I had already been active as a young Socialist, participating in antiwar demonstrations in New York's Union Square. Merton, as everyone knows, was a longtime pacifist. I might even say he was a diehard pacifist, but after he committed himself to the monastic life (and thus was not subject to the military draft), it became only a theoretical issue.

In 1939–1940, when the peace movement was disrupted by the deal Stalin made with Hitler, dividing Europe between them and leaving Hitler free to make an all-out attack on Britain, I was persuaded by the likes of Reinhard Niebuhr at Union Seminary, whom I had known in my Young Socialist days, and by Carlton J. H. Hayes, a leading Catholic historian at Columbia, who was active in the Committee to Defend America by Aiding the Allies, to abandon the "Neutrality" movement and support Britain in its resistance to Hitler. My sympathies for this cause led me in 1940 as chair of the Student Governing Board to respond to a request from Eleanor Roosevelt (long a friend of youth movements) to join in a meeting at the White House in support of the Lend-Lease program, by which FDR provided aid (short of war) to the defense of Britain (during the so-called Battle of Britain.) Later, after the Pearl Harbor attack, I was recruited by Naval Intelligence for my Chinese and Japanese language skills (such as they were in those early days) and then was sent to the Pacific for three years. As you know from the *Seven-Storey Mountain*, Merton followed a very different path—the mystical and eremitical—engaged only in nonviolent struggle.

Nevertheless, after having taken a vow of silence as a Trappist, Merton found a way to be highly articulate, and though not engaged directly in a political or social sense, he managed to express himself on many issues that touched upon his own religiosity, especially the forms of Asian mysticism identified with Hinduism, Daoism, and Zen.

Whether Merton's interest in other religions arose from an ecumenical impulse is a real question. He did not pay much attention to the distinctive characteristics of other religions in their ritual, doctrinal, ecclesiastical, or social forms, and he did not engage them too much on other levels than the contemplative. In the introduction to the Japanese edition of his *The New Man*, his first words bespeak his singular focus: "You must be born again."[1]

Merton goes on to explain this in terms that reflect his earlier starting point in the English version of the essay, titled "Rebirth and the New Man in Christianity."

> These mysterious and challenging words of Jesus Christ reveal the inner meaning of Christianity as life and dynamism. More than that, spiritual rebirth is the key to the aspirations of all the higher religions. By "higher religions" I mean those like Buddhism, Hinduism, Judaism, Islam and Christianity, that are not content with the ritual tribal cults rooted in the cycle of the seasons and harvests. These "higher religions" answer a deeper need in man: a need that cannot be satisfied merely by the ritual celebration of man's oneness with nature. . . . Man seeks to be liberated from mere natural necessity, from servitude to fertility and the seasons, from the round of birth, growth and death. Man is not content with being a slave to need: making a living, raising a family, and leaving a good name to his posterity. There is in the depths of man's heart a voice that says: "You must be born again."[2]

There can be little doubt that being reborn is central to the theme of crucifixion and resurrection in Christianity, and Merton goes on to explain how this theme can be understood in those religions he identifies among the "higher religions." These "higher" religions are defined by their supernatural character, their capacity for spiritual freedom from the limits of natural life, in most cases through a meditative or contemplative praxis such as that to which Merton had very early committed himself.

The essence of this is conveyed in his comments when contemplating the monuments of archaic Buddhist civilization at Polonnaruwa, Sri Lanka. Merton said,

> I don't know when in my life I have ever had such a sense of beauty and spiritual validity running together. . . . I mean I know and have seen what I was obscurely looking for. I have now seen and have pierced through the surface and got beyond the shadow and the disguise. This is Asia in its purity, not covered over with garbage—Asian, European or American—and it is clear, pure and complete.[3]

The question of which religions qualify among the "higher" ones is already prefigured by the titles of the books in which he expresses these views: *Seeds of Contemplation*, *The Ascent to Truth*, and *Introductions East and West*, and by his frequent references to "Asian religions" as a coherent class. To a degree, these are an understandable response to the fact that his early bestselling works were quickly translated into Asian languages, and he felt called upon in the *Introductions* to explain how his ideas related to his Asian audiences.

Among the "higher" religions of Asia, however, and among the major systems of Asian thought to be so classed there is one striking omission: Confucianism. One could explain this as simply a matter of definitions. Many people think of Confucianism as a worldly or secular teaching, merely a social ethic. Indeed, there are some grounds for this, insofar as Confucianism does not fit the conventional notion of religion as a cult of devotional worship in the Indo-European or Semitic mold. But that would not be enough to explain Merton's failure at this point to discuss Confucianism as a prominent alternative to the systems he included approvingly among the "higher religions" of Asia, and one that other Christian writers had felt a need to reckon with.

Before proceeding with this other reckoning, however, I feel that in Merton's case there is at least one particular circumstance that leads him in this direction: his obsession with the evil of "modernity." The world he sought to liberate himself from was a world of modernization—thoroughly corrupted by industrialization, capitalism, and war, from which he sought to liberate himself. I believe this was a powerful element in his turning from his revulsion over a thoroughly corrupt modern world toward a life of contemplation, a turn that he saw as the common characteristic of the "higher religions." This same characteristic he did not recognize in Confucianism, however, which for him did not measure up to this lofty liberating ideal.

Indeed, much of Confucianism he saw as devoted to satisfying those "natural necessities"—"making a living, raising a family, leaving a good name"—from which Merton says we should be liberated.

But there is more . . .

> For modern man the old is often paradoxically that which claims to be new. Man in modern, technological society has begun to be callous and disillusioned. . . . The specious glitter of newness, the pretended glitter of a society in which youthfulness is commercialized and the young are old before they are twenty, fill some hearts with utter despair.[4]

In this respect Merton anticipated the Beats, who followed him at Columbia, "beaten" by a corrupt world and driven by revulsion with it into revolt and escape.

In the midst of this Merton says:

> Yet in the deepest ground of our lives we still hear the insistent voice which tells us "You must be born again. . . ." We seek to awaken in ourselves a force which really changes our lives from within. In modern secular life men resort to many expedients. If you can . . . find a good psychiatrist, it is possible that you may appreciate a psychological breakthrough and liberation. . . . But in reality psychoanalysis and psychiatry tend toward more workable compromises which enable us to function without having to

undergo an impossible transformation. We are not born again. We simply learn to put up with ourselves. . . .

More usually the desperation of modern man drives him to seek a kind of new life and rebirth in mass movements. . . . In these he tries to forget himself, in dedication to a more or less idealistic cause. But he is not born again.[5]

It is directly against this predicament of modern man and modern society that Merton poses the need for a radical spiritual transformation, which finds a parallel in Asian religions that put spiritual liberation ahead of any reform of human society. One can understand, then, why for him Confucianism fails to qualify as a higher religion: it sees self-improvement as integrally bound up with this-worldly social obligation and social melioration. Whether this actually precludes spiritual or religious transformation is another matter, to be discussed in what follows.

In judging this question, it is significant for us that Merton relies on scriptural evidence, directly interpreted in terms congenial to his own conception of modern man's spiritual dilemma. While denying Confucianism a place among the "higher religions," he cannot be unaware of the prominence of Confucianism among the major Chinese traditions. He knows that Confucianism is widely referred to both in China and abroad as among the "Three Teachings" (*san jiao*) of China, often referred to as the "Three Religions of China." Merton is quick to dispute this latter characterization because it does not sufficiently differentiate Confucianism from Daoism and Buddhism and tends to treat it on a par with the latter. On the other hand, he cannot deny that Confucian texts recognized as canonical do have definite religious aspects.

Although Merton's writings on the whole have almost nothing to say about Confucianism, he does attempt to deal with this seeming contradiction in a short section squeezed into a book otherwise broadly and loosely entitled *Mystics and Zen Masters*. Here, he refers to major Confucian texts under the headings of "The Great Traditions of China" and "The Sources of Classical Thought," which lead him into a consideration of texts generally considered "classic" that define that early classical tradition.[6]

These are recognized as "authoritative" but nonetheless competing alternatives in early Chinese thought. They include Daoist and Legalist writings, but the main focus is on what Merton calls the "Four Confucian classics," including the *Great Learning*, the *Mean*, and *Mencius*, along with the *Analects* of Confucius. Merton's section also includes the *Classic of Filial Piety* (*Xiao jing*), which he renders as "Filial Love" (not without some justification, since it combines both love and piety).

Taking these texts as representative of classical Confucianism, Merton has some extraordinarily positive things to say about the Confucian classics themselves, along with other things that would explain why Confucianism as an organized teaching succumbed ultimately to negative forces.

First, some of the strong positive evaluations: Speaking of "Confucian humanism" as found in the classics, he says: "The foundation of the Confucian system is first of all the human person and then his relations with other persons in the society. . . . Confucianism is therefore a humanist and personalist doctrine, and this humanism is religious and sacred." Moreover, "Confucianism is not just a set of formalistic devotions which have been loosely dismissed as 'ancestor worship.' The Confucian system of rites was meant to give full expression to that natural and humane love which is the only guarantee of peace and security in society. For Merton, the true and essential Confucianism was seen in the *Analects* and *Mencius*, which "continued to be the most vital and effective spiritual force in China."[7]

If this is so, however, one naturally asks: why did or does Confucianism not qualify as one of the "higher religions"? Why does it not stand on a par with the other two of the "Three Teachings"? Merton does not address this question in the essay under consideration here, but we get clues along the way as to how, despite this enduring, vital essence of Confucianism as seen in the classics, the teaching came to be vitiated by powerful decadent forces.

As I say, we get only clues, not a full explanation, but these clues fall into a pattern. Explaining a crucial historical development in the third century b.c.e., the unification of China by the totalitarian Legalist movement, Merton says of the latter "that they brought the most vital and productive age of Chinese thought to a close and perhaps did more than anything else to create a society that would guarantee the formalization and even the ossification of Chinese thought for centuries to come. At any rate by the third century the really great development of Chinese philosophy ceased."[8]

So stated, the increasing decadence of Confucianism is explained in terms of external forces and circumstances, but there are also hints that the teaching itself acquiesced in or succumbed to this "ossification" process in the longer run, when a Confucian ideal that had been basically personalistic yielded to "the rigid formalism of Confucian ethics and became, over two thousand years, a suffocating system." Against this, we have contrasting assertions in the same essay. "But in spite of this corruption, the iniquity, the pessimism of human nature that were able to flourish in this climate of official cynicism, [Confucian] scholars remained untouched by what was around them and the Confucian tradition remained pure."[9]

What are we to make of this juxtaposition of two thousand years of decadence and suffocation with Merton's affirmation of the surviving purity of Confucian tradition? I believe what he means is that the institutionalized forms of Confucianism, especially as sponsored by the state, were corrupted by the systemic process, yet individual Confucians, drawing directly on the inspiration of surviving classics, remained true to the original teaching.

These relatively isolated and exceptional cases, however "spirited" they might be, still did not qualify as a "religion," much less as a "higher religion."

At this point, one begins to wonder if this contradictory representation of Confucianism reflects not just the "facts" but some common assumptions in modern Western thought. One of these sees religions in general as tending to fall away from their original inspiration and succumb to a process of inevitable corruption in the all-too-human hands of those who claim its sanction for their own self-interested uses. The other tendency draws from this the further conclusion that organized religion is inherently corrupt as compared to personal "spiritualities" that rely on direct intuitive experience through forms of contemplative praxis that transcend religious dogma and sectarianism. Fortunately, we have more than such suppositions to help us in arriving at a fair judgment, and these appear in the same collection of disparate thoughts collected under the upside-down umbrella of Merton's *Mystics and Zen Masters*.

Under that same heading, we find a section called "The Jesuits in China." Here, drawing mostly on the work of George H. Dunne,[10] Merton credits the early Jesuit missionaries to China in the late sixteenth and early seventeenth century with a remarkable accommodation to Chinese culture, including most notably the sympathetic efforts of Matteo Ricci to achieve a genuine understanding of Confucianism.

Merton's title, "The Jesuits in China," is right in drawing attention to the large contributions of the Jesuits as a group—including other Jesuits in China, such as Adam Schall von Bell (1592–1669), and also those who performed a similar mission, such as Roberto DiNobile (1577–1656) in India and Alexandro Valignano (1539–1606) in Japan—who led in a similar adaptation of Christianity to the native cultures, different as these were from each other, to Hinduism in India and to a Zen Buddhism already much adapted to Shinto and Japanese culture.

Spectacular as each of these cases was in their own local setting, together they could also be seen as an outgrowth of a fundamental impulse in the founding of the Jesuit order in the wake of the European Renaissance, which from the start sought to harmonize Judeo-Christian piety with the classical culture then being revived from Greece and Rome. Jesuits in each of these different cultural settings produced distinctive results, yet this success was not just in adapting Christianity to native cultures but in creatively reviving some of the essential elements in native philosophy and religion itself.

Merton's high estimate of Ricci in these respects is confirmed by the eminent European sinologue Wolfgang Franke (unknown to Merton):

Looking back with our present understanding of Chinese civilization of the late Ming period, we find it almost incredible that a foreigner—however well educated and intelligent he might be—without any previous knowledge of the Chinese language and civilization was able within less than twenty years to take up residence in the capital, become a prominent member of this society, make friends with a number of the most eminent scholar-officials of the time, and even convert some of them to his Christian faith. . . . This accommodation included a thorough Chinese literary education in order to carry on discussions with Chinese scholars and to talk to them on the achievements of European science and development of thought in their own terms. Ricci himself was particularly able to master a highly sophisticated form of accommodation, and was therefore accepted by the Chinese scholar-officials as one of their own.

Ricci's ingenious, gentle and kindly nature conformed to the highest Chinese standards. . . . It inclined him to appreciate and value the essence of Chinese culture. All in all Ricci may be considered the most outstanding cultural mediator of all times.[11]

Ricci's achievement in this respect is typified by his extraordinary effort to learn and master classical Chinese (simply as a missionary he would have had plenty to do just by learning vernacular Chinese so as to communicate with and convert ordinary people). But Ricci recognized the importance of educated Chinese leadership, and he did not just dismiss or sidestep them in the way that Merton tends to do when he denigrates Confucian scholars as in the following: "All China, at least all the ruling class of China, was supposed in theory to be educated along Confucian lines, but many and not the least successful of Chinese statesmen were men who with the outward facade of Confucianism, were inwardly either pedants, rigid and heartless conformists, or unprincipled crooks."[12]

Ricci himself could easily have taken Confucianism at this low level and used it to his own advantage in converting people from a debased Confucianism to an unsullied Christianity. As a post-Renaissance man, however, and like Erasmus a Christian humanist, Ricci was disposed to take the classical Chinese tradition at its own best professions and attempt to reconcile Confucianism with Christianity at the highest level.

That Ricci was successful in this is attributable not only to his own openness of mind but to a similar openness of many Confucian scholars whom he sought to engage in active dialogue. Reciprocity was at work here, not just solitary genius being impressed on credulous others. And this openness of his Chinese partners (so much in contrast to Merton's characterization of the Confucians as rigid, heartless pedants) reflected something in the Confucians' own background that contrasts with Merton's routine characterization of them.

This new element is to be seen in a revival of Confucianism that had started in the eleventh century. It has been called Neo-Confucianism because it was not only a revival of the old but a reformulation of it to meet the new needs of Song-dynasty China. History was not just to be seen as a tired repetition of ancient platitudes by entrenched bureaucrats but a concerted response by thoughtful Neo-Confucians to the challenge of a new situation.

In the eleventh century, this new situation arose from the need of the new Song dynasty both to stabilize society, after years of civil war, and to address the economic and social problems of a society that had developed and expanded to a new level. Hu Yuan (993–1059) was one of a generation of Confucian scholars who responded to this new need by his formula of "substance, function, and literate discourse." By "substance" he meant enduring truths in the Confucian classics still relevant to the solution of contemporary problems (their "function" or "application"), and by literate discourse he meant the need for open, public discourse by which people could arrive at common agreement or consensus on what to do about their shared problems. The test of timeless truths was their adaptability to the needs of human society. These could be based on shared natural feelings, but they had to be expressible, communicable, or they would be as unavailable for practical use as the wordlessness of Laozi or the *koans* of Zen Buddhism were in dealing with the rampant civil war and suffering that had prevailed in the ninth and tenth centuries, while Buddhism and Daoism were flourishing (except for a prohibition on Buddhism in 845 engineered at court by the rival Daoists).

Politically in the eleventh century, this new Confucian reform movement called for a "restoration of the ancient order" (here in an idealized form), and its political and economic program was called the New Laws or New System (*Xin fa*). (In the twentieth century, it is sometimes analogized to Franklin D. Roosevelt's New Deal.) Although the success of this movement waxed and waned in time, its institutional ideals continued to inspire successive generations of new reformers. But among these ideals the most enduring (yet also much conflicted) was a new ideal of "classical" education based on a new curriculum.

By the end of the twelfth century, this new curriculum had been shaped for the long term by the great Neo-Confucian philosopher Zhu Xi (1130–1200), who was no less an educator than a metaphysician and who provided Confucianism with a curricular core that far outlasted and outdistanced the reformers' limited success in achieving universal schooling. Despite the failure of at least nominal attempts to implement universal schooling in China, the new core curriculum made its way in different parts of East Asia and on different levels down into the twentieth century.

Zhu Xi's core curriculum was identified by what were called the Four Books and Five Classics, of which the key and crucial components were the *Great Learning*, the *Analects* of Confucius, the text of Mencius, and the *Mean* (*Zhong yong*). Since together with the Five Classics the Four Books came to be known as "the classics," it is important to recognize that actually they were a very select group of texts, singled out for special attention by Zhu Xi. The *Great Learning* and the *Mean* were separate chapters drawn from a traditional classic known as the *Record of Rites* (*Li ji*), a large collection of materials dealing with ritual under many diverse headings, both theoretical and practical. Zhu Xi, following up on an earlier trend among his Song predecessors, singled these out because they provided a brief compact formulation of the basics of all learning, here made to serve as a guide to one's reading of the other classics. Indeed, Zhu Xi's formulation was so succinct and focused that it readily became the heart of a new Confucian education. First adopted on the local level in Song private academies, next under the Mongol Yuan dynasty in the curriculum of the Imperial College, then in the civil-service examination system, ultimately it reached beyond the borders of China into the schools of Korea, Japan, and Vietnam. In fact, so succinct, manageable, and memorable was this core formulation that it persisted even in the household instruction of many families not able to afford formal instruction.

I have already spoken of the enormous outreach of Zhu Xi's "core" in chapter 9, but let me offer just one recent example of its perduring influence: In 1989, when the Chinese Communist regime reversed Mao's anti-Confucian campaign (the Cultural Revolution), I was invited to speak on Confucianism at a state-sponsored celebration of Confucius's birthday in Beijing. On that occasion, I had a conversation with the president of the People's Republic of China, Jiang Zemin, who fondly recalled his childhood education, before he became caught up in the Chinese Communist revolution, when his father instructed him at home in the Four Books. These homespun lessons stayed with him through the years and were no doubt part of the underlying sensibility that led Jiang, Deng Xiaoping, and other moderates to recoil from the excesses of Mao Zedong and the so-called Gang of Four.

The relevance of all this to Thomas Merton is that so widely had the Four Books become accepted as the essential Confucian classics, when Merton chose to talk about the Confucian classics in his *Mystics and Zen Masters*, he referred to these same core texts as representative of classic Chinese thought, calling them not the Four Books but "the Four Confucian Classics."[13] Classic texts they were indeed, but Merton reads them as speaking for the original pure Confucianism, not the later "corrupt" and "decadent" Confucianism he so readily dismisses (as compared to Daoism and Zen Buddhism). He can appreciate these particular "classics" without recognizing them as neoclassical, Neo-Confucian texts because they speak to him personally and directly and are amenable to his own form of higher spirituality.

Another new feature of "Neo"-Confucianism was its development of a method of contemplative praxis (unacknowledged by Merton) to match Daoist and Zen meditation. It was called "quiet-sitting" (*jing zuo*). Since no such explicit practice appears in classical Confucianism, there cannot be much doubt that quiet-sitting was adapted from something like Zhuangzi's "sitting in forgetfulness," in which one was supposed to "forget humaneness and rightness." Mencius's rejoinder to Zhuangzi was that one should "neither forget (natural moral impulses) nor try to abet (or force) them willfully." Neo-Confucians associated this new/old contemplative practice with a holistic experience of "the humaneness that forms one body (including the bodily feelings) with Heaven-and-Earth and all things."

Zhu Xi explained this further in his commentary on the *Great Learning*'s dictum of *ge-wu*, often translated as the "investigation of things," a rendering that appeals to the modern preference for objective investigation but that is better understood as "the recognition of things," which combines both the subjective and objective aspects of knowing or learning. Zhu Xu explains *ge-wu* as follows:

The teaching of the Great Learning insists that the learner, as he comes upon the things of this world, must proceed from principles already known and further fathom them until he reaches the limit. After exerting himself for a long time, he will one day experience a breakthrough to integral comprehension. Then the qualities of all things, whether internal or external, refined or coarse, will all be apprehended and the mind in its whole substance and great functioning will all be clearly manifested.[14]

Quiet-sitting became a widespread practice in Neo-Confucianism and accompanied it to the rest of East Asia. Some schools in Korea and Japan even considered it orthodox praxis. Though obviously this could not be part of any official-examination "orthodoxy" that emphasized measurable objectivity, it satisfied the more personal and subjective side of Cheng-Zhu learning. Its place and status in the whole system is indicated by the fact that while some of Zhu Xi's predecessors went so far as to speak of "spending half the day in reading (study) and half in quiet-sitting," Zhu himself wondered how one could do this and still meet his essential social obligations.

In his section on "The Jesuits in China" (part of what goes under the title of *Mystics and Zen Masters*), Merton dwells not on these developments in Song Confucianism but on the undoubted achievements of Jesuits like Matteo Ricci in coming to terms with the Confucians of that day.

The legend of the subtle Jesuit diplomatist who always has an ace up his sleeve (otherwise known as "Jesuit casuistry") has obscured the true meaning and profound importance of Ricci's originality. He not only made an intelligent diagnosis of a totally unfamiliar condition, but also, by implication diagnosed his own condition and that of western Christian civilization as a whole. Like a true missionary, he divested himself of all that belonged to his own country and his own race and adopted all the good customs and attributes of the land to which he had been sent.[15]

(So much for the typical "colonialist" view of Christian missionaries.)

Merton has much more to say about the Jesuits that need not detain us here. Suffice it for me to quote these lines: "Here were men who three hundred years ahead of their time, were profoundly concerned with issues which are now seen to be so important that the whole history of the church and Western civilization seems to be implicated in their solution."[16] Merton is right, even though he does not himself go as far into the issues (especially the Neo-Confucian ones) as we might like. We can offer two more illustrations of Ricci's accomplishments that confirm what has just been quoted from Merton. The first is Ricci's phenomenal effort to learn classical Chinese and apply it to a pioneering translation into Latin of the Four Books. To this extent Ricci extended the process of spreading Zhu Xi's influence, already felt throughout East Asia, to the West and even to Merton himself.

The second example is Ricci's translation into Chinese of a version of Cicero's *De Amicitia* in response to the ready interest shown by his Confucian scholars in the fundamental and universal value of friendship. Not only did this satisfy a need of sixteenth- and seventeenth-century Neo-Confucian scholars for whom human association was the key to "self-cultivation and human governance" (as Zhu Xi had put it), but it at the same time expressed a strong impulse in the post-Renaissance religious humanism of Erasmus (1466?–1538), shared by Ricci's Jesuits.

From this we can see how these historical developments in both the West and China converged on an enduring universal value— friendship and the virtue of trust or trustworthiness it depended on. From the Renaissance interest in Roman civility to Erasmus's sixteenth-century religious humanism and on to the eighteenth-century Enlightenment, there was an unceasing focus on the key human elements in a civil society. This appealed to sixteenth-century Neo-Confucians who, instead of simply succumbing to the corrupt, despotic tendencies referred to by Merton, were eager to learn from Ricci whatever he could bring from the West that would help them remain true to their principles of civility.

In "The Jesuits in China," Merton is highly appreciative of what Ricci and the Jesuits did, but he has little to say about their Confucian counterparts. Because he does not pay that much attention to Chinese history (except as recurring decline) and does not recognize the much broader significance of Neo-Confucianism and Zhu Xi's core curriculum as it spread to the rest of East Asia, he is in no position to recognize the continuing vitality of Confucianism inside and outside of China. His own "Confucianism," the true kind, is one he can draw directly from a personal reading of "timeless" classics, like the *Analects* and *Mencius*, not from history.

Nevertheless, the original Confucian classics themselves included history, poetry, and much else, and it was only Merton's early initiation into the Four Books that allowed him to take a foreshortened "timeless" view of Confucianism. Another way to look at it, however, is to note that Merton was, from the start, more of a poet than a historian. As a poet, he could resonate with nature—earthly, human, and divine—but he would have had to be more of a historian and perhaps somewhat less of a pure contemplative in order to be brought truly "down to earth" in a Confucian sense. But then, few Confucians themselves were both good poets and historians. And I myself was no poet, despite my association with Lax and Merton (and even being listed on the masthead of *Jester*!)

At least this is my thought or, rather, the open question that I leave with you in conclusion. Perhaps it is more than I could reasonably expect of Merton, the poet, considering all that he did accomplish in his all-too-brief lifetime. Except for his premature death, he might well have caught up with the history—or better yet, since he was not out looking for it, history would probably have caught up with him.

As for myself, since those early days with Merton, I have spent my life rather differently. Instead of listening for the Zen sound of one hand clapping, I have looked for two hands clapping or clasping in support of humanistic learning, liberal education, and humane governance of the university, combining as best I could spiritual cultivation with public service—as a teacher in a collegial core curriculum, as a scholar in the Asian humanities, and as a university administrator, while at home cultivating my organic garden in a suburban cooperative community. Merton, I think, would not have objected to any of that.

Thank you.

Appendix

*Wm. Theodore de Bary: A Life
in Consultation and Conversation*

CHRONOLOGY

1919, August 9	Born in the Bronx, New York, son of William E. and Mildred Marquette de Bary.
1923–1937	Raised in Leonia, New Jersey. Graduated as valedictorian, Class of 1937, Leonia High School.
1937–1941	Attended Columbia College, New York, on Honor Scholarship; Manager of Debate Council; Chair of Student Governing Board; Phi Beta Kappa; Awarded Henry Evans Traveling Fellowship on graduation, June 1941.
1941 Fall	Started graduate study at Harvard, but after December 7 was recruited by Naval Intelligence to attend Navy Japanese Language School in Berkeley, California, and then Boulder, Colorado (1942).
1943–1945	Commissioned as Ensign USNR. Served in Pacific theater: Pearl Harbor, Aleutians campaign, Summer

	1944; Battle of Okinawa, Spring 1945; occupation of Japan, fall 1945; spring 1946 in charge of Far East desk of Office of Naval Intelligence, Washington, D.C., with rank of Lieutenant Commander.
1946 Fall	Graduate study at Columbia University, M.A. earned in 1948. Doctoral research in China 1949 on Fulbright Fellowship. Dissertation approved 1953 with Distinction.
1946–1952	Put in charge of new Oriental Studies program of Columbia College, teaching Oriental Humanities and Oriental Civilizations and preparing texts and translations for use in same (see bibliography, below).
1953–1956	Formal appointment as Assistant Professor and Chair of University Committee on Oriental Studies (name later changed to "University Committee on Asia and the Middle East").
1959–1966	Chair of Department of Chinese and Japanese (name later changed to "East Asian Languages and Cultures").
1960–1972	Director, East Asian Languages and Area Center.
1966–1967	Sabbatical in Kyoto, Japan, and Taipei, Taiwan.
1968–1969	Elected to Executive Committee of Faculty representing Faculty of Philosophy. Joined in setting up new University Senate, then elected Chair of the Executive Committee of the Senate. Wrote report on conduct of Senate, 1976.
1971–1976	Asked to serve as Executive Vice President for Academic Affairs and Provost. Restored University to balanced budget after successive deficits in 1968 and after (see Provost's Report of 1976).
1975	Initiated Society of Fellows in the Humanities.
1976–1977	Sabbatical in Kyoto, Japan, followed by travel in China as guest of People's Republic.
1976	Initiated Heyman Center for the Humanities Project. Center built in 1981.
1978–1989	Returned to teaching. Active as Chair of Publication Committee of the University Committee on Asia and Middle East.

1981–2004	Director, Heyman Center for the Humanities.
1988	Initiated Society of Senior Scholars, Heyman Center.
1989	de Bary Class of 1941 Endowed Professorship in Asian Humanities established.
1989	Invited by PRC Confucian Association to give keynote address at celebration for Confucius's birthday in Beijing.
1989	Formally retired as regular member of faculty but continued to teach *pro bono* as Special Service Professor in Core courses.

POSITIONS

Chairman, University Committee on Oriental Studies, 1953–1961

Director, East Asian Language and Area Center, 1960–1972

Chairman, Department of East Asian Languages and Cultures, 1960–1966

Carpentier Professor of Oriental Studies, Columbia University, 1966–1978

Chairman, Executive Committee, University Senate, 1969–1971

President, Association for Asian Studies, 1969–1970

Executive Vice President for Academic Affairs and Provost, 1971–1978

John Mitchell Mason Professor of the University, 1979–1990

Director, Heyman Center for the Humanities, 1981–2004

Special Service Professor 1990–

FOUNDER

Heyman Center for the Humanities

The Society of Fellows in the Humanities

The Society of Senior Scholars

The University Lectures

Trilling Seminars

The University Seminars in Neo-Confucian Studies and Asian Thought and Religion

Alumni Colloquia in the Humanities

Legacies Series for 250th Anniversary

DISTINCTIONS AND AWARDS

Watumull Prize of the American Historical Association, 1958

Fishburn Prize of Educational Press Association, 1964

Great Teacher Award, Columbia University, 1969

Honorary Doctor of Letters, St. Lawrence University, 1968

Honorary Doctor of Humane Letters, Loyola University of Chicago, 1970

John Jay Award, Columbia College, 1971

Editorial Board, *American Scholar*, 1971–1997

American Academy of Arts and Sciences, 1974; Member of the Council

Guggenheim Fellow, 1981–1982

Ch'ien Mu Lectureship, the Chinese University of Hong Kong, 1982

Award for Excellence, Graduate Faculties Alumni, 1983

Director, American Council of Learned Societies, 1978–1986

Lionel Trilling Book Award, 1983; Mark Van Doren Prize, 1987

Guest Lecturer, College de France, 1986

Inaugural Lecturer, Edwin O. Reischauer Lectureship in East Asian Affairs, Harvard University, 1986

Tanner Lectureship, University of California, Berkeley, 1988

Order of the Rising Sun (Third Class), 1993

Honorary Doctor of Letters, Columbia University, 1994

Alexander Hamilton Medal, 1994, 1999

Frank Tannenbaum Memorial Award, University Seminars

President's Townsend Harris Founder's Day Medal, City College of New York, 1996

American Philosophical Society, 1999

Tang Jun-yi Lectureship, Chinese University of Hong Kong, 2004–2005

Philolexian Society Award, 2010

Thomas Merton Honorary Lectureship, 2010

Honorary Member Japan Academy, 2010

AUTHOR OR EDITOR OF

Sources of Japanese Tradition (1st ed., New York: Columbia University Press, 1958; 2nd ed., vols. 1–2, 2001, 2004).

Approaches to the Oriental Classics (New York: Columbia University Press, 1958).

Sources of Chinese Tradition (1st ed., New York: Columbia University Press, 1960; 2nd ed., vols. 1–2, 1999, 2000).

Sources of Indian Tradition (New York: Columbia University Press, 1960; rev. ed., 1988).

Sources of Korean Tradition (New York: Columbia University Press, 1997; 2nd. ed., 2001).

Sources of East Asian Tradition, 2 vols. (New York: Columbia University Press, 2008).

Translation of *Five Women Who Loved Love* (Rutland, Vt.: C. E. Tuttle, 1956).

A Guide to Oriental Classics (1st ed., New York: Columbia University Press, 1964; 2nd ed., 1975; 3rd ed., 1988).

Approaches to Asian Civilizations (New York: Columbia University Press, 1964).

The Buddhist Tradition (New York: Random House, 1969).

Self and Society in Ming Thought (New York: Columbia University Press, 1970).

Letters from War-Wasted Asia (New York: Kodansha, 1975).

The Unfolding of Neo-Confucianism (New York: Columbia University Press, 1975).

Principle and Practicality: Neo-Confucianism and Practical Learning (New York: Columbia University Press, 1979).

Neo-Confucian Orthodoxy and the Learning of the Mind and Heart (New York: Columbia University Press, 1981).

Yüan Thought: Essays on Chinese Thought and Religion Under the Mongols (New York: Columbia University Press, 1982).

The Liberal Tradition in China (Hong Kong: Chinese University Press of Hong Kong, 1983; New York: Columbia University Press, 1983).

The Rise of Neo-Confucianism in Korea (New York: Columbia University Press, 1985).

East Asian Civilizations: A Dialogue in Five Stages (Cambridge, Mass.: Harvard University Press, 1987).

The Message of the Mind in Neo-Confucianism (New York: Columbia University Press, 1988).

Neo-Confucian Education (Berkeley: University of California Press, 1989).

Eastern Canons: Approaches to the Asian Classics (New York: Columbia University Press, 1990).

Learning for One's Self (New York: Columbia University Press, 1991).

The Trouble with Confucianism (Cambridge, Mass.: Harvard University Press, 1991).

Waiting for the Dawn: A Plan for the Prince (New York: Columbia University Press, 1993).

Confucianism and Human Rights (New York: Columbia University Press, 1997).

Asian Values and Human Rights (Cambridge, Mass.: Harvard University Press, 1998).

Asia in the Core Curriculum (New York: Heyman Center, 2001).

Nobility and Civility: Asian Ideals of Leadership and Civil Society (Cambridge, Mass.: Harvard University Press, 2004).

Living Legacies at Columbia (New York: Columbia University Press, 2006).

Confucian Tradition and Global Education (New York: Columbia University Press, 2007).

Classics for an Emerging World (New York: University Committee on Asia and the Middle East, 2008).

Finding Wisdom in East Asian Classics (New York: Columbia University Press, 2011).

Notes

INTRODUCTION

1. W. T. de Bary, ed., *Sources of Japanese Tradition* (New York: Columbia University Press, 1958), 1:148; cited in the text as SJT.

1. EDUCATION FOR A WORLD COMMUNITY

Reprinted from *Liberal Education: The Bulletin of the Association of American Colleges* 50, no. 4 (December 1964).

1. John W. Nason et al., *The College and World Affairs* (New York: Hazen Foundation, 1964), 1.

2. Mark Van Doren, *Liberal Education* (Boston: Beacon Press, 1959), 90.

3. This is the text of the opening address of the Conference on Undergraduate Instruction in Critical Languages and Area Studies held at Princeton University, October 12–13, 1964.

4. W. T. de Bary, ed., *Approaches to the Oriental Classics* (New York: Columbia University Press, 1959), 4.

5. Nason et al., *The College and World Affairs*, 5.

6. See Van Doren's *Anthology of World Poetry* (New York: Halcyon House, 1939) and his "Great Books, East and West," in *Approaches to the Oriental Classics*, 7–10. Also see A. N. Whitehead's *Religion in the Making* (New York: The MacMillan Company, 1926).

7. Van Doren, *Liberal Education*, 127.

8. *Non-Western Studies in the Liberal Arts College* (Washington, D.C.: Commission on International Understanding, Association of American Colleges, 1964), 11.

9. *Report of the Commission on the Humanities* (New York: American Council of Learned Societies, 1964), 86.

10. Excerpts from this paragraph appeared in a letter to the *New York Times* (September 27, 1964) in support of the Moorhead Bill for a national humanities foundation.

11. Cf. Nason et al., *The College and World Affairs*, 1, "A New Strategy of Liberal Learning."

12. W. T. de Bary and A. T. Embree, eds., *Approaches to Asian Civilizations* (New York: Columbia University Press, 1964), xiii.

13. *Non-Western Studies in the Liberal Arts College*, 40.

14. de Bary and Embree, eds., *Approaches to Asian Civilizations*; E. P. Boardman, ed., *Asian Studies in Liberal Education* (Washington, D.C.: Association of American Colleges, 1959); W. Morehouse, ed., *Asian Studies in Liberal Arts Colleges* (Washington, D.C.: Association for Asian Studies, 1961).

15. de Bary and Embree, eds., *Approaches to Asian Civilizations*, xiii.

16. Salvador de Madariaga, *Swiss Review of International Affairs* (September 1964): 10.

17. *Analects* 4:17.

2. "Starting on the Road" with John Erskine & Co.

Title adapted from John Erskine's novel *The Start of the Road* (1938), about Walt Whitman.

1. John Erskine, *Classics of the Western World* (Chicago: American Library Association, 1927), 11.

2. Timothy P. Cross, *An Oasis of Order: The Core Curriculum at Columbia College* (New York: Office of the Dean, Columbia College, 1995), 29.

3. Erskine, *Classics of the Western World*, 13–14.

4. Ibid., 16.

5. Ibid., 24–25.

4. A Shared Responsibility to Past and Future

1. See their views as expressed in my *Confucian Tradition and Global Education* (Hong Kong: Chinese University of Hong Kong Press, 2007).

2. See W. T. de Bary, A. T. Embree, and A. V. Heinrich, eds., *A Guide to Oriental Classics*, 3rd ed. (New York: Columbia University Press, 1989).

5. Asia in the Core Curriculum

1. See the topics for discussion suggested for each major work included in W. T. de Bary and I. Bloom, eds., *Eastern Canons: Approaches to the Asian Classics*, 3rd ed. (New York: Columbia University Press, 1989).

6. What Is "Classic"?

1. W. T. de Bary et al., *Classics for an Emerging World* (New York: Columbia University Heyman Center for the Humanities, 2008), 28–68.

7. Classic Cases in Point

The three main sections in this chapter are drawn from chapters 3, 16(b), and 17 of W. T. de Bary, ed., *Finding Wisdom in East Asian Classics* (New York: Columbia University Press, 2011).

1. *Proceedings of the Conference on Classics for an Emerging World, Columbia University, January 19–20, 2008* (New York: University Committee on Asia and the Middle East, 2008).

2. Murasaki Shikibu, *The Tale of Genji*, trans. Arthur Waley (New York: Modern Library, 1935), 23; *The Tale of Genji*, trans. Royall Tyler (New York: Viking, 2001), 22–23. References to *Genji* will hereafter be to the Waley translation.

3. *Nippon Gaku Jutsu Shinkō Kai* (Chicago: University of Chicago Press, 1994).

4. W. T. de Bary, *Sources of Japanese Tradition*, 2nd ed. (New York: Columbia University Press, 2001), 1:244, 1:398, 1:418–419.

5. Ivan Morris, *The Pillow Book of Sei Shōnagon* (New York: Columbia University Press, 1967), xii–xiv.

6. Ivan Morris, *The World of the Shining Prince: Court Life in Ancient Japan* (New York: Knopf, 1964), 198.

7. Ibid,. 106.

8. Ibid., 106–107.

9. W. T. de Bary, *Sources of Japanese Tradition*, 2nd ed. (New York: Columbia University Press, 2001), 1:155.

10. *Bulletin of the Institute of Eastern Culture*, ACTA Asiatica, no. 97 (Tokyo: Tōhō Gakkai, 2009).

8. Human Renewal and the Repossession of the Way

Excerpted from W. T. de Bary, *The Liberal Tradition in China* (New York: Columbia University Press, 1983).

1. See my "Neo-Confucian Cultivation and the Seventeenth-Century Enlightenment," in *The Unfolding of Neo-Confucianism*, ed. W. T. de Bary (New York: Columbia University Press, 1975), 162.

2. *Cheng shi jing-shuo*, in *Er Cheng quanshu* (SBBY ed.; Taipei: Zhonghua, 1976), 5:1a, 3a–b, "Mingdao xiansheng kaizheng Daxue," "Yichuan xiansheng Daxue."

3. W. T. de Bary, *Neo-Confucian Orthodoxy and the Learning of the Mind-and-Heart* (New York: Columbia University Press, 1981), 46–47, 141–143. The important account of his self-reformation by Wu Yubi (1392–1469) was originally entitled *Rixin pu* (Account of Daily Renewal), based on this approach to self-cultivation in the *Great Learning*. See M. Theresa Kelleher, *Personal Reflections on the Pursuit of Sagehood: The Life and Journal of Wu Yü-pi* (Ph.D. diss., Columbia University; Ann Arbor: University Microfilms, 1982), 105.

4. Cheng Yi, *Yichuan wenji*, 7:6a–b, 7b, in *Er Cheng quanshu*.

5. Zhu Xi, preface to *Zhongyong zhangju* (hereafter abbreviated as ZGZXMZJC ed.; Taipei, 1979), 18:39–41.

6. Wing-tsit Chan, "Chu Hsi's Completion of Neo-Confucianism," in *Études Song—Sung Studies in Memoriam Etienne Balazs*, ed. Françoise Aubin, ser. 2, no. 1 (Paris: Mouton, 1973), 76, 78.

7. Zhen Dexiu, *Xishan wenji* (Guoxue jiben congshu), 26:449, "Nan Xiong zhou xue si xiansheng citang ji."

8. Ibid., 24:409–410, "Mingdao xiansheng shutang ji."

9. *Xishan wenji*, 26:449.

10. de Bary, *Neo-Confucian Orthodoxy*, 9–13.

11. Charles Frankel, *Liberalism and Liberal Education* (New York: Columbia University Press, 1976), 3–11.

12. *Mingru xuean*, vol. 6, 32:93.

13. Zhu Xi, *Huian xiansheng Zhu Wengong wenji, Zhuzi daquan* (SBBY ed.), 11:3b, "Renwu yingdao fengshi." Hereafter abbreviated as *Wenji*.

14. Ibid.

15. Ibid., 11:33a.

16. de Bary, *Neo-Confucian Orthodoxy*, 27–37, 91–98.

17. Chen Changfang, *Weishi ji* (Siku quanshu zhenben., 1st series; Shanghai: Commercial Press, 1935), 1:1a–3b, "Di xue lun."

18. See de Bary, *Neo-Confucian Orthodoxy*, 129, 189, 211.

19. Zhu, *Zhongyong zhangju*, 45; cf. also *Wenji*, 11:35b–36a.

20. Tang Junyi, "The Spirit and Development of Neo-Confucianism," *Inquiry* 14 (1971): 59–60.

21. Huang Zongxi and Quan Zuwang, *Songyuan xuean* (Taipei: Heluo tushu chubanshe, n.d.), 1:26. Peter Bol, a specialist in these matters, believes that Hu Yuan's follower Liu Yi may have been attributing his own views to his master, but that does not affect the point being made here.

22. Zhen, *Xishan wenji*, 26:448–449.

9. ZHU XI AND LIBERAL EDUCATION

1. Zhu Xi, *Huian xiansheng Zhu Wengong wenji, Zhuzi daquan* (SBBY ed.), 74:1b. Hereafter abbreviated as *Wenji*.

2. Mao Xinglai, *Jinsilu jizhu* (*Siku shanben congshu*, first series ed.; Taipei: Yiwen yinshuguan, n.d.), 2:13b.

3. *Mencius*, 4B:14; translation adapted from D. C. Lau, *Mencius* (London: Penguin, 1960), 130.

4. *Jinsilu jizhu*, 2:32a; Wing-tsit Chan, trans., *Reflections on Things at Hand* (New York: Columbia University Press, 1967), 68. Hereafter abbreviated as *Things at Hand*, or, following references to *Jinsilu*, simply as "Chan."

5. *Lunyu jizhu* (ZGZXMZJC ed.), 7:17a.

6. *Lunyu jingyi* (*Zhuzi yishu* ed.), 7B:22a–b.

7. *Jinsilu jizhu*, 6:1a; cf. Chan, 171.

8. *Wenji*, 74:19b.

9. Abe Takeo, *Gendai no kenkyū* (Tokyo: Sōbunsha, 1972), 45–57.

10. Makino Shūji, "Gendai no jugaku kyōiku," *Tōyōshi kenkyū* 37, no. 4 (March 1979): 71–74.

11. Martina Deuchler, "Self-Cultivation for the Governance of Men," *Asiatische Studien* 34, no. 2 (1980): 16.

12. Chan, *Things at Hand*, 154; Ye Cai, *Jinsilu jijie, Kinsei kanseki sōkan*, 3rd series (Kyoto: Chūbun shuppansha, 1979), 297.

13. See my introduction to *The Unfolding of Neo-Confucianism*, ed. W. T. de Bary (New York: Columbia University Press, 1975), 16–17.

14. *Er Cheng waishu*, 3:1b; *Jinsilu jizhu*, 5:14a; translation adapted from Chan, 165.

15. See Ren Jiyu, "Rujia yu rujiao," *Zhongquo zhexue* 3. See also his "Confucianism as a Religion," *Social Sciences in China* 2 (1980): 128–152. See also Fung Yu-lan, "Lüelun daoxue de detian, mingcheng he xingzhi," *Shehui kexue zhanxian* (1982–1983): 35–43.

16. Robert M. Hutchins, *Education for Freedom* (Baton Rouge: Louisiana State University Press, 1941), 19–64.

17. Mark Van Doren, *Liberal Education* (New York: Holt, 1943), 119–122.

18. Uno Seiichi, *Shogaku* (Tokyo: Meiji shoin, 1965), 2; *Daxue zhangju* (ZGZXMZJC ed.), 2a–b; *Zhongyong zhangju*, 17a; *Daxue huowen*, 4b–5a, 29b–30a; *Wenji*, 94:20a, "Xuexiao keju siyi"; W. T. de Bary, *Neo-Confucian Orthodoxy and the Learning of the Mind-and-Heart* (New York: Columbia University Press, 1981), 54–55, 125.

19. *Luzhai quanshu, Kinsei kanseki sōkan*, 2nd series (Kyoto: Chūbun shuppansha, 1975), 5:15a–b, "Yuzi shike."

20. *Luzhai quanshu*, 4:25b–28a.

21. Uno, *Shogaku*, 139–140.

22. Ibid., 67.

23. *Yanping dawen, Kinsei kanseki sōkan*, 1st series (Kyoto: Chūbun shuppansha, 1972), 34–35.

24. See Conrad Schirokauer, "Chu Hsi as an Administrator," *Études Song—Sung Studies* 1, no. 3 (1976): 208–219.

25. *Wenji*, 100:5b–7a, "Quan yu bang."

26. Ibid., 74:23a–29b.

27. Shimizu Morimitsu, *Chūgoku kyōson shakai ron* (Tokyo: Iwanami, 1951), 540–549.

28. Kimura Eiichi, "Sitte to Shushi no gaku," in *Chūgoku tetsugaku no tankyū* (Tokyo: Sobunsha, 1981), 280.

29. *Wenji*, 100:6a–7a; Kimura, "Sitte," 282–287; Sakai Tadao, *Chūgoku zensho no kenkyū* (Tokyo: Kōbundō, 1969), 39–40.

30. For instance, Wada Sei, *Shina chihō jichi* (Tokyo: Kyūkōshoin, 1939; rev. ed., 1975), 51–52, 119–145, 224–230; Shimizu, *Chūgoku kyōson shakai ron*, 339–349; Sakai, *Chūgoku zensho no kenkyū*, 34–54.

31. See Wing-tsit Chan, trans., *Instructions for Practical Living and Other Neo-Confucian Writings by Wang Yang-ming* (New York: Columbia University Press, 1963), 298–306. Hereafter cited as *Instructions*.

32. Sakai Tadao, "Ri Rikkoku to kyōyaku," in *Higashi Ajia no shisō to bunka* (September 1979), 134–154.

33. *Mencius*, 3A:4.

34. Shujing, "Shun dian," in James Legge, *Chinese Classics* (Oxford: Clarendon, 1893), 3:44.

35. Zhongyong, 20; Wing-tsit Chan, *Source Book in Chinese Philosophy* (Princeton, N.J.: Princeton University Press, 1963), 107.

36. *Analects*, 15:5.

37. *Changes*, hexagram no. 41; see R. Wilhelm and C. F. Baynes, *The I-ching or Book of Changes* (Princeton, N.J.: Princeton University Press, 1950), 159.

38. Hexagram no. 42; ibid., 163.

39. Dong Zhongshu, as quoted in *Han shu*, 56:21b.

40. *Analects*, 12:2; 15:23.

41. *Wenji*, 74:16b–17a; "Bailu dong shuyuan jieshi."

42. *Xiangshan quanji* (SBBY ed.), 34:24a; trans. Julia Ching, "The Goose Lake Monastery Debate," *Journal of Chinese Philosophy* 1, no. 2 (1974): 165.

43. Qisong, *Xinjin wenji* (SBBY ed.), 3:2a–4a, "Yuan xiao."

44. *Tianmu Mingben chanshi zalu*, A:366a, "Jing xiao," in *Dai Nihon zokuzōkyō*, 2.27.4. The passage quoted is from Mingben's "Admonition on Filial Piety" (Jing xiao), trans. Chun-fang Yu as an appendix to her paper on Mingben in *Yuan Thought*, ed. Hok-lam Chan and W. T. de Bary (New York: Columbia University Press, 1982), 459–460.

45. *Wenji*, 74:17b.

46. Ibid., 12:2a–b, "Yiyu nishang fengshi."

47. See de Bary, *Neo-Confucian Orthodoxy*, 29, 86.

48. See W. T. de Bary, *Self and Society in Ming Thought* (New York: Columbia University Press, 1970), 154–206.

49. Jennifer Robertson, "Rooting the Pine: Shingaku Methods of Organization," *Monumenta Nipponica* 5, no. 34 (1979): 311–332.

50. See Tileman Grimm, "Ming Educational Intendants," in *Chinese Government in Ming Times*, ed. Charles Hucker (New York: Columbia University Press, 1969), 135.

51. Sakai, *Chūgoku zensho no kenkyū*, 46–54.

52. *Wenji*, 69:18a–26a, "Xuexiao gongju siyi."

53. Ibid., 69:21b.

54. Qian Mu, *Zhongguo jin sanbainian xueshu shi*, 4–5; Takeuchi Yoshio, *Takeuchi Yoshio Zenshū* (Tokyo: Kadokawa shoten, 1979), 4:207–208.

55. *Wenji*, 69:22a.

10. Confucian Individualism and Personhood

1. *Analects* 2:7; 17:21.

2. Ron Guey Chu, "Rites and Rights in Ming China," paper presented to the Conference on Confucianism and Human Rights, East-West Center, Honolulu, August 14–17, 1995.

3. *Analects* 2:4.

4. Thomas Berry provides a broad conspectus of Western and Chinese views of the individual and person, bringing out both their contrasting and complimentary features, in his "Individualism and Wholism in Chinese Tradition: The Religious Cultural Context," a paper prepared for an ACLS/NEH-sponsored conference, "Individualism and Holism in Chinese Thought," held at the Breckinridge Center in York, Maine, June 24–29, 1981.

5. Anthony C. Yu, "Altered Accents: A Comparative View of Liberal Education," remarks delivered at the fortieth anniversary of Hong Kong Baptist University, April 17, 1996. In *Criterion* 35, no. 2 (Spring/Summer 1996): 10.

6. *Analects* 2:20.

7. *Analects* 18:6.

8. Liji, yueji 1; Legge, *Li chi* (New York: University Books, 1967), 2:97.

9. Burton Watson, trans., *Hsün tzu: Basic Writings* (New York: Columbia University Press, 1962), 89.

10. As shown by the later examples of Huang Zongxi and Lu Liuliang.

11. *Webster's Third New International Dictionary* (Springfield, Mass.: Merriam, 1961), citing M. R. Cohen.

12. W. T. de Bary, "Individualism and Humanitarianism in Late Ming Thought," in *Self and Society in Ming Thought*, ed. W. T. de Bary (New York: Columbia University Press, 1970), 145–247.

13. In its etymology, *zi* is said by Karlgren (no. 1091) to be associated with "nose" and "breath" and thus is perhaps akin to the Sanskrit *atman*, "self" deriving from "breath."

14. See W. T. de Bary, ed., *The Unfolding of Neo-Confucianism* (New York: Columbia University Press, 1975), 169; *Linquan Wu Wengong ji*, Wanli 40 (1612) ed. in National Central Library, Taipei, *Waiji*, 2:10b–11a.

15. E.g., *Zhuangzi*: Harvard-Yenching Index ed. 22/8/31, 77/28/7, 78/28/54; Burton Watson, *Complete Works of Chuang Tzu* (New York: Columbia University Press, 1968), 102–103, 310, 317.

16. Cf. Zhu Xi, *Sishu jizhu*, commentary on *Mencius*, 4B:4; *Jinsilu jizhu*, 2:22b, no. 41; and Cheng Hao, *Yishu*, 11:4a. My translation follows in part the rendering and annotation of Yamazaki Michio in *Shushigaku taikei* [SSGTK], vol. 9, no. 41, rather than that of Wing-tsit Chan, trans., *Reflections on Things*

at Hand (New York: Columbia University Press, 1967), 57–58. Hereafter abbreviated as *Things at Hand*, or, following references to *Jinsilu*, simply as "Chan."

17. Hu Guang et al., *Xingli daquan* (*Siku zhenben* ed., 5th series; Taipei: Commercial Press, 1974), 43:9b, citing *Er Cheng yishu*, 6:6b.

18. *Yishu*, 2A:2a, *Jinsilu jizhu*, 4:6b, no. 14; SSGTK, vol. 9, 4:129, 310; cf. Chan, *Things at Hand*, 128. Here and in the passage that follows my translation benefits from Prof. Chan's but differs somewhat in the handling of the key terms at issue in my discussion of the problem.

19. *Analects*, 8:2.

20. Ibid., 7:37.

21. *Yishu*, 2A:16a; *Jinsilu jizhu*, 4:7a–b, no. 16; SSGTK ed., 4:130, 310; Chan, *Things at Hand*, 128.

22. For a near analogy in the Buddhist tradition, one might compare this with the *jinen honi* of the Pure Land "saint" Shinran in Japan or with the problem of moral effort (*kufū; gongfu*) in the Zen master Dōgen. See W. T. de Bary et al., ed., *Sources of Japanese Tradition* (New York: Columbia University Press, 1958), 212–218, 249–251.

23. Zhu, *Zhongyong zhangju* (ZGZXMZJC ed.), 49, commentary on chap. 1.

24. Wing-tsit Chan, "Chu Hsi's Completion of Neo-Confucianism," in *Études Song—Sung Studies in Memoriam Etienne Balazs*, ed. Françoise Aubin, ser. 2, no. 1 (Paris: Mouton, 1973), 76; on Chen Changfang, see *Song Yuan xue'an* (SYXA), 29:9–10.

25. See Wing-tsit Chan, *Source Book in Chinese Philosophy* (Princeton, N.J.: Princeton University Press, 1963), 465ff.

26. *Jinsilu jizhu*, 2:1a–b; Chan, *Things at Hand*, 37.

27. *Yichuan wenji*, 4:1a–2a; Chan, *Source Book*, 547ff.

28. Chan, *Source Book*, 473.

29. *Yichuan wenji*, 4:1a; Chan, *Source Book*, 548.

30. *Yichuan wenji*, 4:1b–2a.

31. Uno, *Shogaku*, 3:139.

32. *Zhuzi yulei* (Kyoto: Chūbun shuppansha, 1979), 93:9a; cf. Chan, *Things at Hand*, 204–205.

33. *Zhuzi yulei*, 94:8a–b.

34. Chan, *Things at Hand*, 2.

35. Uno, *Shogaku*, 3:139.

36. *Mingdao wenji*, 2:1a, in *Er Cheng quanshu* (SBBY ed.).

37. *Mencius*, 4A:20.

38. Dong Zhongshu, in *Han shu*, 56:6b; and *Dongzi wenji* (*Jifu congshu* ed.), 1:51.

39. *Yishu*, 15:17a; *Jinsilu jizhu*, 8:16b–17a; Chan, 213.

40. *Yichuan wenji*, 1:3a.

41. Zhu, *Wenji*, 11:4b.

42. Cf. Robert Hartwell, "Patterns of Settlement, the Structure of Government, and the Social Transformation of the Chinese Political Elite, ca. 750–1550," paper presented to the Columbia University Seminar on Traditional China (September 9, 1980), 9, 18–19.

43. Fan Zuyu, *Dixue* (ZGZXMZJC ed.), 3:6b–7a.

44. See Saeki Tomi, *Sō no shinbunka* (Tokyo: Jimbutsu ōraisha, 1967), 372.

45. Ibid., esp. 373ff. On the expansion of schools, rise in scholarly population, and increased participation in examinations, see John W. Chaffee, *Education and Examinations in Sung Society* (Ph.D. diss., University of Chicago, 1979), 338ff.

46. There has been extensive scholarly discussion of this question. Those not already familiar with the literature may wish to consult E. Balasz, *Chinese Civilization and Bureaucracy* (New Haven, Conn.: Yale University Press, 1974), chap. 4, esp. 53–54; and Hartwell, "Patterns," 32–33.

47. C. Schirokauer, in *Confucian Personalities*, ed. A. Wright (Stanford, Calif.: Stanford University Press, 1962), 165–166. The conclusion of Wing-tsit Chan, based on many years' study of Chu's life and work, is that he lived in extremely modest circumstances and managed to support himself partly from a small printing business on the side. See Wing-tsit Chan, "*Zhuzi guqiong*," in his *Zhuxue lunji* (Taipei: Xuesheng, 1982), 205–232.

48. See, for example, Wei-ming Tu, "Toward an Understanding of Liu Yin's Confucian Eremitism," in *Yuan Thought*, ed. W. Chan and W. T. de Bary (New York: Columbia University Press, 1982), 259; and John Dardess, "Confucian Doctrine, Local Reform and Centralization," in ibid., 357.

49. *Yishu*, 19:9a–b.

50. *Mencius*, 2B:2.

51. Cheng Yi, *Yichuan wenji*, 4:21b; *Jinsilu jizhu*, 7:8b; Chan, 190. See also Franklin Houn, "Rejection of Blind Obedience as a Traditional Chinese and Maoist Concept," *Asian Thought and Society* 7, no. 21 (1982): 266–269.

52. *Yishu*, 15:3b–4a; *Jinsilu jizhu*, 7:11a; translation adapted from Chan, 193.

53. Julia Ching, "The Goose Lake Monastery Debate," *Journal of Chinese Philosophy* 1, no. 2 (1974): 175.

54. L. C. Goodrich and C. Y. Fang, *Dictionary of Ming Biography* (New York: Columbia University Press, 1976), 426–433, 474–479.

55. Zhu, *Wenji*, 69:18b.

56. Robert Hartwell, "Patterns"; and Shiba Yoshinobu, *Commerce and Society in Sung China,* trans. Mark Elvin (Ann Arbor: University of Michigan, 1970), esp. 45–50, 202–213; Saeki Tomi, *Sō no shinbunka,* 141–168, 370–392.

57. Saeki, *Sō no shinbunka,* 381–385.

58. Zhu Xi, *Wenji,* 47:17b, letter to Lu Zuqian.

59. Saeki, *Sō no shinbunka,* 370ff. On the crisis in education from the lack of a sense of any higher purpose, see Thomas H. C. Lee, "Life in the Schools of Sung China," *Journal of Asian Studies* 37 (1977): 58–59.

60. *Zhongyong huowen* (Kinsei kanseki sōkan shisō sampen ed.; Kyoto: Chūbun shuppansha, 1976), 82. Translation adapted from Chan, *Things at Hand,* 69.

61. *Yishu,* 22A:14a; *Jinsilu jizhu,* 3:10b–11a; Chan, 97.

62. *Yishu,* 15:19b; *Jinsilu jizhu,* 11:7a. Translation adapted from Chan, 264.

63. *Yichuan wenji,* supplement, 3a, letter to Fang Daofu; *Jinsilu jizhu,* 2:14a, no. 15; translation adapted from Chan, 47–48.

64. *Yishu,* 19:11a; *Jinsilu jizhu,* 3:14a, no. 30; Chan, 100.

65. *Yishu,* 19:11a; *Jinsilu jizhu,* 3:16b, no. 38; Chan, 103.

66. *Yishu,* 2A:21a, 6:6b, 19:11a, 22A:2a, 6b; *Waishu,* 3:1a, 5:1b, 12:4b, 6a.

67. *Waishu,* 5:1b; *Yishu,* 11:4a.

68. Zhang Zai as quoted in *Jinsilu,* 3:10b; Chan, 97.

69. *Waishu,* 11:2b; Chan, 94.

70. *Zhangzi quanshu* (Kinsei kanseki sōkan ed.), 7:5a.

71. Zhu, *Wenji,* 47:30a–b, letter to Lu Zuqian; and *Jinsilu jizhu,* 3:10a; Chan, 96.

72. See his *Jukyō no mokuteki to Sōju no katsudō* (Tokyo: Taishūkan, 1926), 798.

73. de Bary, ed., *Unfolding,* 143–147.

74. W. T. de Bary et al., ed., *Sources of Chinese Tradition* (New York: Columbia University Press, 1960), 492–509; James T. C. Liu, *Ou-yang Hsiu* (Stanford, Calif.: Stanford University Press, 1967), 90–102; and Hok-lam Chan, "'Comprehensiveness' and 'Change' in Ma Tuan-lin's Historical Thought," in *Yüan Thought,* pp. 41–45.

75. Cf. Chan, *Things at Hand,* 88–122.

76. *Yishu,* 24:7b; *Wenji,* 5:11b.

77. *Zhuzi yulei,* 4:12b, 112.

78. Ibid., 67:6b, 2628.

79. Ibid., 12:9b, 334.

80. *Xishan wenji,* 24:410.

81. *Siku tiyao* (Shanghai: Commercial Press, 1933), 36:742.

82. See Christian Murck, *Chu Yün-ming (1461–1527) and Cultural Commitment in Su-chou* (Ann Arbor: University Microfilms International, 1979), 2:311–312.

83. *Zhangzi quanshu*, 7:5a.

84. Murray, *Liberality and Civilization*, 30–31.

11. Zhu Xi's Educational Program

1. Li Jingde, comp., *Zhuzi yulei* (repr; Kyoto: Chūbun shuppansha, 1979), 49:5a; translation from Wing-tsit Chan, trans., *Reflections on Things at Hand* (New York: Columbia University Press, 1967), 94; hereafter cited as *Things at Hand*.

2. Thomas Carter and L. C. Goodrich, *The Invention of Printing in China and Its Spread Westward* (New York: Ronald, 1955), 83.

3. See ibid., 26–28, 38–51, 57–58, 63–65.

4. See W. T. de Bary, ed., *The Buddhist Tradition* (New York: Modern Library, 1969), 208.

5. Qian Mu, *Zhuzi xin xue'an* (Taipei: Sanmin shuju, 1971), 1:160–167.

6. See Jan Yunhua, "Chinese Buddhism in Ta-tu," in *Yuan Thought*, ed. Hok-lam Chan and W. T. de Bary (New York: Columbia University Press, 1971), 388, 397; and Chun-fang Yu, "Chung-fen Ming-pen and Chan," in ibid., 448–449; also "Introduction," 15–22.

7. See Okada Takehiko, "Shushi no chichi to shi," in *Chūgoku shisō ni okeru risō to genjitsu* (Tokyo: Mokujisha, 1983), 391–392.

8. See W. T. de Bary, *Liberal Tradition in China* (Hong Kong/New York: Chinese University of Hong Kong/Columbia University Press, 1983), 21–24.

9. Mary C. Wright, *The Last Stand of Chinese Conservatism* (Stanford, Calif.: Stanford University Press, 1957), 4.

10. Zhu Xi, *Daxue zhangju*, in *Sishu zizhu*, (Zhongguo zixue mingzhu jicheng ed., Taipei, 1979), preface, 1, 2.

11. Ibid., 1b.

12. Ibid., 2a.

13. See de Bary, *Liberal Tradition*, 24–27.

14. *Lunyü jizhu*, in *Sishu jizhu*, 3:19b (216).

15. Morohashi Tetsuji, *Daikanwa jiten* (Tokyo: Taishūkan, 1955), 4:10478–73.

16. Mao Xinglai, *Jinsilu jizhu* (*Siku shanben congshu*, 1st series; Taipei, Yiwen yinshuguan, n.d.), 9:5b. Excerpted and abridged from *Mingdao xiansheng wenji*, 2:2b–3a, in *Er Cheng quanshu* 55 (Kinsei kanseki sōkan ed.), 485;

Wing-tsit Chan, trans., *Reflections on Things at Hand* (New York: Columbia University Press, 1967), 219.

17. See Chan, *Things at Hand*, chap. 14.

18. Zhu Xi, *Zhongyong zhangju*, preface in *Sishu jizhu*, 37–43.

19. Zhu Xi, *Daxue zhangju*, preface 2b (4).

20. *Liji*, 36 *xue ji* (*Shisanjing zhushu fujiaokanji*) (*Yiwen yinshuguan* reprint of Jiaqing 20 [1815 ed.]), 36:3a (649), trans. adapted from James Legge, *Li chi: Book of Rites* (repr; New York: University Books, 1967), 2:83.

21. Mao, *Jinsilu jizhu*, 9:4b–6a.

22. Zhu Xi, *Daxue zhangju*, 2b–3a (10–11).

23. Ibid., 2a (9).

24. Ibid., 6a–6b (17–18).

25. Liu Shuxian, "The Functions of Mind in Chu Hsi's Philosophy," *Journal of Chinese Philosophy* 5 (1978): 204.

26. To To, *Song shi* (Peking: Zhonghua shuju, 1977), 432:12837–12838. Huang Zongxi and Quan Zuwang, *Song Yuan xue'an* (Taipei: Holo tushu chubanshe, n.d.), 1:25–26. In the SYXA account there is some question as to whether Liu Yi may not be attributing his own views to Hu Yuan, but that does not affect the issue here because Zhu Xi and Lü Zuqian appear to have accepted both the attribution and the idea.

27. *Song shi*, 334:10729.

28. Mao Xinglai, *Jinsilu jizhu*, 11:4b–5a; quoting *Er Cheng yishu*, 2:7a; trans. Chan, 262–263.

29. Mao Xinglai, *Jinsilu jizhu*, 11:5a.

30. On the relationship of schools to Cheng Hao's political philosophy, see Ishida Hajime, "Tei Meidō shōkō—jiseki, shimpō, gakkō kyōiku," in *Rekishi ni okeru minshū to bunka* (Tokyo, 1982).

31. See W. T. de Bary, *Neo-Confucian Orthodoxy and the Learning of the Mind-and-Heart* (New York: Columbia University Press, 1981), 59–60.

32. Wu, of course, may also have had access to the original sources from which these excerpts were drawn. See *Wu Wenzheng gong quanji* (*Chongren Wan Huang jiaokanben*, 1756), *juan shou* 34b, suppl. *juan* 1:1a–8b; de Bary, *Neo-Confucian Orthodoxy*, 59; David Gedalecia, *Wu Cheng: A Neo-Confucian of the Yüan* (Ann Arbor: University Microfilms, 1971), 369, 382.

33. Zhu Xi, *Huian xiansheng Zhu Wengong wenji* (Kyoto: Chūbun shuppansha, 1977), 74:18a (1368); hereafter cited *Wenji*. "Bailudong shuyuan jieshi." See also John W. Chaffee, "Chu Hsi and the Revival of the White Deer Grotto Academy, 1179–1181," *T'oung Pao* 61 (1985): 40–62.

34. de Bary, *Liberal Tradition*, 37.

35. Zhu Xi, *Wenji*, 74:18b (1368).

36. Ibid., 74:18b–19a.

37. Zheng Duanmeng (1143–1191), native of Jiangxi and disciple of Zhu Xi, for whom the latter wrote, besides this postscript, several letters and a funerary inscription. See Zhu, *Wenji*, 90:16a (6367); SYXA, 69:13; and *Buyi*, 69:34. Wing-tsit Chan, *Zhuzi menren* (Taipei: Xuesheng shuju, 1982), 245–246; Dong Zhu (1152–1214), a disciple of whom Zhu Xi was particularly fond; SYXA, 69:14; Bui, 69:47; Chan, *Zhuzi menren*, 276–277.

38. Zhu Xi, *Cheng Dong er xiansheng xueze* (CSJC ed.), 3–4.

39. Ibid., 4.

40. *Cheng Dong er xiansheng xueze*, postscript of Rao Lu, 5.

41. Ibid.

42. Zhu, *Wenji*, 69:20–28b (2269–1273).

43. Ibid., 69:21b.

44. Ibid., 69:22a.

45. Ibid., 23b.

46. Ibid., 24a.

47. Ibid., 69:24a; de Bary, *Liberal Tradition*, 41–42.

48. Zhu, *Wenji*, 24b.

49. Ibid., 69:25a, 26a.

50. Ibid., 69:24a.

51. Ibid., 69:20b.

52. de Bary, *Neo-Confucian Orthodoxy*, 38–44.

53. Ibid., 53–60.

54. Ibid., 62–63.

55. This side of Zhu's career emerges with particular clarity in Conrad Schirokauer's account of "Zhu Xi as an Administrator," *Études Song* 1, no. 3 (1976): 207–236.

56. Cheng Duanli, *Chengshi jiashu tushu fennian richeng* (CSJC ed.), 1–43; hereafter cited as *Chengshi . . . richeng*. Summarized and excerpted in John Meskill's *Academies in Ming China: An Historical Essay* (Tucson: Monograph Series of the Association for Asian Studies, University of Arizona Press, 1982), 160–166.

57. Meskill, *Academies*, 61. See also Makino Shūji, "Gendai no jugaku kyōiku," in *Tōyōshi kenkyū* 37, no. 4 (March 1979): 71–74; and Chaffee, "Revival," 18.

58. Cheng Duanli, *Chengshi . . . richeng*, 1:9; SYXA, 87:62.

59. See the discussion of the *Daily Schedule* that follows.

60. Cheng Duanli, *Chengshi . . . richeng*, 1:14; SYXA, 87:65.

61. Ibid., 1:1–2, 3:110–118.

62. Ibid., 1:1–2, preface of Cheng Quanli.

63. Ibid., 1:1–2, 2:23.

64. de Bary, *Neo-Confucian Orthodoxy*, 52–53, 59–60.

65. Zhang Boxing, personal preface to the *Chengshi . . . richeng, Zhengyitang quanshu* (Fuzhou zhengyi xueyuan ed. of Tongzhi 7 [1868]), 1:1.

66. *Song shi* 423:12638; SYHA, 87:1.

67. SYHA, 87:50.

68. Song Lian, et al., *Yuan shih* (Beijing: Zhonghua shuju, 1976), 190:4343.

69. SYHA, 87:54.

70. Zhu, *Wenji*, 99:2b (1758). See Wing-tsit Chan, "Zhu Ziguqiong," in *Zhuxüe lunji* (Taipei: Hsüehsheng shuchü, 1982), 205–232.

71. Cheng Duanli, *Chengshi . . . richeng*, 3:45.

72. Ibid., 1:9; 3:120. "Jiqing lu jiangdong shuyuan jiangyi."

73. See Theresa Kelleher's chapter in *Neo-Confucian Education*.

74. See Zhu, *Wenji* (Kyoto: Chūbun), 14:11a–14a (204–206). *Xinggong biandian zoujiaer*; 74:25a–26a, "Dushu zhi yao," *Zhuzi yulei* (repr; Kyoto: Chūbun shuppansha, 1979), *juan* 10–11, pp. 255–316; Cheng Duanli, *Chengshi . . . richeng* (CSJC ed.), 1:9, 3:120; Hu Guang, *Xingli daquan* (Kyoto: Chūbun shuppansha, 1981), *juan* 53–54, pp. 818–842; Li Guangdi, ed., *Xingli jingyi* (ed. of Daoguang 30, 1850), 8:31b–44b. Qian Mu, *Zhuzi xin xue'an*, 4:613–687.

75. Mao Lirui et al., comps. *Zhongguo gudai jiaoyushi* (Peking: Beijing shifan daxue, 1980), 398–400.

12. SELF AND SOCIETY IN MING THOUGHT

1. Cf. Hu Shi, *The Chinese Renaissance* (repr. of 2nd ed., New York: Paragon Book Reprint Co., 1963), 66–70.

2. *Tinglin shi wenji* 3/1a–2a. As translated in W. T. de Bary et al., eds., *Sources of Chinese Tradition* (New York: Columbia University Press, 1960), 608–609.

3. Cui Shu, *Kaoxin lu tiyao* (CSJC ed.), A/22, as translated in *Sources of Chinese Tradition*, 623.

4. Liang Qichao, *Intellectual Trends in the Qing Period*, trans. Immanuel Hsü (Cambridge: Cambridge University Press, 1959), 28.

5. To cite only two prominent examples among many, there are Wang Yangming in his *Instructions for Practical Living,* trans. by Wing-tsit Chan (New York: Columbia Universty Press, 1963), 119–120, *passim*; and Huang Zongxi in his *Mingyi daifang lu* (as excerpted and translated in *Sources of Chinese Tradition*, 593). Cf. also David Nivison, "Protest Against Conventions and

Conventions of Protest," in *The Confucian Persuasion*, ed. Arthur F. Wright (Stanford, Calif.: Stanford University Press, 1960), 177–201.

6. As one apt example we might cite the discussion of the "discriminating" mind (so deprecated by Gu Yanwu) by He Xinyin, one of the most original and "progressive" thinkers of the late Ming and one who suffered martyrdom for his opposition to the established regime. Cf. Rong Zhaozu, *He Xinyin ji* (Beijing: Zhonghua shuju, 1960), 33.

7. *Mingru xuean* (Wanyou wenku ed.), 1/*Fan lie*.

8. That this was the case from the outset of the Ming is admirably illustrated by Frederick Mote's study of Gao Qi's relations with the founder of the Ming dynasty and Gao's tragic end. Cf. *The Poet Kao Ch'i, 1336–1374* (Princeton, N.J.: Princeton University Press, 1962), esp. chap. 9.

9. The confrontation between Ming despotism and the Confucian conscience is well delineated in Charles Hucker, "Confucianism and the Censorial System" in *Confucianism in Action*, ed. David Nivison and Arthur Wright (Stanford: Stanford Universtiy Press, 1959), 199–208. Cf. also R. B. Crawford et al., "Fang Hsiao-ju in the Light of Early Ming Society," *Monumenta Serica* 15: 303–327.

10. Cf. Jiang Fan, *Hanxue shicheng ji* (Shanghai: Commercial Press, 1934), 13, Fan lie.

11. Cf. Ping-ti Ho, *The Ladder of Success in Imperial China* (New York: Columbia University Press, 1962), 216.

12. For a brief resumé of these changes and the nature of the Ming examinations, see Nivison, "Protest Against Conventions," 193–194.

13. Obviously, this is not a question of numerical minorities but of an organized group capable of acting in opposition to the dominant power or of representing some social segment or class. Any such alignment was condemned as factionalism, and while a Confucian could claim to speak in the general interest, he dared not identify himself as spokesman of a party or organized minority.

14. Cf. Ping-ti Ho, *The Ladder of Success in Imperial China*, 212–214, 255–256, 258–259, 261.

15. Cf. Saeki Tomi, *Sō no shin bunka* (Tokyo: Jinbutsu Ōraisha, 1967), 384. There are already signs of it in Lu Xiangshan; cf., S. C. Huang, *Lu Hsiang-shan* (New Haven, Conn.: Yale University Press, 1944), 32, 58, 62.

16. Chuanxi lu (in *Wang Yangming quanjiah*, Datong ed.; Shanghai, 1935), 1/22; Wing-tsit Chan, *Instructions for Practical Living* (New York: Columbia University Press, 1963), 62–63.

17. *Chuanxi lu*, 1/22 [Cai] Xiyüan wen; trans. adapted from Chan, *Instructions*, 60–61.

18. *Ming shi* (Guofang Yanjiuyuan ed.; Taipei, 1962), 195/2277 can.

19. Cf. Conrad M. Shirokauer, "Chu Hsi's Political Career," in *Confucian Personalities*, ed. Arthur F. Wright and Denis Twitchett (Stanford, Calif: Stanford University Press, 1962), 162–188.

20. *Baishazi quanji* (Temple edition of 1771), V, 6/2b; see also Ken Yuwen, "Chen Xianzhang's Philosophy of the Natural," in *Self and Society in Ming Thought*, ed. W. T. de Bary (New York: Columbia University Press, 1970), 56–57, 61, 79–80.

21. *Ming shi* 282/3171; 283/3181–3182. To say that they were reclusive does not imply that their philosophies were necessarily quietistic: my point is simply that the retreat from book learning was a common response to a common problem among Confucians whose engagement with life took different forms.

22. *Baishazi quanji*, 3/22b–23a.

23. *Nianpu* A/6 Zhengde 3, in *Wang Yangming quanji*, vol. 1.

24. Cf. Wing-tsit Chan, "How Buddhistic Is Wang Yang-ming?" *Philosophy East and West* 11, no. 3–4; Kusumoto Fumio, *Ōyōmei no zenteki shisō kenkyūa* (Nagoya: Nisshindo Shōten, 1958).

25. Cf. Shimada Kenji, *Chūgoku ni okeru kindai shii no zasetsu* (Tokyo: Chikuma Shobō, 1949), 19–35.

26. Translated by Wing-tsit Chan in *Sources of Chinese Tradition*, 524–525; and in his *Source Book in Chinese Philosophy* (Princeton, N.J.: Princeton University Press, 1963), 497.

27. Among innumerable other references one might cite Wang Yang-ming's eloquent statement of the idea in the opening lines of his "Inquiry on the Great Learning" (*Daxue wen*)ak (see Chan, *Instructions*, 272n). Cf. also Shimada's extensive discussion of this theme in "Subjective Idealism in Sung and Post-Sung China: The All Things Are One Theory of Jen," *Tōhōgakuho* 28 (March 1958): 1–80. Shimada sees this theory not only as a powerful force in Ming thought but as an influence on reformist thought at the end of the Qing, especially in Tan Sitong.

28. *Baishazi quanji*, V, 6/2a.

29. Ibid., III, 3/62b.

30. I.e., in his famous dictum that the noble man should be "first in worrying about the world's troubles and last in enjoying its pleasures." For the significance of this motto in relation to the Buddhist ideal of the Boddhisattva, see my article "Buddhism and the Chinese Tradition," *Diogenes* 47 (1964): 120–122.

31. *Analects* II/4.

32. Cf. his "The Heavenly Ordinance in Pre-Ch'in in China," *Philosophy East and West* 11, no. 4; 12, no. 1; and his more recent *Zhongguo zhexue yuan lun* (Hong Kong: Jiulong: Rensheng chubanshe, 1966), 508–521.

33. See C. T. Hsia, "Time and the Human Condition in the Plays of T'ang Hsien-tsu," in *Self and Society in Ming Thought*, ed. W. T. de Bary (New York: Columbia University Press, 1970), 249–290.

34. See my "Individualism and Humanitarianism in Late Ming Thought," in *Self and Society in Ming Thought* (New York: Columbia University Press, 1970), 145–247.

13. THE RISE OF NEO-CONFUCIANISM IN KOREA

1. See Taga Akigoro, ed., *Kinsei Ajia kyōiku shi kenkyū* (Tokyo: Bunrui shoin, 1966), appendix 2, article in Japanese by Lothar Knauth, "Meishin hōgan no ryūtsū to Hispania Yaku no mondai [The *Myŏngsim pogam*: its diffusion and translation into Spanish]," 851–879. See also Sakai Tadao, *Chūgoku zensho no kenkyū* (Tokyo: Kōbundō, 1960), 451, 483; Kim Chung-Kuk, *Myung-Sim-Bo-Kam: Mirror of Clear Mind* (Seoul: Sŏnggyun'gwan University, 1959), 1–11; *Kosŏ mongnok* (Seoul: Sŏnggyn'gwan University, 1979), 50; Richard Rutt, "Chinese Learning and Pleasures," *Transactions of the Korea Branch of the Royal Asiatic Society* 36 (April 1960): 37. Despite its syncretic character as a popular morality book, quotations from Cheng-Zhu schoolmasters down to Zhen suggest that it was an outgrowth of the spread of Neo-Confucianism from Yuan China to Korea, in which Zhen's writings figured prominently.

2. See Wing-tsit Chan, "Chu Hsi and Yüan Confucianism," in *Yüan Thought*, ed. H. L. Chan and W. T. de Bary (New York: Columbia University Press, 1983).

3. See W. T. de Bary, *Neo-Confucian Orthodoxy and the Learning of the Mind-and-Heart* (New York: Columbia University Press, 1981), 1–66.

4. Fung Yu-lan, *History of Chinese Philosophy*, vol. 2, trans. Derk Bodde (Princeton, N.J.: Princeton University Press, 1953); Carsun Chang, *The Development of Neo-Confucian Thought* (New York: Bookman Associates, vol. 1, 1957; vol. 2, 1962); Alfred Forke, *Geschichte der neueren Chinesischen Philosophie* (Hamburg: Cram, De Gruyter, 1964), book 1, chap. 1.

5. Fung Yu-lan, *Zhongguo zhexue shi* (Shanghai: Commercial Press, 1934), vol. 2, chaps. 10–15.

6. Fung, *History*, 2:631.

7. Shimada Kenji, "The Thought of Miura Baien," *Tōyōshi kenkyū* 38, no. 3 (December 1979): 23–24.

8. See Conrad Schirokauer, "Neo-Confucianism Under Attack: The Condemnation of Wei-hsüeh" in *Crisis and Prosperity in Sung China*, ed. John W. Haeger (Tucson: University of Arizona Press, 1975), 163–198.

9. See chapter 11 in this volume.

10. Cf. W. T. de Bary and Irene Bloom, eds., *Principle and Practicality* (New York: Columbia University Press, 1979), 5–15; and W. T. de Bary et al., eds., *The Unfolding of Neo-Confucianism* (New York: Columbia University Press, 1975), 15–22.

11. In the explanatory note (*fanli*) of the *Mingru xuean*.

12. See his "Personal Proposals for Schools and Examinations" in *Huian xiansheng Zhu Wen-gong wenji* (SBBY ed.), 69:24ab. For Chŏng To-chŏn, see herein, Chung Chai-sik, in *The Rise of Neo-Confucianism in Korea*, ed. W. T. de Bary (New York: Columbia University Press, 1985), 59–87.

13. See note 3.

14. *Yi T'oegye chŏnjip* (Tokyo: Ri Taikei kenkyūkai, 1975), 2:260–261.

15. Fung, *History*, vol. 2, chap. 14.

16. Ibid., 585.

17. Zhu Xi, *Sishu jizhu* (Taipei: *Zhongguo zixue mingzhu jicheng zhenben chubian*, 1978), 18. *Daxüe huowen, Kinsei kanseki sōkan*, 3rd series (Kyoto: Chūbun shuppansha, 1976), 20b–21a (40–41).

18. Fung, *Zhongguo zhexue shi*, 2:938.

19. de Bary, *Neo-Confucian Orthodoxy*, 28–35, 91–98.

20. Zhen Dexiu, *Xishan wenji* (GXJBS ed.), 24:409–410.

21. Yi T'oegye, *Songgye Wŏn Myŏng ihak t'ongnok* in *T'oegye chŏnjip* (Seoul: Sŏnggyun'gwan University, 1959), 3:249–551, esp. 254, 513.

22. Takahashi Tōru, "Richō-jugakushi ni okeru shuriha shukiha no hattatsu," in *Chōsen Shina bunka no kenkyū* (Keijō [Seoul]: Keijō teikoku daigaku, 1934), 141–281.

23. Yamanoi Yū, in Onozawa Seiichi et al., *Ki no shisō* (Tokyo: Tokyo University Press, 1978), 355–513; and his *Min-shin shisōshi no kenkyū* (Tokyo: Tokyo University Press, 1980), esp. 149–199.

24. See Martina Deuchler, "Neo-Confucianism: The Impulse for Social Action in Early Yi Korea," *Journal of Korean Studies* 2 (1980): 80, 94; and Han Young-woo, *Chosŏn chŏn'gi ŭi sahoe sasang* (Seoul, 1976), 53–61.

25. See my introduction and article in de Bary and Bloom, *Principle and Practicality*, 12–13, 132–135, 141, 178–179.

26. Zhen, *Xishan wenji*, 25:425.

27. Kusumoto Masatsugu, *Chūgoku tetsugaku kenkyū* (Tokyo: Kokushikan daigaku, 1975), 353–390.

28. *Yiguan wenji* (SBBYed.), 5:12b.

29. Zhu Xi, *Yenping zawen*, in *Kinsei kanseki sōkan, shisōhen* (Kyoto: Chūbun shuppansha, 1972), 70, 89–92, 99–103,.111.

30. Xu Heng, *Xu Lu zhai xinfa* (Ming ed. of 1522), 1b.

31. See de Bary and Bloom, *Principle and Practicality*, 93–96, 129, 131, 165, 273–275, 286–287, 421, 433.

32. Cheng Hao, *Er Cheng yishu* (SBBY ed.), 24:2a.

33. Okada Takehiko, "Practical Learning in the Chu Hsi School," in de Bary and Bloom, *Principle and Practicality*, 283.

34. Cf. de Bary, *Neo-Confucian Orthodoxy*, 44–47, 54–55, 125.

35. de Bary and Bloom, *Principle and Practicality*, 26; R. Tsunoda, W. T. de Bary, and D. Keene, *Sources of Japanese Tradition* (New York: Columbia University Press, 1958), 348–350.

36. Martina Deuchler, "Self-Cultivation for the Governance of Men: The Beginnings of Neo-Confucian Orthodoxy in Yi Korea," *Asiatische Studien* 34, no. 2 (1980): 9–39.

37. de Bary and Bloom, *Principle and Practicality*, 32.

38. See JaHyun Kim Haboush, "A Heritage of Kings: One Man's Monarchy in the Confucian World" (Ph. D. diss., Columbia University; Ann Arbor, Mich.: University Microfilms, 1978), 36–40.

39. *Proceedings of the 2nd Academic Conference for Asiatic Studies* (Seoul: Sŏnggyun'gwan University, 1980), 82–99, 273–288.

40. Yi T'aejin, "The Socioeconomic Background of Neo-Confucianism in Fifteenth- and Sixteenth-Century Korea," draft prepared for the Conference on Korean Neo-Confucianism (August 1981), 27–28.

41. de Bary, *Neo-Confucian Orthodoxy*, 136–141.

42. Makino Shūji, "*Gendai no jugaku kyōiku*," *Tōyōshi kenkyū* 37, no. 4 (March 1979): 64–76.

43. Caolu xiansheng [i.e., Wu Cheng], *Wu wenzheng gong quanji* (1756 ed.), *juan shou* 34b; suppl. chap. 1:1a–8b.

44. *Kyŏngguk taejŏn* (repr; 1934), 212, 214.

45. *Ming Xuanzong shilu, Zhongyang yanjiuyuan* ed. 22:4b Xuande, 10th mo., *xinwei*.

46. *Kosŏ mongnok*, Catalogue of the Central Library, Sŏnggyun'gwan, (Seoul, 1979), 205. Lee Choon-hee, *Yijo sŏwŏn mun'go ko* (Seoul: Sŏnggyun'gwan, 1969), 8, 60, 80, 110.

47. See Wing-tsit Chan, "*The Hsing-Li Ching-i* and the Ch'eng-Chu School of the Seventeenth Century," in de Bary, ed., *Unfolding*, 543–579.

48. de Bary, *Neo-Confucian Orthodoxy*, 61, 134–135.

49. Deuchler, "Neo-Confucianism," 86.

50. de Bary, *Neo-Confucian Orthodoxy*, 188–191.

51. See Lee Choon-hee, *Yijo sŏwŏn*, passim.

52. Deuchler, "Neo-Confucianism," 87–88, 90–91.

53. The foregoing are discussed in de Bary, *Neo-Confucian Orthodoxy*, 28–35, 93–94.

54. This is a main theme in Ray Huang's *1587, a Year of No Significance* (New Haven, Conn.: Yale University Press, 1980).

55. Chŏng Tojŏn, *Chosŏn kyŏnggukchŏn*, in *Sambongjip* (Seoul: Kuksa p'yŏn-ch'an wiwŏnhoe, 1961), 227.

56. These are discussed extensively in Kusumoto Masatsugu, *Chūgoku tetsugaku kenkyū*, 327–352, 359–360.

57. de Bary, *Neo-Confucian Orthodoxy*, 24, 133.

58. Edward W. Wagner, *The Literati Purges: Political Conflict in the Early Yi Dynasty* (Cambridge, Mass.: Harvard University Press, 1974), 2.

59. Uno Seiichi, ed., *Shōgaku (Xiaoxue)*, sec. 6, *Shinshaku kambun taikei*, 3 (Tokyo: Meiji shoin, 1965), 377.

60. See Martina Deuchler, "The Tradition: Women During the Yi Dynasty," in *Virtues in Conflict*, ed. Sandra Mattielli (Seoul: Royal Asiatic Society, Korea Branch, 1977), 1–47.

61. *Jinsilu jizhu* (Taipei: Yiwen reprint, Siku shanben congshu), 9:72a–73b; Wing-tsit Chan, trans., *Reflections on Things at Hand* (New York: Columbia University Press, 1967), 237.

62. E.g., the Kōrakuen Park in Okayama.

63. Huang Zongxi and Quan Zuwang, *Song Yüan xüean* (Taipei, Holo tushu ed., n.d.), 1:26.

64. Cf. Etienne Balazs, *Chinese Civilization and Bureaucracy* (New Haven, Conn.: Yale University Press, 1964), 278–286.

65. Cf. Hermans Ooms, "Neo-Confucianism and the Formation of Early Tokugawa Ideology: Contours of a Problem," in *Responses to Neo-Confucianism in Tokugawa Japan*, ed. Peter Nosco (Princeton, N.J.: Princeton University Press, 1984).

66. In the Korean case, it is obviously not a question of original legitimization but of the Confucian sense that a dynasty's mandate must be constantly renewed by moral effort and political reform if it is to survive. On the Chinese case, see the important studies of John Dardess on the Yuan and Ming respectively: *Confucians and Conquerors* (New York: Columbia University Press, 1973); and *Confucianism and Autocracy* (Berkeley: University of California Press, 1983).

67. See my *Neo-Confucian Orthodoxy*, 41.

68. Ibid., 74.

69. See Sakai, "Yi Yulgok and the Community Compact," 332–334.

70. To the extent that Neo-Confucians promoted local interests in the academies, it would presumably derive from their preference for political

decentralization, emphasizing the dispersion and sharing of power, not from any common rural background or personal identification with the local landed aristocracy. Edward Wagner in "The Social Background of Early Yi-Dynasty Neo-Confucianists" calls into question their having a common social background and emphasizes instead, as the defining characteristic of the *sarim* group, their common outlook as Neo-Confucians. See the proceedings of the Ninth International Seminar, October 1981, entitled *Neo-Confucianism* (Taegu: Kyungpook National University, 1982), 155–175.

71. See my *Neo-Confucian Orthodoxy*, 31–37.

72. See JaHyun Kim Haboush, "A Heritage of Kings," 92.

73. See Lee Ki-moon, "Foundation of Hunmin chŏngŭm," *Korea Journal* 23, no. 6 (June 1983): 4, 8.

74. See Tu, "Yi T'oegye's Perception of Human Nature," 244, 260.

75. See Julia Ching, "Yi Yulgok on the 'Four Beginnings and the Seven Emotions,'" 318–319.

76. The earliest text reported by Professor Eikemeir is dated 1475. See D. Eikemeir, "Some Thoughts Surrounding the Community Pacts in Korea," draft prepared for the Conference on Korean Neo-Confucianism, August 1981.

77. Deuchler, "Reject the False and Uphold the Straight," in *The Rise of Neo-Confucianism in Korea*, 376.

78. Ibid., 388, 392.

79. See de Bary, *Neo-Confucian Orthodoxy*, 9–13.

80. Deuchler, "Reject the False and Uphold the Straight," 392–393.

81. "Orthodoxy and Heterodoxy in Seventeenth-Century Korea," in *The Rise of Neo-Confucianism in Korea*, 427–433.

14. CONFUCIANISM AND HUMAN RIGHTS

Excerpted from W. T. de Bary, ed., *Confucianism and Human Rights* (New York: Columbia University Press, 1998), 1–26.

1. Howard French, "Africa Looks East for a New Model," *New York Times* (February 4, 1966).

2. By Ho Shen, wife of Liu Shipei, founder of the Anarchist movement in China. Ho Chen, "Nuzi fuchou lun," *Tianyi bao* 3, no. 10: 7–13. Trans. Peter Zarrow.

3. Lawrence G. Thompson, *Ta T'ung Shu: The One-World Philosophy of K'ang Yu-wei* (London: George Allen and Unwin, 1958), 183.

4. See Twiss's article and Tu's epilogue in W. T. de Bary, ed., *Confucianism and Human Rights* (New York: Columbia University Press, 1998, for elaboration of this point.

5. See the article by the prominent liberal philosopher Morris Cohen, in the *Encyclopedia of Social Sciences*.

6. Mencius, trans. D. C. Lau (London: Penguin, 1970), IB:8, 68.

7. Ibid., 18:6.

8. W. T. de Bary, *Waiting for the Dawn* (New York: Columbia University Press, 1993), 117–141.

9. See de Bary, ed., *Confucianism and Human Rights*, 1–24, and chapter 1 in this volume.

10. Ibid., 83–93.

11. Ibid., 117–137.

12. Ibid., 142–153.

13. Ibid., 154–168.

14. Ibid., 168–178.

15. Ibid., 179–192.

16. See W. T. de Bary et al., eds., *Sources of Chinese Tradition* (New York: Columbia University Press, 1960), 1:735.

17. de Bary, ed., *Confucianism and Human Rights*, 193–208.

18. Ibid., 209–233.

19. Ibid., 234–250.

20. See de Bary et al., eds., *Sources of Chinese Tradition*, 1:735.

21. de Bary, ed., *Confucianism and Human Rights*, 261–269.

22. Ibid., 270–296.

15. China and the Limits of Liberalism

This chapter is taken from W. T. de Bary, *The Liberal Tradition in China* (Hong Kong: Chinese University Press, 1983), 91–108.

1. On Wu Han, see Fang Zhaoying, in Goodrich and Fang's *Dictionary of Ming Biography* (New York: Columbia Universty Press, 1976), 478–479; and H. L. Boorman, ed., *Biographical Dictionary of Republican China* (New York: Columbia University Press, 1970), 425–430; James R. Pusey, *Wu Han, Attacking the Present Through the Past* (Cambridge, Mass.: Harvard University Press, 1969).

2. See Wu Han, *Hai Rui Dismissed from Office*, trans. C. C. Wang, with an introductory essay by D. W. Y. Kwok (Honolulu: University of Hawaii Press,

1972); Clive Ansley, *The Heresy of Wu Han: His Play* Hai Jui Dismissed from Office *and Its Role in China's Cultural Revolution* (Toronto: University of Toronto Press, 1971). For a fuller discussion of issues involving Wu, see Merle Goldman, *China's Intellectuals: Advise and Dissent* (Cambridge, Mass.: Harvard University Press, 1981), 26–27, 32–37, 118–124, 233–234.

3. W. T. de Bary, ed., *Sources of Chinese Tradition* (New York: Columbia University Press, 1960), 925–928.

4. Marvin Harris, *Cannibals and Kings, the Origins of Cultures* (New York: Vintage, 1977), 240; see also Karl A. Wittfogel, *Oriental Despotism, A Comparative Study of Total Power* (New Haven, Conn.: Yale University Press, 1957).

5. Inge Morath and Arthur Miller, *Chinese Encounters* (New York: Farrar, Straus and Giroux, 1979).

6. Orville Schell, in the *New York Times Book Review* (October 14, 1979): 43.

7. *Mingshi* (Peking: Chung-hua Book Co., 1974), 174:5927–5933. Cf. also Ernst Wolff, "A Preliminary Study of Hai Rui: His Biography in the *Ming shi*," *Journal of the Oriental Society of Australia* 7, nos. 1–2 (December 1970).

8. See biography and bibliography by Frederick Mote in *Dictionary of Ming Biography*, 426–433.

9. Zhang Boxing, *Zhengyi tang quanshu*, Tongzhi 5 (1866) edition, *Fang Zhengxue ji* 7 juan; *Hai Gangfeng ji* 2 juan; Rong Zhaozu, *Mingdai sixiang shi* (Taipei: Taiwan Kaiming Bookstore, 1962).

10. Neil G. Burton and Charles Bettelheim, *China Since Mao* (New York: Monthly Review Press, 1978), 9–13, 37–116.

11. The conflicted nature of this relationship is ably discussed by Goldman in *China's Intellectuals*.

12. See Yamanoi Yū, *Min-Shin shisōshi no kenkyū* (Tokyo: Tokyo University Press, 1980), 223ff.

13. de Bary, ed., *Sources of Chinese Tradition*, 814–818.

14. Ibid., 768–770, 809.

15. I have already pointed this out in relation to developments in seventeenth- and eighteenth-century thought in Tokugawa Japan and extend the discussion to China in W. T. de Bary, "Sagehood as a Spiritual and Secular Ideal in Tokugawa Neo-Confucianism," in *Principle and Practicality* (New York: Columbia University Press, 1979), 139–172.

16. W. T. de Bary, ed., *The Unfolding of Neo-Confucianism* (New York: Columbia University Press, 1975), 32.

17. Qian Mu, *Cong Zhongguo lishi lai kan Zhongguo minzuxing ji zhongguo wenhua* (Hong Kong: Chinese University Press, 1979), 73.

18. Ibid., 74.

16. Huang Zongxi and Qian Mu

1. Qian Mu, *Cong Zhongguo lishi lai kan Zhongguo minzuxing ji Zhongguo wenhua* (Hong Kong: Chinese University Press, 1979), 12–15.

2. Qian Mu, *Zhongguo jin sanbainian xueshu shi* (Shanghai: Commercial Press, 1937), 1:1–7.

3. *Mingru xuean* (Wanyou wenku ed.; Taipei: Commercial Press, 1965), "Fanli," 1.

4. Sun Chifeng, *Lixue zongzhuan* (Taipei: Yiwen yinshuguan, 1969; reprint of 1666 ed.), chaps. 7, 9, 17, 21, 26.

5. *Mingru xuean*, "*Zixu*" and "*Fanli*"; and in his *Bo xie lun*, 1a–b, in *Lizhou yizhu huikan* (Shanghai, 1910), vol. 13.

6. Charles Frankel, "Intellectual Foundations of Liberalism," in *Liberalism and Liberal Education* (New York: Columbia University Program of General Education, 1976), 3–11.

7. Gilbert Murray, *Liberality and Civilization* (London: Allen and Unwin, 1938), 46–47.

17. Tang Junyi and New Asia College

1. W. T. de Bary, ed. *The Unfolding of Neo-Confucianism* (New York: Columbia University Press, 1975).

2. Ibid., 305–22.

18. Ryūsaku Tsunoda Sensei

An address delivered at the Memorial Service, St. Paul's Chapel, Columbia University, December 15, 1964.

19. Thomas Merton, Matteo Ricci, and Confucianism

1. Thomas Merton, *Introductions East and West* (Greensboro, N.C.: Unicorn, 1981), 110.

2. Ibid.

3. Thomas Merton, *Thoughts on the East* (New York: New Directions, 1968), 84.

4. Merton, *Introductions*, 111.

5. Ibid.

6. Thomas Merton, *Mystics and Zen Masters* (New York: Farrar, Straus and Giroux, 1961).

7. Ibid., 51, 52, 58.

8. Ibid., 48.

9. Ibid., 78, 63.

10. George H. Dunne, SJ, *A Generation of Giants* (South Bend, Ind.: University of Notre Dame Press, 1962).

11. L. C. Goodrich and C. Y. Fang, *Dictionary of Ming Biography* (New York: Columbia University Press, 1976), 2:1143–1144.

12. Merton, *Mystics*, 53.

13. Ibid., 57.

14. W. T. de Bary et al., eds., *Sources of Chinese Tradition* (New York: Columbia University Press, 1991), 1:729.

15. Merton, *Mystics*, 83.

16. Ibid., 89.

Index